Engaging Language Learners through CALL

Advances in CALL Research and Practice
Series Editor: Greg Kessler, Ohio University

This series is published in cooperation with the Computer Assisted Language Instruction Consortium (CALICO). Each Spring just prior to the CALICO annual conference the series publishes one volume comprised of original studies on a specific topic.

Published:
2016
Landmarks in CALL Research
Edited by Greg Kessler

2017
Learner Autonomy and Web 2.0
Edited by Marco Cappellini, Tim Lewis, and Annick Rivens Mompean

2018
Assessment Across Online Language Education
Edited by Stephanie Link and Jinrong Li

Engaging Language Learners through CALL

From Theory and Research to Informed Practice

Edited by Nike Arnold and Lara Ducate

CALIC◌

SHEFFIELD UK   BRISTOL CT

Published by Equinox Publishing Ltd.

UK: Office 415, The Workstation, 15 Paternoster Row, Sheffield, South Yorkshire
      S1 2BX
USA: ISD, 70 Enterprise Drive, Bristol, CT 06010

www.equinoxpub.com

First published 2019

British Library Cataloguing-in-Publication Data

A catalogue record for this book is available from the British Library.

ISBN-13   978 1 78179 828 7   (paperback)
ISBN-13   978 1 78179 829 4   (ePDF)

Library of Congress Cataloging-in-Publication Data

Names: Arnold, Nike, editor. | Ducate, Lara, editor.
Title: Engaging language learners through CALL : from theory and research
to informed practice / edited by Nike Arnold and Lara Ducate.
Description: Sheffield, UK ; Bristol, CT : Equinox Publishing Ltd, 2019. | Series:
Advances in call research and practice | Includes bibliographical references and
index.
Identifiers: LCCN 2018035469 (print) | LCCN 2018051357 (ebook) | ISBN
9781781798294 (ePDF) | ISBN 9781781798287 (pb)
Subjects: LCSH: Second language acquisition—Computer-assisted instruction.
| Language and languages—Computer-assisted instruction for foreign speakers. |
Language and languages—Study and teaching—Audio-visual aids.
Classification: LCC P118.2 (ebook) | LCC P118.2 .E58 2019 (print) |
DDC 418.0078/5—dc23
LC record available at https://lccn.loc.gov/2018035469

Typeset by S.J.I. Services, New Delhi

Contents

Introduction

Nike Arnold and Lara Ducate

We are pleased to present the third edition of this CALICO volume. Looking at the technology developments of the eight years since the publication of the last edition, it was high time for an updated overview of the field of computer-assisted language learning (CALL).[1] Touch screen tablets have made their way into many households and advances in artificial intelligence have drastically changed how we interact with these devices (e.g., Apple's Siri and Microsoft's Cortana). Virtual reality has become more mainstream including educational and training applications (e.g., healthcare, military, driving). But there has not only been excitement; there are increasing concerns about our digital footprint, the trustworthiness of online information (e.g., fake news), and technology's effects on our social lives, mental health, and cognition.

Not surprisingly, education has been impacted by these changes as well. The increase in tablet and smartphone ownership has meant that some students even rely on a mobile device for their school work. Technology also plays an increasing role in the delivery of instruction, such as flipped classroom or fully online formats.

Despite these changes, other aspects have practically remained the same. Even in the US, technology access and infrastructure remain hurdles for some, just one way in which technology contributes to inequity (Ortega, 2017). Broadly speaking, CALL, that is, any process in which learners use a computer or mobile device to support their learning of an additional language (definition adapted from Beatty, 2003), has not yet been nominalized. Books like this one are still needed because, unlike the textbook and board, CALL remains "a separate concept and field of discussion" (Bax, 2003: 23). There is also widespread support for the educational value of CALL (e.g.,

---

1   The two previous editions were titled *Calling on CALL: From theory and research to new directions in English Language Teaching* (2006) and *Present and future promises of CALL: From theory and research to new directions in English Language Teaching* (2011).

American Council on the Teaching of Foreign Languages, 2013, 2017), which demonstrates that CALL skills are central for language educators (e.g., Healey et al., 2011). Supporting CALL teacher education, the CALL research base continues to grow, but groups that have arguably the most to gain from its use (e.g., immigrants, who have urgent real-life needs to use the language, often in technology-mediated contexts) are all but absent. In other words, we know very little about how to support "under-served and marginalized multilinguals" (Ortega, 2017: 305) with CALL.

This edited volume begins with two big-picture chapters. Youngs describes the intersection of second language acquisition (SLA) research and CALL to provide a backdrop to the volume and to illustrate how technology can facilitate key pedagogical processes. The second chapter, by Goertler, is dedicated to online and hybrid language courses, which are becoming more common in the educational landscape. The next eight chapters focus on the use of CALL for specific language skills or other learning goals. Last but not least, Hubbard rounds off the volume with a discussion of ways to evaluate courseware and apps.

Each chapter follows a similar structure. It begins with preview questions to encourage readers to think about what they already know on the topic and have perhaps already experienced. In order to provide an evidence-based foundation for the pedagogical implications mentioned later in the chapter, the body of each chapter begins with an overview of the most relevant and recent research in the field. The literature review is followed by implications for teaching based on the research findings, which include how the findings can inform pedagogical practice and how to design and assess tasks. In contrast to the previous two versions of this volume, there is not a separate chapter on assessment here; rather each chapter discusses assessment in its own specific context. The main discussion of the chapter is followed by questions for reflection to engage readers with the information from the chapter and apply what they have learned in order to deepen their understanding of the topic. Case studies describe issues raised in the chapter in concrete settings that illustrate how they could manifest in practice. The case studies are followed by ideas for action research: a list of ideas for small research projects related to the topic that readers can carry out alone or in groups. Each chapter concludes with a list of resources, including tools that could be useful when implementing the ideas mentioned in the chapter. With the fast pace of developments in technology, some of these resources could become out-of-date not long after the publication of this volume. However, they will hopefully provide ideas of other resources that could be useful.

While each chapter in this volume focuses on developing a specific skill, there are themes that run through many of the chapters. As will be demonstrated throughout this volume, technology can be used to promote pedagogical processes thereby creating unique learning opportunities. Since technology shapes so many aspects of our lives (e.g., education, career, social life, parenting), it is also essential to use technology in its own right, that is, to prepare students to make effective use of technology in each of these areas. Another attribute of CALL that appears in several chapters is its ability to overcome constraints of time, space, interlocutors, etc. No matter if technology is used to support learning processes, build digital literacies, or overcome the limitations of the classroom; there are three basic roles it can play, all of which are described in this volume: the role of tutor, tool, or medium (Kern, 2006). As a tutor, CALL provides instruction, feedback, or assessment (e.g., a screencast explaining the difference between two tenses). In the tool role, technology provides access to information (e.g., websites, online dictionaries). As a medium, CALL facilitates communication (e.g., blogs, social networking sites, text chat). We would even suggest a fourth category where technology provides a multimodal immersive experience, in gaming with virtual or augmented reality. In this additional role, the computer enables learners to step into a new world with a new identity to interact with the game itself and possibly other participants in the virtual world(s). As these examples show, CALL is not limited to applications specifically made for language learning, such as the pronunciation software mentioned by O'Brien in this volume. Using CALL research and SLA theory as guides, language instructors can also integrate applications originally developed for other purposes, as illustrated in the chapters by Abrams with Twitter, blogs, Facebook groups, and Skype; by Elola & Oskoz in regard to wikis, blogs, Twitter, and digital storytelling; and by Sykes, Holden, & Knight in relation to gaming.

One of the overarching themes of the volume is CALL's ability to engage learners with autonomous and student-centered activities that model authentic uses of technology. They can be integrated into a classroom but our ultimate goals should be to encourage and enable learners to work independently outside the classroom to support their lifelong language learning or to pursue their interests. With CALL, both are much easier. Instructors should consider their learners' use of technology in general as well as of specific applications, whether that use aligns with the goals of the course, and, if necessary, how to reconcile the two, as pointed out by contributors Sykes, Holden, & Knight and Reinhardt & Thorne. For example, students may already use Facebook in their daily lives, but visiting a Facebook group as a class assignment and in another language has different expectations and rules of engagement. Instructors cannot assume that students will automatically know how to behave in a French Facebook group, even though they visit Facebook daily to communicate with friends. Teachers should provide the necessary scaffolding and preparation for students to enter these authentic contexts, but, as Taylor, Guth & Helm, Montero Perez, and Reinhardt & Thorne argue in this volume, instructors should not and cannot be in control of everything. Students need the freedom to explore, and possibly even make mistakes. They will need these skills to use technology more independently. In some cases, powerful learning opportunities can even arise from such "failures" (O'Dowd & Ritter, 2006). Furthermore, too much teacher control can make an activity artificial and ultimately less useful. And, let's face it, with technology, we are never fully in control because technology fails, not only in the classroom. That means that instructors have the opportunity to authentically model problem solving, ideally in collaboration with students. In doing so, instructors can position students as experts and reduce the typical institutional power difference between instructor and students.

Along with the unique opportunities offered by CALL come challenges and important considerations. While CALL is its own field, informed by a variety of methodologies and theories, it is important to remember that the use of technology is not neutral. Technology is implemented based on different methodologies or theoretical views which shape how it is used and for what purpose. Instructors must consider their own theoretical or methodological lens to be sure that the use of technology aligns with the teaching methods and learning outcomes of the course. But even the technology itself is not neutral since applications reflect cultural values and ideologies such as anonymity, informality, and speed (Reeder et al., 2004) or the native speaker ideal for pronunciation. In those respects, technology is similar to textbooks and other teaching materials. At a fundamental level, however, they are very different, and, as described by Hubbard, must therefore be evaluated differently.

As these themes demonstrate, CALL provides an array of affordances and, sometimes, challenges. It is our hope that this third edition will continue to support readers in implementing a research-based CALL pedagogy and updating their practice as technology and research findings change.

Acknowledgments

We would like to thank the authors for their valuable contributions to the volume, the reviewers for their constructive feedback on the chapters, the

CALICO board for entrusting us with the editing of this updated volume, and Greg Kessler for his support in the process.

References

American Council on the Teaching of Foreign Languages (2013). *ACTFL/CAEP program standards for the preparation of foreign language teachers.* Retrieved from https://www.actfl.org/sites/default/files/CAEP/ACTFLCAEPStandards2013_v2015.pdf

American Council on the Teaching of Foreign Languages (2017). *Statement on the role of technology in language learning.* Retrieved from https://www.actfl.org/news/position-statements/statement-the-role-technology-language-learning

Bax, S. (2003). CALL – Past, present and future. *System*, 31(1), 13–28. https://doi.org/10.1016/S0346-251X(02)00071-4

Beatty, K. (2003). *Teaching and researching computer-assisted language learning.* Harlow, UK: Pearson Education.

Healey, D., Hanson-Smith, E., Hubbard, P., Ioannou-Georgiou, S., Kessler, G., & Ware, P. (2011). *TESOL technology standards: Description, implementation, integration.* Alexandria, VA: TESOL Press.

Kern, R. (2006). Perspectives on technology in learning and teaching languages. *TESOL Quarterly*, 40(1), 183–210. https://doi.org/10.2307/40264516

O'Dowd, R., & Ritter, M. (2006). Understanding and working with "failed communication" in telecollaborative exchanges. *CALICO Journal*, 23(3), 623–642. https://doi.org/10.1558/cj.v23i3.623-642

Ortega, L. (2017). New CALL-SLA research interfaces for the 21st century: Towards equitable multilingualism. *CALICO Journal*, 34(3), 285–316. https://doi.org/10.1558/cj.33855

Reeder, K., MacFadyen, L. P., Roche, J., & Chase, M. (2004). Negotiating cultures in cyberspace: Patterns and problematics. *Language Learning & Technology*, 8(2), 88–105. Retrieved from https://scholarspace.manoa.hawaii.edu/bitstream/10125/25242/1/08_02_reeder.pdf

About the Authors

Nike Arnold (PhD, University of Texas at Austin) is Associate Professor of Applied Linguistics at Portland State University in Oregon, USA. Ever since the online discussions in a graduate seminar helped her overcome her insecurities about knowing nothing about Pavlov's drooling dogs, she has been fascinated by educational technology, especially how it intersects with affect. Nike has published on online collaborative learning in foreign language learning and language teacher education in a variety of venues.

Lara Ducate (PhD, University of Texas at Austin) is a Professor of German and Applied Linguistics at the University of South Carolina in Columbia, SC, USA. Ever since she was "stuck" taking German in high school and quickly won over by her inspiring teacher, she has been fascinated with the German language and culture and with figuring out the best ways to train teachers to motivate their students in the same way she was energized by effective teaching. Lara's research focuses on intercultural learning in a study abroad context, teacher training, and various applications of CALL. Her work also appears in a variety of venues.

1   SLA Theories and Practices in CALL

Bonnie L. Youngs

Preview Questions

If you are currently teaching, answer these questions based on your own classroom. If you are not currently teaching, use a sample course from a second/foreign language (L2) target language/content instructor to help you answer them.

1. What technology is associated with your (sample) course materials? Do you see evidence that second language acquisition (SLA) research guided the implementation of the technology being used?
2. Think back to an activity or a task that "failed" in a class you taught or took. Why did it fail? If you had used technology for that activity or task, would it have failed? Explain.
3. Many computer-assisted language learning (CALL) practitioners believe that the use of technology should be seamless in face-to-face (F2F) language classes. Should the use of technology in distance/hybrid classes be as seamless as in F2F classes? How would it look different in distance/hybrid classes?
4. Write down any of your personal hesitations for using CALL to promote L2 learning. Is it because you don't think it works or can make a difference in learning, you don't think you have the time to integrate CALL well, you don't think that you have the necessary skill set to integrate CALL into your teaching, or…? Should all teachers have the knowledge to be able to produce or advise on CALL development projects?

1   Introduction

Influenced by behaviorist theory, the first CALL tools in the 1950s focused on rote learning through drills. In the 1980s, communicative methodology influenced a move to more production-oriented tasks, but actual language production was still limited. CALL turned to a more multimedia-oriented approach in the 1990s by integrating graphics, sounds, and animation in addition to text. Interaction became the focus, providing an environment for students to "communicate" with the computer in as authentic a manner as possible. Beginning in the 2000s, CALL became even more communicative by allowing learners to interact with other language users via computer-mediated communication (CMC), social media (Lomicka & Lord, 2016), and gaming (e.g., Chapelle & Sauro, 2017; Farr & Murray, 2016; Thorne & Fischer, 2012; Thorne, Black, & Sykes, 2009; Zourou, 2012). These developments have shown, however, that "… media are mere vehicles that deliver instruction but do not influence student achievement any more than the truck that delivers our groceries causes changes in our nutrition" (Clark, 1983: 445). How, then, can we create CALL environments in which students might learn a new language effectively?

As described above, over the past seven decades our field has witnessed CALL implementations in myriad teaching approaches and methods, proving CALL's flexibility, which, however, should not be taken lightly. Flexibility in L2 teaching and learning can be beneficial, but we should still make informed decisions about how and when to implement CALL. For example, L2 instructors can consider how their students would benefit best from a methodology informed by SLA research, which should then lead to technology-based questions regarding the appropriateness of the CALL tool in their instructional context: Does this CALL tool or task provide enhanced input or encourage pushed output? Can the tool individualize instruction by accommodating different learning preferences or allowing students to work at their own pace? Does the tool or task engage learners in collaboration and authentic language use including negotiation of meaning? Would the task be better suited for technology A or technology B, or should technology be avoided altogether for this particular task?

Looking ahead to their students' future, instructors can also ask if their learners will make progress toward digital literacy by using these tools. For example, Guichon & Cohen (2016) describe three key literacies that could enhance language learning and digital literacy: the ability to communicate using different mediational means; the ability to cooperate in net-based interactions; and the ability to create different types of information such as webpages. These sorts of questions allow us to make pedagogically sound decisions about tool selection and task design in order to create a more effective learning environment for our students.

CALL, as it deals with language learning, logically leads to a discussion of SLA. SLA research describes the diverse conditions that facilitate or impede language acquisition (Chapelle, 2000; Doughty & Long, 2003; Ellis, 1986; Freed, 1991), and includes studies on, for example, the acquisition of pronunciation, vocabulary, grammar, pragmatics, syntax, and the development of language skills (e.g., speaking). It examines all aspects of language learning and loss, and can lead to the development of teaching methodologies and improved pedagogy. SLA also elaborates on theories of L2 learning, for example, interactionist, cognitive, and sociocultural, and CALL researchers work to discover how SLA theories can improve CALL.

It would be impractical in one chapter to discuss every SLA theory that has been described since the 1950s. There are more complete articles and books on these topics that describe each theory in great detail (Brown, 1994; Burnaby, 1997; Doughty & Long, 2003; Mitchell & Myles, 1998; Omaggio Hadley, 2001; Schachter, 1997; Shirai, 1997; Shohamy, 1997). Additionally, linking SLA, CALL, and L2 pedagogy would be impossible to do completely in this chapter given the amount of history and research that has been done. Existing resources explain the intricacies between and among these fields (Blake, 2008; Chapelle, 1998, 2009; Debski, 2003; Farr & Murray, 2016; Fischer, 2008; Hubbard, 2008; Lafford, 2009; Thorne & Payne, 2005; VanPatten & Williams, 2015; Zhao, 2003). For the purposes of this volume, the present chapter deals with questions about the relationships between CALL and SLA, which, when combined, can improve L2 teaching and learning.

This chapter has two specific goals: (1) to focus on select SLA theories and concepts and their integration into CALL, and (2) to emphasize the importance of grounding the design and practice of CALL in SLA theory, and for practice to inform theory. Such a mutually informative cycle of theory/application/research and further theory development will help us grow as professional CALL practitioners and researchers. According to Hulstijn (2000: 39), "... theories and methods influence each other. New theories may lead to the search for and invention of new methods and tools, whereas new tools and methods may give rise to new theoretical thinking". Hegelheimer and Chapelle (2000: 42) focus on CALL:

> CALL developers and users constantly seek pedagogical principles that can guide their construction of CALL tasks to make them effective for SLA. At the same time, some SLA researchers seek to improve the ecological validity of studies by conducting them in settings where L2 learners are eager and motivated participants. CALL activities designed in view of hypotheses about ideal conditions for SLA can meet both objectives. This symbiotic relationship between CALL and SLA is maintained through a combination of theoretically-based hypotheses to inform the design of CALL

materials that incorporate SLA concepts and pedagogical principles, and empirically-based research which evaluates both theory
and materials.

Some examples of the principles and research mentioned above form the
balance of this chapter. Specifically, the discussion focuses on Interactionist
Theory, Cognitive Theory, and Sociocultural Theory. After that, affective,
social, motivational, and pedagogical principles concerning learners are
introduced as topics that can be addressed with technology.

2   CALL and SLA: Interactionist Theory

This section highlights CALL's potential to create a rich linguistic environment, the focus of Interactionist Theory (Chapelle, 2005) whereby social
interaction triggers learner-internal processes that promote L2 learning.

2.1   Input, Intake, Noticing

A rich linguistic environment is essential for L2 learning. When describing
the linguistic environment, we usually begin with input, not only because it
is the first phase of the learning process but also because of its vital importance. Input is any language with a communicative intent to which the
learner is exposed (VanPatten & Williams, 2014). Without such linguistic
data produced by other users, L2 learning simply cannot take place (Gass,
1997). Input provides positive evidence of well-formed sentences that can
serve as models for output, which then allow the learner to form linguistic
hypotheses; furthermore, input creates "communicative pressure" to stimulate language learning (Gass, 2008: 224).

One of CALL's strengths is the capacity to provide learners with large
amounts of authentic input, which is to say materials designed by native
speakers for native speakers, whether through spoken or written text, and
this is one of the most obvious and easy ways to employ technology in
the L2 classroom. The Internet offers audio (O'Brien & Hegelheimer,
2007; Stanley, 2006), video, visuals, and texts, and addresses the types of
"communicative practices in which students either already are or want to
become engaged for interpersonal, recreational, and professional purposes"
(Thorne & Reinhardt, 2008: 566). YouTube videos, restaurant menus, social
media posts, and chat opportunities are plentiful.

Although there has not been research that explicitly investigates the use
of authentic materials through CALL, many studies use authentic materials

in research: blogs (Ducate & Lomicka, 2008), reading (Arnold, 2009), cultural information (Hager, 2005), videos (Herron et al., 2002), and Twitter (Antenos-Conforti, 2009). In these studies, students were able to engage directly with authentic artifacts in order to improve their language proficiency and knowledge of the target culture. When used judiciously, input in the form of authentic materials carries multiple advantages over the use of teacher-designed texts developed solely for student use. As Shrum & Glisan (2010) note, these materials allow students access to real language that serves a purpose and is rich in cultural content, reflecting culture and societal values. Furthermore, even though teacher-created materials can be used effectively, it is important to remember that authentic texts can "present learners with real-life challenges" yet "offer … infinite possibilities for content exploration" (Leaver & Willis, 2004: 187).

CALL technologies profit from Internet sources to develop new learning opportunities and create entirely new types of input. For example, due to its integration of multimedia and hyperlinked, nonlinear organization, the Internet has not only introduced a new genre of text but also changed the process of reading that relies on different strategies. Reading online texts, for example, is a very nonlinear and discontinuous process (Sutherland-Smith, 2002). Another example is CMC, particularly its synchronous form (SCMC), which combines aspects of oral and written discourse as well as its own unique features to provide a communicative environment with new rules, demands, and expectations (Crystal, 2006; Payne & Whitney, 2002).

This leads us to the question of what type of input we "should" present to learners. Krashen (1985) proposed that only the right kind of input promotes acquisition, namely comprehensible input that is slightly above the learner's current level ($i+1$). While several researchers (e.g., Swain, 1985) have argued against Krashen's claim that comprehensible input is sufficient for acquisition, learners must have access to input that they are able to process. To make input comprehensible, it is often necessary to modify it according to the learners' current level, which might involve simplification, elaboration, or increased redundancy (Chapelle, 1998). Technology can help guide such modifications. Corpus-based tools like Lextutor, for example, can provide a lexical profile of a text (e.g., lexical coverage provided by high vs. low frequency items). Based on this information, educators can then modify a text to better match the learners' proficiency.

But what constitutes comprehensible input? Collentine's study (2013) suggests strong links between input about people, things, and events in non-complex structures, and the students' output with respect to complexity and lexical density. She studied the input encountered by 60 third-year learners of Spanish using a 3D world and its attendant crime-solving tasks, for example collecting notes, reading diaries, and "interviewing," and the students' subsequent output which consisted of spontaneous writing in SCMC. Collentine concludes that "certain linguistic features in the input are necessary for learners to generate linguistic complexity in their output when engaged in a task" and moreover that "input should be rich in information to affect linguistic complexity in learner output" (Collentine, 2013: 63).

CALL offers extensive options to teachers for modifying input based on learners' individual needs, for example in the forms of repetition, simplification through restatements, nonverbal cues, decreased speed, reference materials, and change of input mode in anticipation of problems. Moreover, learners too should be allowed to request modifications of input. If the input presented in instructional multimedia is intended to expand the learner's linguistic knowledge, then choices, for example, adding subtitles, decreasing audio speed, repeating exercises, and viewing assessment results, are vital.

As an example of choices offered to students, Hegelheimer & Tower (2004) worked with learners of English as a foreign language who engaged with a software program outside of class. The study showed evidence of the variability with which students used the various options to modify the input. Some of the modification options were not used at all and others were accessed frequently. Furthermore, independent of which modifications were requested, students were more successful at completing the tasks when they took advantage of the options provided. These findings indicate that technological tools can successfully promote comprehension while accommodating learners' personal preferences.

Comprehensible input can be a first step to L2 learning, but related to input is the act of intake, which is to say, the language data that learners hold and process in their working memory and have comprehended semantically as well as syntactically (Hegelheimer & Chapelle, 2000; VanPatten, 2003; Wong, 2018). SLA research shows that acquisition can take place when input, gathered through apperception or comprehension, becomes intake through input processing (Gass, 1997; Schmidt, 1995, 2010; Sun, 2008). Intake results from learner engagement with the input (VanPatten, 2003), and one such form of engagement is noticing. When students become aware of a new form or notice a gap in knowledge (Schmidt 1990, 1995, 2010), input is more likely to become intake.

The visual nature of many CALL applications seems to promote noticing. For example, Payne & Whitney (2002) reported that almost two-thirds of their participants noticed other students' mistakes more often during written synchronous chat than during F2F interaction. Their research shows that the written chat logs led to increased awareness, which could promote more syntactic processing and increased noticing of gaps in linguistic knowledge.

Noticing is also promoted by input enhancement, in other words typographic (e.g., font size and color) or phonological techniques (e.g., stress, volume changes) to highlight specific features of a text (Smith, 1993). Collentine (2000) illustrated that CALL can create effective conditions for the active construction of grammar knowledge, in this case indirect speech in Spanish. After viewing short videos of indirect discourse, third-year Spanish students completed a set of online exercises with the new structure visually highlighted in the input and feedback. This input enhancement helped students produce the structure in their own output without explicit instruction.

2.2   Output

Although the availability and comprehension of linguistic data play a pivotal role in language learning, the production of communicative language, in other words output, is also crucial. Attempting to communicate meaning pushes learners to pay closer attention to input. "[L]earners coming to the awareness that they need a form or structure because of their output" (VanPatten, 2003: 69) causes a shift from semantic to syntactic processing, which ultimately affects the learner's developing system (interlanguage). Producing output also creates opportunities for hypothesis testing and the development of automaticity (Gass, 2008). Furthermore, producing output transforms declarative/explicit knowledge into procedural/implicit knowledge and thereby enhances fluency (DeKeyser, 2007). However, it must be noted that "whether output practice leads to L2 development heavily depends on various factors, including learners' psycholinguistic readiness and linguistic features of the target form" (Muranoi, 2007: 60).

Given these important functions of output, instructors must provide learners with frequent opportunities to produce communicative and meaningful output (Wong, 2013). In a traditional classroom setting, this can be challenging, especially for oral interpersonal communication. A teacher-fronted classroom severely limits student participation (Lee, 2000) and group work, which keeps learners significantly more engaged, offers only limited possibilities for teacher monitoring and guidance. Technology, in the form of CMC, can create opportunities for student participation as well as teacher monitoring. The fact that learners produce more and sometimes better quality output in CMC than in F2F interactions has been documented by several studies (Beauvois, 1998; Chun, 1994; Smith, 2016; Warschauer, 1996; see Lin, 2014 for a meta-analysis of 12 years of CMC and SLA research), which have also pointed toward archived transcripts as a unique opportunity for teachers and learners alike to review student contributions (Beauvois, 1998). These texts allow teachers to identify issues that need to be addressed (e.g., common errors), as well as the structures learners are ready to learn based on their developmental stage (Smith, 2009). Transcripts help hold students accountable and lead them to reflection (i.e., self-assessment) and to revisit their output with a focus on form (i.e., self-correction).

When producing output, learners often rely on what Krashen (1982) refers to as the monitor. Assuming learners know the rule, focus on form, and have time, they can plan, edit, and correct their output based on the rules in their learned system. However, overuse of the monitor can hamper output, as Zhang's study (2009) found, showing limited oral output from Chinese students learning English who focused too much on forms. Text-based CMC can provide an environment that allows learners to make use of this editing function. Although written synchronous chat is interactive, similar to oral interpersonal discourse, it provides more time for processing, which in turn allows learners to focus on form and monitor their output.

Self-repair indicates that a learner has monitored their output, noticed a production error, and subsequently attempted a correction. Smith (2008) used screen-capture software to investigate so-called covert instances of self-repair that occur before a message is sent and therefore do not appear on transcripts. Completing jigsaw tasks with a partner, the learners of German in his study self-repaired about six times per 100 words, most of which occurred before the message was posted. Smith (2008: 97) concludes that "the visual saliency of the text as well as the permanency of the written word, which enables one to review the previous 'utterances,' allows learners to focus their attention on the formal aspects of their output without disrupting the flow of communication."

This unique feature of SCMC has received significant attention from researchers who call it a "conversation in slow motion" (Beauvois, 1998: 198) that functions as a "conversation simulator" (Payne & Whitney, 2002: 25) and seems to result in gains in oral ability. Payne & Whitney (2002) investigated whether SCMC can directly improve L2 proficiency and compared two groups of third-semester learners of Spanish, in F2F and SCMC environments. Although both groups demonstrated significant improvement at the end of the semester, the SCMC group outperformed the control group. In an attempt to explain these findings, the researchers propose that the following features of online study can enhance the development of speaking skills: (1) the lack of limited traditional turn-taking allows participants to produce more output than in a conventional classroom, (2) language production is required to establish a presence in a chat room, (3) due to the lack of visual cues, participants cannot rely on paralinguistic communication strategies and instead have to encode all meaning through language (pushed output), and (4) the chat log allows learners to reread previous comments.

Consequently, if we as L2 instructors assume that F2F speech is the only way to develop conversational ability, we may in fact be disadvantaging a significant portion of our students. For students who find L2 oral production an overwhelming task and tend to tune out when the linguistic data generated in F2F conversational settings becomes too great, online synchronous interaction appears to provide an opportunity to develop L2 oral proficiency (Payne & Whitney, 2002). Although replication studies are needed to support their findings, Payne & Whitney present evidence that SCMC can provide learners with unique advantages.

2.3   Output and Negotiated Interaction

Output can also trigger negotiated interaction. Negotiated interaction is at the heart of Long's interaction hypothesis (1996), which is based on the assumption that "conversation is not only a medium of practice, but also the means by which learning takes place" (Gass, 1997: 104). Comprehension checks, recasts, paraphrasing, and other adjustments provide modified input and can focus the learner's attention on form as well as provide negative evidence, or feedback, about the incorrectness of their utterances. This, in turn, leads to the creation of new knowledge or the restructuring of existing knowledge (Gass, 2008; Gass & Mackey, 2007; Pica, 1996).

Interactive forms of CALL provide ample opportunities for negotiation of meaning. González-Lloret (2003) designed a web simulation called "En busca de esmeraldas," which, as part of its plot, asks students to find a missing document. The program provides students with reading and listening choices to obtain information for their search and to follow instructions while navigating a three-dimensional environment (one student gives directions while the other works in the virtual environment). González-Lloret found that learners engaged in negotiation of meaning while using the program. Although she had few subjects in her study, she maintains that "the language produced by the participants during the simulation was typical of negotiation for meaning, where the main emphasis is on the completion of the task, and where language is used with its main communicative purpose in an economical way, without paying attention to the production of long, accurate constructions" (González-Lloret, 2003: 98).

Whereas González-Lloret's participants interacted in the same physical space while working with her web simulation, Kötter's (2003) students of German and English interacted via CMC. Comparing their CMC

interactions to F2F discourse, Kötter found notably more instances of negotiation of meaning, for example clarification requests, elaborations, and
reformulations of others' contributions. The students alternated deliberately
between their L1 and L2 to facilitate communication, and "[a]lmost all
appeals for help were answered within a matter of turns .... Moreover, about
a third of all requests for lexical assistance led to the provision of additional
background information about the usage of a word, or sparked a short discussion about the term or concept" (Kötter, 2003: 155).

Pellettieri (2000), in a study investigating negotiation during SCMC,
also found that learners provide each other with feedback. Dyads of
intermediate-level learners of Spanish completed five closed tasks (e.g.,
jigsaw) during which they engaged in a large number of negotiations
about lexical items. The findings showed that the form-focused tasks triggered more morphosyntactic negotiations. In addition, participants offered
explicit as well as implicit corrective feedback that was correct 80% of the
time. In turn, this feedback resulted in high degrees of lexical, morphosyntactic, and semantic structural modifications, which showed that the participants used the feedback (Pellettieri, 2000).

2.4   Feedback

Throughout the cycle of input, output, and negotiation of meaning, learners constantly receive feedback. In the classroom, feedback can come in the
form of visual cues (e.g., a look of surprise), audio cues (e.g., an agreement
or a request for clarification), or input from the teacher (e.g., error correction, agreement). CALL also provides feedback intended to promote learning, but research has shown its successes and failures in this domain.

As seen in the previous subsection, interaction can provide learners
with valuable feedback. In a CALL environment, such feedback can occur
either from interaction between a learner and other users or from the computer itself. In Heift's study (2004), the computer provided learners of
German enrolled in the first three levels of language courses with feedback as they used an e-tutor to practice vocabulary and grammar. Working
through almost four chapters and 50 individual exercises over the course
of 15 weeks, students had access to four different exercise types: build-a-
sentence, dictation, fill-in-the-blank, and translation. For these exercises,
the program provided error-specific feedback and additional options, such
as a dictionary and individualized grammar help. Her findings showed that a
particular type of feedback can positively influence learner uptake. Students
were most likely to revise their grammar and vocabulary errors when they

received very explicit and prominent feedback, a finding independent of students' proficiency and gender.

Cornillie et al. (2013) explored learners' choices to use corrective feedback (CF) or not during a murder mystery presented in a task-based tutorial CALL environment. Their study explored "whether learners actually made use of optional CF (embedded with highlights and non-embedded), and whether this usage was related to the perceived usefulness of the CF to learners' explicit L2 knowledge, or, ... to their achievement goal orientation" (Cornillie et al., 2013: 23–24). The study showed that the majority of learners perceived the CF as quite useful, especially if they found it easy to use. However, the research also showed that students with a higher explicit knowledge of the L2 found the CF more easy to use and were able to apply the optional CF metalinguistic information more often. The results did not show any relationship between the learners' achievement goal orientation and their use of CF.

Feedback is also widely available to teachers and learners through online learning dashboards (LD). Information included in LDs varies greatly, for example, students can indicate how they are feeling on a particular day, students can see their achievement results in relation to those of the rest of the class, and teachers can see how, when, and what students are doing when working online. However, despite Fischer's (2007) plea to track student learning, logged data from online courses are very difficult to assess in their raw form. At this time, LDs offer much information but little insight into student behavior online and even less insight into appropriate types of feedback that would benefit learners in their studies and instructors in their teaching (Youngs, Prakash, & Nugent, 2017).

As this brief review has illustrated, CALL can play a prominent role in the interactionist cycle. Therefore, "it is useful to view multimedia design from the perspective of the input it can provide to learners, the output it allows them to produce, the interactions they are able to engage in, and the L2 tasks it supports" (Chapelle, 1998: 26).

3   Cognitive Theory

This section discusses theories that take a cognitive, or individual and internally-focused, approach to language learning. Based on the view that language is a mental construct, the cognitive approach places heavy emphasis on knowledge representation, processing, and recall (Chapelle, 2009; Larsen-Freeman, 2007). Indeed, some believe that all language learning is cognitive and that discussions center not on whether language learning is cognitive but rather on how it is learned, for example, through predisposition (Universal Grammar), socially (Sociocultural Theory), or by skill development (Skill Acquisition Theory) (Ortega, 2015).

Mayer's cognitive theory of multimedia learning explains the cognitive processes involved in multimedia learning (Mayer, 1997; Mayer & Moreno, 2002). According to this theory, when students are presented with written or aural and visual information in a multimedia environment, they are more easily able to organize the information into their own mental representation. CALL, with its opportunities for building tasks using various types of multimedia, has considerable potential for creating such ideal learning environments, which several studies have explored (DeHaan, Reed, & Kuwada, 2010; Jones, 2004; Jones & Plass, 2002; Yoshii, 2013). For example, while investigating multimedia annotations in the context of listening comprehension, Jones & Plass (2002) found that students who had access to both written and pictorial annotations performed better on comprehension tests and vocabulary recognition tests than those students who either did not have annotations or who had only either written or pictorial annotations. Relating their results to Mayer & Moreno's (2002) cognitive theory of multimedia learning, Jones & Plass (2002) concluded that being able to access verbal and visual mental representations allowed students to more easily integrate the new material into their already existing schemata and thereby more easily recall the information.

Adding the variable of physical interaction with multimedia, DeHaan, Reed, & Kuwada (2010) explored whether the cognitive load of video games, which simultaneously present text, audio, and animation, helped or hindered the learning of English vocabulary. Since those learners who simply watched the video game performed better on vocabulary posttests than those who actually played the game, the researchers concluded that the physical interactivity of the game added too much cognitive load for schema development, which is to say, playing the game impeded the learners' cognitive awareness of vocabulary (DeHaan, Reed, & Kuwada, 2010: 84).

In another study that examined multimedia and vocabulary learning, Winke, Gass, & Sydorenko (2008) investigated the effects of captioning when students of Arabic, Chinese, Spanish, and Russian watched videos. Comprehension and vocabulary tests showed that learners who saw the videos with captions both times performed better on the post-vocabulary tests than those who viewed the videos without captions. Additionally, when learners watched the video once with captions and once without, they performed better when they watched with captions the first time. The authors conclude that captions seemed to draw students' attention and focus to important vocabulary. When interviewed, the students confirmed that the captions helped to focus their attention on new vocabulary, helped them comprehend the videos better, and reinforced what they already knew.

In addition to studies on multimedia and vocabulary learning in relation to cognitive theory, there have also been studies related to working memory (Payne & Whitney, 2002; Payne & Ross, 2005). Payne & Ross (2005) investigated individual differences in working memory capacity with third-semester Spanish students who engaged in regular synchronous chat sessions. Analysis of chat transcripts and the data from two instruments measuring executive function and phonological working memory revealed that participants with low phonological working memory had a different chatting style. The researchers hypothesized that the fact that these students produced longer utterances than their high-span peers could be a sign that they "were taking advantage of the reduced cognitive burden introduced by the chatroom to produce more extensive and elaborate constructions" (Payne & Ross, 2005: 48–49) and that they used the chat room as a "compensatory mechanism" (Payne & Ross, 2005: 49). Given the results of these studies, it is obvious that CALL provides many opportunities for SLA research within cognitive theory, including research on memory, multimedia, and schemata (Guichon & Cohen, 2016).

4   Sociocultural/Constructivist Theory

Sociocultural Theory (SCT)[1] states that young learners work together with a caregiver who provides a supportive environment and tools for the learner, until an action, such as tying shoes, can be accomplished alone (Vygotsky, 1978). This space or transition between what learners are able to accomplish with the help of another peer or expert and what they can eventually accomplish alone is known as the zone of proximal development (ZPD) (Vygotsky, 1978). Applied to L2 learning, a learner's ZPD can change or develop during interaction. Teachers are thus charged with developing tasks that include problem solving and truly challenge learners to go beyond their current state of knowledge. Donato (1994) believes that students who scaffold one another develop the skills to eventually move from being dependent to independent learners.

Sociocultural Theory suggests that students are their own best teachers and can rely on their previous knowledge and experience of the world

---

1   Sociocultural Theory is also referred to as socioconstructivism since it combines the social aspect of learning with the claim of constructivism that learning takes place within the individual.

as they collaborate with each other in order to improve the learning environment and move beyond their current level of mastery (Chapelle, 1997; Collentine, 2000; Dalgarno, 1996; Jonassen, 1999; Jonassen, Mayes, & McAleese, 1993; Lantolf, 2000; Lomicka & Lord, 2009; Stepp-Greany, 2002; Uzum, 2010; Vygotsky, 1978; Warschauer, 2005). Collaboration, not competition, becomes the main focus of the learning environment. Students collaborate with each other to solve problems, scaffold, and create solutions, all of which is facilitated by the teacher. Context is thus imperative for the learners because experience and knowledge cannot be used in situations that are, first, outside of the learners' experience, and second, not applicable to a real-world scenario. Many of the characteristics of socioconstructivism fit learners who tend to prefer to learn collaboratively and have "expectations for peer review and support, [and] the need for structure, hands-on learning, the use of technology in the classroom, and opportunities for personal creativity" (Spodark, 2008: 27–28). Spodark (2008) refers to the blending of the use of technology with the tenets of socioconstructivism as technoconstructivism, which is believed to appeal to some learning preferences.

Spodark (2008) integrated ideas of technoconstructivism into a fifth-semester French class when she required students to read francophone stories and legends and then write their own stories in French through a multi-step process. As a pre-writing task, students chose a topic by exploring francophone websites to learn about francophone countries and then organized their findings on a class webpage as an annotated bibliography. After peer reviewing their outlines, the students completed the first draft of their stories to again be evaluated by their classmates. After several drafts, students presented the final draft to their classmates in an oral presentation. Spodark (2008) noted that by designing the tasks to encourage collaboration and the use of CALL through every step of the process, students were engaged in several tenets of technoconstructivism, including peer review, teamwork, hands-on learning, creativity, and the use of technology.

4.1   Collaboration in SCT

Collaborative learning is normally associated with sociocultural theory because it has the potential to engage learners in social learning and help them scaffold new material to ultimately internalize it as their own. Collaboration can (1) help students to produce better final products when working collaboratively on a project, such as a wiki page (Arnold, Ducate, & Kost, 2009; Arnold et al., 2009; Elola & Oskoz, 2010; Kessler, 2009; Ho & Savignon, 2007); (2) engage students in deeper reflection (Arnold &

Ducate, 2006) or peer review (Ho & Savignon, 2007); (3) provide students with native or non-native speaker interlocutors (Cooke-Plagwitz, 2008; Sadler, 2007); and (4) connect students with classmates or others with similar interests through social networking, blogs, photo-sharing sites, podcasts, and video-sharing sites (Dieu & Stevens, 2008).

In collaborative writing studies, Bikowski & Vithanage (2016) found that ESL students working together online improved their writing skills over students who worked individually online, and Yeh (2014) found that collaborative text-based synchronous dialogues during the entire writing process improved students' products. Similarly, Elola & Oskoz (2010) investigated collaborative behavior in a wiki task and compared working strategies and final products when eight Spanish students in an advanced writing class worked collaboratively and individually. The researchers found that students working collaboratively addressed issues related to the structure of the essay early in the writing process, for example, determining the thesis, and addressed grammar issues throughout the writing process. Working alone, students worked on essay structure, and edited grammar and vocabulary mainly on their final draft. However the students, acknowledging that collaborative work produced a better final product and appreciating input from their partners, reported preferring writing individually to maintain autonomy over their choices, develop their own personal writing style in Spanish, and work according to their own schedule.

Helm & Guth (2016) explain eTandem and the Cultura models of (S)CMC telecollaboration, highlighting the advantages of sociocultural oral interactions between learners of different languages. The pairs communicate synchronously or asynchronously, in their L1 or L2; then in class, instructors help students understand the mostly cultural information gained from the partnerships. Students engage primarily in task-based activities in which they get to know each other, find out information that only their partner would know, for example, on cultural practices, and negotiate to produce an artifact, for example, a cultural analysis of a world event.

A particular use of collaborative and socioconstructivist learning can be seen in virtual learning environments (VLEs or VEs), massive multiplayer online gaming spaces (MMOGs), and synthetic immersive environments (SIEs). Sykes, Oskoz, & Thorne (2008) believe that these virtual worlds encourage learners to interact and become socialized in the target language in a context specific to the genre of the environment. In virtual environments such as *World of Warcraft* (WOW) and SIEs like *Croquelandia*, "… [l]earners are able to practice … in order to improve their pragmatic competence in a low-risk, yet emotionally engaging, immersive space" (Sykes, 2008: 537). In multiuser virtual environments (MUVEs) such as

Second Life, learners have the opportunity to engage in realistic "linguistic and cultural immersion" (Cooke-Plagwitz, 2008: 555). Grantham O'Brien, Levy, & Orich (2009) discuss another type of virtual environment, CAVEs (CAVE Automatic Virtual Environment), an immersive environment for virtual reality. CAVEs are spatially "real" in that in a darkened room, the learner has the impression of being physically in the reality of the game, which is interactive and takes place in real time (see also Polisca, 2006 and Sykes, Holden, & Knight in this volume).

In addition to virtual environments, Web 2.0 programs can be potentially beneficial to language learners and promote social learning (Lomicka & Lord 2009). This more socially connected and communicative second generation of the World Wide Web can facilitate activities such as blogging, collaborative writing, file sharing, tagging, and social networking (Thorne, Black, & Sykes, 2009) and can promote the formation of learning communities. No matter the environment, learners seek out opportunities to be socially active participants, collaborate with other learners, and teach each other. Some preliminary research has seen tension, however, between the roles of the instructor and the learner, as each participant attempts to understand his or her "new" role in a VLE (Chateau & Zumbihl, 2012; Comas-Quinn, de los Arcos, & Mardomingo, 2012; Bayle & Youngs, 2013).

Collaborative projects can help students produce richer final products and reach higher levels of understanding; however, students still tend to prefer to work alone for logistical reasons and need to be convinced of the benefits of collaboration, trained for how to successfully manage it, and monitored by the teacher throughout the process.

4.2   The Role of Task Design in SCT

Although task-based language teaching (TBLT) is not directly connected to SCT, both share certain philosophies. TBLT includes many of the components noted above by Spodark (2008) and is an important component of L2 teaching that encourages learners to focus more on the purpose of using the L2 rather than on the language forms.

When learning through TBLT, students should focus on expressing themselves, and making and interpreting meaning in context (Lee, 1995). Certainly many CALL tasks fit in the category of TBLT due to their contextualized nature and focus on meaning, and there have been studies that directly examine task design in CALL. Hampel (2006) describes the approach, design, and procedure of CALL-based task development in which she and her colleagues provided opportunities for students to complete contextualized tasks to prepare for and engage in synchronous interactions. Each learner had a role in a specific scenario, such as town-planning developments in an East German spa town; a meeting of newspaper editors deciding on a page 1 story; an interview with a film director; organizing an event around environmental issues; or putting together an exhibition about German history. In this example of TBLT, students worked collaboratively with authentic materials to prepare for their synchronous chats during which they had to focus on meaning in order to reach a decision and complete the assigned task. Hampel (2006) also noted that students' interactions contained examples of negotiation of meaning and, even though they were not required to focus on form, discussions of linguistic features or specific vocabulary.

Collentine (2009) investigated learners' discourse-pragmatic and socio-cultural behaviors in task-based SCMC between intermediate and advanced learners of Spanish. Results from her study indicate that both task type and developmental level influenced the types of holistic language units that learners produced. Based on her finding that lower-level learners used "a restricted repertoire of holistic language moves" (2009: 80), Collentine suggests that in order for learners to use a variety of discourse-pragmatic and sociocultural behaviors in task-based SCMC, they need a higher level of proficiency due to the extra linguistic load of task-based learning. She found that lower-level learners were so focused on the task that they seemed less able to attend to metalinguistic issues, whereas higher proficiency students were even able to joke or engage in off-task behavior.

Learners who collaborate through effectively designed tasks can create an environment that not only facilitates learning, but builds community as well. In order to effectively accomplish both learning and community-building, Gánem Gutiérrez points out that computer-mediated tasks require two levels of analysis: "descriptive, to observe and account for the nature of collaborative activity, and analytical, to discuss the quality of collaborative activity" (Gánem Gutiérrez, 2003: 110). For example, the nature of a collaborative task requires that students aim to solve the problem before them and focus on form. During this process, students co-create, using knowledge common to some but not all, in order to complete the task. The descriptive phase therefore permits instructors to review whether a task was indeed collaborative. The analytical phase illustrates the quality (or lack thereof) of the collaborative task. Gánem Gutiérrez (2003) shows whether students provided each other with necessary scaffolding and whether their output was sufficient to complete the task.

In a later study, Gánem Gutiérrez tested three tasks to understand which ones allowed learners to produce the most high-quality collaboration (HQC), defined as when learners, "working within a zone of proximal development (ZPD), are able to co-construct language related knowledge" (Gánem Gutiérrez, 2006: 238). Her findings show that the type of task, macro problem-solving or micro problem-solving, provided different results in the amount of language-related episodes (LREs) produced by the students when working with a computer or on paper. As the studies described here demonstrate, task-design is an integral part of L2 learning and can have a substantial effect on students' orientation towards and performance in an activity.

5   Affective, Social, and Pedagogical Principles

Technology routinely plays a role in differentiated instruction and permitting universal access to online materials. In this section, we discuss how CALL facilitates the work of instructors in creating successful opportunities for every type of learner.

5.1   Differentiated Instruction

Differentiated instruction offers a framework for addressing learner variance as a critical component of instructional planning (Tomlinson & McTighe, 2006). Learners, even those within the same classroom, can differ in terms of "… culture, race, language, economics, gender, experience, motivation to achieve, disability, advanced ability, personal interests, learning preferences" (Tomlinson & McTighe, 2006: 1), all of which can influence a student's ability or desire to learn. CALL can offer students multiple ways of approaching and accessing information and learning materials to meet their individual needs. For example, students who prefer listening could first listen to a dialogue before reading it; students who prefer reading and "having a handle" on a text could read it first, then listen to it, with or without the support of the original text or transcriptions of the text provided by the video.

The advantage of CALL is that when we help students to work within the scope of any challenges they may have and discover how they learn best, we can help them to develop language learning strategies and perhaps to maximize their learning (Cohen, 2014; Oxford, 1990, 2016). The role of the instructor in noting learner differences and choosing CALL materials that will facilitate individualized instruction is paramount. With this information, we can focus our students on developing autonomy and hopefully create life-long learners. Richards & Rodgers (2010: 30) describe the fundamentals of individualized instruction:

1. Materials will allow learners to progress at their own rates of learning.
2. Materials will allow for different styles of learning.
3. Materials will provide opportunities for independent study and use.
4. Materials will provide opportunities for self-evaluation and progress in learning.

By the same token, the success of CALL materials in facilitating individualized instruction will be a result of developers, in cooperation with instructors, who are aware of the above-mentioned differentiating factors and will be able to incorporate technical elements that will contribute to successful language learning.

5.2   Learner Autonomy

The development of learner autonomy stems from learners' awareness that successful language learning experiences can be realized by virtue of their own actions. Holec (1980, 1988; see also Oxford 1990, 2016) described learner autonomy as the decisions and responsibilities that the learners take for their own learning. Technology can help them achieve autonomy by providing input that can be decoded, but additionally by personally involving them in "more exploratory and experiential tasks" (Kettemann, 1997: 182). Studies have also been done on learner autonomy (Hamilton, 2013), faculty attitudes and motivation to use VLEs (Al Harbi, 2016), and the fostering of independent language learning (Franc & Morton, 2014).

As demonstrated by multiple studies, CALL can promote learner autonomy. Research has shown that by working on their own with such applications as interactive video (Shea, 2000), language learning software (Farivar & Rahimi, 2015; Ruschoff, 1998), corpus data (Chambers, 2005), website design (Van Lier, 2003), wikis (Arnold, Ducate, & Kost, 2009; Kessler, 2009), blogs (Ducate & Lomicka, 2005), Twitter (Newgarden, 2009), synchronous or asynchronous CMC (Abrams, 2006; Arnold & Ducate, 2006; Darhower, 2002; Dias, 2000; Polat, Mancilla, & Mahalingappa, 2013; Schwienhorst, 2003), web-based games or virtual worlds, scenario-based design (Shin & Wastell, 2001), or extended or Internet-based reading (Arnold, 2009; Brandl, 2002), students are able to progressively gain more independence and confidence. In reflective blogs written after SCMC tandem meetings between students from France and Australia, Garcia, O'Connor, & Cappellini (2017) found a social dimension to autonomy development: for example, in one instance students modified a task in order to promote a more spontaneous discussion. However the researchers also found limitations in this environment with respect to learner goal setting as they found no evidence of this type of reflection in the students' blog posts.

Learning strategies to use CALL effectively can also increase learner autonomy (Farivar & Rahimi, 2015; Mutlu & Eröz-Tuga, 2013). As students work more often outside of the classroom and "on the go" due to the growing popularity of mobile-assisted language learning (MALL) and the use of tablets and phones, they have the opportunity to develop their autonomy both in and outside of the classroom (Chinnery, 2006; Fischer, 2007; Reinders & Hubbard, 2013; Schwienhorst, 2012). Stockwell (2013) found, for example, that students' use of PCs or smartphones was determined more by where they preferred to study, at what time of the day, and what their study goal was (i.e., homework or test preparation). However, students are not automatically ready to direct their own learning simply because they understand how to use personal technologies. Instructors must continue to guide students until they can become independent learners (Fischer, 2007).

In their study, Thang & Bidmeshki (2010) examined autonomy and use of reading strategies (cognitive strategy training, vocabulary exercises, how to use contextual cues and dictionaries) in an online course. ESL undergraduates at a Malaysian university improved their reading skills and strategies while becoming more aware of autonomous learning, and even commented that they took the initiative to find and read online scientific texts on their own. In addition to becoming more autonomous, the instruction of reading strategies also had long-term motivational effects, an important aspect of learner autonomy.

As the findings above indicate, there are many ways to measure autonomy in CALL tasks and promote learner autonomy. Nonetheless, there is still research to be done on the types of CALL tasks and tools in this area, for example the possible long-term effects, as well as the role of the teacher.

5.3   Identity

Similar to motivation and learner autonomy, learner identity is an internal factor that influences language students. For example, students sometimes have difficulty establishing an identity as a speaker of the L2 due to their limited language proficiency. The teacher's physical presence can also make it difficult for learners to overcome their own default subordinate position due to the instructor's inherited power. Along with that is the institutional "persona": students in this class, this course, this school are competitive and talkative or shy and awkward in the real world; these same students can take on a different persona in the virtual world.

In an online environment, learners can create identities that are separate and different from those already established in their F2F classroom. For Chang & Sperling (2014), students are freer when online as opposed to in class because online, they can socialize among themselves as themselves, and are not limited by the instructor who may "permit" socialization or not, depending on the F2F context and rules. In an academic context, Ha's (2009) work describes socialization as a question of how do I fit in, do I belong. In order to do so, tools such as avatars, usernames, visual representations, in essence, new meaning-making tools, can allow students to enhance their identities or overcome identity positions that are uncomfortable or not conducive to learning, for example, those students who might be reluctant to participate in class due to anxiety or shyness. Additionally, and perhaps most importantly, online language learners are sometimes able to emphasize other aspects of their identity that allow them to claim positions as experts in targeted subjects, connect with their peers in new and different ways, and establish that the F2F version that everyone "seems" to know is in fact not the full version of the individual.

Social transfer to online learning, however, is not always smooth. Although the potential for success exists, learners need to be socialized into online discourse and its associated communities. For example, Thorne, Black, & Sykes discuss VLEs' potential for L2 education and SLA research, stating that "what occurs online, and often outside of instructed educational settings, involves extended periods of language socialization, adaptation, and creative semiotic work that illustrate vibrant communicative practices" (Thorne, Black, & Sykes, 2009: 815).

Klimanova found that identity was a moving target for her L2 Russian learners engaging with native speakers (NS) in keypal activities and authentic NS online discussion communities. She describes a continuum of L2 learner identity as they worked toward social acceptance from the native speakers, one that spanned the range from the dependent, needy learner to the self-sufficient multilingual subject (Klimanova 2013: 356). Identity questions arose especially when students chose to be "bystanders" instead of active participants in the authentic online community, as their participation was limited by their level of language skill yet this was where significant learning took place (2013: 354).

5.4   Motivation

Students may learn a language for various reasons and the research defines two broad types of motivation: instrumental and integrative (Gardner, 1991; Masgoret & Gardner, 2003; Ng & Ng, 2015; Oletic & Ilic, 2014).

Instrumental motivation is the drive to learn an L2 for tangible gain, including salary raises or promotions. Integrative motivation describes a learner who is interested in becoming familiar with a particular L2 group or culture, and who shows a desire to interact with, even become part of that group or culture. Students who are not integratively motivated however, can still find a welcoming community in the language classroom. As Van den Branden explains, some studies suggest that "SL [Second Language] classrooms might offer better and safer opportunities [for learners] to practice their communicative skills and build up L2 confidence than the outside world" (Van den Branden, 2007: 173). And once motivation increases, a student may become open to communication with the target culture. Prior to this, though, practicing with technology can be the avenue that students use to communicate prior to stepping out into the real world.

In order for a task to be motivating, it must be appropriately difficult, have meaningful objectives, use varying teaching methods, provide feedback, and facilitate learning (Good & Brophy, 1987 as cited in Dias, 2000). Each of the studies below attempts to incorporate these characteristics of a motivating task. While it can be difficult to measure, many studies have examined the level of motivation when using CALL by surveying students (Ayres, 2002; Genc Ilter, 2009; Thang & Bidmeshki, 2010). Studies showing increases in motivation using specific CALL tools are widespread, for example, video-capture virtual reality technology in a second grade English class in Taiwan (Yang, Chen, & Jeng, 2010), employing a robot to engage with English elementary school learners (Chang & Chen, 2010), providing students with a chatbot as an interlocutor (Fryer & Carpenter, 2006), and engaging students with pace-controlled captioned interactive videos (Shea, 2000; see also Ducate & Lomicka, 2009; Jiang & Ramsay, 2005; Lan, Sung, & Chang, 2007; Lord, 2008; Pérez-Llantada, 2009).

In the study noted above that examined Malaysian students' perceptions of an English for science and technology online course (Thang & Bidmeshki, 2010), the students enjoyed the online format of the course with its online modules, interesting topics, animation, and new and comfortable mode of learning that provided flexibility and autonomy. The students reported that their motivation improved over the semester and continued after the semester ended. Ayres (2002) also examined learner attitudes towards CALL and asked 157 learners to compare their attitudes of computer-assisted instruction to traditional teaching. The learners, non-native English students in New Zealand, reported that CALL was useful and motivating to them and should be used more as long as it is closely integrated into the curriculum and relevant to their coursework. In another survey study, Genc Ilter (2009) found that technology helped to motivate EFL (English as a Foreign

Language) students at a Turkish university and that using different types of technological tools can be motivating in class as long as they are integrated into the course content, take into account students' interests and needs, and are based on good pedagogy.

With the goal of increasing advanced German students' motivation towards reading in the L2, Arnold (2009) conducted a study in which she accompanied her students to the computer lab seven times over the semester for them to engage in extensive reading. Students were given a list of websites to help them in their search for interesting texts, and were asked to write a report summarizing what they read thereby relaying their reactions to the text at the end of the session. The students found it motivating to select texts that they wanted to read based on their own personal interests, which also motivated them to want to learn more about the German language and culture, and hopefully helped to keep them motivated about reading German texts even after the semester ended.

As shown by both the survey studies and the task-based study, when CALL is integrated into the curriculum in a meaningful way in order to facilitate learning, it can also serve to increase students' motivation towards CALL use and L2 learning in general.

5.5   Learner Preferences

As teachers, it is important to consider how our learners learn. Some of us, for example, dislike listening comprehension, but others of us adore watching films. Some of us prefer to make charts, others prefer lists. Although disputed in the literature, learner preferences are one way that we can think about how learners perceive and process information (Shrum & Glisan, 2010). For example, Naimie et al. (2010) conducted observations and interviews of 310 learners in order to quantify their learning styles and to discern how various in-class tasks corresponded to learners' learning styles, which could then determine the effectiveness of teaching and technology use in an EFL class in Iran. The findings revealed that when students' learning styles were taken into account, they performed better and were more motivated towards the tasks.

Scarcella & Oxford (1992: 61) outline five preferences: (1) analytic-global; (2) sensory; (3) intuitive/random and sensory/sequential learning; (4) orientation to closure; and (5) competition-cooperation. Similar to Gardner's (2006) nine multiple intelligences, explained below, learning styles can encourage teachers to reflect on how learners approach a task. Subsequently, teachers can help students become more aware of which technologies might support their learning preferences, thereby creating a more effective learning environment.

CALL offers multiple affordances that address various learning preferences and multiple intelligences. Technology, for example, can supplement class activities with online readings, video clips, simulations, or skills practice to cater to students with different learning styles (Chakraborty, 2010). Due to the multimodal affordances of CALL (e.g., video, audio, text, music, visual art, and photographs), different learning preferences and intelligences can be activated to engage learners and help keep them motivated since the

Table 1 Sample activities for different intelligences

Intelligence	Sample activities
Verbal/linguistic	• read authentic materials • publish online with wikis and blogs • communicate with other learners through email, skype, chat, and discussion boards • create presentations, and record audio
Logical/mathematical	• create graphs, maps, illustrations, spreadsheets, and puzzles • use software to engage in simulations
Visual/spatial	• engage with interactive graphic puzzles • publish using desktop publishing and presentation software • create movies • visit interactive websites
Bodily/kinesthetic	• draw online • manipulate visuals using a whiteboard or tablet • employ digital cameras for project-based learning (in the future, gesture-based computing will add exciting new opportunities for this learning style; New Media Consortium, 2011)
Musical	• listen to or compose music or poetry
Interpersonal	• connect with other L2 learners or native speakers using Skype, email, blogs, chat, CMC, and Twitter • engage with classmates on group projects • use wikis for presentational projects
Intrapersonal	• create individual projects • maintain a blog • do independent research in the form of web searches
Naturalist	• create maps and databases • visit online zoos or museums
Existential	• read literature and tell stories, which could be made more interactive via technology with captions, glossing, and images, and digital humanities options, for example, in creating chronologies (http://www.clas.wayne.edu/ELD/)

tasks appeal to their specific strengths (Chisolm & Beckett, 2003). To provide ideas of how CALL can accommodate learners showing strength in different intelligences, Chisolm & Beckett (2003) provide a list of examples and tools, which we have supplemented with additional ideas in Table 1.

Like learning preferences, an awareness of personality types allows teachers to take into account how individuals prefer to learn and work. Using the Big Five personality inventory,[2] Jones & Holland (2013) found that personality type is linked to students' blogging habits and commentary use. Beauvois & Eledge (1996) used the Myers-Briggs Type Indicator (Briggs-Myers & Briggs, 1985) to examine student reactions to SCMC sessions. Both introverted and extroverted students considered CMC linguistically, affectively, and interpersonally beneficial. "An important finding of this preliminary study is that communication on the L[ocal] A[rea] N[etwork] seems to appeal to both E types [extroverted], who tend to participate in the face-to-face interaction of the traditional class discussion, and to I types [introverted], who are often reluctant to interact with their peers because of their specific work preference" (Beauvois & Eledge, 1996: 35). Only one specific personality type, INTP (introversion, intuition, thinking, perceiving), responded somewhat less positively to the chats.

5.6   CALL, Universal Access, and Universal Design

Students with learning challenges, cognitive or physical, can benefit from appropriately developed and implemented CALL tools (Ehrman, 1996; Hamayan, 1997; Schwarz, 1997; Shrum & Glisan, 2010). Research has been done in the areas of test-taking (Dolan et al., 2005), reading (Hall, Hughes, & Filbert, 2000), and mathematics (Bley & Thornton, 2001) showing that computer-assisted learning combined with good pedagogy can improve overall student learning.

CALL tools can be used to enhance audio or produce audio for students with hearing difficulties or visually challenged students. For example, students with visual difficulties can listen to computer-generated audio or use computer screens designed for optimal accessibility. Enhancing computer screens for learners with vision difficulties creates an effect much like that of large-print library books, but with the opportunity to add, again, a listening component, glossary options, and detailed views of smaller images. Descriptions of artwork using the target language could also encourage

---

2   Jones & Holland (2013: 96) use the Five-Factor test in their research. See
     https://www.123test.com/big-five-personality-theory/ for a quick view of
     the five factors.

practice of listening comprehension and vocabulary development, allowing learners to understand the cultural relevance of art. Students with a physical challenge could use voice-activated programs to engage with software or hardware. Research has also been done on computer-assisted learning for individuals with autism spectrum disorder. Vlachou & Drigas (2017) outline mobile tools for augmentative or alternative communication to aid the development of interaction in social situations and linguistically in the L1.

Universal Design for Learning (UDL) is a research-based framework that provides excellent guidelines for including all students in an improved learning environment. Taking into consideration the needs of all learners, Burgstahler (2012) cites the Center for Applied Special Technology,[3] which proposes that a curriculum, supplemented by technology, can offer

1. Multiple means of representation, to give learners various ways of acquiring information and knowledge;
2. Multiple means of action and expression, to provide learners alternatives for demonstrating what they know; and
3. Multiple means of action and engagement, to tap into learners' interests, offer appropriate challenges, and increase motivation.

In the end, instructors who pay attention to learners' needs and apply pedagogical principles will help encourage them and engage them in the learning process.

6   Pedagogical Implications of CALL

In this chapter, we have discussed how teachers, with background in SLA research combined with knowledge of the affordances of CALL, can advance solutions for effective teaching and learning for all students. There remains one component that must not be forgotten, however, and that is the learner or end-user of CALL. As Winke & Goertler remind us, prior to implementing online courses, "the targeted language learning population needs to be surveyed in terms of their computer access and literacy to understand the potential buy-in and feasibility of the project and to ascertain what types of supplemental access and training need to be provided" (Winke & Goertler, 2008: 483). While these are central considerations for online courses, they are equally important for individual CALL tasks designed to supplement F2F instruction. As language teachers, we may not consider it "our job"

---

3   www.cast.org

to teach students how to use computers, but students still need teachers to help direct their time and energy toward the efficient and effective use of CALL tools. While these students are accustomed to using various Web 2.0 and computer applications in their daily life, they need pedagogical training in order to be able to transform their everyday applications, such as Facebook, chat, blogs, and wikis, and social networking opportunities into tools for language learning (Hubbard, 2004; Lin, Warschauer, & Blake, 2016; Lomicka & Lord, 2016).

Below are some questions to help decide, first, whether to use CALL, and second, how and when. These questions may not necessarily be answered in this order and, furthermore, might need to be revisited if a task or outcome changes.

1. What is my objective? The very first step in designing a curriculum, lesson or task is to determine its learning outcomes before choosing how to achieve them. CALL is no different in that respect.

2. Where do I want my students to achieve this objective? While some objectives can be met outside the classroom, others are more appropriate for class time where the teacher can guide learners. This decision might be driven by practical concerns as well as pedagogical ones.

3. What task do I want the students to take on and which tool is most appropriate? There needs to be a match between the task and its learning objectives on the one hand and the tool on the other. For example, if collaborative writing is the goal, a wiki might be a better fit than a blog or paper-based writing. Consider too which affordances of the tool in question might add or subtract to students' learning, based on the task's learning objectives.

4. What kind of students do I have and how do I need to prepare them for the task? We have already mentioned the importance of considering learners' digital literacy and providing learner training when needed. Are learners generally comfortable with technology? Are they anxious when working with particular CALL tools? Are they familiar and comfortable with using technology for an educational goal, to learn language? Do they know how to type accents and foreign characters? Will they need training on this particular tool, and if so, where will it be done, who will instruct them, how long will it take, and what software/hardware will be needed? If the task is to be completed as homework, do the students have access to the technology at home or at school/on campus? Knowing the students is as important as knowing which CALL tool to use.

5. How will I assess learners? It is important to assess student performance in light of the tasks' objective(s) (Leaver & Willis, 2004; Shrum & Glisan, 2010). For CALL, we need to consider additional aspects with regard to assessment, such as if the nature of the technology warrants any adjustments in assessment (e.g., should the assessment change if a writing task is done online and not on paper?), and including effective and appropriate use of the technology in an assessment can motivate students to focus on both the language and the technology/medium or detract from their language/content learning. Rubrics can be very helpful in establishing guidelines for both instructors and students.

6. How will I as the instructor evaluate the CALL implementation? There are two types of evaluation, formative and summative. Formative evaluation can lead to adjustments that need to be made during the implementation of a task or a course. To create more opportunities for student success, some changes can or even should be undertaken immediately rather than waiting until the next time the task or course is offered. In contrast, summative evaluations are performed after a task or a course is finished. At that point, the teacher or researcher can review the entire implementation and decide what could be improved for the next time.

7   Conclusion

This chapter has emphasized the symbiotic nature of CALL and SLA. Practitioners and researchers interested in improving the effectiveness of CALL for the teaching and learning of second and foreign languages sometimes look for guidance from SLA research with the goal of designing CALL activities to create ideal conditions for SLA. Despite convictions that SLA theory and research should inform CALL development and practice, and vice versa, details of how to form such links still need to be elaborated (Hegelheimer & Chapelle, 2000: 41; see also Hubbard, 2008, 2009). The fields of CALL and SLA sometimes feel fixed on opposite ends of a spectrum and language/content teachers seem to be required to choose either the CALL or the SLA "side." Beneficial to our common goals, however, CALL and SLA researchers and practitioners continue to find research-based ways of integrating the two domains.[4]

Needless to say, language/content teachers will continue to struggle with the effective implementation of CALL as they seek to educate their

4   I might suggest "coleslaw" (CALLSLA).

students. Once a teacher decides on a theoretical framework to guide the pedagogy, the decision to integrate technology into that pedagogy must be made according to learning theory and within the guidelines of the discipline's methodology. In the rest of this volume, it will be important to examine closely the research studies supporting a particular technology, the objectives and the expected outcomes for using that technology, and the tasks and assessments designed to achieve the greatest possible gain for students' benefit. Like the filmstrip, reel-to-reel films, ditto machines, video clips, laser discs, and the Smartboard that came before, any current technology, be it hardware or software, must be chosen with thought and great care to maximize its benefits to our students' learning.

Questions for Reflection

1. Design a plan for one learning objective using ACTFL's 5 Cs[5] World Readiness Standards and the 3 Ps for teaching culture: Perspectives, Practices, and Products.[6] Describe the students' proficiency based either on ACTFL[7] or the CEFR,[8] and use the topic of breakfast where your language is spoken, either in different parts of one country or in multiple countries. You may either use French Online or an app of your choosing.
   Outline the:
   - objective/s – Will your focus be on perspectives, practices, and/or products? Will the students compare breakfasts among many target culture countries and/or to their own culture/s?
   - theoretical framework (Interactionist, Cognitive, Sociocultural, other?)
   - task and the CALL tool to accomplish the task and explain why the affordances of the chosen CALL tool will lead to learning
   - task and tool design to include many types of students
   - assessment (of both student achievement and the task design).

---

5 https://www.actfl.org/publications/all/
   world-readiness-standards-learning-languages/standards-summary
6 https://www.actfl.org/news/press-releases/
   actfl-publishes-position-statement-global-competence
7 https://www.actfl.org/publications/guidelines-and-manuals/
   actfl-proficiency-guidelines-2012
8 https://www.coe.int/en/web/
   common-european-framework-reference-languages/level-descriptions

2. Choose an online application for language learning and link its language learning advantages and disadvantages to the research presented in this chapter or to other studies familiar to you.
    Or, if you'd prefer, visit https://oli.cmu.edu/courses/all-oli-courses/ french-i-course-details/ and on the details page of this course, click on "Register for a sample lesson." There is no need to create an account, simply use the right side of the page for "Enter without an account." Click on the "I am not a robot" and then "Enter the course." This course was written based on the technology available at the time. Working with a partner, choose one section of the course and together discuss how, if new technology were available, the design of the activities could be revised according to the research examined in this chapter.
3. If you were required to use the online application from question 2 in your course, how would you exploit its advantages? Similarly, most CALL tools have some disadvantages. What could you do to overcome some of them, but moreover, would it be work that you would want to take on given the other responsibilities required of teachers?

References

Abrams, Zs. (2006). From theory to practice: Intracultural CMC in the L2 classroom. In L. Ducate & N. Arnold (eds.), *Calling on CALL: From theory and research to new directions in foreign language teaching*, pp. 181–210. San Marcos, TX: CALICO.

Al Harbi, M. (2016). Faculty attitudes toward and motivation for virtual learning environments (VLE) for language studies: A cross-national study in Saudi Arabian universities. *American Research Institute for Policy Development*, 4(2), 100–114. https://doi.org/10.15640/jpbs.v4n2a9

Antenos-Conforti, E. (2009). Microblogging on Twitter: Social networking in intermediate Italian classes. In L. Lomicka & G. Lord (eds.), *The next generation: Social networking and online collaboration in foreign language learning*, pp. 59–90. San Marcos, TX: CALICO.

Arnold, N. (2009). Online extensive reading for advanced foreign language learners: An evaluation study. *Foreign Language Annals*, 42(2), 340–366. https://doi.org/10.1111/j.1944-9720.2009.01024.x

Arnold, N., & Ducate, L. (2006). Future foreign language teachers' social and cognitive collaboration in an online environment. *Language Learning & Technology*, 10(1), 42–66. Available at
http://llt.msu.edu/vol10num1/arnoldducate/default.html

Arnold, N., Ducate, L., & Kost, C. (2009). Collaborative writing in wikis: Insights from culture projects in German classes. In L. Lomicka & G. Lord (eds.), *The next generation: Social networking and online collaboration in foreign language learning*, pp. 115–144. San Marcos, TX: CALICO.

Arnold, N., Ducate, L., Lomicka, L., & Lord, G. (2009). Assessing online collaboration among language teachers: A cross-institutional case study. *Journal of Interactive Online Learning*, 8(2), 121–139.

Ayres, R. (2002). Learner attitudes towards the use of CALL. *Computer Assisted Language Learning*, 15(3), 241–249. https://doi.org/10.1076/call.15.3.241.8189

Bayle, A., & Youngs, B. (2013). Patterns of interaction between moderators and learners during synchronous oral discussions online. In P. Hubbard, M. Schulze, & B. Smith (eds.), *CALICO Journal, Learner-Computer interaction in language education: A festschrift in honor of Robert Fischer*, pp. 66–91. San Marcos, TX: CALICO.

Beauvois, M. H. (1998). Conversations in slow motion: Computer-mediated communication in the foreign language classroom. *Canadian Modern Language Review*, 54(2), 198–217. https://doi.org/10.3138/cmlr.54.2.198

Beauvois, M. H., & Eledge, J. E. (1996). Personality types and megabytes: Attitudes towards computer-mediated communication (CMC) in the language classroom. *CALICO Journal*, 13(2/3), 27–45. Available at https://calico.org/journalTOC.php

Bikowski, D., & Vithanage, R. (2016). Effects of web-based collaborative writing on individual L2 writing development. *Language Learning & Technology*, 20(1), 79–99. http://dx.doi.org/10125/44447

Blake, R. (2008). *Brave new digital classroom: Technology and foreign language learning*. Washington, DC: Georgetown University Press.

Bley, N. S., & Thornton, C. A. (2001). *Teaching mathematics to students with learning disabilities*. Accessed November 12, 2017 at https://eric.ed.gov/?id=ED461975

Brandl, K. (2002). Integrating Internet-based reading materials into the foreign language curriculum: From teacher- to student-centered approaches. *Language Learning & Technology*, 6(3), 87–107. Available at http://llt.msu.edu/vol6num3/brandl/default.html

Brown, H. D. (1994). *Principles of language teaching and learning*. New Jersey: Prentice Hall.

Burgstahler, S. (2012). *Universal design in education: Principles and applications*. Seattle: University of Washington. Accessed February 10, 2018 at https://www.theudlproject.com/uploads/8/8/1/9/8819970/udl_principles_ and_applications.pdf

Burnaby, B. (1997). Second language teaching approaches for adults. In G. R. Tucker & D. Corson (eds.), *Second language acquisition: Encyclopedia of language and education*, volume 4, pp. 95–104. Boston: Kluwer Academic. https://doi.org/10.1007/978-94-011-4419-3_10

Briggs-Myers, I., & Briggs, K. C. (1985). *Myers-Briggs type indicator (MBTI)*. Palo Alto, CA: Consulting Psychologists Press.

Chakraborty, P. (2010). Multiple intelligences, blended learning and the English teacher. *Language in India*, 10(10), 546–555.

Chambers, A. (2005). Integrating corpus consultation in language studies. *Language Learning & Technology*, 9(2), 111–125. Available at http://llt.msu.edu/vol9num2/chambers/default.html

Chang, C., & Chen, G. (2010). Using a humanoid robot to develop a dialogue-based interactive learning environment for elementary foreign language classrooms. *Journal of Interactive Learning Research*, 21(2), 215–235.

Chang, Y. C., & Sperling, M. (2014). Discourse and identity among ESL learners: A case study of a community college ESL classroom. *Research in the Teaching of English*, 49(1), 31–51.

Chapelle, C. A. (1997). CALL in the year 2000: Still in search of research paradigms? *Language Learning & Technology*, 1(1), 19–43. Available at http://llt.msu.edu/vol1num1/chapelle/default.html

Chapelle, C. A. (1998). Multimedia CALL: Lessons to be learned from research on instructed SLA. *Language Learning & Technology*, 2(1), 22–34. Available at http://llt.msu.edu/vol2num1/article1/index.html

Chapelle, C. A. (2000). Innovative language learning: Achieving the vision. *ReCALL*, 13, 3–14.

Chappelle, C. A. (2005). Interactionist SLA theory in CALL research. In J. L. Egbert & G. M. Petrie (eds.), *CALL research perspectives*, pp. 53–64. New Jersey: Lawrence Erlbaum Associates.

Chapelle, C. A. (2009). The relationship between second language acquisition theory and computer-assisted language learning. *Modern Language Journal*, 93(1), 741–753. https://doi.org/10.1111/j.1540-4781.2009.00970.x

Chapelle, C. A., & Sauro, S. (2017). *The handbook of technology and second language teaching and learning.* New Jersey: Wiley. https://doi.org/10.1002/9781118914069

Chateau, A., & Zumbihl, H. (2012). Towards new roles for learners and teachers in a language learning system? *Eurocall: Nottingham.* Accessed November 11, 2017 at http://files.eric.ed.gov/fulltext/ED544444.pdf

Chinnery, G. (2006). Going to the MALL: Mobile assisted language learning. *Language Learning & Technology*, 10(1), 9–16. Available at http://llt.msu.edu/vol10num1/emerging/default.html

Chisolm, I. M., & Beckett, C. (2003). Teacher preparation for equitable access through the integration of TESOL standards, multiple intelligences and technology. *Technology, Pedagogy and Information*, 12(2), 249–275. https://doi.org/10.1080/14759390300200157

Chun, D. M. (1994). Using computer networking to facilitate the acquisition of interactive competence. *System*, 22(1), 17–31.

Clark, R. E. (1983). Reconsidering research on learning from media. *Review of Educational Research*, 53, 445–459. https://doi.org/10.3102/00346543053004445

Cohen, A. (2014). *Strategies in learning and using a second language.* New York: Routledge.

Collentine, J. (2000). Insights into the construction of grammatical knowledge provided by user-behavior tracking technologies. *Language Learning & Technology*, 3(2), 44–57. Available at http://llt.msu.edu/vol3num2/collentine/index.html

Collentine, K. (2009). Learner use of holistic language units in multimodal, task-based synchronous computer-mediated communication. *Language Learning & Technology*, 13(2), 68–87. Available at http://llt.msu.edu/vol13num2/collentine.pdf

Collentine, K. (2013). Using tracking technologies to study the effects of linguistic complexity in CALL input ad SCMC output. In P. Hubbard, M. Schulze, & B. Smith (eds.), *CALICO Journal, Learner-Computer interaction in language education: A festschrift in honor of Robert Fischer*, pp. 46–65. San Marcos, TX: CALICO.

Comas-Quinn, A., de los Arcos, B., & Mardomingo, R. (2012). Virtual learning environments (VLEs) for distance language learning: Shifting tutor roles in a contested space for interaction. *Computer Assisted Language Learning*, 25(2), 129–143. https://doi.org/10.1080/09588221.2011.636055

Cooke-Plagwitz, J. (2008). New directions in CALL: An objective introduction to Second Life. *CALICO Journal*, 25(3), 547–557. Available at https://calico.org/journal-TOC.php; https://doi.org/10.1558/cj.v25i3.547-557

Cornillie, F., Lagatie, R., Vandewaetere, M., Clarebout, G., & Desmet, P. (2013). Tools that detectives use: In search of learner-related determinants for usage of optional feedback in a written murder mystery. In P. Hubbard, M. Schulze, & B. Smith (eds.), *CALICO Journal, Learner-Computer interaction in language education: A festschrift in honor of Robert Fischer*, pp. 22–45. San Marcos, TX: CALICO.

Crystal, D. (2006). *Language and the Internet*. Cambridge, UK: Cambridge University Press. https://doi.org/10.1017/CBO9780511487002

Dalgarno, B. (1996). Constructivist computer assisted learning: Theory and techniques. Retrieved July 29, 2010, from http://www.ascilite.org.au/conferences/adelaide96/papers/21.html

Darhower, M. (2002). Instructional Features of Synchronous Computer-Mediated Communication in the Intermediate L2 Class: A Sociocultural Case Study. *CALICO Journal*, 19(2), 249–277.

Debski, R. (2003). Analysis of research in CALL (1980–2000). *ReCALL*, 15, 177–188. https://doi.org/10.1017/S0958344003000429

DeHaan, J., Reed, M., & Kuwada, K. (2010). The effect of interactivity with a music video game on second language vocabulary recall. *Language Learning & Technology*, 14(2), 74–94. Available at http://llt.msu.edu/vol14num2/dehaanreedkuwada.pdf

DeKeyser, R. M. (2007). Introduction: Situating the concept of practice. In R. M. DeKeyser (ed.), *Practice in a second language: Perspective from applied linguistics and cognitive psychology*, pp. 1–18. Cambridge, UK: Cambridge University Press.

Dias, J. (2000). Learner autonomy in Japan: Transforming "help yourself" from threat to invitation. *Computer Assisted Language Learning*, 13(1), 49–64. https://doi.org/10.1076/0958-8221(200002)13:1;1-K;FT049

Dieu, B., & Stevens, V. (2008). Pedagogical affordances of syndication, aggregation, and mash-up of content on the web. *Teaching English as a Second or Foreign Language*, 11(1), 1–15.

Dolan, R. P., Hall, T. E., Banerjee, M., Chun, E., & Strangman, N. (2005). Applying principles of universal design to test delivery: The Effect of computer-based read aloud on test performance of high school students with learning disabilities. *Journal of Technology, Learning, and Assessment*, 3(7). Accessed November 12, 2017 at https://eric.ed.gov/?id=EJ848517

Donato, R. (1994). Collective scaffolding. In J. Lantolf & G. Appel (eds.), *Vygotskian approaches to second language research*, pp. 33–56. Norwood, NJ: Ablex.

Doughty, C. J., & Long, M. H. (2003). *The handbook of second language acquisition*. Malden, MA: Blackwell. https://doi.org/10.1002/9780470756492

Ducate, L., & Lomicka, L. (2005). Exploring the blogosphere: Use of web logs in the foreign language classroom. *Foreign Language Annals*, 38(3), 410–421. https://doi.org/10.1111/j.1944-9720.2005.tb02227.x

Ducate, L., & Lomicka, L. (2008). Adventures in the blogosphere: From blog readers to blog writers. *Computer Assisted Language Learning*, 21(1), 9–28. https://doi.org/10.1080/09588220701865474

Ducate, L., & Lomicka, L. (2009). Podcasting: An effective tool for honing students' pronunciation? *Language Learning & Technology*, 13(3), 72–92. Available at http://llt.msu.edu/vol13num3/ducatelomicka.pdf;

Ellis, R. (1986). *Understanding second language acquisition*. Oxford, UK: OUP.

Ehrman, M. (1996). *Understanding second language learning difficulties*. London: Sage.

Elola, I., & Oskoz, A. (2010). Collaborative writing: Fostering foreign language and writing conventions development. *Language Learning & Technology*, 14(3), 51–71. Available at http://llt.msu.edu/october2010/elolaoskoz.pdf

Farivar, A., & Rahimi, A. (2015). The impact of CALL on Iranian EFL learners' autonomy. *Procedia – Social and Behavioral Sciences*, 192(24), 644–649. https://doi.org/10.1016/j.sbspro.2015.06.112

Farr, F., & Murray, L. (2016). *The Routledge handbook of language learning and technology*. New York: Routledge.

Fischer, R. (2007). How do we know what students are actually doing? Monitoring students' behavior in CALL. *Computer Assisted Language Learning*, 20(5), 409–442. https://doi.org/10.1080/09588220701746013

Fischer, R. (2008). Introduction to the special issue. *CALICO Journal*, 25, 377–384. Available at https://calico.org/journalTOC.php; https://doi.org/10.1558/cj.v25i3.377-384

Franc, C., & Morton, A. (2014). *The use of VLE for monitoring independent language learning in large cohort provision: The case of French Studies at the University of Manchester*, pp. 709–723. https://doi.org/10.4018/978-1-46666042-7.ch034

Freed, B. F. (1991). *Foreign language acquisition research and the classroom*. Lexington, MA: D.C. Heath and Company.

Fryer, L., & Carpenter, R. (2006). Bots as language learning tools. *Language Learning & Technology*, 10(3), 8–14. Available at http://llt.msu.edu/vol10num3/emerging/default.html

Gánem Gutiérrez, G. A. (2003). Beyond interaction: The study of collaborative activity in computer-mediated tasks. *ReCALL*, 15, 94–112. https://doi.org/10.1017/S0958344003000818

Gánem Gutiérrez, G. A. (2006). Sociocultural theory and its application to CALL: A study of the computer and its relevance as a mediational tool in the process of collaborative activity. *ReCALL*, 18, 230–251. https://doi.org/10.1017/S0958344006000620

Garcia, D. N. M., O'Connor, K., & Cappellini, M. (2017). A typology of meta-cognition: Examining autonomy in a collective blog compiled in a teletandem environment. In M. Cappellini, T. Lewis, & A. R. Mompean (eds.), *Learner autonomy and Web 2.0*, chapter 4, pp. 67–90. Sheffield, UK: Equinox Publishing.

Gardner, H. (2006). *Multiple intelligences: New horizons*. New York, NY: Basic Books.

Gardner, R. C. (1991). Attitudes and motivation in second language learning. In A. J. Reynolds (ed.), *Bilingualism, multiculturalism, and second language learning: The McGill conference in honour of Wallace E. Lambert*, pp. 43–63. New Jersey: Lawrence Erlbaum Associates.

Gass, S. M. (1997). *Input, interaction, and the second language learner*. New Jersey: Lawrence Erlbaum Associates.

Gass, S. M. (2008). Input and interaction. In C. Doughty & M. Long (eds.), *The handbook of second language acquisition, chapter 9*. Oxford: Blackwell.

Gass, S. M., & Mackey, A. (2007). *Data elicitation for second and foreign language research*. Mahwah, New Jersey: Lawrence Erlbaum Associates.

Genc Ilter, B. (2009). Effect of technology on motivation in EFL classrooms. *Turkish Online Journal of Distance Education-TOJDE*, 19(4), 136–158.

González-Lloret, Marta. (2003). Designing task-based CALL to promote interaction: En busca de esmeraldas. *Language Learning & Technology*, 7(1), 86–104. Available at http://llt.msu.edu/vol7num1/gonzalez/default.html

Grantham O'Brien, M., Levy, R., & Orich, A. (2009). Virtual immersion: The role of CAVE and PC technology. *CALICO Journal*, 26, 337–362. Retrieved April 3, 2011, from https://calico.org/journalTOC.php; https://doi.org/10.1558/cj.v26i2.337-362

Guichon, N., & Cohen, C. (2016). Multimodality and CALL. In F. Farr & L. Murray (eds.), *The Routledge handbook of language learning and technology*, chapter 36. New York: Routledge.

Ha, M. J. (2009). *Doing graduate school in a second language: Resituating the self through language socialization in computer-mediated classroom discussions*. Doctoral dissertation. Retrieved from https://repositories.lib.utexas.edu/handle/2152/29596

Hager, M. (2005). Using German web sites to teach culture in German courses. *CALICO Journal*, 22(2), 269–284. Available at https://calico.org/journalTOC.php; https://doi.org/10.1558/cj.v22i2.269-284

Hall, T. E., Hughes, C. A., & Filbert, M. (2000). Computer assisted instruction in reading for students with learning disabilities: A research synthesis. *Education and Treatment of Children*, 23(2), 173–193. Accessed November 12, 2017 at http://www.jstor.org/stable/42940524

Hamayan, E. V. (1997). Teaching exceptional second language learners. In G. R. Tucker & D. Corson (eds.), *Second language acquisition: Encyclopedia of language and education*, volume 4, pp. 85–93. Boston: Kluwer Academic Publishers. https://doi.org/10.1007/978-94-011-4419-3_9

Hamilton, M. (2013). *Autonomy and foreign language learning in a virtual learning environment*. Bloomsbury: London.

Hampel, R. (2006). Rethinking task design for the digital age: A framework for language teaching and learning in a synchronous online environment. *ReCALL*, 18, 105–121. https://doi.org/10.1017/S0958344006000711

Hegelheimer, V., & Chapelle, C. A. (2000). Methodological issues in research on learner computer interactions in CALL. *Language Learning & Technology*, 4(1), 41–59. Available at http://llt.msu.edu/vol4num1/hegchap/default.html

Hegelheimer, V., & Tower, D. (2004). Using CALL in the classroom: Analyzing student interactions in an authentic classroom. *System*, 32, 185–205. https://doi.org/10.1016/j.system.2003.11.007

Heift, T. (2004). Corrective feedback and learner uptake in CALL. *ReCALL*, 16, 416–431. https://doi.org/10.1017/S0958344004001120

Helm, F., & Guth, S. (2016). Tellecollaboration and language learning. In F. Farr & L. Murray (eds.), *The Routledge handbook of language learning and technology*, chapter 17. New York: Routledge.

Herron, C., Dubreil, S., Corrie, C., & Cole, S. (2002). A classroom investigation: Can video improve intermediate-level French language students' ability to learn about a foreign culture? *Modern Language Journal*, 86(1), 36–53. https://doi.org/10.1111/1540-4781.00135

Ho, Mei-Ching, & Savignon, Sandra J. (2007). Face-to-Face and Computer-Mediated Peer Review in EFL Writing. *CALICO Journal*, 24, 269–290. https://doi.org/10.1558/cj.v24i2.269-290.

Holec, H. (1980). *Autonomy and foreign language learning*. Nancy: Centre de Recherches et d'Applications Pedagogiques en Langues. Council of Europe.

Holec, H. (ed.). (1988). *Autonomy and self-directed learning: Present fields of application*. Strasbourg: Council of Europe.

Hubbard, P. (2004). Learner training for effective use of CALL. In S. Fotos & C. M. Browne (eds.), *New perspectives on CALL for second language classrooms*, pp. 45–68. Mahwah, NJ: Lawrence Erlbaum.

Hubbard, P. (2008). Twenty-five years of theory in the CALICO Journal. *CALICO Journal*, 25, 387–399. Available at https://calico.org/journalTOC.php; https://doi.org/10.1558/cj.v25i3.387-399

Hubbard, P. (2009). Developing CALL Theory: A new frontier. *Proceedings of the JALTCALL Conference*, Nagoya, Japan, May 2008.

Hulstijn, J. (2000). The use of computer technology in experimental studies of second language acquisition: A survey of some techniques and some ongoing studies. *Language Learning & Technology*, 3(2), 32–43. Available at http://llt.msu.edu/vol3num2/hulstijn/default.html

Jiang, W., & Ramsay, G. (2005). Rapport-building through CALL in teaching Chinese as a foreign language: An exploratory study. *Language Learning & Technology*, 9(2), 47–63. Available at http://llt.msu.edu/vol9num2/jiang/default.html

Jonassen, D. H. (1999). Constructing learning environments on the web: Engaging students in meaningful learning. *EdTech 99 – Educational Technology Conference and Exhibition 1999: Thinking Schools*. Learning Nation.

Jonassen, D. H., Mayes, T., & McAleese, R. (1993). A manifesto for a constructivist approach to uses of technology in higher education. In T. M. Duffy, J. Lowyck & D. H. Jonassen (eds.), *Designing environments for constructive learning*, pp. 231–247. Heidelberg: Springer-Verlag.
https://doi.org/10.1007/978-3-642-78069-1_12

Jones, L. C. (2004). Testing L2 Vocabulary recognition and recall using pictorial and written test items. *Language Learning & Technology*, 8(3), 122–143.
http://dx.doi.org/10125/43998

Jones, L. C., & Holland, A. (2013). Who blogs? Understanding the correlation of personality and blogging in cultural discussions. In P. Hubbard, M. Schulze, & B. Smith (eds.), *CALICO Journal, Learner-Computer interaction in language education: A festschrift in honor of Robert Fischer*, pp. 92–117. San Marcos, TX: CALICO.

Jones, L. C., & Plass, J. L. (2002). Supporting listening comprehension and vocabulary acquisition in French with multimedia annotations. *Modern Language Journal*, 86(4), 546–561.

Kessler, G. (2009). Student-initiated attention to form in wiki-based collaborative writing. *Language Learning & Technology*, 13(1), 79–95. Available at http://llt.mus.edu/vol13num1/kessler.pdf

Kettemann, B. (1997). Innovative second language education in Western Europe. In G. R. Tucker & D. Corson (eds.), *Second language acquisition: Encyclopedia of language and education*, volume 4, pp. 175–186. Boston: Kluwer Academic Publishers. https://doi.org/10.1007/978-94-011-4419-3_17

Klimanova, Liudmila. (2013). *Second language identity building through participation in internet-mediated environments: a critical perspective*. Doctoral dissertation, University of Iowa. http://ir.uiowa.edu/etd/5001

Kötter, M. (2003). Negotiation of meaning and codeswitching in online tandems. *Language Learning & Technology*, 7, 145–172.

Krashen, S. (1982). *Principles and practice in second language acquisition*. Englewood Cliffs, NJ: Prentice Hall.

Krashen, S. (1985). *The input hypothesis: Issues and implications*. London: Longman.

Lafford, B. (2009). Toward an ecological CALL: Update to Garrett (1991). *Modern Language Journal*, 93, 673–96.
https://doi.org/10.1111/j.1540-4781.2009.00966.x

Lan, Y., Sung, Y., & Chang, K. (2007). A mobile-device-supported peer-assisted learning system for collaborative early EFL reading. *Language Learning & Technology*, 11(3), 130–151. Available at
http://llt.msu.edu/vol11num3/lansungchang/default.html

Lantolf, J. P. (2000). Introducing sociocultural theory. In J. P. Lantolf (ed.) *Sociocultural theory and second language learning*, pp. 1–26. Oxford: OUP.

Larsen-Freeman, D. (2007). Reflecting on the cognitive-social debate in second language acquisition. *Modern Language Journal*, 91, 773–787.
https://doi.org/10.1111/j.1540-4781.2007.00668.x

Leaver, B. L., & Willis, J. R. (2004). *Task-based instruction in foreign language education*. Washington, DC: Georgetown.

Lee, J. F. (1995). Using task-based activities to restructure class discussions. *Foreign Language Annals*, 28(3), 437–446. https://doi.org/10.1111/j.1944-9720.1995.tb00811.x

Lee, J. F. (2000). *Tasks and communicating in language classrooms*. New York: McGraw-Hill.

Lin, C.-H., Warschauer, M., & Blake, R. (2016). Language learning through social networks: Perceptions and reality. *Language Learning & Technology*, 20(1), 124–147. Available at http://llt.msu.edu/issues/february2016/linwarschauerblake.pdf

Lin, H. (2014). Establishing an empirical link between computer-mediated communication (CMC) and SLA: A meta-analysis of the research. *Language Learning & Technology*, 18(3), 120–147. Available at http://dx.doi.org/10125/44387

Lomicka, L., & Lord, G. (2009). *The next generation: Social networking and online collaboration in foreign language learning*, volume 8, CALICO Monograph Series. San Marcos, TX: CALICO.

Lomicka, L., & Lord, G. (2016). Social networking and language learning. In F. Farr & L. Murray (eds.), *The Routledge handbook of language learning and technology*, chapter 18. New York: Routledge.

Long, M. H. (1996). The role of the linguistic environment in second language acquisition. In W. R. Ritchie and T. J. Bathia (eds.), *Handbook of second language acquisition*, pp. 412–68. San Diego: Academic Press. https://doi.org/10.1016/B978-012589042-7/50015-3

Lord, G. (2008). Podcasting communities and second language pronunciation. *Foreign Language Annals*, 41(2), 364–379. https://doi.org/10.1111/1467-9922.00212

Masgoret, A.-M., & Gardner, R. C. (2003). Attitudes, motivation, and second language learning: A meta-analysis of studies conducted by Gardner and associates. *Language Learning*, 53, 123–163. https://doi.org/10.1111/1467-9922.00212

Mayer, R. E. (1997). Multimedia learning: Are we asking the right questions. *Educational Psychologist*, 32, 1–19. https://doi.org/10.1207/s15326985ep3201_1

Mayer, R. E., & Anderson, R. B. (1992). The instructive animation: Helping students build connections between words and pictures in multimedia learning. *Journal of Educational Psychology*, 84, 444–452. https://doi.org/10.1037/0022-0663.84.4.444

Mayer, R. E., & Moreno, R. (2002). Theory of multimedia learning: Implications for design principles. Retrieved July 29, 2010, from www.unm.edu/~moreno/PDFS/chi.pdf

Mitchell, R., & Myles, F. (1998). *Second language learning theories*. London: Arnold.

Muranoi, H. (2007). Output practice in the L2 classroom. In R. M. DeKeyser (ed.), *Practice in a second language: Perspectives from applied linguistics and cognitive psychology*, pp. 51–84. Cambridge, UK: Cambridge University Press. https://doi.org/10.1017/CBO9780511667275.005

Mutlu, A., & Eröz-Tuga, B. (2013). The role of computer-assisted langauge learning (CALL) in promoting learner autonomy. *Egitim Arastirmalari – Eurasian Journal of Educational Research*, 51, 107–122.

Naimie, Z., Siraj, S., Abuzaid, R. A., & Shagholi, R. (2010). Hypothesized learners' technology preferences based on learning style dimensions. *TOJET: The Turkish Online Journal of Educational Technology*, 9(4), 83–93.

Newgarden, K. (2009). Media review of Twitter. *TESOL E-Journal*, 13(2), 1–13.

New Media Consortium. (2011). *The Horizon Report*, 2011 edition. Retrieved from http://www.nmc.org/publications/2011-horizon-report

Ng, C. F., & Ng, P. K. (2015). A review of intrinsic and extrinsic motivations of ESL learners. *International Journal of Languages, Literature and Linguistics*, 1(2), 98–105. https://doi.org/10.7763/IJLLL.2015.V1.20

O'Brien, A., & Hegelheimer, V. (2007). Integrating CALL into the classroom: The role of podcasting in an ESL listening strategies course. *ReCALL*, 19(2), 162–180. https://doi.org/10.1017/S0958344007000523

Oletic, A., & Ilic, N. (2014). Intrinsic and extrinsic motivation for learning English as a foreign language. *ELTA Journal*, 2(2), 23–38.

Omaggio Hadley, A. (2001). *Teaching Language in Context*, 3rd edition. Boston, MA: Heinle & Heinle.

Ortega, L. (2015). Second language learning explained? SLA across 10 contemporary theories. In B. Van Patten & J. Williams (eds.), *Theories in second language acquisition: An introduction*, pp. 245–272. Retrieved from https://ebookcentral.proquest.com

Oxford, R. (1990). *Language learning strategies: What every teacher should know*. Boston, MA: Heinle & Heinle.

Oxford, R. (2016). *Teaching and researching language learning strategies: Self-regulation in context*. New York: Routledge.

Payne, J. S., & Ross, B. (2005). Synchronous CMC, working memory, and L2 oral proficiency development. *Language Learning & Technology*, 9(3), 35–54. Available at http://llt.msu.edu/vol9num3/payne/default.html

Payne, J. S., & Whitney, P. J. (2002). Developing L2 oral proficiency through synchronous CMC: Output, working memory and interlanguage development. *CALICO Journal*, 20(1), 7–32. Available at https://calico.org/journalTOC.php

Pellettieri, J. (2000). Negotiation in cyberspace: The role of chatting in the development of grammatical competence. In M. Warschauer & R. Kern (eds.), *Network-based language teaching: Concepts and practice*, pp. 59–86. Cambridge, UK: Cambridge University Press.

Pérez-Llantada, C. (2009). Textual, genre and social features of spoken grammar: A corpus-based approach. *Language Learning & Technology*, 12(1), 40–58.

Pica, T. (1996). The Essential role of negotiation in the communicative classroom. *JALT Journal*, 18(2), 241–268.

Polat, N., Mancilla, R., & Mahalingappa, L. (2013). Anonymity and motivation in asychronous discussions and L2 vocabulary learning. *Language Learning & Technology*, 17(2), 57–74. http://dx.doi.org/10125/44324

Polisca, E. (2006). Facilitating the learning process: An evaluation of the use and benefits of a virtual learning environment (VLE)-enhanced independent language-learning program (ILLP). *CALICO Journal*, 23, 499–515. Available at https://calico.org/journalTOC.php; https://doi.org/10.1558/cj.v23i3.499-515

Reinders, H., & Hubbard, P. (2013). CALL and learner autonomy: Affordances and constraints. In M. Thomas, H. Reinders, & M. Warschauer (eds.), *Contemporary computer-assisted language Learning*, pp. 359–375. New York: Bloomsbury.

Richards, J. C., & Rodgers, T. S. (2010). *Approaches and methods in language teaching: A description and analysis*. Cambridge, UK: Cambridge University Press.

Ruschoff, B. (1998). Neue Medien als Grundlage neuer Lernwelten für das fremdsprachliche Lernen. *Franzosisch heute*, 1, 21–33.

Sadler, R. (2007). Computer-mediated communication and a cautionary tale of two cities. *CALICO Journal*, 25(1), 12–30. Available at https://calico.org/journalTOC.php

Scarcella, R. C., & Oxford, R. L. (1992). *The tapestry of language learning*. Boston: Heinle & Heinle.

Schachter, J. (1997). Linguistic theory and research: Implications for second language learning. In G. R. Tucker & D. Corson (eds.), *Second language acquisition: Encyclopedia of language and education*, volume 4, pp. 11–19. Boston: Kluwer Academic Publishers. https://doi.org/10.1007/978-94-011-4419-3_2

Schmidt, R. (1990). The role of consciousness in second language learning. Applied Linguistics, 11(2), 129–158. https://doi.org/10.1093/applin/11.2.129

Schmidt, R. (1995). Consciousness and foreign language learning: A tutorial on attention and awareness in learning. In R. Schmidt. (ed.), *Attention and awareness in foreign language learning*, pp. 1–63. Honolulu, HI: University of Hawai`i.

Schmidt, R. (2010). Attention, awareness, and individual differences in language learning. In W. M. Chan, S. Chi, K. N. Cin, J. Istanto, M. Nagami, J. W. Sew, T. Suthiwan, & I. Walker (eds.), *Proceedings of CLaSIC 2010*, pp. 721–737. Singapore: National University of Singapore, Centre for Language Studies.

Schwarz, R. L. (1997). Learning disabilities and foreign language learning. Retrieved July 29, 2010, from http://www.ldonline.org/article/6065

Schwienhorst, K. (2003). Learner autonomy and tandem learning: Putting principles into practice in synchronous and asynchronous telecommunication environments. *Computer Assisted Language Learning*, 16(5), 427–443. https://doi.org/10.1076/call.16.5.427.29484

Schwienhorst, K. (2012). *Learner autonomy and CALL environments*. New York: Routledge.

Shea, P. (2000). Leveling the playing field: A study of captioned interactive video for second language learning. *Journal of Educational Computing Research*, 22(3), 243–263. https://doi.org/10.2190/3NEY-BNT0-FB28-VBWY

Shin, J., & Wastell, D. G. (2001). A user-centered methodological framework for the design of hypermedia-based CALL systems. *CALICO Journal*, 18(3), 517–537. Available at https://calico.org/journalTOC.php; https://doi.org/10.1558/cj.v18i3.517-537

Shirai, Y. (1997). Linguistic theory & research: Implications for second language teaching. In G. R. Tucker & D. Corson (eds.), *Second language acquisition: Encyclopedia of language and education*, volume 4, pp. 1–9. Boston: Kluwer Academic Publishers. https://doi.org/10.1007/978-94-011-4419-3_1

Shohamy, E. (1997). Second language assessment. In G. R. Tucker & D. Corson (eds.), *Second language acquisition: Encyclopedia of language and education*, volume 4, pp. 141–149. Boston: Kluwer Academic Publishers. https://doi.org/10.1007/978-94-011-4419-3_14

Shrum, J., & Glisan, E. (2010). *Teacher's handbook: Contextualized language instruction*, 4th edition. Boston, MA: Heinle & Heinle.

Smith, B. (2008). Methodological hurdles in capturing CMC data: The case of the missing self-repair. *Language Learning & Technology*, 12(1), 85–103. Available at http://llt.msu.edu/vol12num1/smith/default.html

Smith, B. (2009). Task-based learning in the computer-mediated communicative ESL/EFL classroom. *CALL-EJ Online*, 11. Retrieved July 29, 2010, from http://www.tell.is.ritsumei.ac.jp/callejonline/journal/11-1/smith.html

Smith, B. (2016). *Technology in language learning: An overview*. New York: Routledge.

Smith, M. S. (1993). Input enhancement in instructed SLA. *Studies in Second Language Acquisition*, 15, 165–179. https://doi.org/10.1017/S0272263100011943

Spodark, E. (2008). Technoconstructivism and the millennial generation: Creative writing in the foreign language classroom. In M. Cherry & C. Wilkerson (eds.), *Dimension 2008: Languages for the nation*, pp. 27–38. Columbia, SC: Southern Conference on Language Teaching.

Stanley, G. (2006). Podcasting: Audio on the Internet comes of age. *Teaching English as a Second or Foreign Language*, 9(4), 1–7.

Stepp-Greany, J. (2002). Student perceptions on language learning in a technological environment: Implications for the new millennium. *Language Learning & Technology*, 6(1), 165–180. Available at http://llt.msu.edu/vol6num1/steppgreany/default.html

Stockwell, G. (2013). Tracking learner usage of mobile phones for language learning outside of the classroom. In P. Hubbard, M. Schulze, & B. Smith (eds.), *CALICO Journal, Learner-Computer interaction in language education: A festschrift in honor of Robert Fischer*, pp. 118–136. San Marcos, TX: CALICO.

Sun, Y. A. (2008). Input processing in second language acquisition: A discussion of four input processing models. *Columbia University Working Papers in TESOL & Applied Linguistics*, 8(1), 1–10. Retrieved from http://journals.tc-library.org/index.php/tesol/article/download/359/260

Sutherland-Smith, W. (2002). Weaving the literacy web: Changes in reading from page to screen. *The Reading Teacher*, 55, 662–229.

Swain, M. (1985). A critical look at the communicative approach (2). *English Language Teaching Journal*, 39, 76–87. https://doi.org/10.1093/elt/39.2.76

Sykes, J. M. (2008). *A dynamic approach to social interaction: SCMC, Synthetic immersive environments & Spanish pragmatics*. Doctoral dissertation, University of Minnesota, Minneapolis, MN.

Sykes, J. M., Oskoz, A., & Thorne, S. L. (2008). Web 2.0, synthetic immersive environments, and mobile resources for language education. *CALICO Journal*, 25, 528–546. Available at https://calico.org/journalTOC.php; https://doi.org/10.1558/cj.v25i3.528-546

Thang, S. M., & Bidmeshki, L. (2010). Investigating the perceptions of UKM undergraduates towards an English for science and technology online course. *Computer Assisted Language Learning*, 23(1), 1–20. https://doi.org/10.1080/09588220903467269

Thorne, S. L., Black, R. W., & Sykes, J. M. (2009). Second language use, socialization, and learning in Internet interest communities and online gaming. *Modern Language Journal*, 93, 802–821. https://doi.org/10.1111/j.1540-4781.2009.00974.x

Thorne, S. L., & Fischer, I. (2012). Online gaming as sociable media. *Alsic* [online], 15(1). Accessed February 10, 2018 at http://journals.openedition.org/alsic/2450; https://doi.org/10.4000/alsic.2450

Thorne, S. L., & Payne, J. S. (2005). Introduction to the special issue. *CALICO Journal*, 22, 369–399. Available at https://calico.org/journalTOC.php; https://doi.org/10.1558/cj.v22i3.369

Thorne, S. L., & Reinhardt, J. (2008). "Bridging activities," new media literacies, and advanced foreign language proficiency. *CALICO Journal*, 25(3), 558–572. Available at https://calico.org/journalTOC.php; https://doi.org/10.1558/cj.v25i3.558-572

Tomlinson, C. A., & McTighe, J. (2006). *Integrating differentiated instruction and understanding by design*. Alexandria, VA: Association for Supervision and Curriculum Development.

Uzum, B. (2010). An investigation of alignment in CMC from a sociocognitive perspective. *CALICO Journal*, 28, 135–155. Retrieved April 4, 2011, from https://calico. org/journalTOC.php; https://doi.org/10.11139/cj.28.1.135-155

Van den Branden, K. (2007). Second language education: Practice in perfect learning conditions? In R. M. DeKeyser (ed.), *Practice in a second language: Perspectives from applied linguistics and cognitive psychology*, pp. 161–179. Cambridge, UK: Cambridge University Press.

Van Lier, L. (2003). A tale of two computer classrooms: The ecology of project based language learning. In J. Leather & J. van Dam (eds.), *Ecology of language acquisition*, pp. 49–63. Dordrecht, Netherlands: Kluwer Academic Publishers.

VanPatten, B. (2003). *From input to output: A teacher's guide to second language acquisition*. New York: McGraw-Hill.

VanPatten, B., & Williams, J. (eds.). (2014). *Theories in second language acquisition: An introduction*. New Jersey: Lawrence Erlbaum Associates.

Vlachou, J. A., & Drigas, A. S. (2017). Mobile technology for students & adults with autistic spectrum disorders (ASD). *iJIM*, 11(1), 4–17. https://doi.org/10.3991/ijim.v11i1.5922

Vygotsky, L. S. (1978). *Mind and society: The development of higher psychological processes*. Cambridge, MA: Harvard University Press.

Warschauer, M. (1996). Comparing face-to-face and electronic discussion in the second language classroom. *CALICO Journal*, 13(2&3), 7–26. Available at https://calico.org/journalTOC.php

Warschauer, M. (2005). Sociocultural perspectives on CALL. In J. L. Egbert & G. M. Petrie (eds.), *CALL Research Perspectives*, pp. 41–52. New Jersey: Lawrence Erlbaum Associates.

Winke, P., Gass, S., & Sydorenko, S. (2008). The effects of captioning videos used for foreign language listening activities. *Language Learning & Technology*, 14(1), 65–86. Available at http://llt.msu.edu/vol14num1/winkegasssydorenko.pdf

Winke, P., & Goertler, S. (2008). Did we forget someone? Students' computer access and literacy for CALL. *CALICO Journal*, 25, 482–509. Available at https://calico.org/journalTOC.php; https://doi.org/10.1558/cj.v25i3.482-509

Wong, W. (2013). Input and output in SLA: Applying theories of mental representation and skill. In J. W. Schwieter (ed.), *Innovative research and practices in second language acquisition and bilingualism*, pp. 23–42. https://doi.org/10.1075/lllt.38.05won

Wong, W. (2018). Input versus intake. In J. I. Liontas (ed.), *The TESOL encyclopedia of English language teaching*, pp. 1–6. New Jersey: Wiley. https://doi.org/10.1002/9781118784235

Yang, J. C., Chen, C. H., & Jeng, M. C. (2010). Integrating video-capture virtual reality technology into a physically interactive learning environment for English learning. *Computers & Education*, 55(3), 1346–1356. https://doi.org/10.1016/j.compedu.2010.06.005

Yeh, H.-C. (2014). Exploring how collaborative dialogues facilitate synchronous collaborative writing. *Language Learning & Technology*, 18(1), 23–37. http://dx.doi.org/10125/44348

Yoshii, M. (2013). Effects of gloss types on vocabulary learning through reading: Comparison of single translation and multiple-choice gloss types. In P. Hubbard, M. Schulze, & B. Smith (eds.), *CALICO Journal, Learner-Computer interaction in language education: A festschrift in honor of Robert Fischer*, pp. 203–229. San Marcos, TX: CALICO.

Youngs, B., Prakash, A., & Nugent, R. (2017 Sept.). Statistically-driven visualizations of students' interactions with a French online course video. *Computer Assisted Language Learning*, 1–20. https://doi.org/10.1080/09588221.2017.1367311

Zhang, S. (2009). The role of input, interaction and output in the development of oral fluency. *English Language Teaching*, 2(4). Accessed February 10, 2018, at https://files.eric.ed.gov/fulltext/EJ1083691.pdf; https://doi.org/10.5539/elt.v2n4p91

Zhao, Y. (2003). Recent developments in technology and language learning: A literature review and meta-analysis. *CALICO Journal*, 21, 7–27. Available at https://calico.org/journalTOC.php; https://doi.org/10.1558/cj.v21i1.7-27

Zourou, K. (2012). On the attractiveness of social media for language learning: a look at the state of the art. *Alsic* [online], 15(1). Accessed February 10, 2018, at http://journals.openedition.org/alsic/2436; https://doi.org/10.4000/alsic.2436

Resources / Professional Journals

CALICO (calico.org)

Computer Assisted Language Learning (http://www.tandfonline.com/loi/ncal20)

Foreign Language Annals (actfl.org) JOLT (jolt.merlot.org)

LLT (http://lltjournal.org)

The Modern Language Journal (http://mlj.miis.edu/)

ReCALL (www.eurocall-languages.org/recall/)

System (www.elsevier.com/locate/system)

TESOL (www.tesol-journal.com)

Universal Design – an example of UDL and how it can be used to improve the learning environment for all students can be found here: http://inclusive.tki.org.nz/guides/universal-design-for-learning/

Web Accessibility Initiative (WAI) https://www.w3.org/WAI/

Conferences & Professional Organizations

See also: http://multilingualbooks.com/forlangassoc.html [accessed February 10, 2018]

CALICO

EUROCALL IALLT

ISTE WorldCALL

National conferences (e.g. ACTFL) and language organizations (like AATF, AATSP, CLTA, NCJLT, TESOL, etc.)

Regional conferences (e.g., CSC, NECTFL, PNCFL, SCOLT, SWCOLT)

State conferences (e.g., NYSAFELT, PSMLA)

About the Author

Bonnie L. Youngs (PhD, University of Pennsylvania) teaches in the under-graduate French & Francophone Studies program and the MA in Applied Second Language Acquisition program, and is the Director of Undergraduate Studies for the Department of Modern Languages at Carnegie Mellon University, Pittsburgh, PA. Her research focuses on using logged online course data and student interviews to understand learners' interactions with online course materials, and providing teachers with data to give effective feedback and guidance to online learners.

2 Normalizing Online Learning: Adapting to a Changing World of Language Teaching

Senta Goertler

Preview Questions

1. Do you have experience teaching or learning online? If so, what is your assessment of the advantages and disadvantages of an online instructional delivery format? If not, how do you imagine that the learning and teaching experience would be different from face-to-face teaching?

2. In Edwige Simon's dissertation (as presented at CALICO in 2010), a participant explained her dislike of online language instruction with the following statement: "I feel that it [online instruction] takes the Human out of Humanities." On the other hand, in their online teaching handbook Carla Meskill & Natasha Anthony claim that: "If we accept as a given that computers are inherently social machines, most pleasurably used for communication and conversation with others, and that learning is best mediated by instructional conversations, then online can be viewed as an optimal venue for language instruction" (Meskill & Anthony, 2015: 70–71). They further argue that "… one of the most critical features of successful online instruction as reported in research studies is the online behaviours of the instructor" (2015: 42). Which one of these two perspectives best matches your own sentiment: (1) online education de-humanizes language instruction; or (2) online learning is a social endeavor in which the teacher plays a key role? Support your opinion.

1   Introduction to the Topic and Definition of Terms

As technologies develop, classroom and office space becomes more limited, institutions attempt to contain budgets and expand access, and students' and faculty's schedules become more hectic, the desire for and the affordances of online language learning increase. In the last iteration of this chapter (Goertler, 2012), I reported that a quarter of university students took at least one online course (Allen & Seaman, 2010). This number has now grown to a third (Allen & Seaman, 2014; National Center for Education Statistics, 2016). Additionally, more and more online resources are available for independent learning or as additions to enrollment in a language class (Meskill & Anthony, 2015).

While institutions and academic leaders overwhelmingly see the benefits of online education (Allen & Seaman, 2014), practitioners and learners continue to have concerns about online and technology-enhanced courses (Allen & Seaman, 2010; Winke, Goertler, & Amuzie, 2010), some of which may be rooted in insufficient information and experience with online learning and teaching (Allen, Seaman, & Garrett, 2007). The Babson Research Group has shown that over time more and more educational leaders express a favorable view of online education except for those at institutions without it (Allen & Seaman, 2014), that is, those lacking experience with online education are more skeptical. According to Allen & Seaman (2014), 90% of academic leaders believe that online learning is likely or very likely to increase, a view confirmed by educational statistics, which in turn means that teaching professionals need to be prepared for and supported in online teaching. This chapter hopes to offer some of this preparation.

The formats of online and blended learning are as varied as the terms used to describe fully and partially online courses (Kraemer, 2008a; White, 2003, 2006). Part of the variance is due to the technologies being used and their purposes, for example, to present and access materials, to build communities, to communicate, to provide feedback, and to act as a resource. Usually four broad categories of delivery format are defined: (A) face-to-face (F2F), (B) technology-enhanced, (C) blended, and (D) online. Adapting the definitions from Allen & Seaman (2010: 4; 2014: 6) and Goertler & Winke (2008) and updating them to reflect current trends, I use the following terms and definitions for instructional delivery formats in this chapter:

A. **Traditional face-to-face instruction** refers to courses that only minimally use technology for either instruction or practice components of a course. These courses meet face-to-face (F2F) only and the technology may be limited to providing the syllabus and the course calendar on a course management system (CMS).

B. **Technology-enhanced instruction** refers to courses that primarily meet F2F. During those F2F meetings, technology is used to varying degrees for instruction and application. These courses may also include online homework assignments. Some class-time, but less than 20% of it, may be replaced with online class periods. This format could include heavy use of technology in class such as working with mobile devices.

C. **Blended instruction**, also called **hybrid instruction**, refers to courses that combine F2F and online instruction and application time. The online components replace 20 to 80% of class-time. The online or technology-enhanced components may be synchronous (in which all participants and teachers are online at the same time working together) or asynchronous, self- or teacher-guided, and use a diverse range of technologies. In recent years, a version of blended learning, **the flipped classroom** (Hojnacki, 2018; Hung, 2015; Mehring, 2016), has gained popularity. The flipped classroom approach takes advantage of class-time for interactive and hands-on learning, while moving the presentation of new information and concepts to at-home interactive online formats.

D. **Open/online instruction** refers to courses that meet F2F minimally, if at all. Most of the instruction and practice time is completed independently and/or online (i.e., more than 80%). Similar to blended instruction, the delivery models of these courses vary greatly. For the purposes of this chapter, this category does not include courses that are paper-based or television-delivered distance learning courses. One especially controversial format in this category, often most closely related to traditional distance learning, is the **Massive Open Online Course (MOOC)** (Dixon & Thomas, 2015). These courses differ from other online courses in that learners are normally not students at the institutions, there is seldom a class size limit, the courses tend to be open access and typically require no tuition, and they often do not offer credit (Allen & Seaman, 2014). The massive size of the course restricts the pedagogical techniques that can be applied yet it enormously increases the possible reach. Despite much attention in the media, only 5% of institutions report offering MOOCs and academic leaders still report being confused about their role in and impact on higher education (Allen & Seaman, 2014).

Table 1 Delivery format comparison

Category	Technologically enhanced	Blended based on flipped model	Online
Time commitment (4 credit course)	600 minutes per week		
Scheduled synchronous meetings per week	Class meets four times a week for 50 minutes in a technology-ready classroom	Class meets three times a week for 50 minutes in a technology-ready classroom	Class breaks up into four groups and each meets once a week online for 50-minutes via video-conferencing
Office hours	2 × 60 minutes F2F		2 × 60 minutes online
Asynchronous and independent learning per week	400 minutes	450 minutes	550 minutes
Presentation of new materials	New grammar, cultural explanations are presented by interactive teacher lecture during F2F meeting	New explanations are presented in recorded lectures with embedded questions	
Grammar practice	Multiple-choice/fill-in-the blank and other form-focused exercises from worksheets and the book are completed in pairs during F2F class meetings and then compared in whole class with teacher feedback	Self-grading multiple-choice/fill-in-the blank exercises from worksheets and online books are completed online individually. Teacher reviews submission reports and uses synchronous time to provide feedback on error patterns and facilitates form-focused, open-ended activities.	Self-grading multiple-choice/fill-in-the blank and open-ended form-focused exercises from online worksheets and the online (work)book are completed individually. Teacher reviews submission reports and open-ended activities and provides feedback on error patterns during synchronous online meeting.

Communication	Communicative tasks (e.g., role-plays, simulations, jigsaws, surveys, interviews, etc.) are completed in pairs or small groups during class time. Answers are compared in a whole class format.	Communicative activities are completed in pairs or small groups during the online meeting using synchronous tools (e.g., break-out rooms in Zoom) or individually or in pairs using asynchronous tools (e.g., VoiceThread, Flipgrid) at other times. Summaries and results are reported in discussion forums or in the online meeting.
Homework	All formats make extensive use of online materials for homework. All use an online workbook and additional online assignments (e.g., web quests, simulated conversations, chats, blogs, wikis, etc.).	
Assessment	Final and midterm exams are taken in person during one of the F2F class periods or specially proctored time slots. For students who are at a remote location, online proctored exams are available. All exams include reading, listening, writing, and speaking components. Speaking components are completed using online asynchronous tools. All major assignments are the same across all three course formats (e.g., quizzes, projects, essays, etc.).	

Table 1 illustrates the differences in the way a variety of curriculum components are presented when a fictitious 4-credit language course is offered in three of these main delivery formats: (1) technology-enhanced, (2) blended, and (3) online. It should be noted that the blended course described below is intended as a flipped model.

Distance learning, and thereby also online learning, have developed with the change of available resources and tools. Yet, as White (2006) points out, all generations of distance learning formats are still present today, contributing to the diversity in implementation and design of courses labeled "online." Many researchers and practitioners have created frameworks through which one can differentiate online instruction. The variables commonly include: (1) level of interactivity; (2) type of media and platforms used; (3) level of synchronicity; (4) instructor and student roles; (5) pedagogical concerns such as teaching approach, curricular goals, and class format; and (6) outcomes and evaluation (Blake, 2009; Means et al., 2009; Meskill & Anthony, 2015).

2   History and Trends in Online Language Education

While online and blended instruction may seem similar on the surface, they have developed out of two different traditions in foreign language contexts. Online courses are the latest version of self-study and distance courses, whose main focus was providing educational opportunities to those who could not come to a campus setting (Hampel & Hauck, 2004) or were not interested in a complete program (Alosh, 2001). Blended courses, on the other hand, were designed for an already existing student population and motivated by institutional and administrative needs (White, 2006) such as the need to make more effective and efficient use of instructional time, space, and resources (Sanders, 2006). The two different goal sets for blended and distance courses necessarily translated to differences in course administration and design features. Today, language programs are mounting online sections within their regular offerings and if other units offer online language courses, they are typically in the form of MOOCs (see for example the German course offered by the University of Pennsylvania) or in non-credit-bearing formats (see for example the language courses offered at the University of Colorado at Boulder).

Blended learning became an attractive solution for administrative and logistical challenges such as increased enrollments (Sanders, 2006). With advances in computing power and speed came the development of computer-mediated communication tools, self-grading exercise programs, and supplemental online materials, which greatly enhanced the feasibility of designing online courses without having to compromise pedagogical goals such as communicative competence.

Regardless of the motivation for moving instruction fully or partially online and regardless of its format, it is here to stay (Allen & Seaman, 2010; Meskill & Anthony, 2015; Murphy-Judy & Johnshoy, 2017), although some researchers speculate that its potential for further growth is limited (Allen & Seaman, 2014). According to data collected in 2004, online courses are more prevalent than blended courses for almost all institutional types (Allen, Seaman, & Garrett, 2007), but the data comparing blended and online enrollments have not been updated. Since blended courses still require classroom space and are usually taught by unit staff using some or all of the same materials as for the F2F courses, blended courses often go unreported (Allen, Seaman, & Garrett, 2007). Recently, Murphy-Judy and Johnshoy (2017) conducted large-scale surveys on online language instruction and found that most online language courses were on the lower level. Spanish courses held the largest share. However, online courses on the upper level were also mentioned and a large variety of languages was represented. Their survey suggests that online language learning has become more common in K-16 contexts in the US.

3   Reasons for and Challenges of Online Language Education

Blended and online learning have become a fixture in language education and, as language educators and researchers, it is important to understand the advantages and disadvantages of moving all or part of the curriculum online. While research results on blended and online learning are encouraging across fields, there are reasons for and against online education in a language learning context. They are discussed below and organized in five sections: (1) logistical, (2) theoretical, (3) pedagogical, (4) curricular, and (5) empirical. Sometimes the same situation can be interpreted from different perspectives in contrasting ways, which will result in some issues being mentioned as both a benefit and a challenge.

3.1   Logistical Factors

Many of the driving forces in curricular redesign projects have included (1) financial considerations such as a need for cost saving or increased revenues and (2) structural considerations such as a need to offer geographical and temporal flexibility for all stakeholders (Meskill & Anthony, 2015; Sanders, 2006). Online courses are beneficial for both reducing demand on classroom space and, through creative staffing, for increasing the student income dollar per staffing expense dollar, which may be the reason they are so popular in lower levels (Murphy-Judy & Johnshoy, 2017). From a logistical perspective, online and blended courses appear on the surface to have many advantages, but hidden problems can negate such advantages and the introduction of such courses requires needs analyses and careful advocacy to ensure stakeholder buy-in. As Gruba et al. (2016) argue, careful review of one's context and its preparedness is necessary before online or blended courses are planned and implemented, which would include these four specific concerns: (1) direct and indirect costs of implementation;

Table 2 Overview of logistical factors

Financial	Potential cost savings:
	• Cut teaching expenses by increasing student-teacher ratio and/or section-teacher ratio (Hampel & Hauck, 2004; Goertler, Bollen, & Gaff, 2012; Sanders, 2006).
	• Use commercial products such as Babel, Duolingo, Rosetta Stone, TalkAbroad and publisher-provided materials to decrease development costs (Lord, 2015; Meskill & Antony, 2015).
	• Recycle and share materials and pre-program feedback which can decrease teacher time commitment (Meskill & Anthony, 2015).
	• Generate revenue through accessing new students (Meskill & Anthony, 2015; White, 2006) and student populations (e.g., non-traditional and/or remote students) (Madyarov, 2009; Meskill & Anthony, 2015).
	Direct and indirect costs:
	• More significant personnel costs, especially if teacher functions as developer, instructor, and technology support (Kraemer, 2008b; Murphy-Judy & Johnshoy, 2017).
	• Retention lower in online courses (Allen & Seamann, 2010; Dreyer, Bangeni, & Nel, 2005).
	• Technology infrastructure is needed (personnel and equipment).
	• Most effective technology tools are still underutilized and often too expensive (Arnold & Ducate, 2015).
	• Ideal target audience (i.e., non-traditional students) may be least prepared for online courses (Goertler, Bollen, & Gaff, 2012; Winke, Goertler, & Amuzie, 2010).
	• Short life-span of tools and high upkeep costs.
Structural	Geographic and temporal flexibility (Meskill & Anthony, 2015)
	• Decrease demand on classroom space.
	• Address increases in student population.
	• Arrange individual learning/teaching time to better match the life, learning, and personality needs of learners and teachers.
	• Collaborate across institutions (e.g., Big Ten Academic Alliance for Less Commonly Taught Languages).
Institutional infrastructure	• Institutional readiness insufficient (Chambers & Bax, 2006).
	• Insufficient understanding of the human, space, and technical resources needed (Gruba et. al, 2016).
	• Teaching online requires a unique skill set (Hampel & Stickler, 2005; Meskill & Anthony, 2015). These skills and training for them are often lacking (Arnold & Ducate, 2015; Kessler, 2006).
	• Students' technology skills are often also insufficient (Gonzalez, 2015; Winke & Goertler, 2008) and are dependent on socio-economic background, ethnicity, and age (Rhinesmith & Reisdorf, 2017), which poses a social justice issue (Ortega, 2017).
	• Adequate solutions need to be found for learners with differing abilities (González-Lloret, 2014) and to protect students' privacy (Zink, 2018).
	• Students and teachers are often apprehensive about online education (Allen & Seaman, 2010; Jaschik & Lederman, 2016), especially those with limited experience with online education.

(2) stakeholder preparedness; (3) technological issues; and (4) stakeholder attitudes. Table 2 provides more detail of benefits and challenges in regard to financial, structural, and institutional concerns.

The checklist below provides instructors with an opportunity to evaluate whether the benefits of online learning outweigh the challenges for their context. The following sections will discuss features and elements that are beneficial in online education from SLA theoretical, pedagogical, and curricular perspectives.

- ✓ Do we need more classroom space or classroom alternatives?
- ✓ Is there a student population who would take our classes, who cannot due to space and/or time concerns? What additional income do we expect?
- ✓ Is there another institution interested in forming an academic alliance?
- ✓ Do we have the technology infrastructure to create, support, and maintain an online course? If not, what would be the cost?
- ✓ Are there online materials available for our language? If not, do we have the resources and skills to create our own? What would it cost?
- ✓ Do our learners and teachers have sufficient technology skills and access for online learning and teaching? If not, what would it cost to provide training and access?
- ✓ Are our learners and teachers willing to learn and teach languages online? If not, what would it take to obtain their buy-in?

3.2   Theory-Based Factors

The theoretical foundation of online language learning goes beyond second language acquisition (SLA) and "literacy studies, discourse analysis, sociocultural theory, sociolinguistics, and anthropology" (Kern, 2006: 201) to include learner autonomy, gaming theory, education, communication, educational technology, and many more. Recently, research on technology-mediated language learning and teaching has asked whether such learning should have its theoretical foundation in SLA or in its own CALL theories (Ortega, 2017). Since readers of this book are likely most familiar with educational and specifically SLA-based theories, these will form the basis of the arguments presented in this section.

From a general education stance, the argument has been made that this and future generations of college students will have formed different learning mechanisms through the use of commercial technology products

(Prensky, 2005). Furthermore, Meskill & Anthony (2015) argue that today's young learners are more comfortable in online communities than face-to-face communities. If so, it is crucial to include learning environments that capitalize on these changed learner behaviors and learning processes. Gaming and virtual worlds are often named as effective environments to address new learner needs (for an overview of gaming in language learning see Sykes & Reinhardt, 2012). Moreover, from a communication standpoint, the contexts in which learners may use the language outside of the classroom has expanded from mere face-to-face conversations to include digitally-mediated interactions as well. As Thorne (2016: 185) argues, "digital communication technologies have amplified the possibilities for communication in the areas of audience, impact, and speed while also facilitating the emergence of distinctive linguistic, multimodal, cultural, interactional, and cognitive practices." This reality poses new demands regarding the goals of language education and the kinds of literacies second language learners need to develop (González-Lloret, 2014; Ortega, 2017), and online language courses are an ideal environment to practice and teach such communication skills.

From early on, CALL researchers, developers, and practitioners have argued for a solid foundation in SLA theory for development, practice and research (Chapelle, 1997, 2009, 2016). As Chapelle (2016) pointed out, SLA theories have expanded in the last decades from mostly cognitive to social perspectives of SLA and from viewing learners as non-native speakers with deficits to learners as members of a language use community (Ortega, 2017). Table 3 summarizes possible features of an online or blended course that are supported by one or more SLA theories (see also Chapelle, 2009).

While blended and online courses can be based on many different theoretical perspectives, there are also theoretical cautions for implementing online and blended learning (Kern, 2006). Most importantly, online learning will necessarily include less synchronous F2F spoken language use. This suggests that the development of oral proficiency and the pragmatic skills needed for F2F interactions might suffer. Moreover, research and experience show that learners can learn a language sufficiently without technology, which for those without the logistical needs discussed in subsection 3.1 above begs the question, why bother? As Doughty & Long (2003) have pointed out, there is no SLA theoretical necessity for the use of technology in L2 teaching and learning.

Table 3 Beneficial features from an SLA theoretical perspective

Flexible	Temporal and geographic flexibility allows for individualized sequencing and pacing of materials and instruction (White, 2006).
Adaptive	Computer-adaptive testing and computer-adaptive learning paths make individualized programs effective and efficient (Blake, 2007; Heift, 2005; Pendar & Chapelle, 2008).
Enhanced	Enhancement through glosses (Lafford, Lafford, & Sykes, 2007) highlighting a particular structure and access to help functions can increase learner attention and noticing (Plonsky & Ziegler, 2016). The slowed-down communication in text-based computer-mediated communication (CMC) and the possibility to adapt the speed of materials give learners the opportunity to process language without pressure (Meskill & Anthony, 2015).
Individualized	Individualized and immediate feedback options based on learner corpora (Blake, 2007; Heift, 2005; Pendar & Chapelle, 2008), learner data (Goodwin-Jones, 2017; Meskill & Anthony, 2015), and parsers (Blake, 2007; Fryer & Carpenter, 2006) will make errors more salient and students can work on their particular problem area (Chapelle & Voss, 2016; Heift, 2010; Simon & Fell, 2013). Built-in intelligent analysis tools (Chapelle, 2016; Goodwin-Jones, 2017; Heift, 2010) give valuable information not just to learners, but also to teachers, and researchers, which can help them improve instruction.
Authentic	Through access to authentic materials and other speakers of the language, learners use and consume language for real purposes (Ortega, 2017).
Communicative	Computer-mediated communication with other speakers of the language or non-player characters/bots provides opportunities to interact, to negotiate for meaning, to notice, to receive modified input, to produce and modify output, and to receive feedback (Blake, 2007; Kern, 2006; Plonsky & Ziegler, 2016). Learners are socialized into digital communities (Ortega, 2017; Thorne, 2016) and can develop effective digital communication skills and multiple literacies, especially since writing conventions in digital communities can differ significantly from traditional formats (González-Lloret, 2014).
Engaging	Learners and teachers can revisit learner language production due to the automatic storing capabilities of programs (Link & Li, 2015). Learners have to actively engage with materials and direct their learning in order to complete the course (Reinders & White, 2016).
Autonomous	Learners have to work through the materials more independently thereby increasing the chances of retention of materials (Reinders & White, 2016).
Multilingual	Activities such as multilingual telecollaboration use several languages of a speaker and acknowledge all languages as resources (Ortega, 2017).

3.3   Pedagogical Factors

As with face-to-face language courses, there are effective and ineffective online and blended language courses. One common misconception about technology and language learning is that online teaching is a teaching method (cf. Blake, 2001), when it is in fact merely a delivery format which can implement a variety of teaching methods: one would design a course following a grammar-translation approach such as, for example, a "German for Reading Knowledge" course quite differently from a communicative language course such as "German for Travel" (González-Lloret, 2014). While the context may limit what pedagogical approaches and activity and task types are appropriate in a course, the delivery format itself does not have such limitations.

As already alluded to, the learning goals for a course will and should drive the decision about teaching approach and therefore also the curricular design process and its evaluation, including whether or not a traditional F2F course can or should be offered as a blended or online course (González-Lloret, 2014; Gruba et al., 2016). As Blake & Guillen (2014) argue: "Our role as language professionals is to focus on designing a superior learning experience for the students, quite apart from any real or supposed economic benefit." This is especially true since, as the Association of Departments of Foreign Languages (ADFL, 2014) reminds practitioners, blended and online learning may not save time or money in the big picture. There might be some immediate cost savings and a potential for increased revenue, as mentioned in subsection 3.1, but there are also associated indirect or hidden costs.

In the language classroom, there are several pedagogical advantages that are particular to online education: (1) connecting speakers/learners inside and outside of the classroom; (2) accessing authentic and up-to-date materials; (3) providing enhanced input and improved feedback loops; (4) developing and reinforcing multiple literacies and digital communication skills; and (5) enabling participatory education.

Connections between learners can be made through online components in several different ways: (1) connections among learners within the group; (2) connections with other learners outside of the class (cf. Zink, 2018); and (3) connections with target language users globally (cf., Goertler et al., 2018: Ortega, 2017; Thorne, Black, & Sykes, 2009). One of the biggest advantages of using CMC in online education is its ability to socialize learners into communities that are safe and rich in interaction, feedback, and authenticity and that foster multilingual communication skills. For more information see also Sykes, Holden, & Knight and Reinhardt & Thorne in this volume.

A second advantage particular to online and blended courses is that authentic and up-to-date materials can be readily integrated into assignments to replace or supplement textbook materials (Goertler & McEwen, 2018). In addition, learners and teachers also have direct access to instructional resources (e.g., online dictionaries, grammar resources, corpora, etc.) which are increasingly available in many languages (Ortega, 2017). When used effectively, these resources can reduce the amount of time an instructor must devote to course preparation, and improve learning (Meskill & Anthony, 2015).

The general advantages of technology for enhancing input and improving feedback loops have already been discussed in the theoretical subsection above. Pedagogically, teachers can utilize these features to make specific materials available to the students in response to their errors and/ or in preparation of the task they have to complete as pre-emptive feedback (Meskill & Anthony, 2015). For example, creating a log of student posts provides an opportunity to document learning for the students, but also to collect a corpus of good examples and typical errors for future students (Meskill & Anthony, 2015). Additionally, the technological platforms allow institutions, programs, and instructors to gather more data about students and their learning engagement, which can be used for more effective curricular planning and teaching (Gruba et. al., 2016; Link & Li, 2015; Youngs, Moss-Horwitz, & Snyder, 2015).

Since online and blended courses require online communication as well as the ability to navigate the content, students naturally have to develop computer, information, critical, multimedia, and computer-mediated literacies (Shetzer & Warschauer, 2000 as cited in González-Lloret, 2014). Meskill & Anthony specify several skills that overlap between online language courses and general online behaviors such as multitasking, bookmarking, updating, self-modulating, conjecturing, exploring, reading discourse contexts, navigating, learning from missteps, representing, reading others' representations, judging, filing, backchanneling (Meskill & Anthony, 2015: 64–68). All of these skills are integral to online learning, yet also necessary to navigate an increasingly digital and multilingual world. For example, planning a trip including purchasing a train ticket is typically completed online these days. Therefore, it is important to practice navigating websites in the target language and participating in online communities such as travel review sites.

And finally, while online education is often criticized for requiring more independence and self-reliance from the students, it is exactly this aspect and the advantages of CMC that can create a more participatory learning environment (Wildner-Bassett, 2008). The anonymous nature of the electronic tools allows for more honest expression of opinions and a student-negotiated democratic classroom-society. Another by-product of online and blended learning is the development of self-responsibility and skills in motivating oneself (Reinders & White, 2016). The typically more open deadlines without direct supervision by a F2F teacher force students to develop their own time-management skills. Program internal components can help learners develop autonomy (Heift, 2005) and learning strategies (Reinders & White, 2016).

From a pedagogical perspective, blended and online courses appear to carry some of the following dangers: (1) lack of personal contact, (2) the possible decreased quality of teaching staff or improperly trained teaching staff, and (3) the culture-bound nature of online materials and presentation, which may make them less accessible for members of other cultures (Kern, 2006).

When asked why they shied away from implementing open and blended courses, program coordinators said that they disapproved of the decrease in personal contact time (Goertler & Winke, 2008). Those at large institutions reported that language classes are often some of the few classes where students have access to professors in a small class environment. Taking away this personal contact with experienced staff may increase the risk of a student's personal or academic problems being detected too late and may lower student retention in the course and the program overall. Effective curricular design components can mitigate such challenges.

From a pedagogical perspective, blended and online courses carry much potential to reach multiple goals, if they are implemented with an awareness of the discussed pedagogical challenges and plans are put in place to safeguard against some of the pitfalls of online and blended education discussed above.

3.4   Curricular Factors

Effective curricula are well articulated within and beyond a program. Many of the best practices for curriculum design for F2F courses also apply to online education. It is simply that in online education, the online platform makes the integration, archiving, and sharing of materials easier and more natural to the format. Meskill & Anthony (2015) argue that for articulation purposes, more fixed elements of a course make curricular articulation easier. Online elements of a course and online education allow us to improve all four aspects of articulation: horizontal, vertical, interdisciplinary, and co-curricular (Goertler & McEwen, 2018).

Horizontal articulation, the articulation across sections such as in the lower levels of a language program, can be improved through online learning, which makes online and blended courses especially popular in the lower-level language classes (Murphy-Judy & Johnshoy, 2017). The advantage of using online and blended formats for delivering the lower levels, which are often taught by less-experienced instructional team members, is that much of the material can be the same across sections and developed by an expert or collaboratively (Goertler & McEwen, 2018). Furthermore, it also allows instructors to form communities for the students across sections thereby further improving articulation and community building as already mentioned earlier (cf. Goertler & McEwen, 2018; Sanders, 2006).

Online and blended instruction can also improve vertical articulation (i.e., articulation across language levels), a problem identified by the MLA (2007) task-force. For example, students can create online portfolios to which they contribute documents each semester; students can have access to and be referred to materials and concepts from previous semesters; or the program could post explicit level goals in the course management system and have students self-assess, if they have met all goals. Especially for improving the language-literature gap, blended upper-level foreign language courses that continue to focus on language through additional language activities online have been suggested and found to be beneficial (Kraemer, 2008b, 2008c; Polio & Zyzik, 2009). Through vertical articulation, programs can slowly increase not only the difficulty of the activities and the language used, but also the number of technological tools used in instruction.

The third form of articulation is interdisciplinary articulation, which stresses the connection among courses in one institution or even across institutions. In an online course, it is more seamless to incorporate other online modules from a related field and to collaborate to create learning activities than in face-to-face courses. For example, an online module created by the library for teaching library skills in our field can be easily inserted in an advanced language course. Content knowledge developed elsewhere in an electronic format, including knowledge of the literary canon, historical information, factual information about the region being studied, or familiarity with the artistic expression of the target culture, may also be easily incorporated in our courses. Many archives and museums can now be visited virtually, which can increase the interactivity with the content materials that a course can offer.

The fourth form of articulation is co-curricular articulation, which means connecting the core curriculum with co- or extra-curricular activities such as education abroad, outreach, internships, etc. For example, the Center for Language Teaching Advancement at Michigan State University offers a teaching internship program in Germany. Students are supported in their education abroad and internship experience through an online course taught at home. In sum, the availability of materials, the opportunity to collaborate, and the ability to store materials in one place, can have a positive impact on all aspects of articulation.

From a curricular perspective, blended and online courses also have drawbacks: (1) course overloading and (2) lack of articulation between online and F2F portions of a course. Moving some of the instruction online may carry the danger of overloading the course with extra assignments as the workload for the independently completed components is no longer as visible to the teacher as those components completed face-to-face. Students often report a higher time commitment (Banados, 2006; Madyarov, 2009; but: Chenoweth, Ushida, & Murday, 2006) as do the teachers. Recent developments in course analytics have, however, made it possible to track students' progress and time commitment in a course. An additional problem is that students are not always able to see the connection between the face-to-face tasks and online tasks, or there simply may not be one. Articulation between online and face-to-face portions of a course, or a program, needs to be a priority (Blake, 2007; Kraemer, 2008b). In sum, as is the case in any delivery format, expert curricular planning is needed to ensure articulation, effectiveness, and appropriate workload for teachers and students.

3.5   Evidence- and Research-Based Factors

To better understand how to effectively design online and blended language courses, research on their effectiveness is reviewed next. A US Department of Education meta-analysis on online learning (Means et al., 2009) concluded that students in online courses outperformed those in the same course in a face-to-face delivery format. The best learning outcomes were in blended courses. Recently, Plonsky & Ziegler conducted a second-order synthesis on the CALL-SLA interface, which outlined various benefits of CALL over non-CALL using F2F teaching environments: most notably "nearly 70% of groups participating in CALL contexts have significantly better learning outcomes than those learners in non-CALL contexts" (2016: 21). Previous synthesis studies on online learning have reported better or equal learning outcomes for online courses and especially for blended courses, as was summarized in Grgurovic's (2007) review of 25 comparison studies. In their meta-analysis Grgurovic, Chapelle, and Shelley (as cited in Chapelle, 2010) found a greater benefit of partially or fully online courses in comparison with F2F courses. Most studies found small or no differences in language development between blended and traditional courses (Chenoweth, Ushida, & Murday, 2006; Sanders, 2006). Studies without comparison groups also reported self-perceived and/or measured language improvements (Banados, 2006; Kraemer, 2008b; Madyarov, 2009). While the research on blended and online learning is still limited, studies from technology-enhanced courses and the existing studies on blended and online L2 learning seem to confirm the overall trend of blended and online learning producing the same or better results as traditional courses. Understanding the effectiveness of online and blended learning in comparison to the existing F2F courses is an important first step in evaluating the benefits and challenges of these delivery formats.

The professional literature on online and blended learning can be divided into three broad categories: (1) practice reports (i.e., descriptive studies), (2) comparative studies (i.e., quasi-experimental studies) such as the studies discussed above, and (3) qualitative studies. Many of the published reports are practice reports summarizing what was done at an institution with few or no objective measures of the effectiveness of the curricular innovation. Comparative studies measure outcomes of online learning against the familiar (i.e., F2F). Hence, these experimental and quasi-experimental studies can show and have shown that online and blended courses can achieve some of the same goals as the F2F courses and can therefore be used as administrative arguments and to reduce some skepticism. However, comparative studies do not explore the potential of online and blended courses. Comparing them to an alleged equivalent in a F2F delivery format assumes similar goals and conditions in each format, when in fact an online course may be an entirely new kind of course and learning success may need to be evaluated differently (Madyorav, 2009).

Since online learning may be an entirely different learning experience, Garrett (1991) and later Blake (2009) argued for treating online learning in its own right and moving away from comparative studies. As Chapelle (2010) pointed out, comparative studies provide interesting information for administrators, but do not add to SLA research. The focus should be on learning processes and not on the tools or the delivery format (Alosh, 2001). Hence, research on blended and open learning should not ask, "does online/ blended learning work better than face-to-face?" but rather, "how is the technology implemented, what learning outcomes were achieved, which technologies worked best for what learning goal, and what learner, etc.?" These questions are often best answered in qualitative or mixed-design studies that provide rich data about a course and its participants (Ortega, 2017). Such rich data can be provided by learner-tracking and corpus-building opportunities within the learning platforms (Chapelle, 2010; Heift, 2010; Sykes, 2008) as well as by screen capture, video recordings, and eye tracking (Smith, 2008, 2010) and must include a variety of data points, sources, and stakeholders (González-Lloret, 2014; Gruba et al., 2016).

Based on the research results discussed above, blended and online language learning does not harm students, but it also may not lead to better language learning results than F2F courses. Furthermore, the advantages and disadvantages of online and blended learning may be measured too narrowly in research studies which only investigated development costs and direct learning outcomes. Most importantly, online and blended learning in itself does not have advantages or disadvantages, it is the implementation that implies advantages and disadvantages (Kern, 2006). It is therefore paramount to consider best practices in the design, implementation, and evaluation of online language courses targeted to specific contexts (González-Lloret, 2014; Gruba et al., 2016).

4   Online Language Education in Practice

After providing the arguments for and against online language education and arguing that the effectiveness of online education is dependent on careful design and implementation, I will now return to the variables mentioned at the beginning of the chapter to provide guidelines and best practices for online language education according to (1) design, (2) technology, (3) roles, (4) interactivity and synchronicity, and (5) outcomes, assessment, and evaluation.

4.1   Design

In adaptation of Barrette (2008) and White (2006), I suggest five main design stages: (1) needs analyses (González-Lloret, 2014; Gruba et al., 2016); (2) curricular planning and material development; (3) implementation; (4) evaluation (Online Learning Consortium, 2014; Quality Matters, 2014); and (5) revisions and adjustments. The design process should be iterative with a design-research-revision approach (White, 2006), which involves as many data points and types and stakeholders as possible (González-Lloret, 2014; Gruba et al., 2016) and follows a backwards-design approach (Wiggins & McTighe, 1998).

Since online and language instruction are context-dependent on the micro, meso, and macro level (Gruba et al., 2016), it is important to conduct needs analyses which include multiple methods (surveys, questionnaires, documentations, focus interviews, observations, review of documents and manuals, etc.), data points, and sources (learners, teachers, parents, administrators, employers, politicians, policy makers, IT personnel, alumni, etc.). Triangulation is needed to validate the data and increase the credibility of the results (González-Lloret, 2014). Unfortunately, these important

Table 4 Guiding questions in a needs analysis

People	• Who are the stakeholders?
Needs	• What are the learners' "language necessities (linguistic and pragmatic)"? (González-Lloret, 2014: 23)
	• What are my learners' and teachers' computer literacy, information literacy, critical literacy, multimedia literacy, computer-mediated literacy, language, and pedagogical skills?
	• What support and access is available to learners and teachers?
	• How are characteristics of learners addressed in the course design? (Ortega, 2017)
Learners	• Are digital literacy and my language-learning objectives supporting each other? (Ortega, 2017)
	• Is the course reaching and representing underserved or marginalized individuals including multilinguals? (Ortega, 2017)
	• Is the course supporting learners as "whole learners developing multilingual repertoires" for multilingual (online) communities? (Ortega, 2017: 305)
Technology	• "What innovations and technological tools are most appropriate" for the curricular goals given the needs? (González-Lloret, 2014: 23)
	• Is my course current events-based, literature-based, culture-based, theme-based, grammar-based, specific purpose-based or function-based? And what are the stakeholder needs based on these organizational principles? (Meskill & Anthony, 2015).
	• Given our context, stakeholder needs, and goals, what is the best delivery format (blended, flipped, online, MOOC, etc.) and appropriate level of autonomy (out of class vs. in-class; informal or formal; non-instructed or instructed; self-directed vs. other-directed)?
	• What is the most appropriate level of interactivity, synchronicity, and technological sophistication?
	• What tasks are best completed in what modality and format?
	• Are the online and the face-to-face components articulated well?
	• "Have I carefully considered in my design bridges between out-of-school digital worlds and classroom technological worlds?" (Ortega, 2017: 305)

needs analyses are expensive and time-consuming and have to be carefully planned, sequenced, and prioritized. Gruba et al. (2016), González-Lloret (2014), and Ortega (2017) provide frameworks and guidelines for conducting needs analyses, which are summarized as guiding questions in Table 4.

The curricular planning phase can be divided into seven subcategories: (a) needs (i.e., the results from the stage described above); (b) curricular specifications (pedagogical approach, delivery format, curricular organizing principle, etc.); (c) tasks and materials; (d) structure and sequencing; (e) student and teacher roles; (f) evaluation; and (g) sustainability plans (e.g., how can this course be maintained and stay [cost-]effective over time?).

Based on previous research and the reports of practitioners, the following elements should be included in the design process (adapted from: ADFL, 2014; Meskill & Anthony, 2015; Murphy, 2005; Pelz; 2004; for blended see Rubio & Thoms, 2012; for flipped see Simon & Fell, 2013).

- ✓ buy-in from all stakeholders with continuous stakeholder feedback;
- ✓ advocacy for and education about online learning;
- ✓ collaborative design;
- ✓ clear objectives aligned with the curricular goals;
- ✓ objectives visible during task completion;
- ✓ guides and other resources for students to navigate tasks and content;
- ✓ purposeful structure and sequence of the course;
- ✓ variation and purpose in grouping;
- ✓ variation and purpose in synchronicity levels;
- ✓ spaces and mechanisms for teachable moments as well as self-discovery;
- ✓ continuous teacher presence through multiple avenues (feedback, postings, surveys, polls, etc.);
- ✓ engaging and interactive course design;
- ✓ consistent, clear, and specific evaluation rubrics;
- ✓ timely quality and individualized feedback;
- ✓ learner-centered design that facilitates active learner responsibilities;
- ✓ continuous monitoring of student learning and teacher involvement as appropriate;
- ✓ inclusion of diverse, authentic materials and voices in a multilingual community;
- ✓ attention to all language skills, especially oral proficiency;
- ✓ an inclusive and safe learning environment that fosters community and curiosity;
- ✓ focus on collaboration and community over competition;

✓ iCALL materials (i.e., materials powered by analytics to provide targeted feedback and present materials in an effective individualized order) whenever feasible.

During the implementation, it is important to remain flexible to make changes as they become necessary and to continuously and openly communicate with all stakeholders to ensure that all understand the iterative design-implementation-evaluation-revision process (Gruba et al., 2016; Madoyrav, 2009). Each stakeholder individually may not understand the complexities of the context, for example the diverse goals, the resources, and the responsibilities and rights of each stakeholder, which means that advocacy work and education about online learning may be necessary.

4.2 Technology

Blake (2001) has argued that pedagogy – not technology – should drive curricular and pedagogical decisions when teaching with technology. Yet as Thorne (2010) pointed out, it cannot be ignored that the medium itself changes the learning and interaction circumstances, and in that sense the technology does in fact matter in the curricular decisions and ultimately the learning experience. Based on the aforementioned needs analyses, the appropriate technologies and their use have to be considered. The most important guiding principle in activity and task design for online learning is to remain focused on the purpose and the desired learning outcomes of your course. Avoid the attraction of technological possibilities presented by the platform or software that are irrelevant to course goals and may detract or distract the learner from them. Meskill & Anthony (2015) recommend using a task toolkit (i.e., https://merlot.org), which guides you through the process, and taking advantage of course management system's task repositories.

Technology in language education plays several different roles: (1) to present and access materials; (2) to establish a community; (3) to provide communication channels, (4) to give feedback; and (5) to serve as a resource. Even face-to-face courses may take advantage of technology for presenting and providing access to materials. In online courses, as mentioned earlier, the teacher has to consider how much support the learners need to easily access the information available and effectively utilize the materials. For blended courses, the flipped classroom has been found to be effective for language teaching, in which new material is presented online with embedded comprehension checks while interactive activities are the focus of the F2F time. In both cases, online materials can and should be enhanced with replay options, intelligent feedback, glosses, and multimodal elements to assist comprehension and improve feedback..

While some believe that the human-interactive experience is critical in language learning and fear that online education cannot adequately provide it, the concern can be successfully addressed if one views community as a key element of course design. Furthermore, technology can connect students with multilingual digital communities, in which linguistic diversity thrives (Ortega, 2017). Additionally, learners must take a more active role in these online learning communities than in F2F courses. Reinders & White (2016) argue that interaction with these digital communities also places learners' lives and experiences at the center of the course, rather than dominating them through teacher-centered activities and communications. As already mentioned, the feasibility of larger and varied communication has become a reality and is continuing to change due to advancing technologies. Multimodality and multilingualism are key features of technology-mediated communication (Ortega, 2017). Specific communication tasks within the course should encourage learners to take advantage of these features. Similarly, feedback options should be optimized with the goal of being efficient, individualized, valid, accurate, and reliable.

One of the central roles of technology is the easy access to resources and tools in support of the learning. In addition to content resources and language resources, such as interactive grammars and dictionaries, training in learner strategy and coaching can be helpful resources in an online course (see Reinders & White, 2016 for examples of such programs).

As mentioned earlier, there is a danger that technology can distract from the pedagogical focus of a learning objective. Additionally, technology may further advantage elite multilinguals and digital natives. Ortega urges that we all "actively strive to combat the well-documented inequities and perils of the complex digital divides in which we are all complicit" (2017: 304). In short, we should use technology to improve the effectiveness of teaching, expand our curricular reach, broaden inclusivity, and maximize the affordances of technology as summarized by Blake & Guillien (2014): flexibility, personalization, autonomy, and automation.

4.3   Roles

Once the curricular needs have been identified, the role of the teachers, students, administrators, support staff (language lab, IT), and the technology must be defined (see White, 2006). While the technology can be a tutor, a tool, a medium, or serve several of these roles, the technology cannot replace the teacher; the teacher role remains crucial for the learning outcomes (Kern, 2006; Meskill & Anthony, 2015). Due to the capabilities of technologies today and the perception that blended and online courses are intended to make teachers unnecessary, it is important to consider the role of the teacher in more detail, especially since it differs from one's role in a F2F classroom (Arnold & Ducate, 2015) and presents special challenges as one adopts a new teacher identity (White, 2007 as cited in Reinders & White, 2016) with differing authorities (Kessler, 2010). As Arnold & Ducate state: "teachers significantly shape the outcomes of CALL through their instructions, scaffolding, feedback and responses to teachable moments" (2015: 1–2). Yet, 79% of the 39% of faculty members who have taught online felt they developed as a teacher and learned new skills as result of the experience (Jaschik & Lederman, 2016).

The teacher plays an important role as a source of feedback, which is also perhaps the biggest difference to F2F teaching. On the one hand, the teachers have more information from course analytics; on the other hand, they cannot as easily provide impromptu feedback or assess learner understanding based on nonverbal information (e.g., facial expressions). It therefore takes more explicit effort for the teacher to serve in the role as source of feedback in online courses. While learners are – or at least can be – more autonomous in online education, their self-study and learning tasks need to be recognized by the teachers, so that students feel validated. This recognition needs to go beyond timely grading, but also include personalized feedback and connecting observations from the assignments in communication to the whole class. Because of the isolation aspect, the teacher will have to take a more social and more motivating role (White, 2006), show more presence, and be a positive example of online interaction (Meskill & Anthony, 2015). The teacher may be the person developing the materials, providing technical support, administering assessment, serving as a personal link with the students, and offering guidance, scaffolding, and feedback (White, 2006). Teacher presence is both static through the materials created prior to course implementation as well as active through interactions during course implementation. Regardless of how many hats the teacher may wear, they must be active in the online environment because students orient toward the teacher (Meskill & Anthony, 2015). For more detailed guides see Hampel & Stickler's (2015) edited volume on online teaching based on the Developing Online Teaching Skills (DOTS) project, as well as Meskill & Anthony's (2015) book which has already been cited repeatedly.

The International Association for K-12 Online Learning (2011) outlines a set of standards for online teaching, which can be used as a guide for effectively fulfilling teacher roles. To summarize, online teachers should be able to design effective online instruction; to skillfully use technology to encourage active learning, interaction, participation, and collaboration; to provide clear expectations, prompt response, and regular feedback; to facilitate legal, ethical, and safe online behavior; to accommodate for diverse learners; to design and implement valid, reliable, effective assessments in relation to standard learning goals; to use data from assessment to improve course design; and to communicate effectively and professionally with all stakeholders.

Due to the change in teacher roles, discussed above, there are also necessary changes in the role of the student. Students may require certain characteristics to be successful and adjust to the changed education environment. Some students do not or cannot make these changes, and thus will be less successful learners in an online course. The 2006 Commission of Public Education (as cited in Blake, 2009) summarized characteristics of a successful online learner: highly motivated, mature, and focused on clear learning goals. Arispe & Blake (2012) found that good study habits and skills, a preference to work independently, low verbal skills, introversion, and conscientiousness correlated with success in online Spanish courses. Elsewhere Blake & Guillien (2014) argued that online courses are a good fit for busy students with logistical constraints, who appreciate the freedom and flexibility and who have had prior positive experiences with online education. As one might imagine, students without online experiences may be unaware of the characteristics that predict success in these courses and may have selected an online course because it better fits their schedule and not because their learner persona matches the characteristics of successful online learners (Blake & Guillien, 2014; Goertler, Bollen, and Gaff, 2012). Students need to be prepared for and supported in their role shift to a more autonomous learner through learner trainings, reflection tasks, and the creation of learner networks (Reinders & White, 2016). In our own courses (Goertler & Gacs, 2018), we have seen that the online groups and the F2F groups have no statistically different learning outcomes when comparing exam scores and course grades. However, the standard deviation and score ranges are larger in online versus F2F. The spread indicates that some learners are more and others less suited for online learning compared with students in traditional F2F courses. As Arispe & Blake observe (2012), some learners need better preparation to succeed in online courses and others will thrive in these new environments. Part of the expanded role of the online teacher is to advise students on the appropriate delivery format for them, and if such a format is not available, to better prepare them for the available format.

4.4 Interactivity and Synchronicity

As in traditional classes, instructors must decide if students should complete tasks and activities independently or with the guidance of the teacher, synchronously or asynchronously (Meskill & Anthony, 2015). What is different in the online format is the flow of a lesson, which cannot be adjusted spontaneously. Hence, instructors need to more carefully design activities and select appropriate tools to complete them. Meskill & Anthony (2015) divide instructional time in online language courses into four venues: written asynchronous, written synchronous, oral synchronous, and oral asynchronous. Asynchronous is the most widely used form of online learning (Meskill & Anthony, 2015), but to maximize language learning potential, synchronous formats should not be neglected. Live meetings are challenging logistically, yet they can be a crucial element of effective online language learning and a key component for learning outcomes (Arispe & Blake, 2012). Interpretive, reflective, and presentational tasks are often best accomplished in asynchronous formats, whereas interpersonal ones are best completed in synchronous meetings. Interactivity can be achieved through person-to-person interaction as well as learner-technology interactions.

4.5 Outcomes, Assessment, and Evaluation

Any course has outcome goals, which need to be assessed in order to evaluate the effectiveness of the curriculum. I use outcomes here to refer to the goals of the course, which may include language proficiency goals as well as other academic goals (e.g., digital literacy, academic writing) and non-academic goals (e.g., student retention, student satisfaction). Assessment here means the process of systematically collecting information about learning outcomes. Evaluation here is even broader to include any systematic evaluation of the course including, but also going beyond, outcome goals (e.g., student time-commitment).

Assessment in online and blended courses offers affordances and challenges. For one, online assessment can be adaptive and thereby be targeted to students' needs; it can contain more accuracy in assessing an individual and thereby avoid wasting time presenting the student with inappropriate materials; additionally, adaptive tests are also considered to have high test security and reliability, but they are challenging to design. Other advantages of online assessment are: (A) efficient use of time, if testing during asynchronous online time and reserving synchronous time for interactive activities; (B) multimodality tests that more closely resemble real language tasks; (C) efficient, self-correcting tests that allow for individualized feedback (even in writing through automated writing evaluation); and (D) reports for teachers and learners that guide them in selecting more effective learning pathways for learners. The most recent CALICO monograph provides a great overview of assessment issues in online education (Link & Li, 2018).

Already during the planning phase, an evaluation plan must be designed that will determine whether the curricular innovation was successful and by what criteria. Part of the evaluation plan should be an assessment of whether the stakeholders' goals were reached and whether they are satisfied with the results. Assuming that there will be some problems in achieving goals and reaching satisfied stakeholders, a revision plan and a sustainability plan must be developed. These plans will need to contain specifications of what will be changed and how the unit plans to sustain the quality of the course over time as start-up funds are exhausted and technologies advance. While formal and informal assessments of the revised curriculum are part of the implementation process, the majority of the analysis and the triangulation of the data will likely be completed after the first implementation. During this phase, it is important to communicate initial findings with all stakeholders and discuss the interpretation of the results with them. Most importantly, based on the original innovation, the evaluation plan and the findings, additional revisions to the curriculum may be proposed. Provided the decision-making stakeholders are willing to continue the path of blending or opening the curriculum, further revisions to the curriculum can be developed, as the second iteration of the initial offering begins.

Several organizations have created frameworks for evaluating online education. Below are the components of the two most widely referenced frameworks.

Online Learning Consortium (OLC) (2014):
1. institutional support;
2. technology support;
3. course development and instructional design;
4. course structure;
5. teaching and learning;
6. social and student engagement;
7. faculty support;
8. student support.

Quality Matters Rubric (2014):
1. course overview and introduction;
2. learning objectives and competencies;
3. assessment and measurement;

4. instructional material;
5. course activities and learner interaction;
6. course technology;
7. learner support;
8. accessibility and usability.

I would like to recommend adding a dimension proposed by Ortega: Are outcome measures going beyond form, including multiple data points and showing "multilingual practices and multilingual identities and ideologies?" (2017: 305). Both OLC and Quality Matters frameworks consider elements within and outside the course, yet neither goes beyond the institutional context. Adding Ortega's focus on identity and ideology can incorporate the macro (i.e., global) context. In both frameworks, the stakeholders are the students, the teachers, and the institution, but not language users in general as proposed by Ortega. Common components across the frameworks are: support, infrastructure, curriculum design, and interaction/engagement. The Quality Matters framework is more detailed and also focuses on assessment and issues of accessibility and usability. Thus, when designing and evaluating fully or partially online courses, I recommend the use of the OLC Quality Scorecard Suite (Online Learning Consortium, 2014), which is freely accessible online and presented as easy-to-use checklists.

5   Conclusions

Online language courses have advantages and disadvantages. Careful planning, designing, implementation, and evaluation of online language courses is therefore key to increase the chance of meeting stakeholder needs and outcome benchmarks. One of the greatest advantages of online language education is that it has the potential to create more access to quality language education. However, by moving instruction online, especially if exclusively online, there is also the risk that we widen inequity gaps. As Rhinesmith & Reisdorf (2017) have discussed, digital skills are often lacking in underrepresented minorities. Online language courses are both an opportunity to teach these lacking skills and yet have the potential of excluding underrepresented minorities from language learning opportunities and thereby also from elite multilingualism as Ortega (2017) described it. Careful planning and continuous evaluation are necessary to provide online language education, which equitably takes advantage of the affordances of online learning and teaching. Since online education is here to stay, it is our responsibility as language educators to ensure that we are prepared for online education and that we follow best practices in planning, implementing, and evaluating online education.

Questions for Reflection

1. After reading this chapter, have you changed your mind on any of your answers to the questions from the beginning of the chapter? Why (not)?
2. This chapter has reviewed historical trends in blended and open learning. Based on your understanding of the field of language teaching and your observations of innovative trends in technology tools and their use, how do you foresee the field of language teaching changing?

Get together in a group. Each person has a different role at the University of Y:

a. teacher unfamiliar with technology,
b. teacher familiar with technology,
c. traditional student,
d. non-traditional student,
e. administrator,
f. Instructional Technology person,
g. parent.

UY has decided to move a third of all courses online, a third in a blended format, and keep a third of the courses in a face-to-face technology-enhanced format. Based on what you have read in this chapter:

1. What is your character's opinion on blended and online learning?
2. What concerns might this character have?
3. What goals might this character have?
4. What does this character want from foreign language education?
5. What questions might this character have of the other characters?

Take some notes, so that you can be in character. Hold a town hall meeting with the other people – be sure to stay in character. Be respectful to each other and always remember that each person is simply playing a part and the opinions expressed may or may not reflect actual opinions held. Try to come up with a plan that can work for all.

Case Studies

Research

You are a Language Coordinator at a large public university and coordinate all six sections of second-year French. Two of the sections moved into an online format two years ago. Half the sections are taught by instructors and half by TAs with one TA and one instructor teaching both an online and a face-to-face section. The students in all sections are comparable according to placement mechanisms (either the placement test or the final exam of the previous semester). Use Table 1 from earlier in the chapter to compare the two formats.

Students, colleagues, and especially the Graduate Teaching Assistants have raised concerns about the online courses. They fear that the online sections are more work, lead to greater attrition rates in the program, and that learning outcomes are lower, especially in speaking proficiency. This does not match your impression as the Language Program Coordinator nor the reports from the instructor teaching online. Colleagues have talked to you in faculty meeting, TAs in coordination meeting, and you have received an unusual amount of negative emails from students, especially from the TA's online section. The online instructor reports that more students are participating in the online course and that some students are making exceptional progress in their language development. Since the course has undergone a few iterations, you feel confident that the course is now well-designed. However, the negative reports do have you concerned. You now set out to gather some empirical evidence, so you can understand better what is going on, and so you can (a) improve the course for the future and (b) publish your research findings.

Discussion Questions:
1. What factors may contribute to the different perceptions among stakeholders (colleagues, students, TAs vs. the online instructor)?
2. Based on the description above, what might be differences in learning outcomes between the online and the F2F sections?
3. Which factors identified in question (1) might explain potential differences determined in question (2)?

Based on your discussion of the questions above, design a case study research project by completing Table 5 below.

Table 5 Research planning sheet

Observations	What problems were observed?
Background	What is the theoretical framework and previous research that lead you to RQ 1?
	Same for RQ2
RQs & Hypotheses	RQ 1 and hypothesized answers
Instruments/ Materials data collection	Instruments and materials that will help you answer this question. How and from whom will you collect them? What treatment will the participants receive?
Data analyses	How will you analyze the data collected to answer RQ1?
Results	What are the answers to RQ1?
Conclusions/ Connections	How do your RQ1 results compare to the previous research?
Implications	What do your results mean for theory, practice, and research methods?
Limitations	What possible limitations and complications do you expect? How can you safeguard against them?

Teaching

An experienced instructor is teaching an online course for the first time. After spending the first few weeks familiarizing the students with each other, the course, and the tools used, s/he is now conducting the first live online class session. The class is an advanced Japanese class and the topic for the week is narrating. Below is the teacher's lesson plan with some missing elements and some notes from implementation.

Advanced Japanese

By the end of the lesson students will be able to:

Time (min)	Activity	Annotation
0–5	Synchronous teacher-led presentation and discussion of elements of narration via the video-conferencing platform Zoom.	Lots of echo. Can't see the students. → Makes me nervous.
5–20	Synchronous small group work in Zoom break-out rooms: students are given links to travel blogs about Japan. Students are supposed to analyze elements of narration both in terms of linguistic functions as well as the overall structure of the text.	Group 2 and 4 worked really well together and identified many narrative elements. Group 1 talked about last weekend in English. Group 3 talked about the content of the blog, but not the structure.
20–40	Most of the students have just returned from a summer abroad program in Japan. Using Google Doc and while logged into the Zoom break-out room, students are asked to write a story about their first day in Japan.	Some pairs divided the work (you write the beginning, I write the end); some co-created outlines and filled them in; in other pairs one person told the story and the partner wrote it down.
40–50	Teams are supposed to post their stories in a discussion forum and provide the other teams with feedback on the content and the language with special attention to narrative elements.	Feedback was mostly praise.
50–55	While the teacher continues reviewing the stories in the discussion forum, the students are supposed to watch a pre-recorded presentation presenting the most common grammatical and organizational problems in narrations based on errors from a previous semester.	The stories are interesting, but do not include narrative elements. Most students did not watch the recorded presentation according to the course management viewing report.

55–60	Students individually complete a self-grading quiz in the course management system. The quiz presents them with incorrect sentences from narrations from previous semesters and students have to correct the errors. After submission the system will show them which items they corrected accurately and which they did not. No explanations are offered.	Students did poorly.
60–75	Each student rewrites the story they previously wrote as a pair and puts it in a Dropbox within the course management system for the teacher to review.	Some just uploaded the same story, others made great revisions. Some students now viewed the recorded lecture and clicked on the quiz answers again.
75–90	Students are asked to explore the interactive website of a Japanese museum and prepare a 1-minute presentation for the other students narrating their "field trip." Students are assigned in groups to different museums.	Students had a hard time navigating the site and often were in different places than their group members, which made writing a coherent story challenging.
90–95	Students share their stories.	They had good stories.
95–100	Teacher explains homework: 1. Students are asked to reflect on the process of creating the different narratives in an Audio Dropbox. 2. Students are asked to complete a simulated conversation using Flipgrid to talk about their actual field trip to a museum in Japan during their summer study abroad.	Students expressed a lot of frustration about not knowing, where to go and what to do. Their Flipgrid posts were great.

Based on the annotated lesson plan above:

- What were the goals for the class? Infer them from the description.
- In an overall assessment, was this a successful online class session or was it a failure?
- Which component worked well and why? Which component failed and why?
- In reviewing the guidelines from section 4 of this chapter, how could the teacher improve the lesson?

Try to rewrite the lesson plan and include concrete instructions and criteria.

Ideas for Action Research Projects

Idea 1: Take a syllabus or a lesson plan which you have developed/worked with/ taught from and try to modify it for an online class (period). In your design consider the following questions based on the 10 variables in online education (Means et al., 2009):

1. Pedagogy/Learning experience:
    i.   What are the learning goals?
    ii   What is the teaching approach?
2. Computer-mediated communication with instructor:
    i.   What communication happens with the instructor?
    ii. What technology tools could be used?
    iii. What communication is best done synchronously? What asynchronously?
    iv. Is there any communication with the instructor that could be replaced with automated computer-generated or teacher pre-programmed communication?
3. Computer-mediated communication with peers:
    i.   What communication happens amongst peers?
    ii. What technology tools could be used?
    iii. What communication is best done synchronously? What asynchronously?
    iv. Is there communication with peers that could be replaced with automated interactions with the computer and/or communication with communities outside of the classroom?
4. Media features:
    i.   See questions for (2) and (3).
    ii. What additional training is needed to prepare students for the use of these technologies?
5. Time on task:
    i.   How much time are learners expected to spend on this task?
    ii. How can you evaluate, if learners spent more or less time than intended?
    iii. How much time is needed from the teacher?
6. One-way video or audio:
    i.   Which modality works best for your learning goals and context?

7. Computer-based instruction elements:
    i.   What instruction could be moved to pre-recorded lectures, pre-pared content from elsewhere?
    ii. What resources could be included in the online format?
8. Opportunity for face-to-face time with instructor:
    i.   Would it make sense to include F2F time with the instructor?
    ii. Is it possible to include F2F time with the instructor?
9. Opportunity for face-to-face time with peers:
    i.   Would it make sense to include F2F time with peers?
    ii. Is it possible to include F2F time with peers?
10. Opportunity for practice, and feedback provided:
    i.   Are there ample opportunities to practice?
    ii. Is immediate and intelligent feedback available?

Try to outline a modification plan based on these variables. Make sure to keep the same learning goals – you may add to them, but you cannot eliminate a learning goal.

Now, imagine this lesson as part of a curriculum. Sketch out a curriculum and evaluate your plan using some of the elements from the OLC Quality Score Card:

- ✓ online education is strategic and supported by central administration;
- ✓ it includes reliable, safe, and supported technology;
- ✓ resources are allocated for development, implementation, support, and maintenance;
- ✓ it uses coherent, cohesive curricular planning and design that supports the learning outcomes;
- ✓ it implements an iterative design process and regular reviews;
- ✓ it follows privacy and accessibility laws and regulations;
- ✓ it is student-centered and engaging;
- ✓ it includes appropriate current and emerging technologies;
- ✓ it conducts usability studies;
- ✓ curriculum designer and teaching faculty either are the same person or work closely together;
- ✓ expectations, learning outcomes, learner demands, activity instructions, policies are clear and shared before the course with the students;
- ✓ it provides adequate and equal access and works across platforms;
- ✓ it is rich in resources that are easy to navigate from language resources to academic resources to content resources and includes a FAQ;

✓ it encourages student-student collaboration;
✓ it facilitates communication between faculty and learners;
✓ it includes constructive and timely feedback;
✓ it instructors show presence;
✓ it connects learners to communities of practice outside of the course;
✓ it offers ongoing technical assistance and training for all;
✓ tasks and activities engage the learners with the whole program and institution beyond the course;
✓ tutoring and strategy training is available;
✓ the course is regularly evaluated using a variety of data striving for continual improvement;
✓ goals are reviewed and revised;
✓ assessment procedures and evaluation procedures are clear.

Idea 2: Visit a local high school and assess its use of technology and technology-mediated instruction in the foreign language program. You may want to keep the following questions in mind: (1) What technologies are used? (2) How are these technologies used? (3) Does the teacher seem comfortable with the technology? (4) Are the students able to perform the tasks with the technology? (5) What technology in the room is unused? (6) What technology has to be brought to the room? (7) Based on the teacher's teaching approach, what other technologies would enhance his/her teaching?

Idea 3: Using the Online Learning Consortium's scorecard (https://onlinelearningconsortium.org/consult/oscqr-course-design-review/) review a blended or online course.

If you have access to the Quality Matters matrix (https://www.qualitymatters.org/qa-resources/rubric-standards/higher-ed-rubric) you could also use that one.

References

ADFL (Associations of Departments of Foreign Languages). (2014). Suggested best practices and resources for the implementation of hybrid and online language courses. Retrieved February 7, from https://www.adfl.mla.org/Resources/Policy-Statements/Suggested-Best-Practices-and-Resources-for-the-Implementation-of-Hybrid-and-Online-Language-Courses

Allen, I. E., & Seaman, J. (2010). *Learning on demand: Online education in the United States, 2009.* Babson Research Group. Retrieved July 30, 2010, from http://www.sloanconsortium.org/publications/survey/pdf/learningondemand. pdf

Allen, I. E., & Seaman, J. (2014). *Grade change: Tracking online education in the United States.* Babson Research Group. Retrieved December 28, 2017, from http://www.onlinelearningsurvey.com/reports/gradechange.pdf

Allen, I. E., Seaman, J., & Garrett, R. (2007). *Blending in: The extent and promise of blended education in the United States.* Retrieved July 30, 2010, from http://www.sloanconsortium.org/sites/default/files/Blending_In.pdf

Alosh, M. (2001). Learning language at a distance: An Arabic initiative. *Foreign Language Annals*, 34(4), 347–354. https://doi.org/10.1111/j.1944-9720.2001.tb02067.x

Arnold, N., & Ducate, L. (2015). Contextualized views of practices and competencies in CALL teacher education research. *Language Learning & Technology*, 19(1), 1–9. Retrieved January 26, 2018, from http://llt.msu.edu/issues/february2015/commentary.pdf

Arispe, K., & Blake, R. (2012). Individual factors and successful language learning in a hybrid course. *System*, 40(4), 449–465. https://doi.org/10.1016/j.system.2012.10.013

Banados, E. (2006). A blended-learning pedagogical model for teaching and learning EFL successfully through an online interactive multimedia environment. *CALICO Journal*, 23(3), 533–550. Available at http://calico.org/journalTOC.php; https://doi.org/10.1558/cj.v23i3.533-550

Barrette, C. M. (2008). Program administration issues in distance learning. In S. Goertler & P. Winke (eds.), *Opening doors through distance language education: Principles, perspectives, and practices*, pp. 129–152. San Marcos, TX: CALICO.

Blake, R. (2001). What language professionals need to know about technology. *ADFL Bulletin*, 32(3), 93–99. https://doi.org/10.1632/adfl.32.3.93

Blake, R. (2007). New trends in using technology in the language curriculum. *Annual Review of Applied Linguistics*, 27, 76–97. https://doi.org/10.1017/S0267190508070049

Blake, R. (2009). The use of technology for second language distance learning. *Modern Language Journal*, 93 (Focus Issue), 822–835. https://doi.org/10.1111/j.1540-4781.2009.00975.x

Blake, R., & Guillen, G. (2014). Best practices for an online Spanish course. *FLTMAG*. Retrieved February 7, 2018 from http://fltmag.com/best-practices-for-an-online-spanish-course-2/

Chambers, A., & Bax, S. (2006). Making CALL work: Towards normalization. *System*, 34, 465–479. https://doi.org/10.1016/j.system.2006.08.001

Chapelle, C. A. (1997). CALL in the year 2000: Still in search of research paradigms? *Language Learning & Technology*, 1(1), 19–43. Retrieved July 30, 2010, from http://llt.msu.edu/vol1num1/chapelle/default.html

Chapelle, C. A. (2009). The relationship between second language acquisition theory and computer-assisted language learning. *Modern Language Journal*, 93 (Focus Issue), 741–753. https://doi.org/10.1111/j.1540-4781.2009.00970.x

Chapelle, C. A. (2010). The spread of computer-assisted language learning. *Language Teaching*, 43(1), 66–74. https://doi.org/10.1111/j.1540-4781.2009.00970.x

Chapelle, C. A. (2016). CALL in the year 2000: A lock book from 2016. *Language Learning & Technology*, 20(2), 159–161. Retrieved January 10, 2018, from http://llt.msu.edu/issues/june2016/chapelle.pdf

Chapelle, C. A., & Voss, E. (2016). 20 years of technology and language assessment in language learning and technology. *Language Learning & Technology*, 20(2), 116–128. Retrieved January 24, 2018, from http://llt.msu.edu/issues/june2016/chapellevoss.pdf

Chenoweth, N. A., Ushida, E., & Murday, K. (2006). Student learning in hybrid French and Spanish courses: An overview of Language Online. *CALICO Journal*, 24(1), 115–145. https://doi.org/10.1558/cj.v24i1.115-146

Dixon, E., & Thomas., M. (2015). Introduction. In E. Dixon & M. Thomas (eds.), *Researching language learner interactions online: From social media to MOOCs*, pp. 1–9. San Marcos, TX: CALICO.

Doughty, C., & Long, M. H. (2003). Optimal psycholinguistic environments for distance foreign language learning. *Language Learning & Technology*, 7(3), 50–80. Retrieved July 30, 2010, from http://llt.msu/edu/vol7num3/doughty/

Dreyer, C., Bangeni, N., & Nel, C. (2005). A framework for supporting students studying English via mixed-mode delivery system. In B. Holmberg, M. Shelley, & C. White (eds.), *Distance education and languages: Evolution and change*, pp. 92–118. Clevedon: Multilingual Matters.

Fryer, L., & Carpenter, R. (2006). Emerging technologies: Bots as language learning tools. *Language Learning & Technology*, 10(3), 8–14. Available at http://llt.msu.edu/vol10num3/emerging/default.html

Garrett, N. (1991). Technology in the service of language learning: Trends and issues. *Modern Language Journal*, 75, 74–101. https://doi.org/10.1111/j.1540-4781.1991.tb01085.x

Goertler, S. (2012). Theoretical and empirical foundations for blended language learning. In: F. Rubio & J. Thoms (eds.), *Hybrid language teaching and learning: Exploring theoretical, pedagogical, and curricular issues*, pp. 27–49. Boston: Cengage/Heinle.

Goertler, S., Bollen, M., & Gaff, J. (2012). Students' readiness for and attitudes toward hybrid and foreign language instruction: Multiple perspectives. *CALICO Journal*, 29(2), 297–320. https://doi.org/10.11139/cj.29.2.297-320

Goertler, S., & Gacs, A. (2018). Assessment in online German: Assessment methods and results. *Unterrichtspraxis*, 51(2), 156–174.

Goertler, S., & McEwen, K. (2018). Closing the GAP for generation study abroad: Achieving goals, improving articulation, and increasing participation. *ADFL Bulletin*, 44(2), 41–55.

Goertler, S., Schenker, T., Lesoski, C., & Brunsmeier, S. (2018). Assessing language and intercultural learning during telecollaboration. In S. Link & J. Li (eds.), *Assessment across online language education*, pp. 21–48. Bristol, CT: Equinox.

Goertler, S., & Winke, P. (2008). The effectiveness of technology-enhanced foreign language teaching. In S. Goertler & P. Winke (eds.), *Opening doors through distance language education: Principles, perspectives, and practices*, pp. 233–260. San Marcos, TX: CALICO.

Gonzalez, A. L. (2015). The contemporary US digital divide: From initial access to technology maintenance. *Information, Communication & Society*, 19(2), 234–248. https://doi.org/10.1080/1369118X.2015.1050438

González-Lloret, M. (2014). The need for needs analysis in technology-mediated TBLT. In M. González-Lloret & L. Ortega (eds.), *Technology-mediated TBLT: Researching technology and tasks*, pp. 23–50. Amsterdam: John Benjamins.

Goodwin-Jones, R. (2017). Scaling up and zooming in: Big data and personalization in language learning. *Language Learning & Technology*, 21(1), 4–15. Retrieved from http://llt.msu.edu/issues/february2017/emerging.pdf

Grgurovic, M. (2007). *Research synthesis: CALL comparison studies by language skills/knowledge.* Retrieved November 1, 2007, from http://tesl.engl.iastate.edu:591/comparison/synthesis.htm

Gruba, P., Cardenas-Claros, M., Suvorov, R., & Rick, K. (2016). *Blended language program evaluation.* New York, NY: Palgrave. https://doi.org/10.1057/9781137514370

Hampel, R., & Hauck, M. (2004). Toward an effective use of audio-conferencing in distance language courses. *Language Learning & Technology*, 8(1), 66–82. http://llt.msu.edu/vol8num1/hampel/default.html

Hampel, R., & Stickler, U. (2005). New skills for new classrooms: Training tutors to teach languages online. *Computer Assisted Language Learning*, 18(4), 311–326. https://doi.org/10.1080/09588220500335455

Hampel, R., & Stickler, U. (eds.) (2015). *Developing online language teaching: Research-based pedagogies and reflective practices.* London, UK: Palgrave. https://doi.org/10.1057/9781137412263

Heift, T. (2005). Inspectable learner reports for web-based language learning. *ReCALL*, 17(1), 32–46. https://doi.org/10.1017/S0958344005000418

Heift, T. (2010). Prompting in CALL: A longitudinal study of learner uptake. *Modern Language Journal*, 94(2), 198–216. https://doi.org/10.1111/j.1540-4781.2010.01017.x

Hojnacki, S. (2018). *The flipped classroom in introductory foreign language classes.* Unpublished dissertation, Michigan State University, East Lansing, MI.

Hung, H.-T. (2015). Flipping the classroom for English language learners to foster active learning. *Computer Assisted Language Learning*, 28(1), 81–96. http://dx.doi.org/10/1080/0958821.2014.967701

International Association for K-12 Online Learning. (2011). *National standards forquality online teaching.* Version 2. Retrieved January 10, 2018, from https://www.inacol.org/wp-content/uploads/2015/02/national-standards-for-quality-online-teaching-v2.pdf

Jaschik, S., & Lederman, D. (2016). *The 2016 Inside Higher Ed survey of faculty attitudes on technology.* Washington, DC: Inside Higher Ed.

Kern, R. (2006). Perspectives on technology in learning and teaching languages. *TESOL Quarterly*, 40(1), 183–210. https://doi.org/10.2307/40264516

Kessler, G. (2006). Assessing CALL teacher training: What are we doing and what could we do better. In P. Hubbard & M. Levy (eds.), *Teacher education in CALL*, pp. 23–44. Philadelphia, PA: John Benjamins. https://doi.org/10.1075/lllt.14.05kes

Kessler, G. (2010). When they talk about CALL: Discourse in a required CALL class? *CALICO Journal*, 27(2), 376–392. https://doi.org/10.11139/cj.27.2.376-392

Kraemer, A. (2008a). Formats of distance learning. In S. Goertler & P. Winke (eds.), *Opening doors through distance language education: Principles, perspectives, and practices*, pp. 11–42. San Marcos, TX: CALICO.

Kraemer, A. (2008b). *Engaging the foreign language learner: Using hybrid instruction to bridge the language-literature gap*. Unpublished dissertation, Michigan State University, East Lansing, MI.

Kraemer, A. (2008c). Happily ever after: Integrating language and literature through technology. *Die Unterrichtspraxis*, 41(1), 61–71. https://doi.org/10.1111/j.1756-1221.2008.00007.x

Lafford, B., Lafford, P., & Sykes, J. (2007). Entre diche y hecho ...: An assessment of the application of research from second language acquisition and related fields to the creation of Spanish CALL materials for lexical acquisition. *CALICO Journal*, 24(3), 497–529. Available at https://calico.org/journalTOC.php

Link, S., & Li, Z. (2015). Understanding online interaction through learning analytics: Defining a theory-based research agenda. In E. Dixon & M. Thomas (eds.), *Researching language learner interactions online: From social media to MOOCs*, pp. 369–385. San Marcos, TX: CALICO.

Link, S., & Li, J. (eds.) (2018). *Assessment across online language education*. Bristol, CT: Equinox.

Lord, G. (2015). "I don't know how to use words in Spanish": Rosetta Stone and learner proficiency outcomes. *The Modern Language Journal*, 99(2), 401–405. https://doi.org/10.1111/modl.12234_3

Madyarov, I. (2009). Designing a workable framework for evaluating distance language instruction. *CALICO Journal*, 26(2), 290–308. Retrieved March 25, 2011, from https://calico.org/journalTOC.php; https://doi.org/10.1558/cj.v26i2.290-308

Means, B., Toyama, Y., Murphy, R., Bakia, M., & Jones, K. (2009). *Evaluation of evidence-Based practices in online learning: A meta-analysis and review of online learning studies.* US Department of Education, Office of Planning, Evaluation, and Policy Development, Policy and Program Studies Service. Retrieved July 30, 2010, from http://www2.ed.gov/rschstat/eval/tech/evidence-based-practices/finalreport.pdf

Mehring, J. (2016). Present research on the flipped classroom and potential tools for the EFL classroom. *Computers in the Schools*, 33(1), 1–10. https://doi.org/10.1080/07380569.2016.1139912

Meskill, C., & Anthony, N. (2015). *Teaching language online.* Buffalo, NY [iBook]: Multilingual Matters.

MLA (Modern Language Association). (2007). *Foreign languages and higher education: New structures for a changed world.* New York, NY: Modern Language Association. Available at http://www.mla.org/flreport

Murphy, L. (2005). Attending to form and meaning: The experience of adult distance learners of French, German, and Spanish. *Language Teaching Research*, 9(3), 295–317. https://doi.org/10.1191/1362168805lr160oa

Murphy-Judy, K. A., & Johnshoy, M. (2017). Who's teaching which languages online? A report based on national surveys. *IALLT Journal*, 47(1), 137–167.

National Center for Education Statistics: NCES. (2016). *Table 311.12. Number and percentage of undergraduate students taking distance education or online classes and degree programs, by selected characteristics: Selected years, 2003–2004 through 2011–12.* Retrieved December 28, 2017, from https://nces.ed.gov/programs/digest/d15/tables/dt15_311.22.asp?current=yes

Online Learning Consortium. (2014). *Quality scorecard 2014: Criteria for excellence in the administration of online programs.* Retrieved May 17, 2018, from https://onlinelearningconsortium.org/consult/olc-quality-scorecard-suite

Ortega, L. (2017). New CALL-SLA interfaces for the 21st century: Toward equitable multilingualism. *CALICO Journal*, 34(3), 285–316. Retrieved January 22, 2018, from https://doi.org/10.1558/cj.33855

Pelz, B. (2004). (My) three principles of effective online pedagogy. *Journal of Asynchronous Learning Networks*, 14(1), 103–116. Retrieved July 30, 2010, from http://www.ccri.edu/distancefaculty/Online%20Pedagogy%20-%20Pelz.pdf

Pendar, N., & Chapelle, C. A. (2008). Investigating the promise of learner corpora: Methodological issues. *CALICO Journal*, 25(2), 189–206.

Polio, C., & Zyzik, E. (2009). Don Quixote meets ser and estar: Multiple perspectives on language learning in Spanish literature classes. *Modern Language Journal*, 93(4), 550–569.

Plonsky, L., & Ziegler, N. (2016). The CALL-SLA interface: Insights from a second-order synthesis. *Language Learning & Technology*, 20(2), 17–37. Retrieved from http://llt.msu.edu/issues/june2016/plonskyziegler.pdf

Prensky, M. (2005). "Engage me or enrage me": What today's learners demand. *EDUCAUSE*, 60–64. Retrieved July 30, 2010, from http://net.educause.edu/ir/library/pdf/erm0553.pdf

Quality Matters. (2014). QM rubrics and standards. Retrieved May 17, 2018, from https://www.qualitymatters.org/qa-resources/rubric-standards

Reinders, H., & White, C. (2016). 20 years of autonomy and technology: How far have we come and where to next? *Language, Learning & Technology*, 20(2), 143–154. Retrieved January 22, 2018, from http://llt.msu.edu/issue/june2016/reinderswhite.pdf

Rhinesmith, C., & Reisdorf, B. (2017). Race and digital inequalities: Policy implications. Retrieved on January 17, 2018, from https://ssrn.com/abstract=2944205.

Rubio, F., & Thoms, J. J. (2012). *Hybrid language teaching and learning: Exploring theoretical, pedagogical, and curricular issues.* Boston: Heinle-Cengage Learning.

Sanders, R. (2006). A comparison of chat room productivity: In-class versus out-of-class. *CALICO Journal*, 24(1), 59–76. Available at https://calico.org/journalTOC.php

Simon, E. (2010, June). *Preparing faculty to teach online: A case study.* Paper presented at the annual meeting of the Computer Assisted Language Instruction Consortium (CALICO), Amherst, MA.

Simon, E., & Fell, C. (2013). The flipped classroom. *FLTMAG.* Retrieved on February 7, 2018 from http://fltmag.com/the-flipped-classroom/

Smith, B. (2008). Methodological hurdles in capturing CMC data: The case of the missing self-repair. *Language Learning & Technology*, 12(1), 85–103. Retrieved July 30, 2010, from http://llt.msu.edu/vol12num1/smith/default.html

Smith, B. (2010, June). *Eye-tracking as a measure of noticing in SCMC*. Paper presented at the annual meeting of the Computer Assisted Language Instruction Consortium (CALICO), Amherst, MA.

Sykes, J. (2008). *A dynamic approach to social interaction: Synthetic immersive environments and Spanish pragmatics*. Unpublished dissertation, University of Minnesota, Minneapolis, MN.

Sykes, J., & Reinhardt, J. (2012). *Language at play: Digital games in second and foreign language teaching and learning*. Boston, MA: Pearson.

Thorne, S. L. (2010, June). *Avoiding the worst game ever: Media and emergent semiospheres*. Keynote presented at the annual meeting of the Computer Assisted Language Instruction Consortium (CALICO), Amherst, MA.

Thorne, S. L. (2016). Cultures-of-use and morphologies of communicative action. *Language Learning & Technology*, 20(2), 185–191. Retrieved January 10, 2018, from http://llt.msu.edu/issue/june2016/thorne.pdf

Thorne, S. L., Black, R., & Sykes, J. (2009). Second language use, socialization, and learning in internet interest communities and online gaming. *Modern Language Journal*, 93 (Focus Issue), 802–821.

White, C. (2003). *Language learning in distance education*. Cambridge: Cambridge University Press.

White, C. (2006). Distance learning of foreign languages. *Language Teaching*, 39, 247–364. https://doi.org/10.1017/S0261444806003727

Wiggins, G., & McTighe, J. (1998). *Understanding by design*. Alexandria, VA: Association for Supervision and Curriculum Development. Retrieved from: https://educationaltechnology.net/wp-content/uploads/2016/01/backward-design.pdf

Wildner-Bassett, M. (2008). Teacher's role in computer-mediated communication and distance learning. In S. Goertler & P. Winke (eds.), *Opening doors through distance language education: Principles, perspectives, and practices*, pp. 67–84. San Marcos, TX: CALICO.

Winke, P., & Goertler, S. (2008). Did we forget someone? Students' computer access and literacy for CALL. *CALICO Journal*, 25(3), 482–509.

Winke, P., Goertler, S., & Amuzie, G. L. (2010). Commonly-taught and less-commonly-taught language learners: Are they equally prepared for CALL and online language learning? *Computer Assisted Language Learning*, 23(3), 53–70.

Youngs, B., Moss-Horwitz, S., & Snyder, E. (2015). Educational data mining for elementary French online: A descriptive study. In E. Dixon & M. Thomas (eds.), *Researching language learner interactions online: From social media to MOOCs*, pp. 362–268. San Marcos, TX: CALICO.

Zink, F. (2018). *Facebook zur Telekollaboration im kommunikativen Fremdsprachenunterricht*. Doctoral dissertation, Pädagogische Hochschule Karlsruhe, Karlsruhe, Germany.

Useful Resources

- Computer Assisted Language Learning Consortium: https://calico.org/
- The Flipped Learning Network: http://flippedclassroom.org/
- International Association for K-12 Online Learning: http://www.inacol.org
- Language Learning and Technology: http://llt.msu.edu
- National Foreign Language Resource Center: http://nflrc.hawaii.edu/
- Online Learning Consortium: https://onlinelearningconsortium.org/
- Quality Matters: https://www.qualitymatters.org
- United States Distance Learning Association: https://www.usdla.org

About the Author

Senta Goertler (PhD, University of Arizona) is an Associate Professor of Second Language Studies and German and Language Program Coordinator at Michigan State University. Her research interests are CALL and education abroad.

3 Culture and CALL

Sarah Guth and Francesca Helm

> Language teaching can no longer make do with focusing on the
> target language and target countries – and on cultures as ter-
> ritorially defined phenomena [....] Apart from developing the
> students' communicative (dialogic) competence in the target lan-
> guage, language teaching ought also as far as possible to enable
> students to develop into multilingually and multiculturally aware
> world citizens. (Risager, 2007: 1)

Preview Questions

1. How would you define culture? How do you see the relationship
   between language, culture, and nation?
2. Have you ever been in a situation where people made assumptions
   about your "culture"? Describe the situation. How did you feel?
   How did you manage the situation?
3. Have you ever made assumptions about other cultures? Provide
   examples.
4. What role, and how much responsibility, do you think foreign language (FL) teachers have to address culture in the FL classroom?
5. What impact do you think the Internet and social media have had
   on languages and cultures? How do you think the Internet could be
   used to explore culture in the language classroom?
6. How aware do you think students are of their own cultural identities and the influence of language and location (be it physical or
   online) on their identities?
7. What considerations do teachers need to take into account when
   planning to use CALL for culture and language teaching?

1   Introduction

Ever since scholars began studying and researching culture, there has been debate regarding exactly what is meant by the term "culture." Although it is a word used commonly in everyday language, depending on the context or field of study, it may have very different meanings and there are hundreds of definitions of culture from across various disciplines (Spencer-Oatey, 2012). The field of second/foreign language (henceforth L2) learning and teaching through CALL has not been immune to the difficulty of defining culture.

The Standards for Foreign Language Learning, originally developed in 1996 by the American Council on the Teaching of Foreign Languages (henceforth Standards), were an important step in defining culture for L2 teaching and learning in the US context and have had a significant impact there. One of the five Cs in the Standards is Cultures (the others being Communication, Connections, Comparisons, and Communities, all of which are interrelated). The Standard regarding Cultures (Standard 2) presents the three Ps of culture, a triangular model of *practices*, *perspectives*, and *products*. According to the Standards, *practices* refer to "patterns of behavior accepted by a society and deal with aspects of culture such as rites of passage, the use of forms of discourse, the social 'pecking order', and the use of space" and derive from *perspectives*, which are "the traditional ideas and attitudes [...] of a culture" (p. 50). The Standards recognize that cultural *products* can be tangible or intangible, but it is important for students to be aware that whatever form a product takes, "[...] its presence within the culture is required or justified by the underlying beliefs and values (*perspectives*) of that culture" (p. 51). Standard 2.1 regards students' awareness of the relationship between the first two Ps, practices and perspectives, and Standard 2.2 the relationship between the second two, perspectives and products. The Standards were revised in 2015, and are now called the World-Readiness Standards for Language Learning (National Standards Collaborative Board, 2015). The five Cs have remained, but the goal area for each standard has been clarified and better illustrated in order to guide implementation and assessment, e.g., for each of the standards a series of can-do statements[1] have been developed in order to guide implementation and assessment. For Cultures, the proficiency benchmarks are defined in terms of the ability to *investigate* (e.g., "In my own and other cultures I can make comparisons between products and practices to help me understand

---

[1]   https://www.actfl.org/sites/default/files/CanDos/Intercultural%20Can-Do_
Statements.pdf

perspectives") and to *interact* (e.g., "I can interact at a functional level in some familiar contexts").

Across the Atlantic, in Europe, the Common European Framework of Reference (CEFR) (Council of Europe, 2001) is a key reference document for foreign language educators. The main aim of the CEFR is to provide a European standard for the teaching and assessment of foreign languages in order to promote mobility throughout the multicultural, multilingual European Union.[2] In this document, the key to developing plurilingualism and pluricultural competence is interculturality. The document states that in learning a foreign language:

> [t]he learner does not simply acquire two distinct, unrelated ways of acting and communicating. The language learner becomes *plurilingual* and develops *interculturality*. The linguistic and cultural competences in respect of each language are modified by knowledge of the other and contribute to intercultural awareness, skills and know-how. They enable the individual to develop an enriched, more complex personality and an enhanced capacity for further language learning and greater openness to new cultural experiences. (p. 43)

This notion of interculturality in the CEFR stems from the work of Michael Byram (1997), who has developed a model of *intercultural communicative competence* (ICC) for foreign language learning. ICC comprises different "savoirs," that is, types of knowledge, skills, and attitudes. These include attitudes of openness and curiosity, skills of discovery and interaction, interpretive skills, knowledge of social groups and their products and practices, and finally critical cultural awareness. Like the Standards, the CEFR too has been recently updated with a Companion Volume[3] (Council of Europe, 2017), in which individuals' plurilingual and pluricultural repertoires are conceptualized. Building on the notion of intercultural competence, a

---

2   As described on the official website of the Council of Europe, the CEFR provides thorough descriptions of "[...] i) the competences necessary for communication, ii) the related knowledge and skills and iii) the situations and domains of communication." In addition to descriptions of overall general competences, the CEFR "[...] defines levels of attainment in different aspects of its descriptive scheme with illustrative descriptors scale."

3   A provisional edition of the CEFR Companion Volume with new descriptors was published online in 2017 by the Council of Europe and is available on their website: https://rm.coe.int/common-european-framework-of-reference-for-languages-learning-teaching/168074a4e2

scale of descriptors has been defined for how to exploit one's pluricultural repertoires.

In both the CEFR and the Standards, culture is recognized as an important part of L2 teaching and learning, and is related to knowledge about the cultures being studied and the sociocultural norms and practices required to be effective intercultural communicators. Culture is very much linked to language, but this can reinforce the widespread misconception that *one* language equals *one* culture and that culture is associated with a *nation* (e.g., French culture is that of France). In strong versions of this "national" paradigm, the standard language of the native speaker is idealized and the language learner is seen as aspiring to *the* native model including what is considered to be appropriate behavior in the target culture. This process of *acculturation* assumes that there is indeed a standard language and, consequently, a standard culture. These concepts have been problematized by many applied linguists (Kramsch, 1998; Lamy & Goodfellow, 2010; Ortega & Zyzik, 2008; Piller, 2011; Scollon, 2004). The transnational paradigm (Risager, 2007), for example, challenges the native speaker model and places the learner in a local and/or global context, not the target, national context. L2 learners, who are complex, often multilingual people with multiple identities, *appropriate* the language(s) and cultures studied in a way that they find comfortable, without losing or disguising their original identity/ies. They should aim to become intercultural speakers, able "to see and manage the relationships between themselves and their own cultural beliefs, behaviours and meanings [...] and those of their interlocutors" (Byram, 1997: 12).

This has, in part, been addressed in the revised Standards, and also in the CEFR Companion Volume, which states that "... the aim of language education is profoundly modified. It is no longer seen as simply to achieve 'mastery' of one or two, or even three languages, each taken in isolation, with the 'ideal native speaker' as the ultimate model. Instead, the aim is to develop a linguistic repertoire, in which all linguistic abilities have a place (CEFR Section 1.3)" (Council of Europe, 2017: 143). The concept of a holistic, interrelated plurilingual repertoire was just beginning to emerge when the CEFR was originally published over 15 years before, and since then a great deal of research has been carried out in the field of bilingual studies, both in Europe and the US (Creese & Blackledge, 2010; Garcia, 2009; Garcia & Li, 2014), which supports this conceptualization of the unitary linguistic repertoire. Furthermore, the structural increase in migration to Europe in recent years and the greater linguistic diversity this has led to, especially in areas that were previously predominantly monolingual, has been in part addressed in the CEFR Companion Volume, in which language study and the development of intercultural competence is not framed merely for travel and study abroad, as in the original CEFR, but also for dialogue in multi-lingual and diverse communities.

In this chapter, we assume that cultural identity cannot simply be defined by language or nation-state, and see cultures as complex, diverse, and multi-faceted. In educational, and particularly CALL contexts, what is needed is a fluid definition of culture that incorporates the multiplicity of cultures and subcultures which are present and continuously changing not only within and across societies but online as well. A definition of culture which we feel can accommodate this more fluid view is Pierre Bourdieu's consideration of culture as "field," namely:

> [...] any site or region within which a group acts, communicates, and evolves its characteristic knowledge and identities [...] fur-nished with a tradition of institutions, group behaviours, prag-matic practices, discourses (verbal and otherwise), ideologies, and a characteristic knowledge base. (1993, in Arens, 2010: 321–322)

Ingrid Piller (2011) explores intercultural communication from a critical perspective and sees culture as an ideological construct which is called into play by social actors in order to produce and reproduce social categories and boundaries. What is essential, in her view, is that we understand the reasons, forms, and consequences of making culture relevant. In the context of this chapter, we therefore need to understand why, and how, language educators include culture in their curricula and what the implications of this might be.

2   New Technologies and Culture

As Kramsch has pointed out, the Internet has led to a transformation in global communications, which is "not just a change in degree, but a change in kind" (2003: 3). Furthermore, the common conviction that languages are ultimately learnt for sojourn in foreign countries and that cultural under-standing can only be acquired through residence abroad is being challenged as focus is placed on the promotion of "global competences," which include language learning in local classrooms. Global competence requires numer-ous skills, including the ability to: "communicate in more than one lan-guage; communicate appropriately and effectively with people from other cultures or countries; comprehend other people's thoughts, beliefs and feel-ings, and see the world from their perspectives; adjust one's thoughts, feel-ings or behaviours to fit new contexts and situations; and analyse and think critically in order to scrutinise and appraise information and meanings" (OECD, 2016: 5).

The number of US college students studying abroad for credit is only about 1% of enrolled students, depending on the year.[4] Although that percentage is higher in some other countries, especially in the EU, the OECD 2016 average is just 5.1% for short-cycle tertiary programs.[5] Furthermore, because of security reasons, the most common study abroad destinations tend to exclude many parts of the world where some of the critical languages are spoken (for instance Iran, Turkey, Egypt to name but a few).

In stark contrast to the very small number of American students who study abroad, "[i]n 2016, the proportion of students using social media for at least six hours per week jumped to 40.9%, nearly 14 percentage points higher than the previous high of 27.2% reached in both 2011 and 2014" (Eagan et al., 2017: 20). This increase is likely also due to the increased ubiquity of mobile devices with Internet access. Indeed, the online sphere has become an authentic context of communication in leisure, work, and education. As Thorne (2006: 21) explains, "Internet-mediated communication is now a high-stakes environment that infuses work processes, educational activity, interpersonal communication and, not least, intimate relationship building and maintenance (Castells 1996)."

Since students are already using social media and other online applications both to interact with their peers and to complete coursework, it makes sense that educators would want to exploit this for intercultural learning within the context of their courses by connecting students with peers in geographically distant locations. This practice, called telecollaboration in the field of foreign language learning and teaching, has grown significantly over the past two decades (Helm & Guth, 2016). The practice has also been growing in other educational fields and is referred to with the terms "virtual exchange,"[6] "online intercultural exchange" (O'Dowd & Lewis, 2016), and "collaborative online international learning" (Rubin & Guth, 2015) among others. Intercultural learning is at the core of all these activities.

The role of languages and cultures on the Internet has not been without debate, in particular with regards to issues of power-play and linguistic and

---

4   http://www.nafsa.org/Policy_and_Advocacy/Policy_Resources/
     Policy_Trends_and_Data/Trends_in_U_S__Study_Abroad/
5   http://www.oecd-ilibrary.org/sites/factbook-2015-en/table-148.html?cont
     entType=&itemId=%2fcontent%2ftable%2ffactbook-2015-table148-en&
     mimeType=text%2fhtml&containerItemId=%2fcontent%2fbook%2ffactb
     ook-2015-en&accessItemIds=
6   http://virtualexchangecoalition.org/

cultural hegemony. On the one hand, the Internet is viewed as yet another vehicle for the hegemonizing effect of English as *the* language of communication that spreads Western culture and values (Holton, 2000) and is responsible for cultural homogenization and the extinction of hundreds of "minor" languages. The dominance of English has somewhat declined in recent years,[7] with other languages such as Chinese, Spanish, Arabic, Portuguese, Indonesian, and Russian increasing exponentially in terms of growth in Internet penetration since 2000.[8] However these larger languages are seen to be pushing out "smaller" languages and leading to the risk of their "digital extinction."[9]

On the other hand, there are those who look at how the rise of the Internet has permitted the diffusion of less known cultures and languages to a much wider community. For instance, the Internet is seen to have provided a "home" for languages which have not had or still have no nation such as Kurdish or Armenian (Bakker, 2001) and where activists strive to revitalize languages (Galla, 2016). The Internet also offers many spaces in which translanguaging practices are the norm, as scholars who have researched linguistic practices on the Web have found (Lee, 2017). Furthermore, it has led to the emergence of new digital registers, such as varieties of Colloquial Arabic, known as Arabizi or Arabeezy, which are widely used together with invented English transliterations (Ortega, 2017). This practice is known as "script-focused translanguaging" or "trans-scripting" (Androutsopoulos, 2015: 188).

Language teachers cannot ignore the immensity of the Internet and the range of resources it offers for culture and language learning. However, the exponential rise in available resources for both teachers and students highlights the need for a critical approach in the selection and analysis of resources. Furthermore, as Furstenberg (2010: 329) points out, "the same old questions of how to 'incorporate,' 'integrate,' and 'infuse' foreign language classes with culture and 'what culture' to teach seem to persist even in this medium." The rest of this chapter aims to look at how teachers and researchers have been approaching culture through CALL to try and find answers to these questions.

---

7   http://www.businessinsider.com/english-is-losing-its-status-as-the-universal-language-of-the-internet-heres-why-thats-a-good-thing-2015-12?IR=T
8   Arabic grew by 7,247.3% between 2000 and 2017, Russian by 3,434% and Indonesian/Malaysian by 26,450.1%. http://www.internetworldstats.com/stats7.htm
9   https://www.theguardian.com/education/2014/mar/26/digital-extinction-europe-languages-fight-survive

3   Review of Practice and Research

Internet technologies now include many of the multimedia affordances of the software applications traditionally associated only with desktop CALL applications such as interactive audio and video and multimodal tools. What was once only possible locally, can now be done in a networked way using the World Wide Web. Our review of L2 education practice and research studies indicates that the practice of teaching culture through CALL has indeed focused more and more on online activities and on activities that can be used alone or in combination. We have categorized these as follows:

- **Access**, providing access to a wealth of authentic cultural resources available in a multiplicity of media and the possibility for teachers and students to access resources on the Web;
- **Communicate and collaborate**, exploiting the opportunities for interaction offered by the Internet to set up intercultural exchanges whereby learners interact, and possibly develop meaningful inter-cultural relationships with distant peers; and
- **Bridge**, attempting to bridge learners' Internet use and identities outside class with language learning in formal settings.

In this section, we shall look at examples of these activities in practice and attempt to relate them to the predominant research paradigms found in the literature on Culture and CALL. One area of research that has had a specific focus on culture in language learning is telecollaboration, currently also known as virtual exchange, to which we dedicate considerable space. The framework we have adopted for the research paradigms is that devised by Blyth (2008), who categorizes CMC (computer-mediated communication) research into four main categories: technological, psycholinguistic, socio-cultural, and ecological, on the basis of theoretical, methodological, and linguistic criteria. Like the approaches to teaching culture through CALL described above, these research paradigms have developed chronologically. New approaches often develop as outgrowths of previous approaches and the success of one does not entail the abandonment of the previous ones. There are no strict rules governing which research approach should be used for different uses of CALL for culture learning; the overview we provide merely reflects trends we have found in the literature.

3.1 Access

3.1.1 Practice There have been many national and transnational initiatives by universities, museums, governments, and transnational organizations such as the EU[10] that share historic collections and artistic patrimonies through digital platforms. Furthermore, news, television programs, films, music, videos are widely available. However, with the technologies and resources available today, culture materials can also be produced by anyone with access to the Internet. This gives teachers and learners access to a wide array of genres (cultural *products*), *practices*, "voices," and *perspectives*, which was not previously possible. One of the potential advantages for culture learning is that now it is not only the "dominant" or mainstream cultural voices that we can find on Internet, but also "other" perspectives. These can include those perspectives which the mass media and commercial educational publishers tend to ignore, address superficially or even suppress. Perspectives from the multiplicity of subcultures, indigenous cultures, and nationless cultures have found a voice on the Internet. For example, teachers of French as a foreign language could focus on francophone parts of the world beyond France and Canada (e.g., in North Africa and the Middle East). There are numerous resources available in French about the different cultures in these areas such as a website called Amazigh World which aims "to help educate people about the Amazigh – the language, culture, the people's struggles for the right to self-identification in North Africa."[11] However, these perspectives may be somewhat difficult to find since they are not what usually appears first on the more commonly used websites (Google, YouTube, and Facebook were the top three in 2017).[12] Given the vast range of resources available on the Web, the importance of developing a critical understanding of culture as it is presented on some of these sites is fundamental. Piller (2011: 5) suggests that the fundamental question that should be asked is: "Who makes culture relevant to whom in which context and for which purposes?"

10   The Digital Libraries Initiative "sets out to make all Europe's cultural
     resources and scientific records – books, journals, films, maps, photographs,
     music, etc. – accessible to all, and preserve it for future generations."
     Between the time of writing the first edition of this chapter and this revised
     edition, the number of digital artifacts available on the European portal
     (http://www.europeana.eu/portal/) has increased from 6 million to almost
     60 million – images, texts, sounds, videos – some famous and other hidden
     treasures from Europe's museums and galleries, archives, libraries, and
     audio-visual collections.
11   http://www.amazighworld.org/eng/index.php
12   https://en.wikipedia.org/wiki/List_of_most_popular_websites

In terms of culture as content, the Web abounds with resources presenting "culture" as a country's *asset* as in tourism marketing contexts, in order to draw people to that country for travel and also bring financial resources. There are also many websites offering advice and tips about cultural practices for travelers. These can be of various genres – from the humorous to more serious corporate travel services which provide customized, destination-specific briefings, sometimes for specific audiences (e.g., "cultural tips" for Americans visiting Italy). In these latter contexts, culture is often presented as a *challenge* that needs to be overcome. Very often it is the nation that is presented as the cultural unit rather than, for example, regions, industries, and social groups to name just a few. Most of these types of sites exemplify and reproduce what Piller (2011) describes as "banal nationalism," which essentializes the nation as the locus of culture and communication and presents homogeneous groups with the same kinds of behavior and even emotions. For students of language and culture, this view of culture is theoretically inadequate as it fails to acknowledge the multiplicity of identities and makes irrelevant class, gender, ethnicity, regional background, and any personal traits. Exploring and critically analyzing websites which offer these views of culture is an exercise which can raise students' awareness of this essentialism.

3.1.2 Research There is little research that specifically measures culture learning through multimedia in the CALL literature using what we have called the "access approach." A keyword search of the word "culture" in the major CALL journals, such as *Language Learning & Technology*, *ReCALL*, and the *CALICO Journal*, produces few results, but when present it mainly appears in articles discussing telecollaboration and intercultural exchange, which we will discuss in the next subsection. Other articles fall into what Blyth (2008) would categorize as "technological," that is, they focus on affordances of the particular technologies used, often comparing and contrasting use of these technologies with "traditional" tools and stressing the potential benefits of the said technologies.

An important study on multimedia for language and culture learning is that by Kramsch & Andersen, who acknowledge that multimedia:

> offers the possibility of developing the sociocultural competence
> of language learners more readily than the pages of a textbook or
> the four walls of a classroom. In effect, computers seem to realize
> the dream of every language teacher – to bring the language and
> culture as close and as authentically as possible to students in the
> classroom. (1999: 31)

However, simply providing multimedia clips illustrating language in context is not sufficient, because watching a video clip lacks much of the contextual and background information that is present in face-to-face contexts. Kramsch & Andersen argue that for context "[...] to be made learnable, especially in an academic setting, it has to be transformed into analyzable text" (1999: 33) and that multimedia offers great possibilities for this. The authors illustrate the process of textualization, that is the presentation and analysis of different resources which can contribute towards the understanding of a "text," for example: a scene based on an ethnographic film of a hearing in a village in Peru can be enriched with the addition of interviews with a native consultant/anthropologist, and a written ethnography. Technologies for delivery of multimedia materials may have changed over the past two decades, but it remains important to support learners' development of media literacy and the ability to deconstruct mediated "texts," whatever technology is used. This can be done through approaches such as discourse analysis and critical ethnography.

Other studies have looked at the use of the Internet through guided tasks for language and culture learning (Gaspar, 1998; Osuna & Meskill, 1998), and the design of pedagogical reading tasks about culture which make use of the Internet (Brandl, 2002). Reported advantages are measured through feedback collected from students in pilot studies and include the authenticity and currency of materials, visual stimuli and multimodality, the interest and enjoyment it arouses, as well as the information provided about cultural products. Few experimental studies which actually seek to "measure" cultural knowledge acquired through Internet-mediated cultural learning have been carried out, with the exception of Dubreil, Herron, & Cole (2004), who conducted an empirical investigation of whether authentic websites facilitate intermediate-level French language students' ability to learn culture. Through pre- and post-tests, the researchers measured gains in cultural knowledge as regards cultural products and practices and found that use of the Internet (information pages and static images) led to a gain in knowledge about cultural products, which was confirmed by student perceptions as measured through an evaluation questionnaire. This quantitative approach is found to be useful in measuring the knowledge component of culture learning, that is, the acquisition of factual knowledge about particular cultural products or practices, but it does not measure sophisticated understanding of different cultural perspectives, or the development of intercultural communicative competence.

An exploratory study by Drewelow & Mitchell (2015) sought to explore learners' rating of culture in relation to other concepts in advanced Spanish courses through a survey with open-ended questions. It found that culture was largely conceptualized as products and practices and that very few students embraced a critical perspective towards the concept of culture. They associated culture mainly with travelling or study abroad. The authors of the study concluded that there was a strong need for advanced-level courses to devise strategies that adopt a "reflective, interpretative, historically grounded, and politically engaged pedagogy" (Kramsch, 2014: 296). Finally, accessing the Internet as a resource is what Levy (2007) describes as a "receptive means" of accessing culture, which does not take advantage of the most revolutionary feature of the Internet, that is, the possibilities it offers for communication and more productive and interactive ways of engaging in culture learning and developing intercultural communicative competence. These approaches will be discussed below.

3.2   Communicate and Collaborate

3.2.1 Practice A large part of the literature on CALL and culture in the past decade in particular has focused on telecollaboration and virtual exchange. This approach is based on a social constructivist view of learning inspired by Vygotskian theories of learning as a social activity and importance is given to the development of intercultural communicative competence, as defined by Byram (1997), as well as language learning.

Traditional models of telecollaboration such as the *Cultura* model (Furstenberg et al., 2001) and institutional forms of *eTandem* learning (Kötter, 2002; O'Rourke, 2005) involve language learners in geographically distant locations engaging in bilingual exchanges (Thorne, 2006). The *Cultura* model is based on a comparative approach to cultural learning and is very structured. Initially students respond to a series of questionnaires in their native language (L1) and compare responses individually and in their classes. They then discuss their hypotheses through online interaction with foreign peers, again in L1. In the expansion phase, they go beyond small student group interactions and enter the online world of opinion polls, films, historical documents, and archives to obtain a more transversal and synoptic perspective – an essential step for moving beyond the simplistic, binary, checklist approach to learning culture (Furstenberg & English, 2016). Although it may initially seem odd that students in an L2 course are using their L1 with their foreign peers, the authors of the project argue that only in the L1 can students truly express the complexity of their own ideas and culture with their peers abroad. L2 learning is supported by students reading their peers' entries in the online forums and through classroom and homework activities.

Whereas the main goal of *Cultura* (as the name itself implies) is to focus on intercultural issues, eTandem models have a more language-development focus. Again, as the name implies, tandem learning is based on reciprocal giving and sharing and is, by definition, a bilingual practice, boding well for multilingualism, as Ortega (2017) writes. eTandem also offers learners the opportunity for learners to negotiate and perform multiple identities (Yang & Yi, 2017).

During the first decade and a half of telecollaboration implementation, practitioners mainly focused on written communication, both asynchronous and synchronous, because, from a technological point of view, video-conferencing was the only viable means available for oral communication but was costly and logistically complex to organize. The increase in freely available audio and video applications that do not require powerful Internet connections and/or do not consume large amounts of data (e.g., Skype, Zoom, FaceTime, WhatsApp, or even video calling on Facebook Messenger) has led to a greater number of telecollaboration exchanges organized around oral communication. The Teletandem Brasil Project of UNESP – Universidade Estadual Paulista in Brazil,[13] for example, makes use of these technologies to partner university students with peers in other countries learning Portuguese and other languages. Two models of institutional Teletandem Brasil are offered, integrated and not-integrated. The former includes teletandem sessions as a mandatory part of the curriculum, carried out during lesson time and with assessment and grades for participation. Non-integrated exchanges are not included in curricula and are carried out during students' own time, though they can receive certificates of recognition for their activity. Partners speak for an hour, usually half an hour in each students' L1, and then de-brief with their instructors in "mediation sessions" to discuss what they have learnt in terms of language, culture, and relationship with their partner.

Two features of teletandem are fundamental to its success. The use of video in teletandem is seen as a key component because it allows participants to engage on a deeper level than text-based exchanges. The webcam and the image it projects of the self (as well as one's partner) serve as a mirror for interactants as they can actually see themselves as they interact. Telles (2009) also uses the mirror as a metaphor to describe the teletandem process, as it offers the opportunity to look at one's self and language from a foreign perspective (that of the partners), which can trigger a reflective process. The mediation sessions with teachers are seen as fundamental, for though the sessions between students are "replete with opportunities for the

13   http://www.teletandembrasil.org/

expression of subjectivities or ideologies, [... these] might go unnoticed if not appropriately dealt with by the teachers who are responsible for the session mediations" (Telles, 2015: 23).

In setting up telecollaboration projects, practitioners have not only responded to the new tools available, but also to different possible configurations, for example, heritage speakers (HS) paired with language learners (Blake & Zyzik, 2003; Hughes, 2010; Yang & Yi, 2017; King, 2010) or groups of non-native speakers using a foreign language as a "lingua franca" (Basharina, 2007; Helm, Guth, & Farrah, 2012) to exchange perspectives on their respective cultures as well as on global issues.

3.2.2 Research While initial research into telecollaboration, and still some research today, focused on technologies, the trend has increasingly been to adopt psycholinguistic and sociocultural approaches to better understand the type of language and culture learning that takes place in these contexts. The psycholinguistic approach tends to focus on language development, whereas the sociocultural approach, as its name suggests, is more relevant to the study of culture learning. Most of the research using the psycholinguistic approach has focused on linguistic issues such as negotiation of meaning (Blake, 2000; Pellettieri, 2000), communication strategies (Chun, 1994; Lee, 2001), and questions and requests for clarification or more information (Abrams, 2001; Chun, 1994; Sotillo, 2000). However, recently there has been an interest in pragmatic aspects of language use. For instance Tudini (2007) investigated the development of ICC among Australian learners of Italian by analyzing the language they used in online chat rooms with native speakers. Through her analysis, she identified a new category she calls "intercultural negotiation," which included intercultural-pragmatic triggers such as respecting rules of politeness and adjacency pairs in conversational openings and closings, introductions and thanking routines. She argues that, although this quantitative study focused on lexis, "[...] *formulaic* aspects of vocabulary, alongside idiomatic and figurative expressions [...] should be distinguished as an intercultural-pragmatic aspect of language learning [as they are] an important part of learners' socialization into the chat environment" (Tudini, 2007: 581). She notes that her findings show that the informal setting of the chat room encouraged the sort of self-initiated negotiation sequences that indicate the skills of discovery and interaction identified by Byram (1997) with reference to the "intercultural speaker" in face-to-face contexts.

What interculturalists see as a drawback to psycholinguistic approaches to telecollaboration research is their focus on language with no consideration of sociocultural context. As Reinhardt (2008: 229) writes: "[i]t is difficult to consider the negotiation of pragmatic, interactional, or interpersonal meanings in an analysis that does not consider the context of situation and individual learner motivations and histories in interpretation." The development of pragmatic competence, i.e., the ability to *effectively* communicate with others, which is considered a part of learning culture, cannot be adequately addressed by a psycholinguistic approach to research. This, together with the deficit orientation of many SLA studies which see language learners as less competent than native speakers, contributed to the "social turn" in SLA studies (Block, 2003) with an ever-growing emphasis on contextual factors.

Much of the literature which focuses on culture and intercultural learning is based within a sociocultural paradigm. Warschauer (2005) describes the three main notions of Vygotskian thought which are important for an understanding of sociocultural perspectives on CALL: mediation, social learning, and genetic analysis. Mediation is the notion that "all human activity is mediated by tools or signs" (Warschauer, 2005: 41) and that what is significant about these tools is not their properties, but rather how they affect and transform human action and, at times, society itself. The concept of social learning, the view that learning occurs collaboratively through interaction, is also fundamental to the sociocultural approach and is particularly relevant to culture in language learning through CMC.

Socially-oriented research studies are generally qualitative and tend to look not only at communication generated by authentic tasks carried out in telecollaboration exchanges (forum discussions, emails, wikis, blogs, chat transcripts) but also texts produced by learners during exchanges such as reflective diaries (Hauck, 2007; Helm, 2009), final projects (Müller-Hartmann, 2006), and contextual factors related to the learners themselves and the classroom context. Information about learners can be collected through questionnaires, attitudinal surveys, interviews, assessments of language, and intercultural awareness. Other contextual information ranges from the classroom level (e.g., tasks, teaching approach, assessment methods) to the institutional level (e.g., constraints, regulations, policies, procedures) and higher up to the geopolitical level (e.g., national policies and curricula). The model of intercultural learning which is used in these studies tends to be Byram's model of intercultural communicative competence and researchers analyze and code data from student interactions, productions and interviews for evidence of attitude, skills, knowledge, and sometimes critical cultural awareness (see, e.g., Liaw, 2006). A limited number of studies have used quantitative tools, such as adaptations of Chen & Starosta's (2000) Intercultural Sensitivity Scale, in combination with qualitative ethnographic data (e.g., Jin, 2008).

The learning outcomes of telecollaboration practice reported in socially-oriented studies include: linguistic and sociolinguistic advances (Kötter, 2003), "communication" skills development (Egert, 2000; Lee, 2004), construction of new intercultural knowledge (Chun & Wade, 2004), intercultural communicative competence and critical cultural awareness (Liaw & Johnson, 2001; Müller-Hartmann, 2000; O'Dowd, 2003), as well as gains in motivation and learner autonomy (Fuchs, Hauck, & Müller-Hartmann, 2012). Key issues that have been addressed include task-design (Dooly, 2011; Müller-Hartmann, 2016), the role of the instructor (Dooly, 2015; Müller-Hartmann, 2006; Ware & Kramsch, 2005), cultural patterns of use (Kramsch & Thorne, 2002; Thorne, 2003, 2016), multimodality (Hauck, 2010; Guichon & Cohen, 2016; Malinowski & Kramsch, 2014; Satar, 2013), and failed communication (O'Dowd & Ritter, 2006).

This last topic has drawn significant interest on the part of researchers, but rather than seeing tensions in communication as obstacles and problems to be avoided, there is a growing tendency to see them as opportunities for intercultural development (Helm, 2013; Kramsch & Thorne, 2002; Ware, 2005; Ware & Kramsch, 2005). Researchers following this line see instances of contestation as "rich points" (Agar, 1994) which should be addressed and dealt with as a productive source for learning in a dialogic approach to online exchanges. Schneider & von der Emde (2006) try to make the dialogic approach more explicit to help students feel more at ease with conflict rather than encourage them to avoid conflict and seek immediately to find common ground. In their study, the authors report on two American learners insistently posing questions until they receive a response from their uncomfortable German partner, and they see this in a positive light as it helped them learn about Germany's "complex" relation to its past. They also report how in their project work, students "used their engagement with the target culture to shine a critical light on their own" (Schneider & von der Emde, 2006: 191) and thus gain a sense of critical cultural awareness. Key to this approach is an emphasis on reflection and meta-reflection which, they believe, allows conflicts to become opportunities for learning.

Potential problems with qualitative research in this field include the risk of researcher bias in the content analyses (Belz, 2003a), generic claims of ICC learning which are unsubstantiated by evidence, and a lack of attention to negative results and limitations of studies (Huh & Hu, 2005). Another drawback is that the majority of studies in the literature are case studies that focus on single exchanges and often just one of the classes engaged in the exchanges. Increased interest in telecollaboration and virtual exchange has made funding available for larger-scale studies on the impact and outcomes of this activity. For example, at the time of writing, the European Policy

Experiment EVALUATE (Evaluating and Upscaling Telecollaborative Teacher Education)[14] is supporting the implementation of 30+ telecollaborative projects involving pre-service teachers and will collect and analyze data from all the exchanges. The researchers have adapted and/or designed both quantitative and qualitative tools that will be investigating the development of digital literacies, intercultural awareness, and foreign language skills.

Although the psycholinguistic and sociocultural approaches have been presented as distinct, the former predominantly quantitative and the latter qualitative, increasingly "mixed methods approaches" are being adopted which combine features of each. Several studies have looked at the development of pragmatic competence in terms of pronoun use (e.g., Kinginger, 2000; Thorne, 2008) and how it develops through interaction in telecollaboration exchanges. They have used a mixed approach which combines linguistic data analysis with information about the sociocultural context and the significant characteristics of this context.[15] Belz laments that the development of intercultural competence has not been investigated in linguistic terms and calls for researchers to "[…] broaden the investigative focus on *what* learners say to include *how* they say it" (2003b: 69) through linguistically grounded analyses, such as Appraisal Analysis (Martin, 1995; White, 1998), which she uses in her study of the development of attitudes of curiosity and openness in telecollaboration (Belz, 2003b). Her study combines the quantitative analysis which characterizes much of the psycholinguistic SLA research with attention to social aspects of the participants and the telecollaboration project she describes. Appraisal Analysis has also recently been used to explore evaluative language for rapport building in telecollaboration (Vinagre & Esteban, 2017).

3.3   Bridging

3.3.1 Practice In telecollaboration contexts, as in the examples mentioned above, it is often the teacher who chooses the online resources and the partner class, and sets up the tasks. Some scholars, however, have begun to argue that this is too restrictive and if we really want to tap into our students' existing online practices and want them to be exposed to a wide variety of the *online cultures* present on the World Wide Web, maybe we need to "let

14   http://www.evaluateproject.eu/
15   This approach is also known as a sociocognitive approach (see Reinhardt 2008).

them go" and provide them with the tools they need to survive, and learn, out on the Web. As de Nooy states:

> despite the promise of the Internet to "connect learners with authentic culture" and serve as "a gateway to the virtual foreign world where *real people* are using real language in *real context*" (Osuna & Meskill, 1998), discussion activities – whether email exchange or discussion lists – are often limited to teacher-determined topics and the cultural comfort zone of student-student interaction. [...] Students are still safely within the classroom, virtual though it might be, and despite its advantages, it suffers the limitations of any language classroom in providing genuine opportunities to engage with the "target culture" in roles other than that of student. (2006: 73)

The question posed here is whether or not we are truly doing our students, especially more advanced ones, a service by "controlling" their learning environments. If our ultimate aim is to help students become autonomous intercultural communicators, it may be worthwhile to expose them to authentic environments where they have to engage both their linguistic, intercultural communication and online literacy skills in order to be effective communicators.

In 2003, Hanna & de Nooy began to explore whether or not linguistic competence and cultural knowledge were enough to allow students to participate effectively in an authentic context of online fora such as those on the website of the French newspaper *Le Monde*.[16] The authors saw these online environments as virtual locations where members from numerous cultural backgrounds come together for a specific purpose, i.e., to discuss a topic. From the researchers' point of view, they were interested in understanding the culture, in particular the practices of online fora and how to equip students with the necessary tools to be effective in these environments; from a pedagogical point of view, they were interested in promoting language and cultural learning.

Hanna & de Nooy focused on four students who participated in an online discussion forum on the *Le Monde* website. They found that the most "successful" student actually used French very little and chose to take part in the French discussion forum using his native language, English. Rather than being excluded from the community because he did not use French, he was included because of his engagement in the discussion. On the contrary, two British students who were consistently apologizing for "their French," even though it was quite good, were not included in the online community

16   http://forums.lemonde.fr/perl/wwwthreads.pl

because they were not willing to fully participate in the discussion at hand. Although the authors found several instances of the members of the forum explicitly or implicitly trying to "teach" these students the acceptable rules in their subculture, the students were not able to step out of their learner shoes. In the forum, understanding and being able to negotiate the rules and behaviors of the online community's culture were prerequisites for success-ful participation and the process was relational, not unilateral. On public Internet fora, the other participants are not there to help students learn, they are there to discuss, debate, and interact. Apart from a degree of competence in the language(s) used in the forums, the type of "cultural knowledge" required, as in any online communities (or cybercultures), involves proposi-tional knowledge of the community's topics as well as knowledge of norms of interaction established by the online community, some of which may be stated on the website in terms of guidelines or rules, but many of which are to be inferred as one begins to engage with the community.

Allowing students to venture out into the *real* "virtual" world within an institutional course clearly requires preparation, awareness raising, and monitoring. Examples of successful and failed communication could be used to expose students to the types of skills they will need when posting to the forum, or other online environment, as may be the case. The behavior patterns of members of online communities are unpredictable so teachers need to prepare students for the often harsh reality of online communi-cation and scaffold them throughout the experience with effective moni-toring. Hanna & de Nooy conclude that despite the challenges, students "[l]earn by participating in the cultural practice rather than asking for spe-cial, student-centered experiences focusing on themselves" (2003: 78). Though not stated explicitly, the "cultural practice" they refer to is not limited to the culture of people from France, but rather includes the online culture that characterizes the forum in *Le Monde*.

An alternative approach is suggested by Thorne (2010), who argues that rather than leading students into teacher-chosen media on the Web (e.g., Hanna & de Nooy above), we should tap into students' existing online per-sonas and exploit the learning that is already going on "out there." He calls this "intercultural communication in the wild," which he defines as learning experiences that are "[s]ituated in arenas of social activity that are less con-trollable than classroom or organized online intercultural exchanges might be, but which present interesting, and perhaps even compelling, opportu-nities for intercultural exchange, agentive action and meaning making" (Thorne, 2010: 144).

Sauro (2017) provides examples of language and culture learning that takes place among avid users of fan-fiction sites. She argues that "our growing understanding of online fan practices can motivate the design of computer-mediated tasks or the integration of social media into formal language teaching" (2017: 1). Fan fiction refers to "writing that continues, interrupts, reimagines, or just riffs on stories and characters other people have already written about" (Jamison, 2013: 17 in Sauro 2017). These sites are based around popular cultural artifacts, such as the *Harry Potter*[17] series or popular television series like *Sherlock*.[18] Participants often come from varied cultural-linguistic backgrounds so that even when there is an "official" language, plurilingual communication tends to be the norm and, as in the discussion fora mentioned above, successful participation in these communities may depend more on intercultural competence and understanding the "culture" of the online environment (i.e., values, interactional aims, and practices of the community) than on language proficiency. In these online communities, newcomers often receive comments for improvement and encouragement from more experienced or established members. Thorne (2010) argues that this context supports the Vygotskian principles of social learning within the Zone of Proximal Development. He provides examples from the work of Black (2005, 2006, 2008), who has shown that English language learners actively participating in fan-fiction sites make linguistic, affective, and intercultural improvements by developing relationships with individuals who share the same interests.

The question that remains, however, is how to integrate this type of learning into the formal, institutional language learning environment. Language teachers face the conflict of having to choose between "[t]he critical importance of high stakes power genres (i.e. formal registers of language taught in schools) and the emergent-contingent logics of digital vernaculars" (Thorne, 2010: 156). In an attempt to work around this conflict, Thorne & Reinhardt (2008) propose a pedagogical framework called "bridging activities" to bring these potential learning experiences into the classroom. They suggest a three-phase activity. First, students bring digital vernacular texts (cultural products) they have produced or been engaged in, into the classroom. Then, together with the teacher and peers, they analyze the texts to identify ways in which they differ and align with conventional literacy and genre forms. Finally, students are "sent back out into the wild" to implement what they have learned in class in the online cultures they participate in as part of their private sphere. Though appealing, this proposal presupposes that students are "willing" to share their personal online identities with classes in formal settings and that, indeed, students have online

17   https://www.fanfiction.net/book/Harry-Potter/
18   https://www.fanfiction.net/tv/Sherlock/

identities to share. Sauro (2017) suggests designing teaching activities that draw on the practices of fans as their inspiration but do not actually require students to enter fan spaces, thus respecting the culture and autonomy of the fan communities.

3.3.2 Research The concept of bridging informal and formal language and culture learning is very much in its infancy as, inevitably, is research in this area. What the research community has recognized, however, is the need for a more holistic approach to research, synthesizing the different fields of research rather than creating dichotomies, and giving increasing importance to the context of language and culture learning. A new metaphor has been found in the "ecological" approach to language and culture learning which represents, according to Van Lier (2004), a natural continuation of socio-cultural theory and CMC approaches to research, expanding the focus of sociocultural approaches to include more and more contextual information. Lam & Kramsch write:

> A critical ecological perspective on SLA does not mean replac-ing schools with computers that simulate the process of socializa-tion in more "natural" or loosely institutionalized environments. It means examining the relationship between the learner and the context, and how a particular metaphor of SLA is part and parcel of a self-organized, self-regulating ecology of language learning. In other words, we need to examine how different parts of an envi-ronment fit together to constitute a system that has its own logic of functioning. (2003: 156)

An ecological approach views learners "as living organisms engaged in a complex network of relationships with the other elements in the envi-ronment" (Blyth, 2008: 54). It places an integral focus on person, process, context, and time. The unit of analysis is the learner, and researchers exam-ine how learners use language and other tools, hence also technologies, to create context and to construct identities and communities.

Lam & Kramsch (2003) present the ecological perspective in their case study of a Hong Kong Chinese learner of English who experienced failure and discrimination in a US school context but then successfully socialized into a global, online, English-speaking community. The case study provides detailed descriptions of the learner's social status and context as well as the offline and online environments in which he used English. The authors also analyze data from interviews with the learner, his website, and tran-scripts of online chats. Through the case study they show how the ecol-ogy metaphor allows consideration of social and political conditions that determine a learner's adaptation to the circumstances of language use. "The ecology metaphor of language learning as socialization through symbolic interaction with other individuals engaged in a shared common activity and participating in a shared social community" (Lam & Kramsch, 2003: 155) aptly describes the web-based acquisition environment in which the learner developed his English language competence. It is important to point out that though Lam & Kramsch are concerned with the acquisition of English language in this study, they reveal how the learner was initiated into a new culture defined not by geographic boundaries but by an online environment. It is thus an illustration of how such an ecological approach can be useful for documenting culture learning in online contexts. The multidimensionality of the ecological approach is believed by researchers to be able to meet the challenge of analyzing language use and language learning in multilingual and multicultural settings (Blin, 2016; Kramsch & Whiteside, 2008) and thus seems suitable for addressing research on culture through CALL, where culture is viewed in the sense we described in the introduction to this chapter, as a fluid, ever-changing context co-constructed by its participants and surrounding histories and ideologies.

4   Pedagogical Implications

At the end of section 2 above, we cited valid questions posed by Furstenberg (2010: 329): "how to 'incorporate,' 'integrate,' and 'infuse' foreign language classes with culture and 'what culture' to teach." Up to now, we have provided a survey of what has been done. The rest of the chapter will be dedicated to providing more practical examples of what teachers and learners can do, and what skills and competences they need to answer the questions posed by Furstenberg.

In teaching culture through CALL, language teachers have, as we explained above, a variety of options available to them. They can:

- access resources which provide for culture learning about products, practices, and perspectives;
- communicate and collaborate through the practice of telecollaboration whereby learners interact, and hopefully develop meaningful intercultural relationships with distant peers;
- bridge learners' Internet use and identities outside class with language learning in formal settings.

These options are not mutually exclusive, of course. For example, teachers can choose to set up telecollaboration exchanges which involve learners exploring, sharing, and discussing resources with distant peers and then have learners collaboratively create their own resources which can be made available to the outside world. Whatever the choice, it needs to be well-informed, taking into consideration the operational skills required on the part of both the teacher(s) and learners, awareness of the complexity of culture learning, and a critical approach to all activities. The teacher(s) and learners must also be aware of the need to be flexible and adapt what has been "planned" to what actually "happens." Below we discuss some key issues for teachers to consider for each of the approaches.

4.1   Access: Selecting Resources

The vast array of resources available on the Internet means that, yes, culture learning can be enhanced by accessing a wide variety of multimedia resources, but this availability can be disorienting and overwhelming. Resources can be used in many ways and indeed it is how a resource is used that is more important than the quality of the resource itself. For example, a website containing stereotypical and reductionist representations of "the target culture" may be deliberately chosen for a task involving critical analysis. The teacher's role lies in the selection of appropriate resources to meet the needs of the task(s) in mind and in guiding learners in the reading and interpretation of the cultural resources selected. Teachers may want to ask themselves some of these questions:

- Who produced the resource and for what purpose and/or audience was it originally intended?
- What are the underlying theories and values of the resource?
- How does the resource represent language and its cultures and subcultures – multiple, diverse, dynamic and changing or monolithic and static? Does it represent an "online culture" and/or culture(s) in the "physical world"?
- Does the resource help learners to make connections between products, practices, and perspectives?
- Does the resource allow learners to make connections between their lives and experiences and those represented?
- What opportunities for exploration does the resource afford learners?

- To what kind of opportunities for interaction does the resource lead learners (e.g., email address, discussion forum, link to Facebook page)?
- Is the resource appropriate for the intended learners? For example, do they have the background knowledge and/or experience to be able to effectively interpret and understand the resource? Alternatively, is it a resource that may be out of the learners' comfort zone (e.g., sensitive issues such as religion and politics)? In this case does the teacher have specific facilitation skills to manage classroom discussions about these topics?

If the materials chosen are stimulating and the learners motivated, they will also want and need to move on to their own cultural explorations, thus the teacher also needs to help them acquire the necessary practical, but also critical skills necessary to search, find, and evaluate their own resources and learn from them.

In order to move beyond information retrieval, learners should start reflecting, comparing, and analyzing cultural artifacts together with their classmates. Traditionally, contrastive approaches have focused on comparing and analyzing the products and practices of two nationally-defined cultures. However, it is also possible to compare different perspectives, for example, how different cultural groups view a particular global issue, how these views are or can be transmitted through different media in different countries, and the impact of the choice of media and language on the message. Such an activity is facilitated, but also complicated, by the quantity of information available on the Web today and, therefore, involves promoting media literacy (e.g., considering the cultural context of the online world in addition to the culture of the source of information).

4.2   Communicate and Collaborate

4.2.1 Choosing an environment and communication modes The practice of telecollaboration for culture learning makes a great deal of demands on teachers in terms of organization and collaboration with partner teachers and classes. It is, in all its aspects, a lesson in intercultural development for the teacher too, who has to find a partner teacher with whom s/he can collaborate effectively and who shares the same goals and pedagogical approach. In addition, calendars have to be established and the communication tools chosen. Two issues arise here: whether to use one institution's closed proprietary system as opposed to another online space such as social media, and whether to engage in synchronous or asynchronous communication, or both. With regards to the former point, Guth & Thomas point out that Learning Management Systems (LMSs) often reflect "the cultural and educational bias of that particular institution and/or culture" (2010: 48). Furthermore, using an LMS involves issues of ownership, access, and familiarization. Regarding mode of communication, some practitioners prefer asynchronous communication as it allows students the time to reflect both on what they have read and want to say, thus enriching the cultural exchange. Others argue for synchronous communication because it helps students learn the skills required in real-time cultural exchange and it more easily promotes relationship building. Ideally, an exchange would involve both forms of communication, which are now permitted on many learning management platforms (e.g., Moodle with Big Blue Button; see the TILA project),[19] social networks (e.g., Facebook; see Woodman & Kazoullis, 2013), and messaging tools (e.g., Skype; see Martí & Fernández, 2016).

4.2.2 Designing and sequencing tasks for telecollaboration Telecollaboration projects are made up of a series of tasks, which should follow a certain order to lead learners through a process of developing language and intercultural skills and competences. The literature on online learning (Salmon, 2000, 2002) and telecollaboration (Kurek & Müller-Hartmann, 2017; O'Dowd & Ware, 2009) indicates that successful learning in such contexts progresses from initial phases of socialization and familiarization, followed by tasks which involve comparison and analysis, to finally collaborative tasks. The types of tasks which appear in the early stages should focus on exchanging information in order to "get to know" one another and the online environment. Table 1 shows the pre-exchange tasks for an English as a Lingua Franca (ELF) exchange between students in Italy and students in Germany using a wiki for asynchronous communication and Skype for synchronous communication. As can be seen, points 1, 2, and 6 aim to familiarize students with the wiki environment whereas points 3, 4 and 7 aim to "get students thinking" and to get to know one another before having to speak during the first Skype session.

Subsequent tasks can become more complex as learners engage in interaction and knowledge construction through activities of comparison and analysis. Whereas exchanging information merely involves learners sharing what they know about themselves and their culture, when comparing and analyzing, learners interpret cultural products and practices, discussing the perspectives that may be behind them. When parallel texts or films exist, they can be a salient source of perspectives and practices to be critically

19   http://www.tilaproject.eu/

Table 1 Pre-exchange tasks in an English as a lingua franca German-Italian tele-collaboration project using a wiki and Skype

1. Our course website is a wiki! What is a wiki? Watch the Common Craft video on Teacher Tube for an explanation.
2. Sign up to be a "writer" of this wiki webspace by clicking on the "To join this workspace, request access" link on the right.
3. Individually, in your respective classrooms, on your own time, watch the video *Single Story*, in English (the lingua franca of the exchange). Then write a short comment on the same page explaining *what* your single story of the "other" country is and *where* you think it comes from, e.g. media, books, family, vacations, etc. Comments on this page function like a discussion forum in the sense that BEFORE you write your comment, read those that come before yours in order to relate back to other ideas and avoid repeating the same thing over and over again.
4. On your personal page post a brief introduction of yourself.
5. Complete the Pre-Exchange Questionnaire.
6. In-class or on your own time, "play around" with the wiki in order to become more familiar with it using the tutorials on the Trouble Shooting page. Doubts or questions can be posted as comments to this page.
7. Read each other's introductions and single story comments.

analyzed by learners. Teacher guidance during this stage is extremely important in order to lead students beyond superficial observation to critical thinking. Even when there are no useful parallel texts, the representation of a specific aspect of cultures can be compared by analyzing different media. For example, in an Italian-American bilingual exchange, students were asked to watch *The Godfather: Part I* (Coppola, 1972) and *I Cento Passi* (Giordana, 2000) in order to compare representations of the Italian mafia in American cinema and in Italian cinema. They were also asked to access different online media, from YouTube to online newspapers in "third" countries such as the English version of *Al Jazeera*, to compare and contrast how the Italian mafia is represented in different cultures and different media. Through this process, students, in this case the Italian students in particular, are engaged in a process of learning about their own culture and how it is viewed by others not only abroad, but in different regions of their own country as well.

A third stage, possible only once learners have become familiar with the online environment and tools and have established a relationship with one another, can engage learners in tasks that require collaboration and product creation. The complexity of this stage is indeed heightened by the degree of collaboration required as learners negotiate roles, set deadlines, come up with workplans, etc. This sort of activity is complex enough in face-to-face contexts and even more so in the online intercultural context of telecollaboration, where students may have to reflect on, interpret, and overcome cultural differences (e.g., by providing and receiving peer feedback).

Table 2 provides an example of the collaborative project in the Italian-American exchange mentioned above. In groups of 4–6, students were to produce an L2 text on the wiki and encouraged to interpret "text" in the broadest sense possible in order to include various media and cultural products (see Step 3). One of the most challenging aspects in this stage, however, is respecting deadlines and coming to an agreement on content. For this reason, each group has to assign a leader and the roles of the other members (see Step 2). Nonetheless, it is important that teachers monitor the progress of the various groups in order to guarantee full participation. Teacher guidance is also useful during Step 5, when students have to provide one another with feedback both on the language used and the contents. In this exchange, for example, the American students found the feedback provided by their Italian peers to be too "direct" whereas the Italians felt their American peers were not "clear" or "straightforward." Teacher intervention can use this "conflict" as an opportunity for culture learning.

Reflective practice between sessions, in the form of both classroom discussions and individual learner diaries, should be an integral part of any exchange. As Guth & Marini-Maio argue: "[i]t is just as important for students to step back and reflect on what they are learning and saying about their own culture as it is to have synchronous conversations with peers about the 'other' culture" (2010: 419). Following the compare and contrast example provided above, one Italian student wrote in her learner diary:

> Reading the articles I read (from different countries) and watching the Godfather, I directed my attention to the different situations that Italy faces, I'm lucky because I don't live in a society dominated by Mafia, but for people (above all common people) who have to, I think it's terrible. I'm astounded by the conspiracy of silence which reigns among those people, but, in a way, I also understand them because they live in a dangerous situation. I don't know if in their shoes I would be braver.

This student comes from the north of Italy and is learning to reflect on the situation of her fellow citizens in other parts of the country. As we have stated above, culture learning should be transversal, i.e., rather than focusing solely on one "target" culture, even in a bilingual exchange, telecollaboration should offer learners the opportunity to become more aware of the various "cultures" that exist both in the "foreign" country as well as in their own.

Table 2 Final project in a bilingual Italian-American exchange using a wiki and Skype

---

FINAL PROJECT

Aim
The aim of this final project is to create a bilingual wiki page on the mafia (organized crime) and related issues in the US and Italy.

General Description
The final wiki page will be divided into sections, much like magazine articles are. In your groups you will work on one section in the language you are studying and help your peers edit their work. When each group has completed "their" part, the instructors will then assemble these in the wiki to make a coherent, single piece.

Tasks
Step 1: Choosing topics
In class, the American groups will choose/be assigned one of the topics. The topics include history and structure of the mafia in Italy and the US, other mafia-like organizations, the mafia today, organized crime and illegal immigration, mafia and politics.

Step 2: Roles and workplan
In school and work, when working in groups, it helps if roles are assigned. Use the comment function in your group page to do this or you can contact one another via Skype, email, instant messaging, Facebook, etc. However, since it is Thanksgiving in the States this week, your communication will have to be "on your own" time and asynchronous.

First of all, choose a group leader. This person will be responsible for making sure that each team member is doing their part, and report back to the instructors should there be problems with participation.

Then decide who is going to focus on what, and by when.

Write the name of your group leader and the students' names with their specific assignments in the table.

Step 3: Research
Research your topic on the Web. Wikipedia should be seen as a STARTING POINT and NOT the only reference for your research. When you find useful information and sites, copy and paste the URLs onto your group pages or personal pages.

Since the Americans are writing about Italy and the Italians about America, you may be able to help one another locate "good" resources on the Web, e.g., online newspapers, government sites, etc., to help your peers in their research.

Finally, since we are using digital text, you can add images, graphs, videos, etc. to your pages in a way that is not possible on paper. Please take advantage of this!

Step 4: Writing
Each person should write a minimum of 400 and a maximum of 500 words for their part. Therefore, your aim is to be clear and concise rather than long-winded, and to identify only the MOST relevant information for your part. Again: quality not quantity and cite your sources!

Step 5: Editing and peer feedback

Once each person has produced their "text," you should give peer feedback. You can do this by using the Comment section or by directly editing your peer's work (you can then use the "history" function and "compare versions" to see the changes that have been made). Each group should decide how the members would like to give and receive feedback on their use of the language (vocabulary, syntax, tone, etc.), style, and organization. You will also decide "who" is going to correct "whose" work. The project is collaborative, therefore helping each other is permitted and welcome, provided that the groups comply with three basic rules: (1) each group should write its own piece in the target language, (2) the edits are explained and understood on both sides, (3) all this work is clear and can be traced in the wiki ("comment," "history," or "compare versions" functions). Please take this part of the project as a great learning opportunity!

Step 6: Project due

Once each group has finished with the editing, the project is ready to go. After December 18, 11:59 pm, no more changes will be possible and the instructors will start working on the formatting of the "web-magazine."

Step 7: Survey

All students will fill out a brief survey in order to provide feedback about their own and their partners' contributions in the project. The survey is anonymous and will help the instructors to assess the students' work.

5   Assessment

The issue of how to evaluate outcomes in the context of culture learning is complex and brings up ethical and moral issues. While cultural knowledge is often measured by discrete item tests or written essays, more complex and controversial aspects of ICC, such as attitudes of openness and curiosity, are difficult to measure. Several quantitative tools for measuring cross-cultural, intercultural, or global competence have been developed,[20] many for the field of business. However, in foreign language education there has been a growing interest in student motivation, learner autonomy, and the involvement of students in the learning and assessment process. Research has shown that having learners regularly and frequently participate in establishing goals and monitoring and documenting their progress increases language and academic achievement and enhances motivation (Little, 2003; Little, Goullier, & Hughes, 2011; Moeller, Theiler, & Wu, 2012; Ziegler, 2014).

In 2017, a series of Can-Do Statements for Intercultural Communication and a Reflection Tool for Learners was published by NCSSFL-ACTFL (see

20   See Fantini's list of assessment tools at http://www.sit.edu/
SITOccasionalPapers/feil_appendix_f.pdf

Table 3 for two examples). In this document, intercultural communicative competence (ICC) is defined as:

> the ability to interact effectively and appropriately with people from other language and cultural backgrounds. ICC develops as the result of a process of intentional goal-setting and self-reflection around language and culture and involves attitudinal changes toward one's own and other cultures. Intercultural communicative competence is essential for establishing effective, positive relationships across cultural boundaries, required in a global society.[21]

The Can-Do Statements are seen to support learners in self-assessment and goal-setting, and they can support teachers and learners in the creation of rubrics for performance-based grading. The statements for intercultural

Table 3 Two examples of NCSSFL-ACTFL Can-Do Statements for Intercultural Communication

	Novice	Intermediate	Advanced	Superior	Distinguished
Investigate	In my own and other cultures I can **identify** products and practices to help me understand perspectives.	In my own and other cultures I can **make comparisons** between products and practices to help me understand perspectives.	In my own and other cultures I can **explain** some **diversity** among products and practices and how it relates to perspectives.	In my own and other cultures I can **suspend judgment while critically examining** products, practices, and perspectives.	In my own and other cultures I can **objectively evaluate** products and practices and mediate perspectives.
Interact	I can interact at a survival level in some familiar everyday contexts.	I can interact at a functional level in some familiar contexts.	I can interact at a competent level in familiar and some unfamiliar contexts.	I can interact in complex situations to ensure a shared understanding of culture.	I can engage with complexity and pluricultural identities and serve as a mediator between and among cultures.

21   https://www.actfl.org/publications/guidelines-and-manuals/ncssfl-actfl-can-do-statements

Table 4 Performance indicators for NCSSFL-ACTFL Can-Do Statements for Intercultural Communication at an advanced level

INVESTIGATE	In my own and other cultures I can explain how people's practices of contribute to environmental problems or solutions.
INTERACT	I can write a blog entry about how to respect and conform to local environmental practices and respond to comments.

communication with proficiency benchmarks for the different levels are outlined in Table 3.

Performance indicators and sets of examples are also provided, which make links between investigation and interaction; see Table 4 for examples at an advanced level. The intention is for these examples to be customized according to the school curriculum or individuals' learning goals.

Identifying learning outcomes and goals is a first step, but to move on to intercultural learning, reflection is a crucial step (Byram 1997; Deardorff, 2006; Fantini & Tirmizi, 2006). Having an experience is not enough for learning to occur beyond a superficial level. It is the examination of one's own values and attitudes and how these influence one's engagement with the "other" that can lead to a deep understanding, engagement with otherness, and learning to see with multiple lenses. Reflective activities such as in-class discussions and individual reflective writing are seen as supporting this type of understanding, and reflective essays and portfolios can be used for assessment.

Several models of portfolio have been developed, many following the model of the European Language Portfolio,[22] which has three sections: a Passport which includes bio-data and information about assessments and certification, a Biography in which learners are asked to report and reflect on their personal intercultural experiences, and finally a Dossier in which learners are required to provide evidence for their intercultural learning. More recently in the US, the LinguaFolio® was developed by members of the National Council of State Supervisors for Languages (NCSSFL), based on the European Language Portfolio (ELP) and the NCSSFL-ACTFL Can-Do Statements. Like the ELP, it is composed of a Passport, Biography, and Dossier.[23] For assessment purposes, however, it is often the Dossier component of a portfolio which learners are asked to produce, which can be assessed in and of itself or through oral interviews in which the portfolio is discussed. O'Dowd argues that questions and sections of both rubrics

22   http://www.coe.int/t/dg4/portfolio/
23   http://ncssfl.org/linguafolio/

and portfolio design, shared with students at the onset of an intercultural experience, "are vital for increasing student awareness of what the learning outcomes of telecollaborative activity can be" (2010: 355). In other words, students can be presented with rubrics throughout a course, or asked to gradually compile documents for a portfolio, and through teacher guidance and classroom discussion, these can promote culture learning through formative assessment.

6   Conclusion

In this chapter we have sought to present discussions surrounding culture and language teaching and relate these to the use of CALL. The key point we hope to have made is that L2 educators, now more than ever, need to take into account the complex, multifaceted, ever-changing nature of culture that characterizes today's world – physical and online. This certainly makes addressing culture in L2 teaching a more complex task than representing a monolithic, static view of culture, yet it opens the doors to an exciting, dynamic, but also critical approach which can be enhanced through CALL and in particular Internet technologies.

The view of culture learning we have presented pertains not only to knowledge of cultural products, practices, and perspectives but also to the acquisition of intercultural competence and awareness, which is not specific to any culture but is transversal and allows individuals to "step outside of their own shoes" and effectively communicate in varying physical and online cultural contexts and understand different perspectives. The Internet offers a rich source of authentic cultural material and an environment for intercultural learning to take place with multiple channels for exploration and modes of interaction with distant learners. However, as we hope we have shown, it is not the technology or the resources themselves which enhance culture learning but the uses to which they are put, and the tasks and activities which are designed to lead the learner through a journey of intercultural understanding where they can develop the attitude, knowledge, skills, and critical awareness to become active citizens of the world. Learner-centered teaching approaches which foster the adoption of ethnographic techniques in explorations of other cultures through online resources and communities can arouse students' curiosity in other cultures and lead to intercultural learning.

The factors that can contribute to or hinder learning are many, and increase with technological and social changes. Future researchers will have to find methods which can account for this multiplicity of factors – the diversity of individual language learners but also of their educational, social, and political environments; the interaction of global, local, and emergent online cultures; the affordances of different online environments and tools for culture learning; and the relationship between formal and informal learning. Despite the many challenges, we believe that we cannot ignore the educational value of teaching and learning about different cultures and perspectives, acquiring an intercultural stance, and developing a sense of critical cultural awareness.

Questions for Reflection

1. After having read this chapter, if you were asked to define "culture," what definition would you give and how would you go about "teaching" this concept?
2. Which of the practices described in the chapter do you think you could implement? Provide a specific example of what you might implement in the classroom and how.
3. Type the name of a national culture, e.g., "Italian culture," in the YouTube search box. Explore some of the results and ask yourself questions such as: who makes culture relevant to whom in which context and for which purposes? What kind of information does it provide about the "target culture(s)"? How could you use it with your students?
4. Find an Internet resource that you feel would be useful for focusing on products and perspectives of any cultural group that is NOT a "national culture," e.g., football culture or gaming culture. Find a similar resource for practices and perspectives. Develop a lesson plan for using these resources with your students.
5. Which way of assessing intercultural competence described in the chapter appeals to you the most? How do you assess your learners' cultural knowledge or intercultural communicative competence, if at all? What factors influence your approach?
6. Would you be prepared to dedicate the time and energy to designing, setting up, and monitoring a telecollaborative exchange for your learners? How would you ensure their active participation in the exchange? How do you think you would feel about conflicts if they occurred during an exchange?

Cases

Research Case

An instructor of second-semester beginners' Chinese has set up a telecollaboration project with Chinese students because her American students were very keen to learn more about the culture(s) related to that language. Specifically, in response to questionnaires at the end of the first semester, her students indicated a desire to better understand the relationship between certain practices and perspectives because they felt that some practices that they had read about in their first-semester materials were very different from their own and they had difficulty understanding and even accepting them. Because her students' competence in Chinese was not sufficient for them to discuss issues in the L2, she decided to set up the project using English as the main language of communication. The partners she found for her students were Chinese students who had resided in the US for at least 3 years and were enrolled in an advanced English course. She decided to dedicate one of the four 50-minute weekly classroom sessions to Skype sessions with these Chinese peers to discuss culture-related issues stemming from short texts they had read or extracts from films (with English subtitles). At the same time, the American students were open to answering any questions their Chinese peers might have about American culture. Students were asked to record their discussions and make these accessible to their instructor. After their chats, they wrote journal entries reflecting on their cultural learning. One additional 50-minute weekly session was then dedicated to focusing on language using the contents of students' Skype exchanges. Gradually the teacher encouraged students to attempt to "try out" some of the language they were acquiring in the classroom with their online peers. Students were very enthusiastic about the exchange, but a few weeks after the beginning of the exchange, the head of department told her that she was concerned that the students were spending too much time communicating and writing in English and that there was no need for the Skype sessions.

Discussion Questions:
1. From an intercultural competence perspective, what arguments could you use to support the integration of the mainly English-language telecollaboration exchange in the Chinese course?
2. How could you demonstrate that culture learning was taking place?
3. How could you demonstrate a connection between the culture learning taking place in the Skype chats and the language learning taking place in the other three classroom sessions?

4. Outline a research project based on the data you have from student interactions and journals that would look into students' understanding of the relationship between practices and perspectives (Standard 2.1) and perspectives and products (Standard 2.2).

Teaching Case

An instructor of intermediate Spanish has set up a telecollaboration project using Spanish and English between her students in the US and intermediate students of English in Guatemala. The aim of the project is for students to learn about each other's cultures and also to discuss global issues which are important to students on both sides (e.g., human rights and poverty). Every week there is a one-hour video-conference where students are divided into small groups. The students in Guatemala are participating from a computer lab which is well equipped with webcams, high-speed Internet, and technicians on hand to help if necessary, and they are all in the lab twice a week, once for video-conference and another session to work on a wiki which has been created for the project. Some students do not have access to Internet from their homes, however, so they need to do all of their work in the lab. The university limits access to certain websites, in particular social networking sites, and Skype is not available on computers. A proprietary software is used for video-conferencing sessions which take place through the Guatemalan University's account. Students in the US on the other hand have one session a week in the lab for the video-conferences, and the rest of the time they connect from their dorms or libraries where there is a good connection, and no regulations regarding social networks.

After the first two weeks of getting to know each other and exchanging personal information, the students are asked to start working on a collaborative wiki about human rights in the US and Guatemala and are organized into 3 groups of about 8 students each, with equal number of partners from both countries. After a few weeks, the teachers explore the wiki to see how students are progressing and notice that there is a considerable amount of content on the wiki pages about each individual country, but suspect that much of it is simply copied and pasted from other websites. Looking at the history of the wiki pages, they notice that few of the pages have been edited by more than one person, and on the discussion pages little activity has occurred. Asked if they have had contact with their peers, some students report having established contact on Facebook and/or via email, others complain that they have tried engaging with their peers outside of the sessions but never get responses to their mails or messages. Both teachers are disappointed, and wonder how to get their students to collaborate on the wiki pages, and engage more deeply in the issues and in dialogue with their distant peers (i.e., compare and contrast the situations in the two countries, explore underlying issues and causes, begin to understand the diversity within each of the countries, understand different perspectives and practices).

Discussion Questions:

1. What was the pedagogical objective for this task? What were the conditions of this activity (group constellation, specifics of the assignment)? Would you consider this activity a "disappointment"? In what way? From the information you have, what do you think was lacking in this project? What do you think were the causes of the lack of communication?
2. What would be the challenges of collaborative "product creation" activities? What could the instructor have done to avoid students' copying and pasting content? How could dialogue between the distant peers have been promoted?
3. Could this activity have been preceded by other tasks? What kind of support could the learners have been given?

Ideas for Action Research Projects

*   How do I approach culture teaching in my classes? Do I focus more on products, practices and/or perspectives? Do I focus on one specific target culture, various target cultures (as may be the case, for example, with Spanish or English), online cultures, or global cultures? How can I enable my students to interpret the cultural perspectives that underlie cultural products and practices? Keep a journal recording your plans and aims for class sessions on culture; after these sessions, write your reflections in the journal. Regularly go back and read through your journals to develop hypotheses about your practice. Throughout the course, you may want to conduct informal interviews with students to investigate whether students' impressions of your teaching match yours. You could also develop an end-of-course questionnaire with the same aim.
*   Set up a virtual exchange between your class and students from another culture. As you go through the process of developing the project and then implementing it, keep an observation log where you include the decisions you and your partner teacher make, the discussions you have (e.g., emails you have exchanged and/or

recordings of synchronous video sessions you have), and observations you make of your students' work, how their distant partner groups are or are not working, what tasks are eliciting the desired outcomes and which ones are not, etc. When the exchange is over, look back on your observation log and reflect on what worked in the exchange and what didn't. Discuss this with your partner teacher and agree on changes you will make for the second iteration of the project.

- What are the global issues that my students are interested in? How could I enable them to learn about different cultural perspectives on these same issues? Choose one specific current topic and ask students "where" they get their information regarding the topic: e.g. online newspapers (which ones?), television (which channels and programs?), blogs, forums, etc. Record this information in a format where it can be retrieved (learning management system, a wiki, or even paper!). Then provide students with 3 or 4 "alternative" sources of online information and ask them to search for additional ones for homework. Encourage students to search for resources where users contribute either through forums, Twitter, or wiki-based collaborative production. Develop a chart or guidelines for students to follow to compare the perspectives provided in the various resources. Record the following classroom session in which students are asked to engage in discussion on what they have found. Analyze the recording to identify salient points and bring it to the classroom the following session to discuss these points with students.

- Do my students participate in "online cultures"? If so, would they be willing to share their knowledge and experience of these cultures with me and the rest of the class? How could I use their experience and the products, practices, and perspectives they bring to share with the class for culture learning? Carry out a survey on your students' online activities out of class using, for example, the form function on Google docs. Ask students with interesting experiences if any of them would be willing to share their experience and some examples or samples of their online cultures with you and the class. Discuss these individually with the student(s) involved in order to find out more about them before designing a class activity they would feel comfortable with. Ask the student(s) to provide specific examples of language in use in their online context and develop an in-class task to analyze and discuss what language and culture

mean and their role in this specific context. Carry out the activity
in class and collect feedback from students.

- How aware are my students of the origin of their own values and
beliefs? How can I help them to develop critical cultural awareness? Develop a series of activities which will encourage learners to reflect on the origin of their own values and beliefs and to
compare their values to those of others. For example, the *Cultura*
project has an archive of results from student responses from different cultures to word association questionnaires, sentence com-
pletions, and situation questionnaires (e.g., "What would you do if
you saw a parent slap their child in a supermarket?"). You could
have your students respond to the same questionnaires and then
compare them with those available in the *Cultura* archive. Ask students to keep journals from the very beginning of these experiences, providing them with prompts for reflection. You may want
to discuss with students whether they wish to share these journals
with other students, e.g., on a blog or wiki, or if they want to keep
private journals to hand in to you regularly. Analyse students' diaries looking for evidence of which activities proved most fruitful in
stimulating reflection and critical cultural awareness.

References

Abrams, Zs. (2001). Computer-mediated communication and group journals:
Expanding the repertoire of participant roles. *System*, 29(4), 489–503.

Agar, M. (1994). *Language shock: Understanding the culture of conversation*. New
York: William Morrow.

American Council on the Teaching of Foreign Languages (1996). *Standards for foreign language learning. Preparing for the 21st century: Executive summary*.
Retrieved December 15, 2017, from
http://www.actfl.org/files/public/StandardsforFLLexecsumm_rev.pdf

Androutsopoulos, J. (2015). Networked multilingualism: Some language practices
on Facebook and their implications. *International Journal of Bilingualism*,
19(2), 185–205.

Arens, K. (2010). The field of culture: The Standards as a model for teaching culture. *Modern Language Journal*, 94(2), 321–324.

Bakker, P. (2001). *The Internet crusade*. Paper prepared for the 2001 International
Studies Association Annual Convention. *International relations and the new
inequality: Power, wealth, and the transformation of global society at the
beginning of the twenty-first century*. Chicago, IL, February 20–24, 2001.
Retrieved December 15, 2017, from
http://citeseerx.ist.psu.edu/viewdoc/download?doi=10.1.1.101.3066&rep=rep
1&type=pdf

Basharina, O. K. (2007). An activity theory perspective on student reported contradictions in international telecollaboration. *Language Learning & Technology*, 11(2), 82–103.

Belz, J. A. (2003a). From the special issue editor. *Language Learning & Technology*, 7(2), 2–5.

Belz, J. A. (2003b). Linguistic perspectives on the development of intercultural competence in telecollaboration. *Language Learning & Technology*, 7(2), 68–117.

Black, R. W. (2005). Access and affiliation: The literacy and composition practices of English-language learners in an online fan fiction community. *Journal of Adolescent and Adult Literacy*, 49(2), 118–128.

Black, R. W. (2006). Language, culture, and identity in online fan fiction. *E-Learning*, 3(2), 170–184.

Black, R. W. (2008). *Adolescents and online fan fiction*. New York: Peter Lang.

Blake, R. (2000). Computer-mediated communication: A window on L2 Spanish interlanguage. *Language Learning & Technology*, 4(1), 120–136.

Blake, R., & Zyzik, E. (2003). Who's helping whom? Learner/heritage speakers' networked discussions in Spanish. *Applied Linguistics*, 24(4), 519–44.

Blin, F. (2016). Towards an "ecological" CALL theory: Theoretical perspectives and their instantiation in CALL research and practice. In F. Farr & L. Murray (eds.), *The Routledge handbook of language learning and technology*, pp. 39–54. New York and London: Routledge.

Block, D. (2003). *The social turn in second language acquisition*. Edinburgh: Edinburgh University Press.

Blyth, C. (2008). Research perspectives on online discourse and foreign language learning. In S. Magnan (ed.), *Mediating discourse online*, pp. 47–73. Amsterdam: John Benjamins. https://doi.org/10.1075/aals.3.05bly

Brandl, K. (2002). Integrating Internet-based reading materials into the foreign language teaching curriculum: From teacher- to student-centered approaches. *Language Learning & Technology*, 6(3): 87–107.

Byram, M. (1997). *Teaching and assessing intercultural communicative competence*. Clevedon: Multilingual Matters.

Chen, G. M., & Starosta, W. J. (2000). The development and validation of intercultural communication sensitivity scale. *Human Communication*, 3, 1–15.

Chun, D. M. (1994). Using computer networking to facilitate the acquisition of interactive competence. *System*, 22(1): 17–31.

Chun, D. M., & Wade, E. R. (2004). Collaborative cultural exchanges with CMC. In L. Lomicka and J. Cooke-Plagwitz (eds.), *Teaching with technology*, pp. 220–247. Boston: Heinle.

Coppola, F. F. (1972). *The Godfather*.

Council of Europe (2001). *The Common European Framework of Reference for Languages: Learning, teaching, assessment*. Retrieved November 24, 2017, from https://rm.coe.int/1680459f97

Council of Europe (2017). *The Common European Framework of Reference for Languages: Learning, teaching, assessment. Companion Volume with new descriptors. Provisional edition*. Retrieved November 24, 2017 from https://rm.coe.int/common-european-framework-of-reference-for-languages-learning-teaching/168074a4e2

Creese, A., & Blackledge, A. (2010). Translanguaging in the bilingual classroom: A pedagogy for learning and teaching? *Modern Language Journal*, 94(1), 103–115.

de Nooy, J. (2006). Border patrol in the borderless world: Negotiating intercultural Internet discussion. *Language, Society and Culture*, 19.

Deardorff, D. (2006). Identification and assessment of intercultural competence as a student outcome of internationalization. *Journal of Studies in International Education*, 10(3), 241–266.

Dooly, M. (2011). Divergent perceptions of telecollaborative language learning tasks: Tasks-as-workplan vs. task-as-process. *Language Learning & Technology*, 15(2), 69–91.

Dooly, M. (2015). Learning to e-function in a brave new world: Language teachers' roles in educating for the future. In A. A. Turula, B. Mikolajewska, & D. Stanulewicz (eds.), *Insights into technology enhanced language pedagogy*, pp. 11–25. *Warsaw Studies in English Language and Literature*, Vol. 18, J. Fisiak (ed.). Bern/Vienna: Peter Lang.

Drewelow, I., & Mitchell, C. (2015). An exploration of learners' conceptions of language, culture, and learning in advanced-level Spanish courses. *Language, Culture and Curriculum*, 28(3), 243–256.

Dubreil, S., Herron, C., & Cole, S. P. (2004). An empirical investigation of whether authentic websites facilitate intermediate-level French language students' ability to learn culture. *CALICO Journal*, 22(1), 41–61.

Eagan, M. K., Stolzenberg, E. B., Zimmerman, H. B., Aragon, M. C., Whang Sayson, H., & Rios-Aguilar, C. (2017). The American freshman: National norms fall 2016. Los Angeles: Higher Education Research Institute, UCLA. Retrieved December 9, 2017 from
https://www.heri.ucla.edu/monographs/TheAmericanFreshman2016.pdf

Egert, C. (2000). FORUM: Language learning across campuses. *Computer Assisted Language Learning*, 13(3), 271–280.

Fantini, A., & Tirmizi, A. (2006). Exploring and Assessing Intercultural Competence. *World Learning Publications*, 1. Retrieved October 9, 2018, from
https://digitalcollections.sit.edu/worldlearning_publications/1

Fuchs, C., Hauck, M., and Müller-Hartmann, A. (2012) Promoting learner autonomy through multiliteracy skills development in cross-institutional exchanges. *Language Learning & Technology*, 16(3), 82–102.

Furstenberg, G. (2010). Making culture the core of the language class: Can it be done? *The Modern Language Journal* 94(2), 329–332.

Furstenberg, G., & English, K. (2016). CULTURA revisited. *Language Learning & Technology*, 20(2), 172–178. Retrieved November 24, 2017, from
http://llt.msu.edu/issues/june2016/furstenbergenglish.pdf

Furstenberg, G., Levet, S., English, K., & Maillet, K. (2001). Giving a virtual voice to the silent language of culture: The CULTURA project. *Language Learning & Technology* 5(1), 55–102.

Galla, C. G. (2016) Indigenous language revitalization, promotion, and education: Function of digital technology, *Computer Assisted Language Learning*, 29(7), 1137–1151.

García, O. (2009). *Bilingual education in the 21st century: A global perspective.* Malden, MA and Oxford: Blackwell/Wiley.

García, O., & Li, W. (2014). *Translanguaging: Language, bilingualism and education.* New York: Palgrave Macmillan. https://doi.org/10.1057/9781137385765

Gaspar, C. (1998). Situating French language teaching and learning in the age of the Internet. *French Review*, 72(1), 69–80.

Giordana, T. (2000). *I Cento Passi.*

Guichon, N., and Cohen, C. (2016) Multimodality and CALL. In F. Farr and L. Murray (eds.), *The handbook of language learning and technology.* Abingdon: Routledge.

Guth, S., & Marini-Maio, N. (2010). Close encounters of a new kind: The use of Skype and wiki in telecollaboration. In S. Guth & F. Helm (eds.), *Telecollaboration 2.0: Language, literacies and intercultural learning in the 21st century*, pp. 413–426. Bern: Peter Lang.

Guth, S. & Thomas, M. (2010). Telecollaboration with Web 2.0 tools. In S. Guth & F. Helm (eds.), *Telecollaboration 2.0: Language, literacies and intercultural learning in the 21st century*, pp. 39–68. Bern: Peter Lang.

Hanna, B., & de Nooy, J. (2003). A funny thing happened on the way to the forum: Electronic discussion and foreign language learning. *Language Learning & Technology*, 7(1), 71–85.

Hauck, M. (2007). Critical success factors in a TRIDEM exchange. *ReCALL*, 19(2), 202–223.

Hauck, M. (2010). Telecollaboration: At the interface between multimodal and intercultural communicative competence. In S. Guth & F. Helm (eds.), *Telecollaboration 2.0: Language, literacies and intercultural learning in the 21st century*, pp. 219–248. Bern: Peter Lang.

Helm, F. (2009) Language and culture in an online context: What can learner diaries tell us about intercultural competence? *Language and Intercultural Communication*, 9(2), 91–104.

Helm, F. (2013). A dialogic model for telecollaboration. *Bellaterra Journal of Teaching & Learning Language & Literature*, 6(2), 28–48. Retrieved December 15, 2017, from http://revistes.uab.cat/jtl3/article/view/522/571

Helm, F. and Guth, S. (2016). Telecollaboration and language learning. In F. Farr & L. Murray (eds.), *The Routledge handbook of language learning and technology*, pp. 241–254. New York: Routledge.

Helm, F., Guth, S., and Farrah, M. (2012) Promoting dialogue or hegemonic practice: The use of ELF in telecollaboration. *Language Learning & Technology*, 16(2): 103–127.

Holton, R. (2000). Globalization's cultural consequences, *Annals of the American Academy of Political and Social Science*, 570, 140–152.

Hughes, J. (2010). The multilingual Internet. In S. Guth & F. Helm (eds.), *Telecollaboration 2.0: Language, literacies and intercultural learning in the 21st century*, pp. 249–274. Bern: Peter Lang.

Huh, K., & Hu, W. (2005). Criteria for effective CALL research. In J. L. Egbert & G. M. Petrie (eds.), *CALL research perspectives*, pp. 9–24. New York: Routledge

Jin, L. (2008). Using instant messaging interaction (IMI) in intercultural learning. In S. Magnan (ed.), *Mediating discourse online*, pp. 275–304. Amsterdam: John Benjamins. https://doi.org/10.1075/aals.3.16jin

King, T. (2010). The Cross Call Project: Cross-sector computer-assisted language learning. In S. Guth & F. Helm (eds.), *Telecollaboration 2.0: Language, literacies and intercultural learning in the 21st century*, pp. 437–452. Bern: Peter Lang.

Kinginger, C. (2000). Learning the pragmatics of solidarity in the networked class-room. In J. K. Hall & L. S. Verplaestse (eds.), *The development of second and foreign language learning through classroom interaction*, pp. 23–46. Mahwah, NJ: Lawrence Erlbaum.

Kötter, M. (2002). *Tandem learning on the Internet: Learner interactions in online virtual environments*. Frankfurt: Lang.

Kötter, M. (2003). Negotiation of meaning and codeswitching in online tandems. *Language Learning & Technology*, 7(2), 145–72. Retrieved December 15, 2017 from http://llt.msu.edu/vol7num2/kotter/default.html

Kramsch, C. (1998). *Language and culture*. Oxford: Oxford University Press.

Kramsch, C. (2003). Introduction: How can we tell the dancer from the dance? In C. Kramsch (ed.), *Language acquisition and language socialization: Ecological perspectives*, pp. 1–30. London: Continuum.

Kramsch, C. (2014). Teaching foreign languages in an era of globalization: Introduction. *The Modern Language Journal*, 98(1), 296–311. https://doi.org/10.1111/j.1540-4781.2014.12057.x

Kramsch, C., & Andersen, R. W. (1999). Teaching text and context through multi-media. *Language Learning & Technology*, 2(2), 31–42. Retrieved December 15, 2017, from http://llt.msu.edu/vol2num2/article1/

Kramsch, C., & Thorne, S.L. (2002). Foreign language learning as global communi-cative practice. In D. Block & D. Cameron (eds.), *Globalization and language teaching*, pp. 83–100. London: Routledge.

Kramsch, C., & Whiteside, A. (2008). Language ecology in multilingual set-tings. Towards a theory of symbolic competence. *Applied Linguistics*, 29(4), 645–671.

Kurek, M., & Müller-Hartmann, A. (2017). Task design for telecollaborative exchanges: In search of new criteria. *System*, 60, 7–20. Retrieved on December 15, 2017, from http://www.sciencedirect.com/science/article/pii/S0346251X16304092; https://doi.org/10.1016/j.system.2016.12.004

Lam, E., & Kramsch, C. (2003). The ecology of an SLA community. In J. H. Leather & J. van Dam. (eds.), *Ecology of language acquisition,* pp. 141–158. Boston, MA: Kluwer Academic Publishers.

Lamy, M.-N., & Goodfellow, R. (2010). Telecollaboration and learning 2.0. In S. Guth & F. Helm (eds.), *Telecollaboration 2.0: Language, literacies and inter-cultural learning in the 21st century*, pp. 107–138. Bern: Peter Lang.

Lee, J. W. (2017). *The politics of translingualism: After Englishes*. New York: Routledge.

Lee, L. (2001). Online interaction. Negotiation of meaning and strategies used among learners of Spanish. *ReCALL*, 13, 232–244.

Lee, L. (2004) Learners' perspectives on networked collaborative interaction with native speakers of Spanish in the US. *Language Learning & Technology*, 8(1), 83–100. Retrieved December 15, 2017, from http://llt.msu.edu/vol8num1/lee/default.html

Levy, M. (2007). Culture, culture learning and new technologies: Towards a pedagogical framework. *Language Learning & Technology*, 11(2), 104–127.

Liaw, M. (2006). E-learning and the development of intercultural competence. *Language Learning & Technology*, 10(3), 49–64. Retrieved December 15, 2017, from http://llt.msu.edu/vol10num3/pdf/liaw.pdf

Liaw, M. & Johnson, R.J. (2001). Email writing as a cross-cultural learning experience. *System*, 29(2), 235–251.

Little, D. (ed.) (2003). *The European Language Portfolio in use: Nine examples*. Strasbourg, France: Council of Europe. Retrieved December 15, 2017, from https://www.coe.int/en/web/portfolio

Little, D., Goullier, F., & Hughes, G. (2011). *The European Language Portfolio: The story so far* (1991–2011). Strasbourg, France: Council of Europe. Retrieved December 15, 2017, from https://www.coe.int/en/web/portal/home

Malinowski, D., & Kramsch, C. (2014). The ambiguous world of heteroglossic computer-mediated language learning. In A. Blackledge and A. Creese (eds.), *Heteroglossia as practice and pedagogy*, pp. 155–178. Berlin: Springer.

Martí, N., and Fernández, S. (2016). Telecollaboration and sociopragmatic awareness in the foreign language classroom. *Innovation in language learning and teaching*, 10(1), 34–48. Retrieved December 9, 2017, from http://www.tandfonline.com/doi/abs/10.1080/17501229.2016.1138577?journalCode=rill20\\; https://doi.org/10.1080/17501229.2016.1138577

Martin, J. (1995). Interpersonal meaning, persuasion and public discourse: Packing semiotic punch. *Australian Journal of Linguistics*, 15, 33–67.

Moeller, A., Theiler, J., & Wu, C. (2012). Goal setting and student achievement: A longitudinal study. *The Modern Language Journal*, 96, 153–169.

Müller-Hartmann, A. (2000). The role of tasks in promoting intercultural learning in electronic learning networks. *Language Learning & Technology*, 4(2), 129–147.

Müller-Hartmann, A. (2006). Learning how to teach intercultural communicative competence via telecollaboration: A model for language teacher education. In J. A. Belz & S. L. Thorne (eds.), *Internet-mediated intercultural foreign language education*, pp. 63–84. Boston: Thomson Heinle.

Müller-Hartmann, A. (2016). A task is a task is a task is a task ... or is it? Researching telecollaborative teacher competence development – the need for more qualitative research. In S. Jager, M. Kurek, & B. O'Rourke (eds.), *New directions in telecollaborative research and practice: Selected papers from the second conference on telecollaboration in higher education*, pp. 31–43. Research-publishing.net. Retrieved December 15, 2017, from https://research-publishing.net/display_article.php?doi=10.14705/rpnet.2016.telecollab2016.488

National Standards Collaborative Board. (2015). *World-Readiness Standards for learning languages*. 4th ed. Alexandria, VA: National Standards Collaborative Board.

O'Dowd, R. (2003). Understanding the "other side": Intercultural learning in a Spanish-English email exchange. *Language Learning & Technology*, 7(2), 118–144.

O'Dowd, R. (2010). Issues in the assessment of online interaction and exchange. In S. Guth & F. Helm (eds.), *Telecollaboration 2.0: Language, literacies and intercultural learning in the 21st century*, pp. 337–360. Bern: Peter Lang.

O'Dowd, R., & Lewis, T. (eds.) (2016). *Online intercultural exchange: Policy, pedagogy, practice*. New York and London: Routledge.

O'Dowd, R., & Ritter, M. (2006). understanding and working with "failed communication" in telecollaborative exchanges. *CALICO Journal*, 23(3), 623–642. https://doi.org/10.1558/cj.v23i3.623-642

O'Dowd, R., and Ware, P. (2009). Critical issues in telecollaborative task design. *Computer Assisted Language Learning*, 22(2), 173–188. https://doi.org/10.1080/09588220902778369

O'Rourke, B. (2005). Form-focused interaction in online tandem learning. *CALICO Journal*, 22(3), 433–446.

OECD (2016). Global competency for an inclusive world. Retrieved on December 15, 2017 from https://www.oecd.org/education/Global-competency-for-an-inclusive-world.pdf

Ortega, L. (2017). New CALL-SLA research interfaces for the 21st Century: Towards equitable multilingualism. *CALICO Journal*, 34(3), 285–316. https://doi.org/10.1558/cj.33855

Ortega, L., & Zyzik, E. (2008). Online interactions and L2 learning: Some ethical challenges for L2 researchers. In S. Magnan (ed.), *Mediating discourse online*, pp. 331–356. Amsterdam: John Benjamins. https://doi.org/10.1075/aals.3.19ort

Osuna, M. M., & Meskill, C. (1998). Using the World Wide Web to integrate Spanish language and culture. *Language Learning & Technology*, 1(2), 71–92.

Pellettieri, J. (2000). Negotiation in cyberspace: The role of chatting in the development of grammatical competence. In M. Warschauer & R. Kern (eds.), *Network-based language teaching: Concepts and practice*, pp. 59–86. Cambridge: Cambridge University Press. https://doi.org/10.1017/CBO9781139524735.006

Piller, I. (2011). *Intercultural communication: A critical introduction*. Edinburgh: Edinburgh University Press.

Reinhardt, J. (2008). Negotiating meaningfulness: An enhanced perspective on interaction in computer-mediated foreign language learning environments. In S. Magnan (ed.), *Mediating Discourse Online*, pp. 219–244. Amsterdam: John Benjamins. https://doi.org/10.1075/aals.3.13rei

Risager, K. (2007). *Language and culture pedagogy: From a national to a transnational paradigm*. Clevedon: Multilingual Matters.

Rubin, J., and Guth, S. (2015). Collaborative online international learning: An emerging format for internationalizing curricula. In A. Schultheis Moore and S. Simon (eds.), *Globally networked teaching in the humanities: Theories and practices*, pp. 15–27. New York and London: Routledge.

Salmon, G. (2000). *E-moderating: The key to teaching and learning online.* London and Sterling, VA: Kogan Page Limited. https://doi.org/10.4324/9780203465424

Salmon, G. (2002). *E-tivities: The key to active online learning.* London and Sterling, VA: Kogan Page Limited.

Satar, H. M. (2013). Multimodal language learner interactions via desktop video-conferencing within a framework of social presence: Gaze. *ReCALL,* 25(1), 122–142.

Sauro, S. (2017). Online fan practices and CALL. *CALICO Journal* 34(2), 131–146. https://doi.org/10.1558/cj.33077

Schneider, J., & von der Emde, S. (2006). Conflicts in cyberspace: From communication breakdown to intercultural dialogue in online collaborations. In J. A. Belz & S. L. Thorne (eds.), *Internet-mediated intercultural foreign language education,* pp. 178–206. Boston: Thomson Heinle Publishers.

Scollon, R. (2004). Teaching language and culture as hegemonic practice. *The Modern Language Journal,* 88, 271–275.

Sotillo, S. (2000). Discourse functions and syntactic complexity in synchronous and asynchronous communication. *Language Learning & Technology,* 4(1), 82–119.

Spencer-Oatey, H. (2012). What is culture? A compilation of quotations. GlobalPAD core concepts. Available at GlobalPAD Open House. Retrieved November 29, 2017 from http://www.warwick.ac.uk/globalpadintercultural

Telles, J. A. (2009). Do we really need a webcam? – The uses that foreign language students make out of webcam images during teletandem sessions. *Letras & Letras,* 25(2), 65–79.

Telles, J. A. (2015). Teletandem and performativity/Teletandem e performatividade. *Revista Brasileira de Linguistica Aplicada,* 15(1). https://doi.org/10.1590/1984-639820155536

Thorne, S. L. (2003). Artifacts and cultures-of-use in intercultural communication. *Language Learning & Technology,* 7(2), 38–67.

Thorne, S. L. (2006). Pedagogical and praxiological lessons from Internet-mediated intercultural foreign language education research. In J.A. Belz & S.L. Thorne (eds.), *Internet-mediated intercultural foreign language education,* pp. 2–30, Boston: Thomson Heinle.

Thorne, S. L. (2008). Transcultural communication in open Internet environments and massively multiplayer online games. In S. Magnan (ed.), *Mediating discourse online,* pp. 305–327, Amsterdam: John Benjamins. https://doi.org/10.1075/aals.3.17tho

Thorne, S. L. (2010). The "intercultural turn" and language learning in the crucible of new media. In S. Guth & F. Helm (eds.). *Telecollaboration 2.0: Language, literacies and intercultural learning in the 21st century,* pp. 139–164. Bern: Peter Lang.

Thorne, S. L. (2016). Cultures-of-use and morphologies of communicative action. *Language Learning & Technology,* 20(2), 185–191. Retrieved December 15, 2017, from http://llt.msu.edu/issues/june 2016/thorne.pdf

Thorne, S. L., & Reinhardt, J. (2008). "Bridging activities," new media literacies and advanced foreign language proficiency. *CALICO Journal,* 25, 558–572.

Tudini, V. (2007). Negotiation and intercultural learning in Italian native speaker chat rooms. *The Modern Language Journal*, 91(4), 577–600. https://doi.org/10.1111/j.1540-4781.2007.00624.x

Van Lier, L. (2004). *The ecology and semiotics of language learning: A sociocultural perspective.* Dordrecht: Kluwer. https://doi.org/10.1007/1-4020-7912-5

Vinagre, M., & Esteban, A. C. (2017): Evaluative language for rapport building in virtual collaboration: an analysis of appraisal in computer-mediated interaction, *Language and Intercultural Communication*, 1–19.

Ware, P. (2005). "Missed" communication in online communication: Tensions in a German-American telecollaboration. *Language Learning & Technology*, 9(2), 64–89.

Ware, P., & Kramsch, C. (2005). Toward an intercultural stance: Teaching German and English through telecollaboration. *The Modern Language Journal*, 89(2), 190–205. https://doi.org/10.1111/j.1540-4781.2005.00274.x

Warschauer, M. (2005). Sociocultural perspectives on CALL. In J. L. Egbert & G. M. Petrie (eds.) *CALL research perspectives*, pp. 41–52. New York: Routledge.

White, P. (1998). *Telling media tales: The news story as rhetoric*. Doctoral dissertation. Retrieved from: https://www.researchgate.net/profile/Peter_White17/publication/268256149_Telling_Media_Tales_the_news_story_as_rhetoric/links/55508cae08ae956a5d24df70.pdf

Woodman, K., & Kazoullis, V. (2013). Facebook, telecollaboration, and international access to technology in the classroom. In Francisco V. Cipolla Ficarra, K. Veltman, D. Verber, B. Novak, P. Fulton, & D. Edison (eds.), *Fourth international conference on advances in new technologies, interactive interfaces and communicability*, pp. 116–124. Huerta Grande, Cordoba, Argentina: Blue Herons Editions.

Yang, S., & Yi, Y. (2017). Negotiating multiple identities through eTandem learning experiences. *CALICO Journal*, 34(1), 97–114. https://doi.org/10.1558/cj.29586

Ziegler, N. (2014). Fostering self-regulated learning through the European Language Portfolio: An intervention mixed methods study. *The Modern Language Journal*, 98(4), 921–936. https://doi.org/10.1111/modl.12147

Resources

It is not possible to provide resources for the multiplicity of languages and cultures which are taught, so the resources provided below regard websites which we feel provide interesting perspectives from a multiplicity of cultures, in particular voices which are perhaps not so commonly heard, resources with news, statistics, and surveys from many different countries, and finally links to websites related to telecollaboration.

Perspectives

- *Global Voices* is a community of more than 300 bloggers and translators around the world who publish reports from blogs and citizen media around the world, with emphasis on voices that are not ordinarily heard in international mainstream media. This resource is plurilingual. http://globalvoicesonline.org/
- *7 Billion Others* offers clips from 6000 interviews with the inhabitants of 84 countries on issues such as family, love, happiness, war, values, and beliefs. http://www.7billionothers.org

International News, Statistics and Surveys

- International News http://www.abyznewslinks.com/
- *NationMaster*: A compilation of data from sources such as the CIA World Factbook, UN, and OECD which allows for comparison on a host of statistics, and easy generation of maps and graphs on all kinds of statistics. http://www.nationmaster.com
- *World Values Survey* http://www.worldvaluessurvey.org/
- *Pew Global Attitudes Project* http://pewglobal.org/

Telecollaboration

- *Cultura*: This website provides information for teachers about the Cultura project, a teachers' guide, model site and an exchange tool which will allow teachers to design their own exchange with questionnaires, resources and online fora. http://cultura.mit.edu/
- *UNICollaboration Virtual Exchange Platform:* This platform allows university educators to look for partner classes for telecollaboration projects, it also has a database of training materials, tasks to engage students in, a series of sample telecollaboration projects, and a forum for practitioners. https://uni-collaboration.eu
- *UNICollaboration Academic Organization*: a cross-disciplinary professional organisation for telecollaboration and virtual exchange in higher education. https://www.unicollaboration.org
- Teletandem Brasil: This website provides information about Teletandem Brazil and information for teachers interested in partnering their students. The site also has a list of publications about Teletandem and professional development for teachers. http://www.teletandembrasil.org

About the Authors

Sarah Guth teaches English as a foreign language (EFL) at the University of Padova, Italy. She was the Program Coordinator at the SUNY COIL Center from February 2013 to June 2014. Her research focuses on tele-collaboration, intercultural communication, and the normalization of virtual exchange in higher education. She is the President of the UNI Collaboration Organisation. She has published numerous articles and book chapters on language learning and testing, computer-mediated communication, intercultural competence, and culture learning. She co-edited the book *Telecollaboration 2.0: Language, literacies and intercultural learning in the 21st century* with Francesca Helm.

Francesca Helm is Assistant Professor of English at the Department of Political Science, Law and International Studies, University of Padova, Italy. She obtained her MA from the University of London, and PhD from the Universitat Autònoma de Barcelona. She served as a member of the executive board of Eurocall for six years, and is currently vice-chair of the Education Innovation working group of the Coimbra Group University network. She is on the editorial board of the journals *ReCALL* and *System*. Her research has focused on telecollaboration and virtual exchange, internationalization of higher education, identity, intercultural dialogue, and multimodality. She has published articles in international journals and books on these subjects.

4 Technology-Enhanced Listening: How does it look and what can we expect?

Maribel Montero Perez

Preview Questions

1. What are your personal experiences with listening in a foreign language? Are you often exposed to situations in which you have to listen in a foreign language? If so, which types of listening situations are you confronted with (e.g., video, podcasts, face-to-face conversation)?
2. Do you think listening can stimulate any kind of L2 learning? Why or why not?
3. What kind of listening materials would you use in an L2 course and how would you justify your choice?
4. Would you allow your students to use help or support options such as subtitles, transcripts, etc. when listening in a foreign language? What could be the advantages or disadvantages of these support options?
5. Which criteria would you use to select listening materials for L2 learners? For instance, how would you decide whether the difficulty level of the selected materials is appropriate?
6. Do you think some kind of listening instruction is important and how could you organize this?
7. How can we encourage language learners to engage in listening situations outside the formal classroom?

1 Introduction: Listening and Multimodality

With over 1 billion hours of YouTube per day, more than 200 million subscriptions to websites such as Netflix and HBO, the overall accessibility of DVD, TV, and Internet, people are constantly engaging in multimedia listening situations. These types of media do not only reflect media use in the mother tongue (L1), they also provide us with numerous opportunities to listen in a second language (L2). Recent studies have shown that these types of media can, for instance, be linked to opportunities for out-of-class language learning and vocabulary development (e.g., Lindgren & Muñoz, 2013; Peters, 2018). They can also be used to expose language learners to different genres such as, for instance, documentaries, news clips, and fiction in the target language, and can be implemented in different types of electronic as well as mobile learning environments that are available on a broad range of devices (laptop, tablet, mobile phone, etc.). In these technology-enhanced learning environments, materials can be further exploited or modified by adding specific instructions and tasks as well as support options such as on-screen text, advance organizers, etc. Listening opportunities can be based on authentic input, that is, materials that are created for a native speaker audience such as TED-talks, programs and clips of TV channels in the foreign language, or movies. Yet, materials can also be specifically created for pedagogical purposes, which is often the case for reading-while-listening activities (i.e., a combination of reading and the spoken version of the text) or digital storybooks that are adapted for a given proficiency level in the second language.

What the aforementioned types of materials have in common is that they can be characterized as multimodal (Kress & Van Leeuwen, 2001) since they expose learners to different types of semiotic resources such as imagery, voice or audio input, written text, etc. As argued by The Douglas Fir Group, language learning is per definition "semiotic learning" (2016: 27): As language learners we are exposed to a wide array of semiotic resources (including, for instance, intonation, facial expressions, body language) that can be combined in order to comprehend and interpret information. These resources "are conceived as an open set of ever-evolving multilingual and multimodal possibilities for making meaning" (p. 37). Therefore, language learning as such is necessarily multimodal learning.

Multimodality is also a key feature of CALL environments (Chapelle, 2009). During the last decade, we have seen an increasing number of studies on the role of multimodal texts and how these may stimulate L2 learners' listening as well as their language (i.e., vocabulary) development. As we will show in this chapter, these studies deal with questions of how to present content in listening activities in order to make them as effective as possible.

The outline of this chapter is as follows: in section 2, we will briefly look into a number of theoretical aspects related to listening as well as theories that have inspired research on technology-enhanced listening. Section

3 discusses the role of technologies for developing aspects of fluent listening. In section 4, we focus on listening as a source of meaning-focused input that may stimulate vocabulary learning. A number of aspects related to the assessment of listening in technology-enhanced contexts will be discussed in section 5 before looking into the conceptualization of listening activities in section 6. We conclude this chapter with some reflections on the role of technology for future research into L2 listening.

2   Listening in Technology-Enhanced Environments: Defining Constructs and Frameworks

2.1   Listening

Rost (2014: 281) argued that the "key to defining 'fluency in listening' lies in understanding that while most listening behavior is not visible, listening actually does involve real mental processes that can be regulated by the listener." Indeed, listening has been described as a learner's ability to use an interaction of bottom-up and top-down processing (Vandergrift, 2004). Top-down processes refer to the use of context as well as of conceptual and prior knowledge (e.g., topic familiarity, culture, expectations) in order to actively construct meaning. Taking into account the multimodal character of CALL-based listening, top-down processes may also include knowledge that can be extracted from imagery including facial expressions and gestures. Bottom-up processes, on the other hand, refer to the ability to segment and decode the speech stream, to identify word boundaries, to recognize words and to use this information for further interpretation. As argued by Field (2008), these also include recognizing suprasegmental features such as liaison, assimilation, and elisions. Being able to successfully recognize words in the input is necessarily linked to a learner's vocabulary knowledge. Studies (e.g., Matthews, 2018; Staehr, 2009) have shown that learners with more vocabulary knowledge are more successful in listening comprehension, presumably because they have more chances to know the words in the input, which may subsequently "strengthen learners' ability to successfully cope with the heavy online processing demands of listening" (Staehr, 2009: 589).

When information is processed by using a combination of bottom-up and top-down processes, successful comprehension can take place. Yet, the speed with which the input is delivered is often perceived as one of the main obstacles for L2 listeners (Graham, 2006). Indeed, bottom-up and top-down processes need to take place in real-time since L2 learners are in most cases "forced to process speech in the same speed with which it is produced by the speaker" (Hulstijn, 2003: 420). In order to become fluent in listening, listeners thus need to develop "the ability to deal with progressively more fluent speech [...], to decode incoming language quickly, and to a large extent automatically" (Rost, 2014: 281). In order to overcome problems related to speed of delivery and breakdowns at the level of bottom-up and top-down processes, instructional interventions can be considered. These do not only focus on developing and supporting the aforementioned processes, but also aim at helping learners to apply the appropriate listening strategies such as guessing the meaning and using visual cues to compensate for deficient vocabulary knowledge.

As we will show in this chapter, CALL-based approaches to listening are particularly beneficial for developing listening fluency as well as for providing learners with assistance on demand (e.g., media players that allow for easy adjustment of speed of delivery, presence of on-screen text, etc.). This may not only foster top-down and bottom-up processing but also comprehension and language learning.

2.2 Theoretical Frameworks That Have Inspired Technology-Enhanced Listening

Two main theoretical frameworks can be identified in research on technology-enhanced listening: studies that are based on an interactionist perspective of SLA and studies that focus on the concept of multimodality and applications of multimedia learning theory. These perspectives should, however, not be seen as mutually exclusive, since most of the studies are actually based on a combination of both, or how multimedia can be used to realize the central components of language acquisition from an interactionist perspective (see Plass & Jones, 2005 for a detailed description of this framework).

2.2.1 Interactionist theory In her 2003 book, Chapelle outlined the role of an interactionist SLA perspective for CALL research. An interactionist SLA framework underscores the role of three central components: input, interaction, and output. In this perspective, input plays a crucial role as the features of the input are closely linked to acquisition. Yet, in order to increase the likelihood of acquiring new elements from the input (i.e., to stimulate noticing), researchers have argued that the input should be enhanced (see Sharwood Smith, 1993). Chapelle stated that input enhancement can be realized in three different ways: (1) input can be made salient in order to stimulate noticing (e.g., adding highlights in subtitled video, emphasizing words in speech), (2) input can be modified (e.g., adding subtitles to video), or (3) elaborated (e.g., adding a grammatical phrase). The goal of these enhancements is to make the input more understandable and to stimulate language learning. As argued by Chapelle (2003: 54) "one of the key features of enhanced input in CALL is that it is almost always provided interactively." While interaction was originally used to refer to interpersonal interaction, Chapelle extended this concept by including human-computer interaction in contexts where learners interact with electronic learning tasks. The goal of this interaction is then to obtain enhanced input which can be considered a support for language comprehension and learning.

Numerous CALL studies on listening can be situated within this interactionist framework since they focus on the affordances of a type of input (e.g., audio, video), how this input can be enhanced, and what this means in terms of comprehension as well as language learning (e.g., Grgurovic & Hegelheimer, 2007; Winke, Gass, & Sydorenko, 2010).

2.2.2 Multimedia learning theory Another framework that has inspired CALL listening studies (e.g., Jones & Plass, 2002; Rodgers & Webb, 2017) is dual-coding theory (Paivio, 1986) and the more recent multimedia learning theory (Mayer, 2005). Dual-coding theory postulates that the brain has distinct channels for the processing and storage of verbal and nonverbal information, that is, a verbal and imagery system, both of which are limited in capacity. Even though these channels work independently, they are most effective when they are activated simultaneously, resulting in better encoding and recall of information. This perspective was subsequently included in Mayer's cognitive theory of multimedia learning.

Multimedia learning theory is based on a set of principles with the multimedia learning principle at its center. This principle holds that people "learn better from words and pictures than from words alone" (Mayer, 2005: 63), which indicates that a combination of different types of modalities is expected to enhance learning. Looking at the literature on technology-enhanced listening, we found references to the multimedia principle (e.g., Jones & Plass, 2002) but also to other principles such as the split-attention principle (e.g., Winke, Gass, & Sydorenko, 2013), which states that presenting words and pictures in an integrated fashion results in better learning. Rodgers (2018) focused on the role of the spatial contiguity principle, which holds that words and pictures are best presented simultaneously to stimulate learning.

These principles are very informative for listening environments since they provide concrete guidelines on how to implement a combination of modalities in learning activities. Yet, it should also be stressed that multimedia learning theory was initially designed in a native language science learning context, which may have effects on the validity of certain principles in the context of L2 learning. One specific example is the redundancy principle, which states that "people learn more deeply from graphics and narration than from graphics, narration, and on-screen text" (Mayer, 2005: 183). In the context of L2 learning, however, numerous studies have shown that redundant information may actually improve performance in terms of speech decoding (see subsection 3.1), comprehension (see subsection 3.4), and language learning (see subsection 4.2).

3   Technology-Enhanced Approaches to Stimulate Listening Fluency and Comprehension

It has been shown that an interaction between bottom-up and top-down processes is necessary in order to become a more proficient listener (Yeldham & Gruba, 2014) and that these processes "can be targeted for improvement by L2 learners" (Rost, 2014: 281). One way to develop listening fluency is to stimulate learners to engage in extensive listening programs, which consist in exposing learners to considerable amounts of listening materials. Even though research on the benefits of such an approach is scarce, there is now beginning evidence that exposure to listening and reading-while-listening input (i.e., providing learners with auditory input that is accompanied by the written account) in extensive programs is conducive to listening development (e.g., Chang, 2012; Chang & Millett, 2016) if a sufficient amount of exposure takes place within a given period.

Yet, even though large exposure is crucial (Renandya & Farrell, 2011; Rost, 2006), learners might be unable to deal with the complex nature of listening situations without explicit instructional interventions (Cross, 2009). Therefore, numerous researchers have looked into the role of interventions that target bottom-up and top-down processes. These instructional approaches are crucial since learners who do not have the necessary bottom-up or top-down fluency may use up their attention resources at the decoding level as a result of which they have no capacity left to "concentrate on higher levels of information, that is, on semantics and content" (Hulstijn, 2003: 419). This may lead to a number of listening problems or even listening anxiety (for more information on listening problems, see Goh, 2000 and Graham, 2006).

3.1   Developing Bottom-Up Processes

Approaches that aim at developing L2 learners' bottom-up processes are mainly focused on the importance of automaticity of aural word recognition. These interventions are crucial since successful speech segmentation and word boundary identification were found to be among the main problems of L2 listeners (Goh, 2000; Graham, 2006; Renandya & Farrell, 2011) and inevitably hinder further parsing and processing of the input. Two main types of approaches can be identified in the CALL literature: (1) tools that create conditions for repeatedly listening to an audio excerpt in order to stimulate word recognition and (2) the addition of a written version of the auditory input in the form of captioned video (i.e., video with subtitles in the L2) or reading-while-listening activities.

3.1.1 Repeated and intensive listening The first set of interventions to be discussed aims at stimulating automaticity of word recognition (e.g., Hulstijn, 2003; Matthews, Chang, & O'Toole, 2014). Generally speaking, the aim of these approaches is to provide learners and teachers with a computer-based platform to conduct repeated or intensive listening activities, which consist of (repeatedly) listening to a specific excerpt, often segment by segment "for precise sounds, words, phrases, grammatical units and pragmatic units" (Rost, 2002: 138). In the study by Matthews, Chang, & O'Toole (2014), for instance, students used a web-based application to listen to an audio fragment, to transcribe the corresponding segment and to receive feedback in the form of the correct transcription of the audio fragment or an indication of the number of words that they transcribed correctly themselves. It was found that participants who had used such an application showed significantly more improvement in word recognition from speech than a control group who had not used such an application. In addition, this type of repeated listening approach may be combined with other options that facilitate word recognition such as the possibility to slow down the speech rate of the input (see subsection 6.2). Providing learners with input in which the speech rate is slowed down has been shown to lead to increased listening abilities, presumably because this approach is beneficial for developing bottom-up skills (McBride, 2011) and word recognition (East & King, 2012).

3.1.2 Combining written and auditory input A second set of interventions that addresses the development of bottom-up processes has activities in which written and auditory modalities are combined. Examples of this input combination are reading-while-listening activities (see Figure 1) and captioned video, that is L2 video enhanced with L2 on-screen text (see

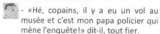

En sortant de la cabane, les garçons rencontrent Rufus.

- «Hé, copains, il y a eu un vol au musée et c'est mon papa policier qui mène l'enquête!» dit-il, tout fier.

Figure 1 Example of a reading-while-listening activity in which learners listen to an audio story while having the transcript (and in this example also a corresponding image) on the screen.

Ben, mon père, il a des tableaux cent fois mieux à la maison...

Figure 2 Example of a captioned video (both audio and on-screen text are presented in the L2 = French).

Figure 2). It should be noted that we systematically use the concept of "captions" to refer to video with on-screen text in the L2 while the concept of "subtitles" is used to refer to on-screen text in the native language (L1).

What captioned video and reading-while-listening have in common is that they provide a written account of the audio in order to support learners' speech segmentation and decoding of the spoken input. Yet, this kind of approach has often been criticized based on the argument that the presence of a written account of the audio would prevent learners' processing of the auditory input and have them rely exclusively on their processing of the written text. Yet, there is now beginning evidence (e.g., Bird & Williams, 2002; Charles & Trenkic, 2015; Mitterer & McQueen, 2009) that providing learners with a written account actually facilitates speech perception and decoding (for a comprehensive review, see Yeldham, 2017), even after relatively brief exposure to captioned video (e.g., Mitterer & McQueen, 2009) or reading-while-listening materials (e.g., Chang, 2012). It has also been argued that when a video is shown twice, it seems most effective to provide captions during the first viewing since this may help learners to focus on the language in the clip which subsequently stimulates efficient listening without captions during the second viewing (Winke, Gass, & Sydorenko, 2010). Yet, this was only found for target languages that are based on the same orthography as the learner's L1 (e.g., English-speaking learners of Spanish). In addition, bimodal input exposure may not only lead to enhanced auditory processing for known words (e.g., Mitterer & McQueen, 2009) or sentences (Charles & Trenkic, 2015), but it may also lead to enhanced processing "that generalizes beyond the programmes watched" (ibid.).

Together, these studies tend to suggest that supporting L2 learners' listening by means of a written account of the auditory input does not hinder listening or auditory processing but may actually facilitate automaticity of spoken word recognition, which is in turn crucial for successful listening and comprehension.

3.2   Developing Top-Down Processes

CALL-based listening activities may stimulate top-down processes in different ways. Some studies have looked into the role of specific interventions such as advance organizers as a means to activate relevant background knowledge and stimulate comprehension. These studies draw on the advance organizer principle of the multimedia learning theory, which holds that "students acquire language better when they view an advance organizer before receiving input in reading or listening activities" (Plass & Jones, 2005: 481). It has been shown that (teacher-aided) advance organizers containing, for instance, prior knowledge or topic-related texts make it possible to integrate information more easily, hence resulting in better comprehension (Chang & Read, 2006; Yang, 2014), and that advance organizers presented in visual and verbal modes are more effective than those presented without visuals (Plass & Jones, 2005: 481). Advance organizers can also include other types of pre-listening tasks such as pre-teaching new vocabulary or previewing comprehension questions (Chang & Read, 2006; Chung, 2002).

As argued in the introduction of this chapter, the multimodality of the materials used in CALL-based listening makes it possible to extract meaning from different types of semiotic resources. These do not only include linguistic but also nonlinguistic resources such as imagery. In this respect, Rodgers (2013) argued that the imagery or the use of visuals in video-based listening have the potential to contribute to top-down processing and subsequent comprehension, which was also found by Bianchi & Ciabattoni's data (2008) on beginning learners and Cross's study (2011). Rodgers (2013), as well as Webb & Rodgers (2009), pointed out that this may also explain why L2 learners can achieve adequate understanding of video input with a more limited vocabulary size than would be the case for written input (see subsection 6.1). Not only images, but also related series or storylines have the potential to contribute to more effective top-down processing since learners build specific knowledge with regard to characters and topics that a specific series focuses on (Rodgers, 2013).

Some studies have looked at how learners deal with the different types of input modalities (audio, images, on-screen text) when watching captioned video by using eye-tracking methods. These studies show that the presence of captions does not prevent learners from processing the visuals (Bisson et al., 2014; Winke, Gass, & Sydorenko, 2013) and that learners are capable of switching their attention between different sources of information, which confirms the idea that these sources can be used for information extraction. Yet, even though imagery may stimulate comprehension processes, it should be noted that not all types of video input provide informative visuals. In addition, images may aid comprehension at one point in a program, but they may be uninformative at another.

3.3   The Role of Strategy Instruction

Proficient listeners not only use a combination of bottom-up and top-down processes, but they also rely on a wider range of listening strategies (for more information on strategies for listening, see, for instance, Vandergrift & Goh, 2012) than less skilled listeners (e.g., Roussel, 2011; Vandergrift, 2003). It has therefore been argued that listening instruction should also include activities that teach listeners "how to listen" (Cross, 2014: 8) and that raise their "metacognitive awareness of the cognitive processes underlying successful L2 listening" (Vandergrift, 2007: 198). Metacognitive awareness reflects learners' management of listening activities including planning, monitoring, and evaluating the listening process (see Goh, 2005 and Vandergrift, 2007, for a detailed description) and learners' abilities to regulate these processes. As argued by Vandergrift (2004), such an approach may be particularly useful for fostering top-down processes.

The potential of strategy instruction is now increasingly targeted by listening researchers as a means to enhance and support learners' listening abilities. It has, for instance, been reported that explicit strategy instruction might be particularly beneficial for less skilled learners (Vandergrift & Tafaghodtari, 2010) and that these lower-level learners might benefit more from a strategy instruction approach than an approach that combines strategies and bottom-up training (Yeldham, 2016).

So far, however, the role of strategy instruction in multimedia listening remains difficult to characterize. Results in technology-enhanced settings suggest that metacognitive instruction has a beneficial impact on multimedia listening comprehension (Bozorgian & Fakhri Alamdari, 2018) and that strategy instruction may help learners to deal with the complexities of multimedia input such as videotexts (Cross, 2009). Strategy instruction may also help learners to become better autonomous listeners, which is crucial when working individually in electronic learning environments (Vandergrift, 2007) or with materials such as podcasts (Cross, 2014). We are, however, not aware of studies that have used technology-enhanced environments in order to stimulate listening strategies (e.g., CALL exercises on strategy use). CALL platforms may, nonetheless, be helpful to gain insight into learners' processes and use of strategies while listening. Roussel (2011), for instance, found that learners' use of media control buttons (pausing, rewind, forward), recorded by means of screen-capturing tools, is indicative of their metacognitive strategies. Future studies might investigate how these strategies can be trained using CALL platforms and how these impact listening ability.

3.4   Supporting Comprehension

It is safe to say that the bulk of research into L2 listening has focused on the product of listening, i.e., the effect of certain variables or modifications on the input on learners' comprehension (Vandergrift & Tafaghodtari, 2010). Building on the importance of bottom-up and top-down processes for fluent listening, most studies have looked at the role of interventions that may facilitate the aforementioned processes in order to subsequently measure their impact on global or detail comprehension of the content.

It has been shown that listening to audio excerpts accompanied by multimedia annotations which contain word-related information such as definitions or pictures, may stimulate comprehension from auditory input (e.g., Jones & Plass, 2002). It might also be beneficial to give learners control over the speech rate (e.g., pause or rewind) in order to improve their comprehension (Zhao, 1997). So far, however, the majority of CALL-based listening research has looked into the effect of on-screen text such as captions, L1 subtitles, and keyword captions on content comprehension.

There is ample evidence that the presence of captions leads to better input comprehension compared to conditions where no form of on-screen text was available (see Montero Perez, Van Den Noortgate, & Desmet, 2013 for a meta-analysis on this topic). This finding has been explained by the fact that learners need less cognitive resources in order to decode or segment the speech stream and can therefore spend more time interpreting the message (Montero Perez et al., 2014). In addition, results of an eye-movement study showed that there was a correlation between actual reading behavior and performance (Kruger & Steyn, 2014). More particularly, it was found that learners who had captions and who actually read the captions outperformed participants who had on-screen text but did not (entirely) process the text, on a comprehension test. The listening materials used in the aforementioned studies are, however, relatively short videos. Studies that have looked at the effects of captions on comprehension over time are scarce. One exception is the study by Rodgers & Webb (2017), which investigated the effect of captioned video in ten 42-minute episodes of a TV series on L2 learners' comprehension. Their results revealed that captions may aid comprehension but significant differences were only found for the most difficult episodes.

While the effects of L2 captions on comprehension seem clear-cut, the role of L1 subtitling is still a matter of debate. Guichon & McLornan (2008) did not find differences between L1 and L2 subtitles on intermediate students' comprehension tests. In the research by Markham, Peter, & McCarthy (2001) and Markham & Peter (2003) involving intermediate-level students, the highest comprehension scores were reported for students who were given L1 subtitles and who significantly outperformed the control group. The captioned group, in turn, outperformed the video-only condition. Markham & Peter therefore proposed a "developmental progression" (2003: 399) which consists of providing learners with different types of support options in different viewings. For instance, learners could first view the video with the L1 subtitles before viewing the same excerpt with L2 captions. Such an approach could help students to progressively ameliorate their level of comprehension in relation to the type of (enhanced) video used. Moreover, such a developmental or staged approach could be used to help learners gain adequate and detailed comprehension before training their L2 skills by means of captioned video (Markham, Peter, & McCarthy, 2001). Yet more research is needed in order to empirically validate the potential of a staged video approach.

Other types of captioning, that is, variations on standard full captioning, might also be considered (e.g., Mirzaei et al., 2017; Montero Perez et al., 2014; Montero Perez, Peters, & Desmet, 2014). Building on two earlier studies on the use of keyword or partial captions (Guillory, 1998; Park, 2004), these studies were inspired by the fact that full captions may present too much textual density on the screen which could hamper learners' listening experience. The idea behind keyword or partial captions is that only the important ideas of the sentence are visualized in the on-screen text area. Yet, empirical research into the effects of partial captions has reported mixed findings. While some studies revealed that keywords and full captions are equally effective in order to stimulate comprehension (Mirzaei et al., 2017; Montero Perez, et al., 2014), others found that full captioning may be more effective (Montero Perez, Peters, & Desmet, 2014).

4 Listening as a Source of Meaning-Focused Input

In the previous section, we argued that different types of technological components may support different aspects of listening. In this section, we will study the role of listening as a source of meaning-focused input and how listening may stimulate language learning.

4.1 Listening and Incidental Learning

An increasing number of studies are now focusing on the role of listening as a type of input that may foster language development and more specifically vocabulary acquisition. Nation (2007) argued that an effective and well-balanced language course consists of four different components or "strands" of which two are meaning-focused: language learning through receptive (reading and listening) and productive activities (speaking and writing). The other two strands, "deliberate learning" and "fluency development," should also be considered in a language program.

In order to effectively use listening as a type of meaning-focused input, a number of prerequisites need to be met: learners need to be focused on the message, the input should contain a number of unfamiliar items, the input should be understood and noticing of the unfamiliar items needs to take place (Nation, 2001: 390). Learning through meaning-focused input has also been qualified as incidental learning, or the "picking-up" (Hulstijn, 2001: 349) of language while performing an activity in which a learner is focused on the meaning and comprehension of the input (e.g., watching TV, reading a book). It is now commonly accepted that effective vocabulary development is not only based on intentional learning (i.e., deliberately trying to learn a new word) but also on incidental learning (Webb & Nation, 2017). While incidental learning is a very slow process which generally results in modest learning gains, research underlines the value of this type of learning since it "puts knowledge to use, enriching it, reinforcing it, and making it fluently available for use" (Webb & Nation, 2017: 168). Building on the importance of incidental learning for L2 learners' vocabulary development, numerous studies have sought to understand this process and have looked at ways to use and enhance listening activities in order to stimulate the pick-up rate of new words from listening.

When we look at studies that have focused on the use of some type of listening activity as meaning-focused input, we can broadly distinguish three types of input: audio (e.g., van Zeeland & Schmitt, 2013), reading-while-listening (e.g., Webb & Chang, 2015), and video (e.g., Peters & Webb, 2018). While the effectiveness of these different types of input may slightly differ, results suggest that all three types stimulate incidental learning. In studies on the role of viewing video, for instance, researchers have reported learning gains between 2 and 6 words after different amounts of exposure to video or TV series (Montero Perez, 2017; Peters & Webb, 2018; Rodgers, 2013). While these gains seem very low, they provide encouraging evidence that learners pick up new words incidentally and that longer exposure to these types of materials may lead to more sizeable learning gains.

4.2   Fostering Vocabulary Learning from Listening

In order to boost incidental vocabulary learning through listening or viewing, it has been argued that listening materials need to be enhanced or modified. First, we will look at the role of visualizations and images (4.2.1) as a means to increase the value of listening as a source of meaning-focused input (e.g., Jones & Plass, 2002; Rodgers, 2018). Next, we will look into the role of different types of on-screen text (4.2.2).

4.2.1 The role of imagery Audio-based listening can be enhanced by means of annotations that contain a picture, textual information, or a combination of both. It has, for instance, been found that audio with multimodal annotations which contain a combination of visuals and text may lead to more vocabulary gains than single modality annotations (pictures or text) (Jones & Plass, 2002), as was also suggested by the multimedia learning theory. Yet, a study in the context of mobile assisted listening (Çakmak and Erçetin, 2017) did not find such a modality effect. It was, however, found that listening to a story with annotations is more effective in terms of vocabulary learning than listening only.

What distinguishes the aforementioned types of audio-based listening activities from the more commonly used video-based activities is the presence of dynamic imagery. Rodgers' recent study (2018) investigated the potential of imagery in TV programs for vocabulary learning. It was found that visuals may be more supportive in documentaries than in narrative TV programs, which indicates that the choice of genre may impact the potential of imagery for vocabulary learning. Yet, his results also indicated that images seem to co-occur frequently enough with the spoken input and that this co-occurrence takes place in a timeframe that can stimulate word learning, as has also been defined by the spatial contiguity principle (Mayer, 2005).

4.2.2 The role of audio-visual materials and on-screen text The majority of studies on the effects of CALL-based listening on language development have used audio-visual materials (YouTube clips, TV excerpts, etc.). In order to emphasize the use of audio-visual materials, some of these studies have used the concept of "viewing" (e.g., Montero Perez, Peters, & Desmet, 2018; Peters & Webb, 2018) rather than "listening." Since audio-visual input alone seems to result in very low learning gains, extensive research has investigated the value of enhancing the original audio-visual input by adding a "technological overlay" (Robin, 2007: 109) or "technical attributes" (Vanderplank, 2010: 31). These have been realized in the form of on-screen text such as subtitling (i.e., in the native language) or captions (i.e., in the target language).

The advantage of adding such an overlay is twofold. First, it may amplify learners' chances of correctly processing the auditory input (i.e., their bottom-up processing) and may therefore strengthen their understanding of the message (see section 3). Second, computer-based approaches to enhance listening activities offer learners options that make it possible to "engage with language input in ways not possible with more paper-based media" (Martinez & Schmitt, 2010: 28) which may in turn stimulate learning. Below, we will discuss different types of on-screen text: captions, keyword captions, and subtitles and what we can expect from them in terms of incidental vocabulary learning.

L2 captions A meta-analysis on the effects of captioning for L2 vocabulary learning (Montero Perez, Van Den Noortgate, and Desmet, 2013) in which ten studies were included (e.g., Sydorenko, 2010; Winke, Gass, & Sydorenko, 2010), revealed that the presence of captioning (compared to video only) had a large and significant effect on vocabulary learning. This effect was found irrespective of the proficiency level of the participants and the type of vocabulary post-test used to measure vocabulary learning (recognition or recall). These findings seem to confirm the role of captioning in helping learners to notice new words in the input or their "conscious focusing on the form (especially on correct form), particularly when new or striking expressions are used" (Vanderplank, 1988: 276). Learning gains in these captioning studies were mainly found at the level of form- or meaning-related aspects of word knowledge such as being able to recognize the form as a new word (e.g., Sydorenko, 2010) or to recall word meaning information (e.g., Baltova, 1999; Winke, Gass, & Sydorenko, 2010). It is not surprising that most studies have focused on these aspects of word knowledge since incidental learning results in limited learning gains that are most likely to be found at the earliest stages of acquisition. Yet, captions may also have a positive effect on learners' productive vocabulary use in, for instance, written compositions (Hsu, 2014).

Other types of captions We see a limited yet growing number of studies that investigate the role of variations on standard full captions. Montero Perez et al. (2014) compared vocabulary gains in three conditions which differed with regard to the salience of the lexical items: Lexical items appeared in the standard full captions, or appeared as keyword captions or as highlighted keywords in the full captions. Results showed that the keyword and highlighted keyword groups significantly outperformed the control group on a meaning recognition test. Keywords were also found to lead to more noticing compared to full captions on a form recognition test (Montero Perez, Peters, & Desmet, 2015).

Another way to modify captions is to add glosses which contain meaning-related information such as translations or definitions (Montero Perez, Peters, & Desmet, 2018). It has been shown that glossed keyword captions result in significantly higher scores on the meaning recall test than full or keyword captions. In addition, it was found that using the gloss was significantly and positively related to correctly recalling the meaning of that word.

Together, these findings indicate that variations on standard captioning can stimulate the processes that are required to foster word learning from listening. The disadvantage of those types is that they are based on a lot of manual work such as keyword selections, translations, etc. even though there have been attempts to find ways to create these types of captions automatically. In this respect, Mirzaei et al. (2017) present a system that automatically captions video based on automatic speech recognition. This is a concrete example of how the affordances of technology can be maximized in order to facilitate not only the creation of innovative listening materials but also the learning of vocabulary by using those materials.

Another way to capitalize on the potential of technology-enhanced environments is to provide adaptive captioning. In a study by Hsu (2015), for instance, captions were adapted in function of the vocabulary knowledge of learners in order to provide them with captions which contained words that are more likely to be difficult. It was found that adaptive captions had a positive effect on motivation. Yet, more research on these types of approaches is needed in order to uncover their potential for listening as well as vocabulary learning.

L1 subtitles The role of L1 subtitles for vocabulary learning from listening is less clear-cut.[1] Peters, Heynen, & Puimège (2016) conducted two exploratory studies on the effects of L1 and L2 subtitles on vocabulary learning through short video exposure. In one of the studies, they found that learners with L2 subtitles significantly outperformed learners having L1 subtitles on a form recall test (i.e., provide the L2 word). In a longitudinal study, Frumuselu et al. (2015) investigated the effect of watching 13 episodes of *Friends* with either L1 or L2 subtitles on L2 learners' acquisition of informal and conversational speech (e.g., phrasal verbs, expressions). Their findings indicated that participants in the L2 subtitles group significantly outperformed the L1 group and this effect was found irrespective of participants' proficiency level.

On-screen text and young learners While numerous studies have highlighted the benefits of captions in terms of speech segmentation, comprehension, and vocabulary learning, the value of captions for beginning-level learners and more particularly young learners is still a matter of debate. First of all, researchers have stressed the fact that video materials should be in accordance with the proficiency level of the learner, even when support in the form of captions is offered (Bianchi & Ciabattoni, 2008; Danan, 2004). In addition, Vanderplank (2016: 14) noted that "it is not until they have reached the age of about ten years that native speaker children with normal hearing are comfortable with keeping up with captions on many adult programs, and then only if they are at the upper reading ability." This is an important issue since the use of captions requires "the ability to read and understand at reasonable speed" (p. 85) and thus implies a sufficiently developed reading speed. Issues related to reading speed may however be tackled to some extent by using options to modify or decrease the speed of content delivery which are available in free media players such as the VLC player (see subsection 6.2). Drawing on this age-related issue, Muñoz (2017) compared the reading of L1 and L2 subtitles of different age groups by means of eye-tracking. The eye-movement data indicated that children fixated captions more than L1 subtitles which may reveal that captions were more challenging. She therefore argued that L1 subtitles might be more appropriate for young beginning learners.

4.3   Extensive Viewing

Most of the findings presented above are based on studies in which vocabulary learning gains were measured after a relatively short exposure to L2

---

1   The majority of studies on L1 and L2 subtitles were carried out in the 1990s (e.g., d'Ydewalle & Pavakanun, 1996; d'Ydewalle & Van de Poel, 1999).

input. This explains why learning gains are generally low, even when using types of on-screen text as enhancement technique. Yet, they also provide encouraging evidence that listening may result in learning at the initial stages of acquisition such as the recognition of a word's form and meaning. As argued by Webb (2015), more substantial and sizeable gains can be expected in contexts where there is more extensive exposure to aural input that offers enough repetition to stimulate durable vocabulary learning. This approach has been labeled extensive viewing and aims at preparing learners for independent out-of-class viewing by providing initial classroom-based viewing activities. These are used to "raise awareness of the benefits of L2 television for language learning, teach learners strategies that can be used to support their comprehension, and demonstrate that through implementing a principled extensive viewing approach, comprehension may be sufficient for pleasurable viewing" (Webb, 2015: 160). In order to stimulate vocabulary learning through extensive viewing, Webb noted that programs should be perceived as motivating and interesting by the learners. In addition, in order to have a good global comprehension of TV programs, which is required to stimulate pleasurable viewing, participants' vocabulary knowledge plays an important role (see subsection 6.1).

In order to investigate the role of extensive viewing for vocabulary learning, a CALL platform could be an interesting research tool since it could allow for easy tracking and logging of learners' use of video (time spent viewing, etc.) over a longer period of time as well as their interactions with support options such as captions or subtitles. These types of tracking and logging data could be further linked to their general vocabulary knowledge as well as their listening proficiency in the L2. It could also inspire studies on how learners' interactions with support options evolve over time or in function of the content used in out-of-class contexts.

5   Assessing Listening in a Technology-Enhanced Context

The widespread use of technology for L2 listening inevitably impacts the way in which listening is assessed. Indeed, when we look at research on the use of technology for listening in assessment contexts, we see that there is some discussion with regard to the type of materials that can be used and how those materials should be presented to test-takers. These questions emerged because of the additional choices that technology-enhanced environments offer, such as speed adjustments or the option to simultaneously present exercises and media. In this section, we discuss three issues that we might consider when developing materials for listening tests.

A first question is related to whether video-based or audio-based materials should be used in testing settings. As we have shown in the introduction of this chapter, listening is a very rich source of input which means that learners can use all available resources such as visuals and audio in order to extract meaning. The question then becomes: should the assessment of learners' listening ability be based on "listening only" situations, i.e., situations in which we listen without visual support (e.g., telephone conversations, radio programs, etc.) or on situations in which there is visual support. The latter is said to be more authentic and construct-relevant (Batty, 2015) since it represents "a more realistic replication of real-world listening" (Buck, 2001: 123). Indeed, in the majority of the cases, we have supportive visual information such as body language and facial expression in communication, or imagery in TV programs. The role of visuals in listening assessment contexts remains, however, difficult to characterize. So far, research has shown that L2 test-takers attend to the visuals for approximately 69% of the time but there is also a substantial amount of individual variation (Wagner, 2007). While some studies have shown that visuals may support listening test performance (e.g., Wagner, 2013), other studies did not find differences between the audio- and the video-format of a traditional multiple-choice listening test (e.g., Batty, 2015). Since there are no clear-cut results with regard to this question, it can be argued that it is the task of the test designer to make informed decisions about this particular aspect.

Another question is whether learners can access the questions while or before listening. Results of studies that have investigated this aspect have produced mixed findings. While some studies found no difference on test performance between learners who could access the questions and learners who couldn't (e.g., Wagner, 2013); others found that previewing questions (e.g., questions and multiple-choice options or questions only) had a positive effect on test performance (e.g., Chang & Read, 2006; Koyama, Sun, & Ockey, 2016). Given the potential impact of item preview on performance (see, for instance, the advance organizer principle in subsection 3.2), it is important to consider this aspect when designing a test and to make decisions in function of the operationalization of the listening construct. While item preview might be unnecessary when testing global comprehension, a test that measures detailed aspects or word recognition could benefit from item preview.

Finally, a typical question in high stakes listening tests includes one listening at normal speed in order to guarantee test validity and objectivity. Yet, we also know that a test context in which learners can only listen once may lead to stress and anxiety since input is very often perceived as too fast (Goh, 2000). Therefore, it seems crucial to prepare learners for such a context. In this respect, East & King (2012) investigated the impact of classroom-based preparatory listening activities in which the speed of delivery can be adapted. In order to do so, they used technology to slow down the audio or media that is available in most standard media players such as Windows Media Player, VLC player, etc. Results indicated that slower speed has a positive effect on test performance but the percentage of speed adjustment (15% slower or 30% slower) did not make a difference to performance. Since a reduction of 20% has been defined as a maximum reduction in order to guarantee natural audio input (Buck, 2001; East & King, 2012), a speed adjustment of 15% may be preferable even if 30% might still be appropriate for pedagogical purposes (East & King, 2012).

6   Conceptualizing Listening Activities

In this section, we will look into the pedagogical implications of the research findings outlined above and discuss a number of research-based criteria that teachers and materials designers might want to consider when conceptualizing listening activities. We will also provide some practical information with regard to the creation and presentation of materials.

6.1   The Role of Lexical Coverage

One of the challenges that we are confronted with when selecting multimedia input for L2 learners is to determine beforehand whether the difficulty level of the material will be in accordance with the proficiency level of our students. Even though the use of other support tools such as subtitling or captioning can be considered, research has shown that the material (without support) must still meet the proficiency level of the learner as much as possible. In order to objectively evaluate the difficulty level of a clip, we can consider calculating the lexical coverage, or the percentage of words of a given input that a learner masters in some way, i.e., being able to recognize the meaning (Adolphs & Schmitt, 2003).

From a pedagogical perspective, the question of learners' lexical coverage is crucial since we want to make sure that the selected materials (whether audio or video) are in accordance with learners' vocabulary knowledge in order to allow them to have the vocabulary knowledge that is required for speech decoding and adequate understanding of the input. The question then is how much vocabulary we need in order to adequately understand different types of audio or audio-visual materials. This has been tackled in corpus-driven studies that have analyzed the vocabulary used in different types of materials in order to determine their lexical frequency profile.

With regard to the lexical coverage of television programs, Webb & Rodgers (2009) found that a vocabulary size of the 3,000 most frequent word families would be required to cover 95% of the vocabulary (excluding proper nouns) used in American television programs (e.g., *Friends*, *Will and Grace*, *The Sopranos*). This coverage percentage may be sufficient to adequately understand the input and to incidentally pick up new words while viewing TV programs. Depending on the contribution of imagery, comprehension or vocabulary learning may also take place with lower coverage percentages (cf. subsection 3.2).

Other studies have looked at the role of lexical coverage for understanding spoken input such as audio stories or spoken conversation: van Zeeland & Schmitt (2013) argued that a vocabulary size of 750 to 2,000 words might be sufficient to deal with authentic spoken input, which is in line with Schmitt, Gardner, & Davies (2017), who found that knowledge of the 1,500 most frequent words (dictionary form) can lead to a 95% coverage of spoken conversation. More information on how to calculate lexical coverage can be found in the Appendix.

6.2   Selection and Creation of Materials for L2 Listening

In an attempt to categorize a number of criteria that play a role in the selection of listening materials, we have outlined the main questions in Table 1.

In the remainder of this section, we will, albeit very briefly, discuss a number of more practical aspects that are related to the topics listed in Table 1 under "presentation of content."

(1) In this chapter, we have seen that the presence of on-screen text (keywords, subtitles or captions) has been linked to various listening benefits. While subtitles of movies or series can (at least for English) easily be found online, the majority of video or audio files do not come with this type of on-screen text. Luckily, there are numerous tools available online (SRT editors) that enable us to create subtitle files (i.e., files with .srt extension). SRT (SubRip) editors make it possible to upload the video excerpt that you want to subtitle and to create specific timestamps per subtitle (see Figure 3). This means that a beginning and end time should be specified per subtitle which defines the appearance and duration of the text on the screen. The subtitle can be a full subtitle, a caption, or only a keyword.

Each editor uses different keys to add beginning and end times (e.g., function keys) and this information is generally included in the manual that can be found on the website of the corresponding tool. An example of such

Table 1 Criteria for the selection of listening materials

Goal of the listening activity	What is the goal of the listening activity? Is this an activity that focuses on bottom-up processes, top-down processes, comprehension, or vocabulary learning? Is the activity used to learn to listen (practice setting) or to assess learners' listening (test setting)?
Characteristics of the audio	Is the speed of the input (speech rate) acceptable for the intended audience or are modifications needed? Does the input contain dialects, background noise, or other variables that could affect speech decoding and segmentation?
Characteristics of the visuals (if available)	Are there images available? Are the images supportive of comprehension? Do the images provide information that could clarify the meaning of difficult words, semantics, or content?
Topic	Will learners find the topic of the activity interesting and motivating? Is the topic authentic and relevant? Do learners need specific background knowledge with regard to the topic? Does topic knowledge need to be (re-)activated before the activity?
Lexical profile	What is the lexical frequency profile (e.g., high vs. low frequency words, technical vocabulary, academic vocabulary) of the materials and will the profile be in accordance with my students' vocabulary knowledge?
Presentation of the content	Will there be options to modify the input such as captions, subtitles, keywords, etc.? Can learners listen or view multiple times (repeated listening)? Do learners have control over the input presentation? For instance: Can learners choose to access support options or are these embedded in the materials? Can the speed of audio delivery be adapted? Are materials implemented in a learning platform and on which device will learners access the activities?
Instruction	Do learners need extra assistance or instruction in order to select help options or to deal with the media player control options (pause, forward, etc.)? Would pre-listening tasks (topic, vocabulary, strategies, previewing questions) be helpful?

an SRT editor can be found in Figure 3. Since these types of editors are freely available online and relatively user-friendly, we could also ask students to create and add the on-screen text themselves as part of a repeated or intensive listening activity.

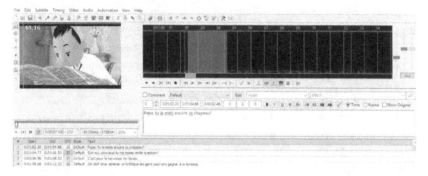

Figure 3 Example of the Aegisub SRT editor with video excerpt and timestamping (see Appendix).

Most of the SRT editors include standards with regard to subtitle presentation such as the maximum characters per subtitle (Díaz-Cintas & Remael, 2014) and specify what should be adapted in the subtitle in order to conform to good subtitling practice. Some tools also allow one to do some basic formatting such as highlighting words in the subtitle or adapting the font size of the text.

Subtitling files (.srt) can subsequently be uploaded with the corresponding video file in media players such as Windows Media Player, Quicktime, or VLC. Some tools, such as the freely available SRT editor "Aegisub," make it possible to "hardsub" the subtitles, which means that the subtitles are burnt in the file and should not be added to the media in other types of media players. The app store also offers tools that make it possible to merge video and SRT files in order to have the subtitles hardcoded.

(2) A different type of modification that may support learners' listening is to adapt the speed of audio delivery. As outlined above, most standard media players make it possible to modify the speed of delivery. This feature is also available on websites such as YouTube, where users can choose to slow down or increase the speech rate per 25%. When we use audio only, tools such as Audacity can be considered. The option to modify the speed of audio delivery is particularly useful for classroom practice since it gives the learners more time to process the spoken input and to understand the excerpt. Excerpts can be played several times with different amounts of speech reduction until the learners are able to process the audio at normal speech rate. Yet, it is possible that not all learners are familiar with these options which is why explicit instruction might be necessary in some contexts.

(3) Another question is related to the amount of control that we give learners when using media and support options. Early research into the use of help options for listening showed that effective and ineffective learners tended to use the same help options (English script, rewind button, and subtitles) but they used them differently (Liou, 1997). While the effective group used the captions most frequently, the ineffective group used the rewind option more frequently. This does, however, not entail that rewinding as such is not effective but rather that learners are not always able to identify help options that might be beneficial for them or for the activity that they need to complete.

Other studies found that learners often tend to ignore help options (e.g., Cárdenas-Claros & Gruba, 2014) or use them less frequently than expected (Grgurovic & Hegelheimer, 2007). This suggests that an important challenge lies in stimulating learners' use of help options, especially in contexts where learners have control over their choices. Teachers play a crucial role in informing learners about the potential benefits and drawbacks of help options. Teachers might also help students to distinguish between practice and test settings and show how specific help options may prepare learners for autonomous listening such as is the case in assessment contexts. Strategy instruction might also be used to have students recognize their listening problems and to help them look for effective strategies to overcome their shortcomings.

The use of support options (e.g., in environments in which learners have control over the activity) may also be triggered by the instructional design of the materials or the learning environment. Yet, few studies have actually investigated the instructional design of listening environments (see, for instance, Cárdenas-Claros & Gruba, 2013 on the role of participatory design methods in designing listening materials). An interesting example can be found in the study by Grgurovic & Hegelheimer (2007). In this study, students were redirected to a video with a help option when they could not answer the comprehension questions correctly. This kind of design does not only trigger learners' use of help options, it also shows them the benefits of activating support tools in terms of comprehension. Yet, more studies are needed in this area in order to clarify the role of instructional design in listening activities.

(4) A fourth aspect that concerns the presentation of the content is the device that will be used to realize the listening activities since the device may, to some extent, have consequences for the design of the materials. In a mobile learning context, for instance, the videos might need to be short and motivating since more distraction might be present in the environment. More difficult learning activities might be more suitable for electronic

learning environments on laptop or PC where a broader range of support tools might aid listeners during task completion (e.g., electronic dictionaries). In contexts where out-of-class exposure to listening or viewing is stimulated, a well-designed user interface as well as the possibility to combine mobile and electronic platforms seem crucial (Gobel & Kano, 2014). Yet, far more research is needed in order to uncover the role of different contexts and devices for technology-enhanced listening.

7   Conclusions and Directions for Future Research

Listening in technology-enhanced contexts can be realized in a variety of ways. As we have seen, different types of listening activities and materials can be considered for different learning goals. Below, we summarize the main findings that have been presented in this chapter.

- Bottom-up processes may be developed by using tools that allow for repeated or intensive listening or that allow one to slow down the speed of audio delivery. Another approach consists of combining written and auditory input modes (e.g., captioned video).
- Top-down processes can be activated through pre-listening tasks such as advance organizers or by using audio-visual input with supportive visuals. Strategy instruction could also be considered in order to help learners become more autonomous listeners.
- Techniques that stimulate top-down or bottom-up processes such as captions or advance organizers may also enhance L2 learners' comprehension.
- Numerous studies have found that listening stimulates incidental vocabulary learning and that this process can be boosted by adding support options that stimulate bottom-up or top-down processes such as L1 subtitles or other types of captions.
- It remains difficult to characterize the types of listening materials that are best used in technology-enhanced testing settings. Yet, preview of questions as well as imagery may be considered depending on the construct that needs to be measured.

While technology-enhanced approaches provide numerous ways to train and develop L2 listening, we also observed that the types of activities and materials studied in existing literature do not always capitalize on the increasing potential offered by technology. Therefore, we list below a number of avenues for future research in which technology can be used to enhance the listening experience as well as to enrich the types of data that can be collected in order to gain a clearer understanding of the product and process of listening.

- *Call for the use of real-time data collection techniques:* more research is needed on how learners deal with listening environments or activities and how they divide their attention over these aspects. Unobtrusive data collection methods such as eye-tracking could clarify how learners use listening activities in electronic or mobile environments and reveal when they need or do not need support options. Eye-tracking could also shed more light on how learners shift their attention between images, on-screen text, and exercises and how that affects performance.
- *Call for the use of learning analytics in order to provide adaptive listening activities:* only a few studies have tried to use technology as a means to automatically adapt materials such as captions in function of learners profiles. Taking into account the potential of learning analytics, future listening research in CALL-based contexts could investigate how materials and support options can be adapted in the function of specific learner profiles. Similarly, the use of learning analytics might clarify when and how learners use support options and when we would need to direct them to these options (e.g., when scores on comprehension items are insufficient, a support layer might need to be activated).
- *Call for more longitudinal studies:* So far, the majority of the studies can be qualified as single-treatment intervention studies in which the treatment phase is relatively short. While these studies provide us with very important information regarding the effectiveness of particular approaches, longitudinal research into listening in technology-enhanced contexts is necessary in order to study the development of listening processes and strategies over time and how learners' underlying listening processes may affect their performance. Learning analytics could be used to refine our understanding of learners' listening and viewing behavior and how individual differences affect behavior and performance. CALL environments are perfect research tools in that they make it possible to present larger numbers of listening activities and to gather enormous amounts of learning analytics over time in formal as well as informal learning contexts.

Questions for Reflection

1. After having read this chapter, if you were asked to create a listening activity for L2 learners, which aspect of listening would you focus on and which materials would you choose?
2. We have shown that successful listening is based on a combination of bottom-up and top-down processes. Reflect on how listening activities can be designed in order to strengthen both types of processes.
3. It has been argued that providing learners with on-screen text in order to stimulate speech decoding and segmentation is an effective technique. Could you think of contexts in which you would definitely use on-screen text and other contexts where you would not allow your students to use such a support option?
4. Would you be willing to prepare your learners for extensive listening or viewing programs and how would you try to motivate them to spend time listening or viewing in the target language outside the classroom?
5. How would you assess your students' listening in the foreign language? Would you use a technology-enhanced environment? Which factors would guide your decisions and which challenges would you have to deal with when designing listening tests?
6. Select a video excerpt in a language that you are familiar with but that is not your mother tongue. Watch the segment without on-screen text and evaluate your comprehension and the difficulties you encountered during the listening process. Next, watch the same excerpt or a similar excerpt with on-screen text in the target language (i.e., captions) and re-evaluate your comprehension and the difficulties you encountered. How would you compare your comprehension in both cases and how do you think the on-screen text did or did not help? How do the results compare to the results mentioned in this chapter?

Case Studies

Research

In this chapter, we have seen that listening is a complex skill that may cause a number of difficulties for L2 learners. In order to support learners, numerous studies have looked into the role of support options such as providing learners with control over the media player, adding on-screen text (in the L1, L2, in the form of keywords, etc.), or instructional interventions such as explicit strategy training. While these different types of support options have various benefits and may support listeners in a variety of ways, studies that have looked at learners' actual use have noticed that listeners often ignore support options or are unable to regulate their own listening by activating support when necessary. One way to deal with this problem could be to explicitly teach students how they can regulate their own listening and show them the different benefits of support options for listening. Yet, there is a lack of empirical research that has investigated the use of support options by L2 listeners and how instruction could help learners to engage in more effective listening training. This would, however, be a first important step towards more autonomous listening and independent out-of-class listening. In order to address this gap, this study will investigate the effectiveness of explicit instruction with regard to support option use in CALL-based listening.

- Design two conditions in which learners have access to a number of listening materials and different types of support options. Which materials would you use and which support options would you give the students access to? In one of the two conditions, students will be taught how to use support options during listening. The other condition will not receive guidance.
- How would you realize the instructional component with regard to help option use?
- Which techniques will you need to gain insight into learners' use of support options (e.g., screen capturing, logfiles, …)?
- In order to verify learners' understanding of the clip, we will also need comprehension tests. What will these tests look like?
- Discuss the pedagogical implications of this study and the potential consequences for the instructional design of listening environments.

Teaching

Diane teaches French as a foreign language to a group of 16-year-old English-speaking learners. Her students have had approximately 6 years of formal instruction (between 3 to 4 hours per week). Diane notices, however, that her students are still stressed and nervous every time they need to listen (for practice or in test settings). This is probably due to the fact that her learners are not regularly exposed to target language (i.e., French) listening situations outside the classroom. Therefore, she decides to work out specific activities that aim at developing learners' listening abilities and at decreasing their anxiety levels in listening situations. She designs an instructional intervention that consists in investing 1 hour per week in listening practice over a period of one semester (12 weeks). While preparing her activities, she decides that she needs to deal with this in a principled way. A systematic approach to teaching listening might help learners to understand the goals and objectives of the listening intervention. Therefore, she decides to create three different listening sequences that are based on a set of prototype activities. The aim of the first sequence is to develop learners' bottom-up processes and to stimulate automaticity at the level of word recognition and speech decoding. The second sequence aims at stimulating top-down processes in order to improve comprehension. The third sequence aims at helping learners become more autonomous and strategic listeners. Each of the three sequences lasts 1 hour and will be repeated four times throughout the semester. Every sequence will be based on new listening materials, which will be chosen in function of the objectives of the cycle (bottom-up, top-down, or strategy training).

Table 2 Operationalization of the sequences per week

Week 1	Week 2	Week 3	Week 4	Week 5	Week 6	...
Sequence 1	Sequence 2	Sequence 3	Sequence 1	Sequence 2	Sequence 3	...

1. Think of activities and materials that Diane can include in each of the three listening cycles. Use Table 1 (see subsection 6.2) in order to describe the materials that will be used, per cycle. Think about which instructional interventions are needed and which types of support options might be useful for the goals of the different pedagogical cycles.
2. Justify why the activities of each cycle were chosen and how they contribute to students' listening abilities.
3. How will Diane be able to help students become autonomous listeners who are able to regulate their listening process and who might eventually be motivated to engage in out-of-class listening or viewing?
4. Do you think that such an approach might have a beneficial effect on learners' perceptions towards listening as well as their (perceived) performance in authentic listening settings?
5. Would it be useful to consider some activities on mobile devices in this program and in which cycle would activities on mobile devices be most appropriate?

Ideas for Action Research Projects

1. Try out tools to calculate the lexical profile (see Appendix) of different types of transcripts such as movies and series which can be found online (the language should be English or French in order to be compatible with the software). Try to discuss the output of the lexical profile and compare the output with your lexical knowledge (www.lextutor.ca). For instance, what is the frequency profile of the words that are unknown to you? This kind of activity may clarify why vocabulary knowledge is a crucial component of listening as outlined in this chapter.

2. As an intensive viewing activity that focuses on bottom-up listening processes, students can use freely available subtitling tools to create and add the on-screen text of a foreign language video. At the same time, this will also be a repeated listening activity since students will have to listen multiple times in order to have the exact transcription of the sentence as well as to synchronize the caption with the soundtrack. What is the effect of such an approach on learners' listening process and the end product (the captioned video)? How do learners perceive the value of this activity?

3. Select a TV series in the foreign language that you are currently learning. Watch the first 8 to 10 episodes and evaluate whether the series has helped you to train your listening comprehension or to notice words or structures that you were not familiar with before encountering the items in the series. Write down your expectations in terms of learning gains before you start watching the series. Evaluate this approach after watching. Did the outcomes meet your expectations? Are there other linguistic benefits that you hadn't thought of before watching the series?

4. Survey learners on their use of audio/video in the foreign language you are teaching. Do they use such materials, in which contexts (in classroom or out-of-class use), how do they use them (with support, without, …) and for which purposes? What could be the implications of their use and attitudes for classroom-based listening?

Appendix

Tools to Create and Add Subtitles or Captions

There are numerous tools available to add on-screen text to images or videos. Tools to create subtitles are, for instance, http://www.aegisub.org/, http://subworkshop.sourceforge.net/, and SRT edit pro (available in the App store). Video editing software such as iMovie or Screenflow can also be considered.

Lexical Profile Analysis and Vocabulary Size Tests

In order to be able to analyze the lexical profile of English or French documents, we can use the Vocabprofile tool that is available on the Lextutor website: https://www.lextutor.ca/vp/ or the RANGE software (Nation & Heatley, 2002) for English documents: https://www.victoria.ac.nz/lals/resources/range.

In order to have a reliable estimate of learners' vocabulary size, different types of frequency-based tests are also available online (e.g., https://www.lextutor.ca/tests/ or http://www.lognostics.co.uk/tools). More information on how to use these tools or how to interpret their results can be found on the corresponding websites.

References

Adolphs, S., & Schmitt, N. (2003). Lexical coverage of spoken discourse. *Applied Linguistics*, 24(4), 425–438. https://doi.org/10.1093/applin/24.4.425; https://doi.org/10.1093/applin/24.4.425

Baltova, I. (1999). *The effect of subtitled and staged video input on the learning and retention of content and vocabulary in a second language.* Unpublished doctoral dissertation, University of Toronto.

Batty, A. O. (2015). A comparison of video- and audio-mediated listening tests with many-facet Rasch modeling and differential distractor functioning. *Language Testing*, 32(1), 3–20. https://doi.org/10.1177/0265532214531254

Bianchi, F., & Ciabattoni, T. (2008). Captions and subtitles in EFL learning: an investigative study in a comprehensive computer environment. In A. Baldry, M. Pavesi, C. Taylor Torsello, & C. Taylor (eds.), *From didactas to ecolingua: An ongoing research project on translation and corpus linguistics*, pp. 69–90. Trieste: Edizioni Università di Trieste.

Bird, S. A., & Williams, J. N. (2002). The effect of bimodal input on implicit and explicit memory: An investigation into the benefits of within-language subtitling. *Applied Psycholinguistics*, 23(4), 509–533. https://doi.org/10.1017/S0142716402004022

Bisson, M.-J., Van Heuven, W. J. B., Conklin, K., & Tunney, R. J. (2014). Processing of native and foreign language subtitles in films: An eye tracking study. *Applied Psycholinguistics*, 35, 399–418. https://doi.org/10.1017/S0142716412000434

Bozorgian, H., & Fakhri Alamdari, E. (2018). Multimedia listening comprehension: Metacognitive instruction or metacognitive instruction through dialogic interaction. *ReCALL*, 30(1), 131–152. https://doi.org/10.1017/S0958344016000240

Buck, G. (2001). *Assessing listening* (5th ed.). Cambridge: Cambridge University Press. https://doi.org/10.1017/CBO9780511732959

Çakmak, F., & Erçetin, G. (2017). Effects of gloss type on text recall and incidental vocabulary learning in mobile-assisted L2 listening. *ReCALL*, 1–24. https://doi.org/10.1017/S0958344017000155

Cárdenas-Claros, M. S., & Gruba, P. A. (2013). Decoding the "CoDe": A framework for conceptualizing and designing help options in computer-based second language listening. *ReCALL*, 25(2), 250–271. https://doi.org/10.1017/S0958344013000049

Cárdenas-Claros, M. S., & Gruba, P. A. (2014). Listeners' interactions with help options in CALL. *Computer Assisted Language Learning*, 27(3), 228–245. https://doi.org/10.1080/09588221.2012.724425

Chang, A. C.-S. (2012). Gains to L2 learners from extensive listening: Listening development, vocabulary acquisition and perceptions of the intervention. *Hong Kong Journal of Applied Linguistics*, 14(1), 25–47.

Chang, A. C.-S., & Millett, S. (2016). Developing L2 listening fluency through extended listening-focused activities in an extensive listening programme. *RELC Journal*, 47(3), 349–362. https://doi.org/10.1177/0033688216631175

Chang, A. C.-S., & Read, J. (2006). The effects of listening support on the listening performance of EFL learners. *TESOL Quarterly*, 40(2), 375. https://doi.org/10.2307/40264527

Chapelle, C. A. (2003). *English language learning and technology*. Amsterdam/ Philadelphia: John Benjamins Publishing Company. https://doi.org/10.1075/lllt.7

Chapelle, C. A. (2009). The relationship between second language acquisition theory and computer-assisted language learning. *The Modern Language Journal*, 93, 741–753. https://doi.org/10.1111/j.1540-4781.2009.00970.x

Charles, T. J., & Trenkic, D. (2015). Speech segmentation in a second language: The role of bi-modal input. In Y. Gambier, A. Caimi, C. Mariotti (eds.), *Subtitles and language learning: Principles, strategies, and practical experiences*, pp. 173–198. Bern: Peter Lang.

Chung, J. (2002). The effects of using two advance organizers. *Foreign Language Annals*, 35(2), 231–241.

Cross, J. (2009). Effects of listening strategy instruction on news videotext comprehension. *Language Teaching Research*, 13(2), 151–176. https://doi.org/10.1177/1362168809103446

Cross, J. (2011). Comprehending news videotexts: The influence of the visual content. *Language Learning & Technology*, 15(2), 44–68. Retrieved from http://llt.msu.edu/issues/june2011/cross.pdf

Cross, J. (2014). Promoting autonomous listening to podcasts: A case study. *Language Teaching Research*, 18(1), 8–32. https://doi.org/10.1177/1362168813505394

Danan, M. (2004). Captioning and subtitling: Undervalued language learning strategies. *META*, 49(1), 67–77. https://doi.org/10.7202/009021ar

Díaz-Cintas, J., & Remael, A. (2014). Audiovisual translation: Subtitling. Manchester: St. Jerome Pub.

d'Ydewalle, G., & Pavakanun, U. (1996). Le sous-titrage à la télévision facilite-t-il l'acquisition des langues? In Y. Gambier (ed.), *Les transferts linguistiques dans les médias audiovisuels*, pp. 217–223. Lille: Presses Universitaires du Septentrion.

d'Ydewalle, G., & Van de Poel, M. (1999). Incidental foreign-language acquisition by children watching subtitled television programs. *Journal of Psycholinguistic Research*, 28(3), 227–245. https://doi.org/10.1023/A:1023202130625

East, M., & King, C. (2012). L2 learners' engagement with high stakes listening tests: Does technology have a beneficial role to play? *CALICO Journal*, 29(2), 208–223. https://doi.org/10.11139/cj.29.2.208-223

Field, J. (2008). *Listening in the language classroom*. Cambridge: Cambridge University Press.

Frumuselu, A. D., De Maeyer, S., Donche, V., & Colon Plana, M. del M. G. (2015). Television series inside the EFL classroom: Bridging the gap between teaching and learning informal language through subtitles. *Linguistics and Education*, 32, 107–117. https://doi.org/10.1016/j.linged.2015.10.001

Gobel, P., & Kano, M. (2014). Implementing a year-long reading while listening program for Japanese university EFL students. *Computer Assisted Language Learning*, 27(4), 279–293. https://doi.org/10.1080/09588221.2013.864314

Goh, C. C. (2000). A cognitive perspective on language learners' listening comprehension problems. *System*, 28(1), 55–75. https://doi.org/10.1016/S0346-251X(99)00060-3

Goh, C. C. M. (2005). Second language listening expertise. In K. Johnson (ed.), *Expertise in second language learning and teaching*, pp. 64–84. Basingstoke: Palgrave Macmillan.

Graham, S. (2006). Listening comprehension: The learners' perspective. *System*, 34(2), 165–182. https://doi.org/10.1016/j.system.2005.11.001

Grgurovic, M., & Hegelheimer, V. (2007). Help options and multimedia listening: students' use of subtitles and the transcript. *Language Learning & Technology*, 11(1), 45–66.

Guichon, N., & McLornan, S. (2008). The effects of multimodality on L2 learners: Implications for CALL resource design. *System*, 36(1), 85–93. https://doi.org/10.1016/j.system.2007.11.005

Guillory, H. G. (1998). The effects of keyword captions to authentic French video on learner comprehension. *CALICO Journal*, 15(1–3), 89–108.

Hsu, C. K. (2015). Learning motivation and adaptive video caption filtering for EFL learners using handheld devices. *ReCALL*, 27(1), 84–103. https://doi.org/10.1017/S0958344014000214

Hsu, W. (2014). The effects of audiovisual support on EFL learners' productive vocabulary. *ReCALL*, 26(1), 62–79. https://doi.org/10.1017/S0958344013000220

Hulstijn, J. H. (2001). Intentional and incidental second language vocabulary learning: a reappraisal of elaboration, rehearsal and automaticity. In P. Robinson (ed.), *Cognition and second language instruction*, pp. 258–286. Cambridge: Cambridge University Press. https://doi.org/10.1017/CBO9781139524780.011

Hulstijn, J. H. (2003). Connectionist models of language processing and the training of listening skills with the aid of multimedia software. *Computer Assisted Language Learning*, 16(5), 413–425.
https://doi.org/10.1076/call.16.5.413.29488

Jones, L. C., & Plass, J. L. (2002). Supporting listening comprehension and vocabulary acquisition in French with multimedia annotations. *The Modern Language Journal*, 86(4), 546–561. https://doi.org/10.1111/1540-4781.00160

Koyama, D., Sun, A., & Ockey, G. J. (2016). The effects of item preview on video-based multiple-choice listening assessments. *Language Learning & Technology*, 20(1), 148–165. Retrieved from
http://llt.msu.edu/issues/february2016/koyamasunockey.pdf

Kress, G., & Van Leeuwen, T. (2001). *Multimodal discourse: The modes and media of contemporary communication*. London: Arnold.

Kruger, J. L., & Steyn, F. (2014). Subtitles and eye tracking: Reading and performance. *Reading Research Quarterly*, 49(1), 105–120.
https://doi.org/10.1002/rrq.59

Lindgren, E., & Muñoz, C. (2013). The influence of exposure, parents, and linguistic distance on young European learners' foreign language comprehension. *International Journal of Multilingualism*, 10(1), 105–129.
https://doi.org/10.1080/14790718.2012.679275

Liou, H. C. (1997). Research of on-line help as learner strategies for multimedia CALL evaluation. *CALICO Journal*, 14(2–4), 81–96.

Markham, P., & Peter, L. (2003). The influence of English language and Spanish language captions on foreign language listening/reading comprehension. *Journal of Educational Technology Systems*, 31(3), 331–341.
https://doi.org/10.2190/BHUH-420B-FE23-ALA0

Markham, P., Peter, L., & McCarthy, T. (2001). The effects of native language vs. target language captions on foreign language students' DVD video comprehension. *Foreign Language Annals*, 34(5), 439–445.
https://doi.org/10.1111/j.1944-9720.2001.tb02083.x

Martinez, R., & Schmitt, N. (2010). Invited commentary: Vocabulary. *Language Learning & Technology*, 14(2), 26–29.

Matthews, J. (2018). Vocabulary for listening: Emerging evidence for high and mid-frequency vocabulary knowledge. *System*, 72, 23–36.
https://doi.org/10.1016/j.system.2017.10.005

Matthews, J., Cheng, J., & O'Toole, J. M. (2014). Computer-mediated input, output and feedback in the development of L2 word recognition from speech. *ReCALL*, 27(3), 321–339. https://doi.org/10.1017/S0958344014000421

Mayer, Richard E. (ed.) (2005). *The Cambridge handbook of multimedia learning*. Cambridge: Cambridge University Press.
https://doi.org/10.1017/CBO9780511816819

McBride, K. (2011). The effect of rate of speech and distributed practice on the development of listening comprehension. *Computer Assisted Language Learning*, 24(2), 131–154. https://doi.org/10.1080/09588221.2010.528777

Mirzaei, Mm. S., Meshgi, K., Akita, Y., & Kawahara, T. (2017). Partial and synchronized captioning: A new tool to assist learners in developing second language listening skill. *ReCALL*, 29(March), 1–22.
https://doi.org/10.1017/S0958344017000039

Mitterer, H., & McQueen, J. M. (2009). Foreign subtitles help but native-language subtitles harm foreign speech perception. *PLOS One*, 4(11), e7785.
https://doi.org/10.1371/journal.pone.0007785

Montero Perez, M. (2017, April). *Incidental vocabulary learning from viewing: The role of vocabulary knowledge and working memory.* Paper presented at the TBLT conference, Barcelona.

Montero Perez, M., Peters, E., Clarebout, G., & Desmet, P. (2014). Effects of captioning on video comprehension and incidental vocabulary learning. *Language Learning & Technology*, 18, 118–141.

Montero Perez, M., Peters, E., & Desmet, P. (2014). Is less more? Effectiveness and perceived usefulness of keyword and full captioned video for L2 listening comprehension. *ReCALL*, 26, 21–43. https://doi.org/10.1017/S0958344013000256

Montero Perez, M., Peters, E., & Desmet, P. (2015). Enhancing vocabulary learning through captioned video: An eye-tracking study. *The Modern Language Journal*, 99, 308–328. https://doi.org/10.1111/modl.12215

Montero Perez, M., Peters, E., & Desmet, P. (2018). Vocabulary learning through viewing video: The effect of two enhancement techniques. *Computer Assisted Language Learning*, 31, 1–26.
https://doi.org/10.1080/09588221.2017.1375960

Montero Perez, M., Van Den Noortgate, W., & Desmet, P. (2013). Captioned video for L2 listening and vocabulary learning: A meta-analysis. *System*, 41, 720–739. https://doi.org/10.1016/j.system.2013.07.013

Muñoz, C. (2017). The role of age and proficiency in subtitle reading. An eye-tracking study. *System*, 67, 77–86. https://doi.org/10.1016/j.system.2017.04.015

Nation, I. S. P. (2001). *Learning vocabulary in another language.* Cambridge: Cambridge University Press.

Nation, I. S. P. (2007). The four strands. *Innovation in Language Learning and Teaching*, 1(1), 1–12. https://doi.org/10.2167/illt039.0

Nation, I. S. P., & Heatley, A. (2002). RANGE: A program for the analysis of vocabulary in texts [software]. Retrieved September 14, 2018, from
http://www.victoria.ac.nz/lals/staff/paul-nation/nation.aspx

Park, M. (2004). *The effects of partial captions on Korean EFL learners' listening comprehension.* Unpublished doctoral dissertation, University of Texas at Austin.

Paivio, A. (1986). *Mental representations: A dual coding approach.* New York: OUP.

Peters, E. (2018). The effect of out-of-class exposure to English language media on learners' vocabulary knowledge. *ITL International Journal of Applied Linguistics*, 169(1), 142–168. https://doi.org/10.1075/itl.00010.pet

Peters, E., Heynen, E., & Puimège, E. (2016). Learning vocabulary through audiovisual input: The differential effect of L1 subtitles and captions. *System*, 63, 134–148. https://doi.org/10.1016/j.system.2016.10.002

Peters, E., & Webb, S. (2018). Incidental vocabulary acquisition through view-ing L2 television and factors that affect learning. *Studies in Second Language Acquisition*, 40(3), 551–577. https://doi.org/10.1017/S0272263117000407

Plass, J. L., & Jones, L. C. (2005). Second language acquisition with multimedia. In R. E. Mayer (ed.), *The Cambridge handbook of multimedia learning*, pp. 476–488. New York: Cambridge University Press.

Renandya, W. A., & Farrell, T. S. C. (2011). "Teacher, the tape is too fast!" Extensive listening in ELT. *ELT Journal*, 65(1), 52–59. https://doi.org/10.1093/elt/ccq015

Robin, R. (2007). Commentary: Learner-based listening and technological authen-ticity. *Language Learning & Technology*, 11(1), 109–115.

Rodgers, M. P. H. (2013). *English language learning through viewing television: An investigation of comprehension, incidental vocabulary acquisition, lexical coverage, attitudes, and captions* (Unpublished doctoral dissertation). Victoria University, Wellington, New Zealand.

Rodgers, M. P. H. (2018). The images in television programs and the potential for learning unknown words: The relationship between on-screen imagery and vocabulary. *ITL International Journal of Applied Linguistics*, 169(1), 191–211. https://doi.org/10.1075/itl.00012.rod

Rodgers, M. P. H., & Webb, S. (2017). The effects of captions on EFL learners' comprehension of English-Language television programs. *CALICO Journal*, 34(1), 20–38. https://doi.org/10.1558/cj.29522

Rost, M. (2002). *Teaching and researching listening*. London: Pearson Education Limited.

Rost, M. (2006). Areas of research that influence L2 listening instruction. In E. Uso-Juan and A. Martinez-Flor (eds.), *Current trends in the development and teaching of the four language skills*. Berlin: Mouton de Gruyter.

Rost, M. (2014). Developing listening fluency in Asian EFL settings. In T. Muller, J. Adamson, P. Shigeo Brown, & S. Herder (eds.), *Exploring EFL fluency in Asia*, pp. 281–296. London: Palgrave Macmillan.

Roussel, S. (2011). A computer assisted method to track listening strategies in second language learning. *ReCALL*, 23(2), 98–116. https://doi.org/10.1017/S0958344011000036

Schmitt, N., Gardner, D., & Davies, M. (2017, March). *How many words does it take to listen and read in English?* Paper presented at the TESOL Conference, Seattle.

Sharwood Smith, M. (1993). Input enhancement in instructed SLA: Theoretical bases. *Studies in Second Language Acquisition*, 15, 165–179. https://doi.org/10.1017/S0272263100011943

Sydorenko, T. (2010). Modality of input and vocabulary acquisition. *Language Learning & Technology*, 14(2), 50–73.

Staehr, L. S. (2009). Vocabulary knowledge and advanced listening comprehension in English as a foreign language. *Studies in Second Language Acquisition*, 31, 577–607.

The Douglas Fir Group. (2016). A transdisciplinary framework for SLA in a multi-lingual world. *The Modern Language Journal*, 100, 19–47. https://doi.org/10.1111/modl.12301

van Zeeland, H., & Schmitt, N. (2013). Incidental vocabulary acquisition through L2 listening: A dimensions approach, *System*, 41(3), 609–624. https://doi.org/10.1016/j.system.2013.07.012

Vandergrift, L. (2003). Orchestrating strategy use: Toward a model of the skilled second language listener. *Language Learning*, 53, 463–496. https://doi.org/10.1111/1467-9922.00232

Vandergrift, L. (2004). Listening to learn or learning to listen? *Annual Review of Applied Linguistics*, 24(May), 3–25. https://doi.org/10.1017/S0267190504000017

Vandergrift, L. (2007). Recent developments in second and foreign language listening comprehension research. *Language Teaching*, 40(3), 191–210.

Vandergrift, L., & Goh, C. C. M. (2012). *Teaching and learning second language listening: Metacognition in action.* New York: Routledge.

Vandergrift, L., & Tafaghodtari, M. H. (2010). Teaching L2 learners how to listen does make a difference: An empirical study. *Language Learning*, 60(2), 470–497. https://doi.org/10.1111/j.1467-9922.2009.00559.x

Vanderplank, R. (1988). The value of teletext sub-titles in language learning. *English Language Teaching Journal*, 42(4), 272–281. https://doi.org/10.1093/elt/42.4.272

Vanderplank, R. (2010). Déjà vu? A decade of research on language laboratories, television and video in language learning. *Language Teaching*, 43(1), 1–37. https://doi.org/10.1017/S0261444809990267

Vanderplank, R. (2016). *Captioned media in foreign language learning: Subtitles for the deaf and hard-of-hearing as tools for language learning.* London: Palgrave Macmillan. https://doi.org/10.1057/978-1-137-50045-8

Wagner, E. (2007). Are they watching? Test-taker viewing behavior during an L2 video listening test. *Language Learning & Technology*, 11(1), 67–86.

Wagner, E. (2013). An investigation of how the channel of input and access to test questions affect L2 listening test performance. *Language Assessment Quarterly*, 10(2), 178–195. https://doi.org/10.1080/15434303.2013.769552

Webb, S. (2015). Extensive viewing: language learning through watching television. In D. Nunan and J. C. Richards (eds.), *Language learning beyond the classroom*, pp. 159–168. New York: Routledge.

Webb, S., & Chang, A. C.-S. (2015). How does prior word knowledge affect vocabulary learning progress in an extensive reading program? *Studies in Second Language Acquisition*, 37(4), 651–675. https://doi.org/10.1017/S0272263114000606

Webb, S., & Nation, I. S. P. (2017). *How vocabulary is learned.* Oxford: Oxford University Press.

Webb, S., & Rodgers, M. P. H. (2009). Vocabulary demands of television programs. *Language Learning*, 59(2), 335–366. https://doi.org/10.1111/j.1467-9922.2009.00509.x

Winke, P., Gass, S., & Sydorenko, T. (2010). The effects of captioning videos used for foreign language listening activities. *Language Learning & Technology*, 14(1), 65–86.

Winke, P., Gass, S., & Sydorenko, T. (2013). Factors influencing the use of captions by foreign language learners: An eye-tracking study. *The Modern Language Journal*, 97(1), 254–275. https://doi.org/10.1111/j.1540-4781.2013.01432.x

Yang, H.-Y. (2014). The effects of advance organizers and subtitles on EFL learners' listening comprehension skills. *CALICO Journal*, 31(3), 345–373. https://doi.org/10.11139/cj.31.3.345-373

Yeldham, M. (2016). Second language listening instruction: Comparing a strategies-based approach with an interactive, strategies/bottom-up skills approach. *TESOL Quarterly*, 50(2), 394–420. https://doi.org/10.1002/tesq.233

Yeldham, M. (2017). Viewing L2 captioned videos: What's in it for the listener? *Computer Assisted Language Learning*, 30(8), 864–883. https://doi.org/10.1080/09588221.2017.1406956

Yeldham, M., & Gruba, P. (2014). Toward an instructional approach to developing interactive second language listening. *Language Teaching Research*, 18(1), 33–53. https://doi.org/10.1177/1362168813505395

Zhao, Y. 1997. The effect of listeners' control of speech rate on second language comprehension. *Applied Linguistics*, 18, 49–68. https://doi.org/10.1093/applin/18.1. 49168

About the Author

Maribel Montero Perez is a postdoctoral researcher at KU Leuven (imec ITEC research group). She has been primarily interested in the role of technology-enhanced interventions for stimulating L2 listening and vocabulary acquisition (such as video with different types of subtitling). Her research has been published in *a.o.*, *Language Learning & Technology*, *The Modern Language Journal*, and *Computer Assisted Language Learning*.

5   CALL and L2 Reading: Current Research and Application

Alan Taylor

Preview Questions

1. What types of texts do you normally read in another language?
2. What are some reading strategies you use to facilitate the reading process?
3. Do you ever read L2 texts online? What resources are you aware of that can be used for reading an L2 text online? Which ones have been the most effective for you?
4. What are some effective smartphone apps for L2 online or hard-copy reading?
5. When reading an L2 text online, are L1 translations usually help-ful? How?
6. Have you ever used Google Docs or another online sharing resource for collaborative reading? If so, what was effective and what was not?

1   Introduction

Since we live in the information age, computers and electronic devices have become, for better or worse, an integral part of our lives (Carr, 2008; 2010; Ducate & Arnold, 2011). Reading, including reading in the L2, is often asso-ciated with technology, which can help us find information about a topic or answer a question. Although printed texts may sometimes be better for overall comprehension for some students (e.g., Singer & Alexander, 2017), the freedom and convenience of the Internet and the ease with which one can acquire a device to access it make CALL reading a very pertinent issue in educational contexts. The ACTFL World Readiness Standard 1.2 states that "Learners understand, interpret, and analyze what is heard, read, or viewed on a variety of topics." (Cutshall, 2012: 35). The Internet, which contains a variety of texts of varying difficulty, is a viable venue for increasing L2 input for intensive as well as extensive reading. This chapter focuses on recent research on interventions to improve CALL L2 reading, including factors associated with success and failure in comprehension. It assesses how research justifies some of the more common ways of facilitating L2 reading in CALL and provides ideas and action research toward improving CALL L2 reading pedagogy.

The debate about CALL's role in L2 learning has shifted from whether CALL resources are helpful, to discussing the extent to which CALL is beneficial in L2 learning generally, including L2 reading (e.g., Plonsky and Ziegler, 2016). CALL reading not only provides L2 input, but also improves students' ability to use technology, which in turn gives them access to more input and, of course, to additional languages (Chun, 2011). In the literature review below, we will discuss the benefits of CALL resources for L2 reading comprehension and vocabulary learning.

2   The Process of L2 Reading

L2 learning success depends to a certain degree on L2 reading competency. Gettys, Imhof, & Kautz noted: "Reading in a second language is an important skill acquired by students in the course of second language study. Apart from being one of the goals of foreign language instruction, reading is also a powerful means of instruction" (2001: 98). Regardless of whether or not reading is done in large quantities, it is an important receptive skill that enhances L2 learning because it provides a potentially rich linguistic environment, exposing the L2 reader to much L2 input (Youngs, Ducate, & Arnold, 2011).

Neil Anderson suggests that L2 reading is:

> An active, fluent process which involves the reader and the reading material in building meaning. Meaning does not reside on the printed page, nor is it only in the head of the reader. A synergy occurs in reading which combines the words on the printed page with the reader's background knowledge and experiences. Readers move through the printed text with specific purposes in mind to accomplish specific goals. (1999: 1)

Reading on the Internet is essentially reading with a purpose since the reader is usually looking for information, reading the news, or completing a school or work assignment. CALL tools such as glosses and embedded links with background knowledge can all help with the fluency of the reading process. If too much time is used to attempt to read online in the L2, reading can become laborious and the ability to maintain concentration becomes more difficult.

There are different ways of supporting the often difficult task of processing L2 text, namely top-down and bottom-up. Top-down refers to support such as activating background knowledge before and during reading. Top-down strategy is supported by Schema Theory, which claims that readers bring past individual experience and understanding (i.e., "schemata") to understand ideas. L2 teaching based on Schema Theory claims that it is easier to understand a text, whether in the L1 or L2, if a certain amount of background knowledge is provided or activated (for a classic article, see Carrell, 1984). An L2 reader activates background knowledge by thinking about (or being prompted to think about) prior knowledge right before reading an L2 text (see Lee & Vanpatten, 1995; Thompson & Phillips, 2009). Thus, information in short-term memory can often facilitate L2 reading because it is more readily accessible, since the information is new and likely more ready to use. When used in combination with information from long-term memory, better comprehension can occur. Indeed, some research suggests that working memory is more predictable for L2 reading comprehension when readers have more background knowledge of an L2 text (Joh & Plakans, 2017). Working memory, which used to be referred to as short-term memory, refers to the cognitive resources that store smaller amounts of information for short amounts of time with relatively little processing (Cohen, 2008). In other words, more knowledge generally equates to more comprehension because it is easier to relate new information acquired in L2 reading to already acquired knowledge that is similar. Such findings suggest that when background knowledge is activated and/or when additional information is provided in pre-reading activities, L2 reading comprehension is enhanced.

On the other hand, bottom-up supports are language-based and help the reader decode the text. Bottom-up support could mean the teacher or author provides translations in the margin of an L2 text, or a lesson could assist the L2 student in learning key vocabulary words or verb conjugations before reading. Bottom-up support via glossing, for example, is a much more traditional way of facilitating L2 reading than top-down support (Taylor, 2002), although both top-down and bottom-up support play important roles in facilitating L2 reading comprehension and are part of interactive approaches to teaching L2 reading (Redondo, 1997). Interactive approaches claim that language and background knowledge interact and because of this, the L2 reader can construct meaning from text (Anderson, 1999; Bernhardt, 1991;

Redondo, 1997) and compensate for lack of knowledge whether top-down or bottom up (Bernhardt, 2005).

Dual coding theory also informs reading comprehension and describes how learners may use at least two different means of processing information into memory, namely language (auditory or written) and nonverbal (imagery, smells, or tastes) channels. Mayer's descriptions of dual coding (1997) involve a series of computer-based studies demonstrating how verbal (both heard and written) and visual aids (videos or pictures) can be more effective when integrated towards completing meaningful tasks. Mayer concluded that especially "the visual-based power of computer technology represents a grossly underutilized source of potential education innovation" (1997: 17) and demonstrated how more than one mode of presentation in a multimedia environment greatly enhanced learning. With regard to CALL reading comprehension, combining pictures with text and auditory glossing can increase L2 reading comprehension (e.g., Lomicka 1998; Salem, 2006). Both can influence L2 reading and can be used to acquire information whether used separately or interactively (Steffensen, Geotz and Cheng, 1999) and may be most effective when used together. For example, L1 textual glosses with pictures and/or video may even be more effective in L2 reading comprehension than they are when used alone (Yanguas, 2009) and in L2 vocabulary learning studies while reading (e.g., Kost, Foss, & Lenzini, 1999).

In addition to background knowledge and linguistic factors, the difficulty of a text in relation to a reader's proficiency level also plays a role in comprehension. Indeed, the match between the readers' proficiency and the difficulty of the text is one of the most important moderating variables in the L2 reading process. If the L2 text is too difficult and the student needs to look up many words, the fluency of reading can be interrupted. Joyce (1997) illustrated this phenomenon, demonstrating that when providing L1 glosses to L2 readers of beginning and intermediate levels, the more advanced-level learners with no glossing actually had higher scores than those with glossing. Thus, glossing *can actually get in the way of reading* at more advanced levels, even for L1 glossing. In general, for intensive reading (as opposed to pleasure reading, also called extensive reading), it is common to have a text that is at least slightly difficult for the L2 learner in order to provide new vocabulary and grammar to the learner so that new words and grammatical structures can be learned (e.g., Thompson and Phillips, 2009). Another factor in L2 reading is the L1-L2 relationship. For example, an English-speaking student reading in French may have the benefit of seeing cognates (i.e., words that look similar in another language and have similar meaning to the L1 word equivalent). However, an L1 English-speaker reading Chinese may not have that benefit, so identifying cognates is not a productive reading strategy for that student. In general, lexical assistance such as glossing may be more effective for reading an online L2 text that is similar to the L1 (Taylor, 2002) although this is not always the case (e.g., AbuSeileek, 2011).

3 The Process of Online/Tech-Mediated Reading

Online reading has obvious significant benefits. First, the CALL reader can access many authentic L2 texts within seconds so extensive reading can occur much more easily online (Arnold, 2009). Accessing more L2 texts can be very helpful since the learner can find and easily discard L2 texts without any pressure of time limits or type of text selected that may exist in the L2 classroom. In addition, the L2 reader can look at L2 texts holistically before looking at the details. For example, an English-speaking learner of French can watch videos, and look up key words, titles, and any known L2 vocabulary more easily while consulting a French news website. However, the additional media on a website can also have a distracting effect on the L2 reader depending on how well it is connected to the topics of the text.

Second, the L2 teacher, if not the L2 reader, can easily use online tools to determine which text fits the reader's level (see Resources at the end of this chapter for details). This is very important since a well-chosen text can mean the difference between successful and limited text comprehension. Third, the online L2 reader has access to many apps (i.e., Google Translate) and resources in order to not only determine which text to read, but also to reduce working memory. For example, there is now an AI- (Artificial Intelligence) powered translator by Microsoft called Microsoft Translator Text API (see Resources), which may be able to translate L2 text with human parity (Perez, 2018). This may assist working memory because students would spend less time guessing meaning of text and trying to relate it to their own linguistic and background knowledge because they would have access to more L2 vocabulary and would thus depend less on previously acquired knowledge. Thus, students can think more about concepts in the L2 text and less about word meaning. Such resources can generally guide students in preparing to read in the L2 or provide assistance during reading to facilitate vocabulary learning and reading comprehension (see Abraham, 2008).

On the other hand, there may be some negative aspects to technology. Singer & Alexander (2017), for example, found that, although learners prefer reading online in their L1, they actually remember details better with print texts, a finding contrary to the L1 readers' own beliefs. Mangen,

Walgermo, & Brønnick (2013) and Kerr & Symons (2006) reported similar results. Furthermore, online L2 reading can be distracting. Videos, pictures, sensationalized texts, ads, etc., are all competing for clicks and views. Similarly, some research has observed that online readers change activities while reading on a digital device every 3 minutes in order to check email or text (Liu et al., 2009). Thus, even when an L1 or L2 reader finds a text to read, the ability to concentrate can be diminished because of the power of online distractions (e.g., Carr, 2008). Even potential tools and resources, such as glossing or reading strategy training, can be less effective because they are sometimes distracting themselves (e.g., Joyce, 1997; Taylor, 2010) and because they may compete with other online interferences (Liu et al., 2009). Of course, to be fair, some CALL resources can minimize distraction as well, which will be discussed more below.

4   How Technology Can Support L2 Readers

L2 readers have several challenges while reading in general. First, the ability to use L2 reading supports with as little distraction as possible is very important. For example, a text with a pop-up translation can be much less distracting than a printed text with many translations in the margin or on the bottom of the page. CALL resources have been shown to be less distracting than paper-based supports (e.g., Taylor, 2006, 2009, 2013). Second, in order to read accurately, L2 learners generally need lexical support, especially at the beginning level (Taylor, 2002). Apps and online dictionaries can provide limitless lexical support. Third, L2 readers need training on how to read L2 texts. Such training can be provided in CALL with videos, pictures and virtual reality games. While the above resources do not mean that CALL is always effective, there are many apps and programs that can be used to enhance L2 reading comprehension and vocabulary learning that should generally be considered helpful.

Technology can support L2 readers with resources such as glossing, strategy training, support for digital social reading (collaborative reading), and digital annotation tools, among other things. For example, there are L2 learning apps that contain spoken L2 texts with explanations or translations which can enhance L2 reading. They can also help true beginners with the phonetic decoding of an L2 text (see Resources). Online dictionaries such as Google Translate, Word Reference and Larousse offer similar support. The following subsections describe in more detail how these CALL resources can be employed to support reading in the L2.

4.1   Glossing

One way to promote reading comprehension is through adjunct aids, which are sometimes called glosses or glossing. Glossing refers to extra information that accompanies a text to assist in understanding words or phrases. The most common type of glosses focus on vocabulary, since it is not easy to infer a word from context unless at least 95% of the text is already understood by the reader (e.g., Laufer, 1996; Laufer & Ravenhorst-Kalovski, 2010; Nation, 2006). To get to this point of comprehension, the L2 reader needs to have a fairly large vocabulary (about 5,000 words) to be able to read most daily texts such as newspapers, magazines, menus, and subtitles on the news (Laufer, 1996).

Through its lexical or grammar content, glossing provides bottom-up support, which allows the L2 reader to use more top-down processes and focus more on textual inferencing and interpretation. If the L2 reader knows most, if not all the words in a text, he or she can focus on other textual aspects such as grammar, context, and author intent, and metacognitively regulate his or her own thinking while reading the text. For example, he or she can reflect upon whether meaning is understood and perhaps reread an earlier portion of the text. Glossing also provides the most basic part of reading comprehension, that is, direct language-oriented information about the L2 itself. Knowing the L2, or at least more about the L2, is almost always helpful to the L2 reader. If the L2 reader has a large vocabulary, however, then bottom-up support becomes irrelevant and perhaps even distracting (Joyce, 1997). So how can CALL glossing be effective? Assuming the text is at an appropriate level for the L2 reader, glossing can help the L2 reader with gaps in knowledge (see Schmidt & Frota, 1986). Thus, when L2 readers are aware of their need of lexical support, they can use CALL glossing to look up an item (i.e., fill in a gap in knowledge) in a timely manner and continue the reading process with as little interruption as possible.

Usually, glossing is most effective when there is not too much or too little glossing. Selecting an L2 text with at least 90% lexical coverage (i.e., 90% of the words are familiar to the reader) and then making use of various CALL glossing resources would be effective since most studies have shown the effectiveness of CALL glossing for 10% glossing or less (Taylor, 2018). In many CALL glossing studies, about 3–5% of the text is glossed, usually in the L1 (e.g., Yanguas, 2009) although some studies have more glossing (e.g., Abraham, 2007; Hayden, 1997; Lomicka, 1998). If there is more, it is usually a dictionary-type gloss (e.g., Plass et al., 2003; Stoehr, 1999; Youngs, 1994). CALL glossing in the L2 can also be effective for L2 readers with more experience with L2 learning (e.g., AbuSeileek, 2011; Stoehr,

1999). Overall, however, L2 glossing has generally been shown to be less effective than CALL L1 glossing (e.g., Taylor, 2009).

Some non-CALL (e.g., Baumann, 1994; Joyce, 1997) and CALL studies (e.g., Chen & Yen, 2013; Coriano Velásquez, 2001; Lomicka, 1998; Plass et al., 2003; Youngs, 1994) have shown a negative effect for glossing, and other studies have shown positive effects of CALL glossing on L2 reading comprehension (e.g., Abraham, 2007; Aweiss, 1994; Goyette, 1995; Hayden, 1997; Knight, 1994; Salem, 2006; Stoehr, 1999; Yanguas, 2009). So what is the overall effect of CALL glossing? Meta-analyses (quantitative syntheses of multiple experimental studies) have shown large effect sizes for the effects of CALL glossing on vocabulary acquisition (e.g., Abraham, 2008; Yun, 2011) as well as reading comprehension (Plonsky & Ziegler, 2016; Stoehr, 1999; Taylor, 2002, 2006, 2009, 2013; Yanguas, 2009). Plonsky and Ziegler's meta-analysis (2016), for example, showed that about 84% of learners with CALL glosses performed (and should perform in the future) better on tests of reading comprehension than those without CALL glosses. This means that not only is glossing generally effective in CALL or non-CALL form (e.g., Taylor, 2002) – it is especially effective in CALL form (Taylor, 2014b). Further, more available glossing does not always result in more comprehension; other variables may be more important, such as learner and text level and whether the glossing is CALL or not (Taylor, 2014b).

There are many different types of CALL glosses, which are summarized in Table 1.

With regard to the medium of glosses, visual glossing such as video or pictorial glossing is often effective along with textual glossing (Abraham, 2007; Hayden, 1997; Salem, 2006; Taylor, 2018). For beginning L2 readers, textual glosses are generally more appropriate than visuals, unless the learner has limited L1 reading proficiency (in which case visual glosses could be useful). However, both are often even better when used together (e.g., Abraham, 2007; Hayden, 1997; Salem, 2006; Taylor, 2018; Yanguas, 2009) perhaps because of dual coding theory mentioned above.

Table 1 Types of CALL glosses

Medium	Content	Presentation	Language
Text	Vocabulary	Pop-up	Target Language
Video	Grammar	Embedded	L1
Pictures	Culture	Link to external content	
		Margin	

The content of glossing can also make a difference in its effectiveness (e.g., Plass et al., 2003). Usually, glosses are lexical (vocabulary words) in nature, which has proven to be effective. Studies utilizing cultural and grammatical glossing have not always shown significant results (Coriano Velàzquez, 2001; Plass et al., 2003; Youngs, 1994).

The presentation of glossing can also be important because if the L2 reader has to move his or her eyes too much, the fluency of reading can be hindered. AbuSeileek (2008, 2011) compared the effects of CALL glosses on L2 reading comprehension and found that the CALL glossing which was closest in proximity to the glossed item produced the best L2 reading comprehension. Interruption of the reading process is an important consideration, since studies show that eye movement is likely a key component in the effectiveness of CALL glossing and in glossing in general (AbuSeileek, 2008, 2011). For example, it is quite probable that marginal glossing is better than glossing at the bottom of a text and especially at the end of a text on another page because of the amount of time it takes for the L2 reader to find the gloss and then get back to the L2 reading. Further, placement is important along with the number of items in the gloss itself. For example, AbuSeileek (2011) found that about four words per gloss was optimum for L2 reading comprehension. In other words, if there are seven words in the gloss, it actually may be as ineffective as only one or two. It is possible that the more time it takes to get meaning from a text, the more interrupted the reading process becomes. L2 reading can even be interrupted by the mere presence of a gloss, if the learner level is too high for the text, since the glossed items become more distracting than helpful because the L2 reader may already have a large vocabulary, or at least large enough to read the text effectively. Of course, for glossing to be effective in every case, the conditions have to optimal. Generally, at the first two years of L2 learning, glossing assistance should help most learners in some way because extra information about the text is provided (Taylor, 2002, 2006).

As mentioned above, the language of the gloss can also have an effect on L2 reading comprehension. For example, L2 readers will generally select L1 textual glosses over L2 glosses in CALL contexts (e.g., Abraham, 2007; Bell & LeBlanc, 2000; Hayden, 1997). CALL textual glossing is usually most effective in the L1, especially for beginning-level L2 readers (e.g., Aweiss, 1994; Bowles, 2004; Guidi, 2009; Taylor, 2018) and L1 glossing can be very effective for intermediate learners (e.g., Abraham, 2007, 2008; Salem, 2006; Taylor, 2002; Yanguas, 2009).

While the above examples of CALL glosses can usually only be incorporated into programs designed for specific texts, there are also more accessible tools for L2 learners when reading any online text. One tool is Google

Translate, a fairly effective app available for download. When viewing a website in Chrome, the L2 reader can right-click on any word to access its dictionary definition. Another resource that may even be more effective for L2 reading is augmented reality with a smartphone with the Google Translate app. Once the app is opened, the camera icon can be selected, and the L2 reader can hold the camera up to a French text, whether online or in print, and obtain a fairly accurate sentence-level translation in English. The app can be programmed for the language, so the L2 and the L1 can be identified, or there is a "detect language" function that can be useful in multilingual contexts. Such resources are very common (and often free) and may be used by anyone with a computer or handheld device.

There are some short-term effects of CALL glossing that seem obvious but merit some mention. CALL glossing provides individualized support for L2 readers and reduces the need for a teacher to assist the L2 reader since it provides immediate to near-immediate feedback. Further, the fluency of CALL reading can be improved with the student feeling a sense of accomplishment. In the short term, general (L1, L2, pictures, videos, etc.) CALL glossing (Abraham, 2008) and especially CALL L1 textual glossing (Taylor, 2006, 2009, 2013) have repeatedly been shown to improve L2 reading comprehension. Other studies have shown otherwise, but they are much fewer and have less robust results (e.g., Coriano Velàzquez, 2001; Youngs, 1994).

Although the long-term research on CALL glossing in L2 reading comprehension is somewhat limited, CALL glossing is very effective in enhancing L2 vocabulary learning, whether short- or long-term. Abraham (2008) observed a large average effect size (1.40) for the general effects of glossing (most studies included various types of glossing with a CALL program) on L2 vocabulary learning, which means that approximately 89% of students with general CALL glossing of various types performed higher on immediate vocabulary tests than those without CALL glossing. An effect size of 1.25 was found for the delayed vocabulary post-test, which means that 87% of L2 readers with CALL glossing performed higher on delayed vocabulary tests than those without CALL glossing. This finding suggests that CALL glossing is very conducive to L2 vocabulary learning, which in turn likely improves future reading comprehension. If the teacher would like to provide the glosses in a CALL text, there are online resources to do so, such as Glossmaker.

4.2 Sociocultural Ways to Improve CALL Reading

Besides glossing, another way to approach CALL reading is from a socio-cultural theory (SCT) perspective. SCT claims that human learning can be assisted by interacting with others and that through the mediation of an instructor or classmate, learners can construct meaning from a text, with the final goal of becoming more independent in L2 reading (Thomas & Poole, 2017).

CALL resources that enable human interaction online can provide a plat-form for such mediation. For example, a digital annotation tool (DAT) such as eComma, can be used collaboratively for annotating (markup, highlight, write on) L2 text. Students can use this digital social reading platform to ask their peers for lexical assistance. eComma can also enable students to "co-construct meaning and scaffold their learning while [being] engaged in close readings of ... texts outside of the physical classroom" (Thomas & Poole, 2017: 38) which gives them the capacity to help each other with dif-ferent perspectives, hypotheses to test, and vocabulary and grammar (ibid.).

Collaborative CALL reading quite often also leads to higher-order think-ing (thinking about the intent/deeper meaning of the text rather than simply decoding the text) and analysis (Thomas & Poole, 2017). A study on digital social reading (ibid.) used a DAT called Hylighter with 18 Spanish-learners to allow them to comment on, write on, and highlight poems. The research-ers found that most comments were not about the language, but more about literary issues such as interpretations of the poems and furthering other stu-dents' thoughts about the poems, which suggests that students were able to more deeply process the text with help from their classmates and the DAT they used.

Interactive and "shadow reading" (reading quietly along with a partner) in non-CALL studies have been shown to positively affect recall, advanced processing, and the use of reading strategies (Commander & Guerrero, 2013; Turnbull & Evans, 2017). Such strategies could easily be incorpo-rated into a CALL environment in which students discuss texts via Google Chat, Google Docs, Skype, or FaceTime, or via the DATs mentioned above.

Besides DATs, online sociocultural learning can be helpful in integrating vocabulary and learning strategies into the L2 learner's developing system. For example, digital game-based learning (DGBL) can potentially facili-tate deeper L2 learning. DGBLs can teach culture, vocabulary, and reading to students via interactive fiction (IF) games in which the students adopt the role of an exchange student in another country, for example. Students involved in IF games may be more able to abstract their knowledge of learned vocabulary for writing assignments (Neville, Shelton, & McInnis, 2009).

In sum, SCT tasks may assist CALL reading comprehension to some degree, especially with a greater capacity to remember L2 text and especially to remember deeper meaning about texts. More research should be conducted on how collaborative learning can facilitate CALL reading, as the body of experimental quantitative research is still quite sparse.

4.3   Reading Strategy Training

Reading strategies are essentially actions taken to achieve certain reading goals. L2 strategy training, in other words the training L2 learners take to engage in certain actions before, after, or during L2 reading to facilitate comprehension, has been generally shown to be effective in L2 learning (e.g., Plonsky, 2011; Taylor, Stevens, & Asher, 2006). However, CALL reading strategy training is an area of CALL research that has much untapped potential although some interesting studies have been conducted.

Reading strategies are often classified into cognitive and metacognitive strategies. Cognitive strategies are those that are used to help the student think while reading a text and metacognitive strategies are those used to help students plan how they will strategically read a text (Anderson, 1999) and help them to monitor their comprehension as they are reading. As examples, but not necessarily recommendations for all reading situations, some cognitive strategies that could be used in CALL reading include the following ideas:

1. Look at pictures accompanying an online text as well as the title and make predictions about the content of a passage.
2. Identify the main idea and conduct a web search on it.
3. Look for cognates in the L2 online text and highlight them.
4. Guess the meaning of vocabulary words in online reading individually or with other students either in a real classroom or via a digital annotation tool (DAT).
5. Use a DAT with highlighting colors to identify themes in a text.
6. Look up the most difficult and relevant words with Google Translate or an online dictionary for print or digital text.
7. Synchronously or asynchronously type a short summary of a text in a Word document and share it in a DAT.
8. Use a DAT to make a mind map of how ideas relate to each other (see "Resources" for specific online mind-mapping tools).

Some metacognitive CALL strategies could include the following activities:

1. Via a DAT, ask other students how they came to certain conclusions about the meaning of a text.
2. Plan online which part of an online text to read first and, especially, how to decide which words to guess or look up.
3. In a DGBL (digital game-based learning) environment, observe what others have done to successfully understand L2 texts and plan the use of similar strategies.
4. For better L2 text comprehension and retention with a DAT, restate in your own words what the text means so others can see.
5. Through a DAT, ask clarifying questions about the text.
6. Write or record a video about a reaction to a text via a DAT.

Of course, many other strategies besides those listed above exist (see Anderson, 1999).

Is strategy training effective? The answer is generally, yes – in paper-based (Taylor, Stevens, & Asher, 2006) as well as in CALL contexts. For example, Liu, Chen, and Chang (2010) showed that the cognitive strategy of CALL concept mapping was especially beneficial in facilitating reading comprehension of weak readers. Culver (1991) also found that after students completed a Reading Mastery Program focused on various reading strategies, most of them increased their reading speed and improved by over one grade level in reading and four grade levels in vocabulary learning.

Since glossing is such a large part of the literature on CALL L2 reading, we could ask whether reading strategies are generally more effective than glossing. To find out, Taylor's (2014a) meta-analysis comparing reading strategy studies with L1 glossing studies found that both are effective, albeit with strategy training slightly less so. This is not to say, however, that strategies are not important; they can be very helpful in facilitating L2 reading comprehension. Very likely, in CALL glossing studies, some reading strategies are being used by the L2 readers either consciously or unconsciously because it is almost impossible to read in an L1 or L2 without at least some strategies. For example, the decision to read the title before the text and to reflect on it is a reading strategy that may often be undertaken unconsciously. Skipping to the end of an online text to see the conclusion after reading the first paragraph is another common strategy that could be used either consciously or unconsciously. In sum, strategy training definitely has a role to play in L2 reading comprehension.

5   Assessing Reading Comprehension

Assessing reading comprehension is an essential curricular component to the reading process. One way to test L2 reading comprehension is recall protocol: after reading an L2 text, students write a complete, detailed summary in the L1 or L2 without looking at the text. The recall is then scored based on a list of central ideas. A big advantage of the recall protocol is that no test-taking (i.e., guessing, deduction, etc.) skills can be applied and there can be no bias from the test maker (Bernhardt, 1991). The weakness of the recall protocol is that it could be perceived and used as more of a memory exercise rather than an analytical sample of what was understood.

Studies assessing reading along with vocabulary acquisition have also used receptive instruments, including multiple-choice tests (e.g., Ko, 1995; Kwong-Hung, 1995). In general, both receptive and productive tests can reliably test L2 reading comprehension with good validity. However, in general, each test, because it examines comprehension in a different way, will sometimes produce different results (Wolf, 1993; Youngs, 1994)). Therefore, "a variety of test items should be used" to test L2 vocabulary and reading comprehension (Chun, 2011: 160). In an ideal world, in order to more accurately test reading comprehension, having students take several types of tests would be best in order to obtain more accurate results. This is not always feasible, however, so tests (especially multiple-choice tests) should be constructed with enough items to accurately test L2 reading comprehension (e.g., Youngs, 1994). Such CALL testing can easily be conducted within online learning management systems (LMS) platforms such as Brightspace, Blackboard, Brainhoney, or Canvas. The advantage of LMS is that set-up is easy and multiple-choice, true-false, and open-ended questions can be scored automatically, and time limits can be set. Further, LMS can be used to provide practice L2 reading comprehension tests, which help the L2 student be more at ease with the CALL testing environment and essentially provide pedagogical feedback to the student of progress made in L2 reading.

6   Pedagogical Implications

This section summarizes the most basic pedagogical implications and conclusions suggested by the results of the current CALL research on facilitating L2 reading comprehension.

6.1   CALL Glossing

CALL glossing can be effective if the teacher can determine which gloss-ing is needed in a text, anticipate the items, construct a vocabulary quiz, administer it to the students, and then decide/confirm which items to gloss in a text. Also, a readability analyzer for ESL or EFL course can be used. CALL glosses should always be used with the goal of the reading activity in mind. The L2 instructor should ask him- or herself: "Why do I want to pro-vide glosses with the text?" to be sure that L1 or L2 glossing is essential to the L2 curriculum or to the goals of the task. A teacher may want to conduct an activity for training students on how to guess meaning from context, for example, instead of relying on glossing (Taylor, 2002).

While there has not yet been substantial research on mobile devices and L2 reading comprehension, they can provide glossing support for L2 read-ing comprehension and should improve L2 reading comprehension. For example, a smart phone with Google augmented reality used on paper or CALL texts should have a similar effect on L2 reading as has been shown in meta-analytic results that have demonstrated that most learners with CALL glossing will comprehend more text than those without CALL glossing (e.g., Taylor, 2013). It should be mentioned, however, that advanced lan-guage learners should not necessarily use L1 glosses regularly in CALL since they have a higher proficiency and should be able to figure out the meaning of words from their context. However, perhaps for advanced-level students, requiring L2 (instead of L1) glossing while reading a text during a test or an assignment may facilitate look-up behavior and help them learn new L2 vocabulary and read in the L2 more effectively (Taylor, 2002). CALL L1 glosses accompanying an L2 text may impede the learners' abil-ity to guess from context (Taylor, 2002, 2006).

6.2   Difficulty Level of the Text and Learner Level

If CALL glosses are to accompany a text, the text chosen should be long enough in order for the glossing to have an effect (Taylor, 2002). Also, L2 teachers should choose online L2 texts that are appropriate for the reading level of the students. Texts that are too easy will be understood regardless of (and sometimes in spite of) the glossing (e.g., Joyce, 1997). Glosses have been shown to not have any effect (or even a lesser effect) on L2 reading comprehension when learner and text level are not optimal for each other (Taylor, 2018).

There is a kind of "fit" between learner and text and if the conditions are not prime, then L2 reading comprehension interventions such as CALL glossing may not be as effective (Taylor, 2002). If the purpose of the reading activity is to cater to the different levels existing in the classroom, the teacher should consider doing the reading activities in a CALL environment with a CALL glossed text. The flexibility of CALL glossing can meet the needs of different student levels. The flexibility of CALL glossing and the tendency of CALL glossing to be less distracting to the L2 reader are some of the key reasons why CALL reading can assist in L2 reading success (Taylor 2006, 2009).

Students now have ubiquitous access to glossing and, especially with augmented reality capability, can access more L2 texts. Because of the likely benefit of CALL resources, more authentic texts can be used inside and outside of L2 classroom contexts and will be accessed more regardless of curriculum because of the ubiquitous nature of the Internet. Authentic texts can be a useful tool in L2 curricula, since there are now better CALL resources to measure text difficulty. In terms of length of authentic texts, the L2 text should be long enough so that there is enough content to assess or conduct post-reading tasks.

6.3   Goals for Reading

If the goal of a CALL reading task is deeper comprehension and analysis of a text, learners can use collaborative resources such as Google Docs, eComma, and Hylighter to share analysis, words, and ideas in order to build their L2 text comprehension together. Such resources could also be used for beginning and intermediate levels, although probably more time will be focused on words than ideas. Further, if the goal is reading an L2 newspaper online for extensive reading purposes, right-clicking in Google Chrome should be a good way to look up words, as shown earlier in this chapter. L2 students could also be trained to watch the videos that sometimes accompany L2 texts in order to guess and make predictions about L2 text content.

6.4   Sociocultural Implications

Digital annotation tools (DATs) can be very useful in online courses to enable individual students or whole classrooms to highlight, modify, or comment on digital texts. Such tools can promote higher-order thinking and analysis and motivate L2 readers to learn vocabulary before discussing an L2 text. DATs can also be used collaboratively in social digital reading contexts in which varying groups of students can scaffold their reading/ analyses either synchronously (at the same time) or asynchronously (at different times) such as in a blog, texting, or email context (Thomas & Poole, 2017). While reading texts with another person online can be effective, screen time can sometimes be detrimental to social interaction due to the mesmerizing and distracting effects of being online. Further, shadow reading, i.e., reading along with another person, may have interesting future research and pedagogical possibilities in CALL contexts due to the benefits of more collaboration and assistance between reading partners for better comprehension of the text (Commander & Guerrero, 2013).

DGBLs can enhance deeper L2 vocabulary learning and reading comprehension, and have tremendous potential because the virtual realities that will likely be created in the future should increase in quality. Teachers should however be aware that it may take time for the teacher and learners to become accustomed to the DGBL and should therefore find its best use at the right learning stage (beginning, intermediate, advanced, etc.) and explain to students its potential learning benefits.

6.5   Assessing L2 Reading Comprehension

If the L2 instructor provides two different CALL tests of L2 reading comprehension to students, they quite often will show two different results, since the CALL assessment is not always extensive enough (i.e., doesn't include enough items on the test) to thoroughly measure L2 reading comprehension (Taylor, 2018). L2 reading comprehension tests should assess both general and detailed information and textual analysis, especially at higher levels.

CALL testing can also be used pedagogically, with the instructor creating practice tests for the L2 reader. Further, although much maligned in the past, multiple-choice testing in the L1 or L2 can be conducted with good reliability and validity in CALL. Multiple-choice testing works very well in a CALL setting because it is easy to set up and grade for classroom and research purposes. Open-ended testing (recall, open-ended questions/answers) can also accurately test CALL reading comprehension. If a recall protocol test is used, the importance of writing *everything* remembered about the text should be emphasized to students. In general, the L1 recall protocol is a valid and likely reliable test for L2 reading comprehension (Bernhardt, 1991). However, the L1 recall protocol's weakness is difficulty in scoring. Besides the open-ended L1 or L2 recall protocol, short-answer tests, or a multiple-choice test, other types of testing exist but they are more instructor-intensive (i.e., the oral recall, think-aloud protocol) and may not be necessary or feasible in the L2 classroom. Further, other types of post-reading tasks besides testing are feasible. For example, students could research the topic they just read and post about it in a blog or on a DAT, participate in a synchronous chat in which they review the main ideas (or details) from the L2 text, or write an analytic or summarizing essay.

6.6　CALL Extensive L2 Reading Integration

The following are a series of questions that logically walk the teacher through the process of deciding how CALL resources can be used for a CALL extensive reading assignment in an intermediate (or advanced)-level classroom. Any of them can be discarded or modified, and may be used to stimulate other ideas.

1. How will the students choose their own online texts? Or, will the teacher provide a list and let the students choose a certain number of them?
2. Has the teacher shown the students how to determine the text level (with a readability analyzer) and offer a recommendation for which level would be good for them?
3. What contingency plan will there be if an online text were pulled from the Internet? Should an extra text (or two) be initially found by the students for such cases?
4. What training will be provided to assist the students? Should a class or a portion of a class be dedicated to showing learners how to use Google Translate on a phone and via computer with right-clicking? Will online dictionary (e.g., Larousse) use (and apps) be part of the training? How long will that take? Should a tech-savvy student be assigned to help with training?
5. What if a student would like to change texts mid-semester? What contingency plan will there be? Will the teacher simply allow the student to change the initial texts selected or will the student be required to be locked into the initial reading choice?
6. How will students be assessed? For example, will the assessment be conducted with a collaborative task online (via a DAT, for example), a reflective journal, an individual reading report, an online multiple-choice test, or any combination of those? Or, should students write their own online tests (for each other or as a retention device) as an assignment with the teacher correcting them?
7. Once an assessment instrument has been selected, how will it be constructed? For example, a reading report (a type of L1 or L2 recall task) could require that students not only summarize the text, but also describe the perceived readers of the text, the tone of the article, what its main goal is, which details seem to be the most

important, etc. (Arnold, 2009). If a multiple-choice test is (part of) the assessment, how many questions or tests will be required?

8. What other steps are necessary to ensure that extensive online reading is a positive experience for the students? What will increase students' motivation to read more in the L2 online on their own?

7 Conclusion

In sum, new technologies are generally helpful for L2 reading comprehension. It is possible that, in the future, there could occasionally be too much help from technology, or that devices could sometimes be more distracting than helpful. Translation may become so accurate that L2 knowledge and ability will only be necessary as interpersonal skills. I personally believe that the more tools the better, and that CALL resources are often excellent for understanding more L2 text and to receive more L2 input. Because better comprehension should occur, there will be better support felt by the student, the affective filter will be lowered, and as a result, students will be more motivated to tackle more difficult L2 texts. The L2 teacher, in turn, should assist the learner in using different CALL resources by testing, implementing, and recommending them to students as well as training students on how and when to use these applications. As technological aids become increasingly available and pervasive, providing students with the necessary training, strategies, and skills for using them to augment their language learning rather than as simply a temporary crutch will be vital for L2 teachers.

Questions for Reflection

1. What are some ways in which translation apps like Google Translate can be used in our L2 courses for reading more texts and learning more L2 vocabulary?
2. Studies have shown that L2 glosses can be effective for some students based on their vocabulary and grammar knowledge. Therefore, how could L2 teachers introduce L2 glosses earlier for beginning or early intermediate learners?
3. CALL glossing has been shown to be effective in L2 reading comprehension as has paper-based glossing, albeit to a lesser degree. Can you think of situations in which CALL glossing is especially effective or can be optimized to a greater degree?
4. How could pictures or videos be used more to provide meaning instead of textual definitions?

5. How might you integrate reading in pairs or groups to facilitate CALL reading in a brick-and-mortar or online classroom?
6. In your L2 classroom, what kinds of assessments or post-reading projects would work best for you and your students?
7. How can you organize your L2 classroom to maximize deeper L2 text reading? How can tutors or advanced students more greatly facilitate deeper L2 reading comprehension?

Case Study 1: Research

A French language teacher provides a CALL L2 text to be read by beginning-, intermediate-, and advanced-level L2 learners. Each group level is randomly assigned to three groups: a control group, a CALL glossing group, and a paper-based glossing group. The control group only reads the online L2 text, while the experimental group reads the online text with the ability to right-click on any word using Google Translate (L1 glossing), whereas the paper-based group reads the text on paper with 5% of the more difficult words glossed in the margin (L1 glossing). After reading the text, participants are then asked to take a 30-item CALL multiple-choice test to assess reading comprehension. Results indicate that, across levels, there is an effect size of 0.8 in favor of CALL glossing and 0.5 for paper-based glossing with a significant difference between groups. For the beginning-level L2 learner, there is a significant difference between control and CALL glossing groups, with the CALL glossing group obtaining a significantly higher mean score on the test when compared to the control group. The paper-based group's results are also significantly higher but less so. The intermediate paper L1 glossing group does not obtain significant results when compared to the control group while the CALL group barely obtains significant results when compared with the control group. For the advanced group, L2 learners who read their CALL L1 glossing text actually have a slightly higher mean score on the reading comprehension test than the control group although it is not significantly higher. The (advanced-level) paper-based L1 glossing mean score is actually lower than the control group but not significantly so.

Discussion Questions:
1. Why did some groups not score significantly higher than other groups?
2. What role did the learner level play?
3. What role did the level of text play?

4. Why would advanced L2 learners not be more influenced by the effects of glossing?
5. How might the choice of text influence the results of the study?
6. Why were the results of paper and CALL glossing so mixed?

Case Study 2: Teaching

In an online 400-level French literature course, a professor has asked students to meet in the virtual class after individually making a list of the ten most descriptive adjectives used in a chapter of an Balzac novel, highlighting them online and posting them via a DAT (digital annotation tool). When class starts, the teacher notices that not everyone has completed the task, so the students are given 20 extra minutes to complete it. Next, the teacher asks the students in pairs to look at each other's list in order to combine their top ten adjectives and to discuss any differences. In looking at the online discussions, the teacher notices during class that there is collaboration, but it is occurring quite slowly. At the end of the class, the students have not finished the collaboration task and the teacher is frustrated because only one group was able to combine their ten adjectives together into one list. The teacher is concerned about getting behind in the curriculum since the activity needs more time during class the following week, which was supposed to be on the next chapter. The teacher is disappointed and is wondering how to restructure the class for better results.

Discussion Questions:
1. What was the pedagogical objective of this task?
2. What were the conditions of this activity?
3. How to you think the teacher needs to restructure this task to make it more productive?
4. How could CALL resources be used more effectively?
5. What kind of assessment tool could be used, if any?
6. What would be the criteria you would set up to evaluate the student's preparation before, during or after class?

Ideas for Action Research Projects

1. Find an L2 passage online of about 300–500 words for your students to read. Randomly assign a third of your students to a group with smartphones with Google Translate that have augmented reality capability, a third with Google Translate in a right-click format

on a desktop computer, and a group that only reads the text. In a learning system such as Brightspace or Blackboard, construct a 20-item multiple-choice test that you can use to compare the groups. Other ideas:

a.   You can write the test in the L2 or L1. I would recommend the L1 for the most accurate results but you could easily write two tests, since the grading of them should be easy. It would also be interesting to see how much the language of the test can moderate the results of such an experiment.

b.   You should make sure your reading test cannot be passed by students with good test-taking ability (e.g, guessing, process of elimination, unintended giveaways of the correct answer). Have other instructors look at the questions to verify they are good samples of reading comprehension. You may have to changes a few questions and maybe eliminate and/or add a few extra questions.

2.   For an EFL or ESL class, select an online text than is perhaps 750–1,000 words for an intermediate-level L2 class. Use the online resource https://readable.io/text/ to determine difficulty and readability of text. The text should be only slightly above the level of your students. Next, record (video) yourself teaching some type of reading strategy training (skimming, scanning, using background knowledge, identifying the main idea, etc.) in the L1 and then in the L2. Then, put the two links (one for the L1 and another for the L2) on YouTube and then link them to their student account on Brightspace, Blackboard, or Canvas. Next, randomly assign students to three groups, a group that only reads the L2 text, a group that watches the L1 video and then reads the L2 text, and a group that watches the L2 video and reads the L2 text. Finally, provide a 20-item multiple-choice test to all three groups.

a.   Ask the students to inform you if they already had background knowledge of the material in the text before reading it, and if so eliminate their scores from the data pool.

b.   When making the video, try to make the L1 and L2 videos about the same length – no longer than 10 minutes – with very similar explanations and examples.

c.   Try to choose a text that is not too difficult, and on which most students will not have too much background information.

d.   The time to read the text and take the test should be limited and uniform across groups, perhaps 15–20 minutes.

N.B. You may consider doing the above experiment with more advanced L2 students and compare the results.

References

Abraham, L. B. (2007). Second-language reading comprehension and vocabulary learning. *Hispania*, 90, 98–108.

Abraham, L. B. (2008). Computer-mediated glosses in second language reading comprehension and vocabulary learning: A meta-analysis. *Computer Assisted Language Learning*, 21, 199–226.

AbuSeileek, A. F. (2008). Hypermedia annotation presentation: Learners' preferences and effect on EFL reading comprehension and vocabulary acquisition. *CALICO Journal*, 25, 260–275.

AbuSeileek, A. F. (2011). Hypermedia annotation presentation: The effect of location and type on the EFL learners' achievement in reading comprehension and vocabulary acquisition. *Computers & Education*, 57, 1281–1291.

Anderson, N. J. (1999). *Exploring second language reading: Issues and strategies.* Boston: Heinle and Heinle Publishers.

Arnold, N. (2009). Online extensive reading for advanced foreign language learners: An evaluation study. *Foreign Language Annals*, 42, 340–366.

Aweiss, S. (1994). Situating learning in technology: The case of computer-mediated reading supports. *Journal of Educational Technology Systems*, 23, 63–74.

Baumann, C. C. (1994). *The effect of previews and glosses on the reading comprehension of beginning and intermediate students of German.* Unpublished doctoral dissertation, University of Minnesota.

Bell F. L., & LeBlanc, L. B. (2000). The language of glosses in L2 reading on computer: Learners' preferences. *Hispania*, 83, 274–285. https://doi.org/10.2307/346199

Bernhardt, E. B. (1991). *Reading development in a second language: Theoretical, empirical and classroom perspectives.* Norwood, NJ: Ablex.

Bernhardt, E. B. (2005). Progress and procrastination in second language reading. *Annual Review of Applied Linguistics*, 25, 133–150. https://doi.org/10.1017/S0267190505000073

Bowles, M. A. (2004). L2 glossing: To CALL or not to CALL. *Hispania*, 87, 541–552. https://doi.org/10.1017/S0267190505000073

Carr, N. (2008). Is Google making us stupid? What the Internet is doing to our brains. *The Atlantic*. Retrieved from http://www.theatlantic.com/magazine/archive/2008/07is-google-making-us-stupid/6868/.

Carr, N. (2010). *What the Internet is doing to our brains: The Shallows.* New York: W. W. Norton & Company.

Carrell, P. L. (1984). Schema theory and ESL reading: Classroom implications and applications. *The Modern Language Journal*, 68, 332–343. https://doi.org/10.1017/S0267190505000073

Chen, I. J., & Yen, J. C. (2013). Hypertext annotation: Effects of presentation formats and learner proficiency on reading comprehension and vocabulary learning in foreign languages. *Computers & Education*, 63, 416–423.

Chun, D. M. (2011). Call technologies for L2 reading post web 2.0. In A. Arnold & L. Ducate, *Present and future promises of CALL: From theory and research to new directions in language teaching*, pp. 131–169. San Marcos, TX CALICO.

Cohen, N. (2008). What are the differences between long-term-short-term and working memory? *Progress in Brain Research*, 169, 323–338.

Commander, M., & De Guerrero, M. C. M. (2013). Reading as a social interactive process: The impact of shadow reading in L2 classrooms. *Reading in a Foreign Language*, 25, 170–191.

Coriano Velázquez, A. (2001). *Vocabulary acquisition through reading: A study of the effectiveness of different CALL based annotations*. Unpublished master's thesis, University of Puerto Rico.

Culver, L. (1991). *Improving reading speed and comprehension of ESL students with the computer*. Unpublished dissertation, Nova University, Florida.

Cutshall, S. (2012). More than a decade of standards: Integrating communication in your language instruction. Retrieved from https://www.actfl.org/sites/default/files/publications/standards/Communication.pdf.

Ducate, L., & Arnold, N. (2011). Technology, CALL, and the Net generation: Where are we headed from here? In A. Arnold, and L. Ducate, *Present and future promises of CALL: From theory and research to new directions in language teaching*, pp. 1–22. San Marcos, TX CALICO.

Gettys, S., Imhof, L. A., & Kautz, J. O. (2001). Computer-assisted reading: The effect of glossing format on comprehension and vocabulary retention. *Foreign Language Annals*, 34, 91–106. https://doi:10.1111/j.1944-9720.2001.tb02815.x

Goyette, E. S. (1995). *The effects of dictionary usage on text comprehension.* Doctoral dissertation, McGill University, Montreal.

Guidi, C. (2009) *Glossing for meaning and glossing for form: A computerized study of the effects of glossing and type of linguistic item on reading comprehension, noticing and L2 learning.* Unpublished doctoral dissertation, Georgetown University, Washington DC.

Hayden, S. (1997). *An investigation into the effect and patterns of usage of a computer-mediated text in reading comprehension in French,* Unpublished doctoral dissertation, University of Pennsylvania, Philadelphia.

Joh, J., & Plakans, L. (2017). Working memory in L2 reading comprehension: The influence of prior knowledge. *System*, 70, 107–120.

Joyce, E. E. (1997). Which words should be glossed in L2 reading materials? A study of first, second and third semester French students' recall. *Pennsylvania Language Forum* (ERIC Document Reproduction Service No. ED 427 508).

Kerr, M. A., & Symons, S. E. (2006). Computerized presentation of text: Effects on children's reading of information material. *Reading and Writing: An Interdisciplinary Journal*, 19, 1–19.

Knight, S. (1994). Dictionary use while reading: The effects on comprehension and vocabulary acquisition for students of different verbal abilities. *The Modern Language Journal*, 78, 285–299. https://doi.org/10.1111/j.1540-4781.1994.tb02043.x

Ko, M. H. (1995). *Glossing in incidental and intentional learning of foreign language vocabulary and reading comprehension.* Unpublished MA thesis, University of Hawai'i, Manoa.

Kost, C. R., Foss, P., & Lenzini, J. J. (1999). Textual and pictorial glosses: Effectiveness on incidental vocabulary growth when reading in a foreign language. *Foreign Language Annals*, 32, 89–113.

Kwong-Hung, L. (1995). *Bilingual texts: A study of the effects of providing L1 Chinese terms in L2 English texts on text comprehension and on English vocabulary acquisition.* Unpublished master's thesis, University of Hong Kong.

Laufer, B. (1996). The lexical threshold of second language reading comprehension: What it is and how it relates to L1 reading ability. *Jyvaskyla Cross-Language Studies*, 17, 55–62.

Laufer, B., & Ravenhorst-Kalovski, G. C. (2010). Lexical threshold revisited: Lexical text coverage, learners' vocabulary size and reading comprehension. *Reading in a Foreign Language*, 22, 1530.

Lee, J, F., & VanPatten, B. (1995). *Making communicative language teaching happen.* New York: McGraw-Hill.

Liu, A., Aamodt, S., Wolf, M., Gelernter, D., Mark, G. (2009, October 14). Does the brain like e-books? *New York Times*, p. 17.

Liu, P., Chen, C., & Chang, Y. (2010). Effects of a computer-assisted concept mapping learning strategy on EFL college students' English reading comprehension. *Computers & Education*, 54, 436–435.
https://doi.org/10.1016/j.compedu.2009.08.027

Lomicka, L. L. (1998). To gloss or not to gloss: An investigation of reading comprehension online. *Language Learning & Technology*, 1, 41–50.

Mangen, A., Walgermo, B. R., & Brønnick, K. (2013). Reading linear texts on paper versus computer screen: Effects on reading comprehension. *International Journal of Educational Research*, 58, 61–68.
https://doi.org/10.1016/j.compedu.2009.08.027

Mayer, R. E. (1997). Multimedia learning: Are we asking the right questions? *Educational Psychology*, 32, 1–19.

Nation, I. S. P. (2006). How large a vocabulary is needed for reading and listening? *The Modern Language Review*, 63, 59–92.

Neville, D. O., Shelton, B. E., & McInnis, B. (2009). Cybertext redux: Using digital game-based learning to teach L2 vocabulary, reading, and culture. *Computer Assisted Language Learning*, 22, 409–424.

Perez, S. (2018, March 14). Microsoft announces breakthrough in Chinese-to-English translation. Retrieved from
https://techcrunch.com/2018/03/14/microsoft-announces-breakthrough-in-chinese-to-english-machine-translation/

Plass, J. L., Chun, D. M., Mayer, R. E., & Leutner, D. (2003). Cognitive load in reading a foreign language text with multimedia aids and the influence of verbal and spatial abilities. *Computers in Human Behavior*, 19, 221–243.
https://doi.org/10.1016/S0747-5632(02)00015-8

Plonsky, L. (2011). The effectiveness of second language strategy instruction: A meta-analysis. *Language Learning*, 61, 993–1038.
https://doi.org/10.1111/j.1467-9922.2011.00663.x

Plonsky, L., & Ziegler, N. (2016). The CALL-SLA interface: Insights from a second-order synthesis. *Language Learning & Technology*, 20, 17–37. http://llt.msu.edu/issues/june2016/plonskyziegler.pdf

Redondo, M. (1997). Reading models in foreign language teaching. *Revista Alicantina de Estudios Ingleses*, 10, 139–161. https://doi.org/10.14198/raei.1997.10.11

Salem, E. B. (2006). *The influence of electronic glosses on word retention and reading comprehension with Spanish language learners*. Unpublished doctoral dissertation, University of Kansas.

Schmidt, R., & Frota, S. (1986). Developing basic conversational ability in a second language. In R. Day (ed.), *Talking to learn*, pp. 237–326. Rowley, MA: Newbury House.

Singer, L. M., & Alexander, P. A. (2017). Reading across mediums: Effects of reading digital and print texts on comprehension and calibration. *The Journal of Experimental Education*, 85, 155–172. https://doi.org/10.1080/00220973.2016.1143794

Steffensen, M. S., Geotz, E. T., & Cheng, X. (1999). A cross-linguistic perspective on imagery and affect in reading: Dual coding in Chinese and English. *Journal of Language Research*, 31, 293–319. https://doi.org/10.1080/10862969909548050

Stoehr, L. E. (1999). *The effects of built-in comprehension aids in a CALL program on student-readers' understanding of a foreign language*. Unpublished doctoral dissertation, University of Texas at Austin.

Taylor, A. M. (2002). *A meta-analysis on the effects of L1 glosses on L2 reading comprehension*. Unpublished doctoral dissertation, Purdue University, West Lafayette, IN.

Taylor, A. M. (2006). The effects of CALL versus traditional L1 glosses on L2 reading comprehension. *CALICO Journal*, 23, 309–318.

Taylor, A. M. (2009). CALL-based versus Paper-based Glosses: Is there a difference in reading comprehension? *CALICO Journal*, 27, 147–160.

Taylor, A. M. (2010). Glossing is sometimes a distraction: Comments on Cheng and Good (2009). *Reading in a Foreign Language*, 22, 353–354. http://nflrc.hawaii.edu/rfl/October2010/discussion/taylor.pdf

Taylor, A. M. (2013). CALL versus paper: In which context are L1 glosses more effective? *CALICO Journal*, 30, 63–81.

Taylor, A. M. (2014a). L1 glossing and strategy training for improving L2 reading comprehension: a meta-analysis. *International Journal of Quantitative Research in Education*, 2, 39–68.

Taylor, A. M. (2014b). Glossing frequency and L2 reading comprehension: The influence of CALL glossing. *CALICO Journal*, 31, pp. 374–389.

Taylor, A. M. (2018). Technology and reading: The effects of CALL glossing. In N. Ziegler, *Routledge Handbook of SLA and Technology*, 2nd ed. New York: Routledge.

Taylor, A. M., Stevens, J. R., & Asher, J. W. (2006). The effects of explicit reading strategy training on L2 reading comprehension: A meta-analysis. In J. Norris

& L. Ortega (eds.), *Synthesizing research on language learning and teaching*, pp. 231–344. Philadelphia, PA: John Benjamins.

Thomas J., & Poole, F. (2017). Investigating linguistics, literary and social affordances of L2 collaborative reading. *Language Learning & Technology*, 21, 139–156.

Thompson, C. P., & Phillips, E. M. (2009). *Mais Oui!* Boston: Houghton Mifflin.

Turnbull, B., & Evans, M. S. (2017). The effects of L1 and L2 group discussions on L2 reading comprehension. *Reading in a Foreign Language*, 29, 133–154.

Wolf, D. F. (1993). A comparison of assessment tasks used to measure FL reading comprehension. *The Modern Language Journal*, 77, 473–489. https://doi.org/10.1111/j.1540-4781.1993.tb01995.x

Yanguas, I. (2009). Multimedia glosses and their effects on L2 text comprehension and vocabulary learning. *Language Learning & Technology*, 13, 49–67.

Youngs, B. L. E. (1994). *CALL and second language acquisition: The use of the 'Reader' computer program to improve student proficient in French.* Unpublished dissertation, University of Pennsylvania Philadelphia.

Youngs, B. L. E., Ducate, L., & Arnold, N. (2011). Linking second language acquisition, CALL, and language pedagogy. In A. Arnold, and L. Ducate, *Present and future promises of CALL: From theory and research to new directions in language teaching*, pp. 23–60. San Marcos, TX CALICO.

Yun, J. (2011). The effects of hypertext glosses on L2 vocabulary acquisition: A meta-analysis. *Computer Assisted Language Learning*, 24, 39–58.

Resources

Microsoft Translator API
(https://www.microsoft.com/en-us/translator/word.aspx)
This is a recent, AI-powered translator that may be more accurate than other translation apps. API offers several other capabilities as well, such as text to text, text to speech, speech to text, and speech to speech translation. This should become a very useful technology in the future.

Brightspace (https://www.d2l.com)
An LMS for course management and for testing reading as well. It requires a bit of a learning curve, but has lots of capability.

Blackboard (http://www.blackboard.com/)
An LMS for course management and for testing reading as well.

Brainhoney (https://www.brainhoney.com/)
An LMS for course management and for testing reading as well. Fairly easy to use.

Canvas (https://www.canvaslms.com/)
An LMS for course management that can be used for testing reading as well.

Duolingo (https://www.duolingo.com/)
This very popular app starts at a very basic level and is useful for not only L2 reading but L2 learning as well.

eComma (https://ecomma.coerll.utexas.edu/)
A DAT that can be used to collaborate online while reading L2 texts.

English Readability Analyser: (https://readable.io/text/)
This is a very user-friendly site into which you can cut and paste an L2 text.

French Readability Analyser: (https://labs.translated.net/lisibilite-texte/)
This is a site into which you can cut and paste a French L2 text.

Glossmaker (https://languagecenter.cla.umn.edu/lcdev/makers/gloss/)
This is a site with which you can create a glossed text.

Google Docs (https://www.google.com/docs/)
This is a very popular site for commenting on group texts.

Google Translate Application (https://translate.google.com/)
Google Translate is a potentially useful app that is very useful for translating. It takes some practice to know how to effectively use it.

Hylighter (https://www.hylighter.com)
This is another useful digital annotation tool.

iClicker Reef (https://app.reef-education.com/#/login)
This is a tool to take polls in class in real time.

Larousse Dictionaries (http://www.larousse.fr/)
This is an online dictionary that has not only translations but pronunciation as well. The Larousse app (in Apple store and elsewhere) is also worth paying for and is a great dictionary for a phone.

Mango (https://mangolanguages.com/)
A good app for learning to read and pronounce dialogues.

MINDMUP (https://www.mindmup.com)
A great app for mind mapping.

NB (http://nb.mit.edu/welcome)
A collaborative reading tool by MIT.

Top Hat (https://tophat.com/)
A tool to take polls in class in real time.

Word Reference (http://www.wordreference.com)
A good dictionary that cross-references with Collins dictionaries and also
has many words pronounced.

About the Author

Alan M. Taylor (PhD, Purdue University) is French Section Head at
Brigham Young University–Idaho. His research areas include CALL and L2
reading, Reading Strategy Training, L1 glossing and meta-analytic methodology in L2 research. He wrote one of the first quantitative meta-analytic
dissertations in the L2 learning field in 2002 and has since published seven
quantitative meta-analyses examining the effects of paper-based glossing,
CALL glossing, and strategy training on L2 reading comprehension. His
work has been published in journals such as *CALICO*, *Reading in a Foreign
Language*, *Language Learning & Technology*, *Journal of Educational and
Behavioral Statistics*, and *Canadian Modern Language Review.*

6 Digital Literacies as Emergent Multifarious Repertoires

Jonathon Reinhardt and Steven L. Thorne

Preview Questions

1. How is literacy traditionally defined, and how has this definition changed in the digital era? How have the concepts of computer, information, and media literacy changed over the past few decades?
2. What tools do you currently use for work and personal communication and how have your communication patterns changed over the past 5 or 10 years? How does your use of online media compare with that of your students?
3. In what ways is using digital tools and media participatory? What particular skills are needed to participate socially in these new contexts?
4. How have the kind, number, and functions of digital tools expanded over the past few decades? How has the Internet become more multimodal, transcultural, and polylingual?
5. Do you think digital literacies have become more everyday, personal, and informal over the past decade? What impact does the everyday use of digital tools have on CALL in the classroom?
6. How might you more closely align your classroom use of digital tools with the digital environments and online communication abilities relevant to your students' present and future lives?

1 Introduction

Throughout history, the development of new technologies has had social impacts leading to new understandings of literacy and new social practices, and the digital era is no exception. For example, the invention and spread of the printing press in 16th-century Europe helped push literacy rates in the UK from 16% in 1550 to 53% in 1650, which contributed to broader scientific literacy (Mitch, 2005). The development of inexpensive printed political pamphlets in the 18th century helped spread enlightenment ideals as "commonsensical" and everyday, which contributed to sociopolitical literacy (Standage, 2013) and ultimately political revolution. In the mid-20th century, television brought access to information and entertainment to millions in the developed world, connecting them into a "global village" (McLuhan, 1964) and blending the "local" and "global" into the "glocal."

Throughout much of the world, literacy practices are central to the cultural organization of social life (Pennycook, 2010). While many literacies are widespread, relatively monolithic and standardized, and state sponsored (i.e., through education), people and communities often learn and use multiple literacies as a function of participating in diverse social contexts. To take a well-known case, among the Via people of Liberia, three literacy practices coexist (Scribner & Cole, 1981). The first is a script indigenous to the Vai people, which is learned outside of school and used for personal and commercial purposes. The second is Arabic, which is learned and used in Islamic religious settings. English, learned in school, is the third literacy system, which is used primarily for public and official governmental functions. In the case of the Vai, each of these literacy practices is situationally and culturally specific in origin and function.

We will argue throughout the remainder of this chapter that digital information and communication environments have created conditions under which a multifariousness[1] of literacy practices coexist, some of which have emerged recently in informal, decentralized, and non-consolidated forms. Presuming that historically important standardized literacies remain at the center of instructed world languages education, a primary issue confronting teachers and students involves deciding how to adequately prepare students for successful interaction in a social universe comprised of multifarious literacies – many of them digital and outside of formal academic domains. As with all pedagogical choices in second and foreign (L2) education, proposed learning outcomes should align with the kinds of linguistic and interactional expertise that support the performance of relevant social and professional identities.

In the text below, we first review studies and describe approaches aimed to support teachers in this effort, beginning with a brief look back to the ways the Internet has transformed our understanding of and possibilities for

---

1   We use the term "multifarious" because of its entailments of diversity and complexity, which the term "multiple" does not necessarily imply.

digitally mediated communication. We then survey research on the topic in two somewhat overlapping literatures. The first focuses on L2 digital literacy development that has been examined as informal, everyday phenomena in the wild, and the second as types and features of digital literacies that can be formally addressed in the L2 classroom. We then offer a pedagogical framework for developing L2 digital literacies formally that complements and supplements the approach we took in the first version of this chapter (Reinhardt & Thorne, 2011). To that end, we examine how "traditional" digital literacies – computer, information, and media literacies – have changed not only paradigmatically to be more social in nature, but also ontologically as comprised of new "stuff" (Lankshear & Knobel, 2006) that is participatory, multifarious, and everyday. Looking at L2 digital literacies as new in this way allows us to implicate new approaches to familiar activities, and to imagine new sorts of activities for the L2 classroom. We conclude by outlining six such activities.

2   An Expanded View of Digital Literacies

The development of the Internet in the late-20th century (i.e., "Web 1.0") challenged earlier text-based and autonomous model of literacy (Street, 1984; Barton, 2007). The autonomous model of literacy assumes that literacy itself has context-independent effects on individual cognition. In contrast, what is termed the ideological model of literacy argues that literacy is both a cognitive and technical skill as well as a *social practice* situated in ecologies of use that will vary across different social contexts (Street, 1995). As described in the above-mentioned example of the three distinctive literacies used by the Via people (Scribner & Cole, 1981), literacy as a vehicle for communicating meaning is always embedded in specific social circumstances.[2] This socially informed definition of literacy acknowledges the cognitive dimensions of literacy but emphasizes that instances of use are mediated by various communities and technologies and grounded in a socially shared symbolic system of communication, namely language. Accordingly, becoming literate in a particular practice (or set of practices, hence "literacies" in the plural) requires the ability to interpret and generate signs that are meaningful to a community of practice (Lave & Wenger,

---

2   This is why academic literacy genres differ significantly from assemblages of literacy practices associated with social media use, synchronous chat channels in online games, and handwritten love letters produced during the Victorian era.

1991), while it also involves the development of an identity appropriate to that practice (Gee, 2004). Group participation involves taking on recognizable social roles (Gee, 1999), or "doing identity" in ways that are recognizable to that group. In short, this more holistic reconceptualization constitutes a new paradigm for thinking about enhancing literacy abilities as processes that relate to the development of dispositions or mindsets (Lankshear & Knobel, 2006).

The "Web 2.0 turn" at the start of the millennium has led to further ontological shifts in the definition of literacy – that is, the nature of literacy has changed in part because meaning-making is increasingly inclusive of post-typographic and multimodal expression, for example the use of emoticons, images, sound, video, and intertextual linkages to other media. Tusting (2017), for example, describes the ways in which contemporary technologies have transformed everyday literacy practices in multiple ways, such as the inclusion and prevalence of multimodal expression and the entwining of written communication with socially relevant issues of participation and identity formation. Similarly, Jewitt (2014) describes the complexity of multimodal semiotic repertoires that can include written and spoken language, image, gesture and haptics, and three-dimensional forms, among others, and explicates these forms of meaning-making through the lens of multimodal social semiotics (e.g., Bezemer & Kress, 2016; Kress, 2010). In particular, Jewitt encourages the use of multimodal analysis in application to school curricula as a way to make visible new forms of learning in digital environments and to enhance the recognition and acknowledgement of multimodal learning both within and outside of classroom contexts. Indeed, the array of technologies now mediating "informal learning" and literacy development are numerous, especially in social media environments and online gaming and virtual worlds, where curation of identities and negotiation of social presence is paramount (e.g., Ito et al., 2010; Thorne, 2012). A narrow focus on text alone may not be adequate to account for the interaction and learning happening in many digital environments.

Another dynamic present in contemporary Web 2.0 environments is that digital content has become not only readable or consumable by millions, but writable or producible as well (Warschauer & Grimes, 2007). An ethos of "remix," where Internet content is no longer "read only" or even "read/write" (Lessig, 2008) but copied, remixed, and shared, now typifies many digital literacy practices, to the point that they involve not just reading and writing but "reprodusage" – a portmanteau of remix, produce, and use. Because these new practices involving "reprodusage" are highly social, interactive, and affinity-based, they are more participatory (Jenkins et al., 2006) and distributed across many more communicative media than are traditional print-based literacy practices. To participate in emergent literacy practices demands facility with multifarious media and modes – text, sound, and image, both dynamic and static.

Within language and literacy education that typically presumes a plurality of monolingualisms (i.e., the coexistence of self-contained and separate languages), it is especially pertinent to underscore that the Internet is a multiplicity of language contact zones unprecedented in human history (see Danet & Herring, 2007). This results in communication activity that can be transcultural and polylingual, as user communities spanning the globe mix different cultural referents and linguistic varieties (Thorne & Ivković, 2015).[3] Despite the fact that "impure" and mixed communicative actions are everyday and sometimes high stakes (e.g., Blommaert, 2010; May, 2014; Pennycook & Otsuji, 2015), such varieties of language and literacy are not typically taught or learned in school settings, even though they are increasingly important for participation in on- and offline interaction. Hybridized literacies are generally acquired informally through the grounded, everyday use of various technologies, with the result that users may not gain critical pragmatic awareness regarding when and with whom to use which genres, registers, and communicative styles.

In view of the sociolinguistic realities described above, L2 instructors and curriculum developers have good reasons to engage with digital literacies development in the classroom. First, digital tools have become vital to everyday and workaday life in the modern world and are becoming increasingly invisible and normalized (Bax, 2011) in classrooms. Explicit instruction in how to use these tools in order to interact in diverse speech communities is warranted, especially instruction with gaining criticality as its focus, precisely because it is not only how we use the tools, but how the tools and the algorithms operating through them influence us. Second, practically speaking, L2 users may experience as many, if not more, opportunities to use their L2 in online digital forms as face-to-face (F2F) or in real life (IRL) forms, and much of their online lives will be polylingual and transcultural – areas that L2 educators are uniquely positioned to address. Moreover,

3   As a brief metacommentary, while multingualism is pervasively visible in digital environments, terminology describing the use of multiple languages within and across communicative encounters has become complex. For example, "plurilingualism" and "multilingualism" are often seen as equivalent terms, but both have been critiqued in recent sociolinguistics research as problematic ideological abstractions since they infer multiple separate and homogeneous linguistic varieties rather than the mixing and hybridity that are often evident in everyday communicative repertoires (e.g., Blommaert, 2010; May, 2014; Pennycook & Otsuji, 2015).

developing L2 digital literacies may impact a learner's overall symbolic competence (Kramsch & Whiteside, 2008), which may apply not only to L2 use but general language use and awareness more broadly. Awareness of, and facility with, the means and purpose of digital meaning-making in an L2 may transfer positively to critical social media literacy in general, a competence that has become more important today than ever. Building from a base in Bourdieu and the notion of *sens practique* (e.g., Bourdieu, 1991; Darvin & Norton, 2015), Darvin & Norton (2015) make a powerful argument for the necessity of attention to how power operates in digital spaces with the implication that language learners and educators should develop a sustained critical stance regarding biases, assumptions, and the ideological work that occurs in online interaction. Recent world events, such as "fake news" and the purported social media tampering with US elections in November of 2016, illustrate the importance of developing a critical stance to information (both on- and offline), by carefully appraising the source of information/authorship and substantiating claims by checking multiple sources representing diverse ideological positions.

3   Research on L2 Digital Literacies Development: In the Wild and in the Classroom

Since digital literacies are prevalent, and even dominant, across both instructional and non-instructional contexts, in this section we review research relevant to L2 literacy development, beginning first with studies that examine the inclusion of digital literacy activities in classroom contexts and then describing the history of research on language development in the wild, defined here as research studies that document language use and learning outside of formal educational settings (e.g., Thorne, 2008; Sockett & Kusyk, 2015; Wagner, 2015).

In early research on L2 digital literacies development in formal or school-related contexts, Warschauer (1999) countered arguments that technology has equalizing effects by showing how learners of English and Hawaiian had different trajectories of electronic literacy development due to differing ecologies of learning and levels of access to technology (see also Kern, 2000). Since then, blogs, wikis, and social networking sites, both vernacular and educational, have been studied as sites for formal L2 digital literacies development (see Thorne & Payne, 2005, for a review of early work in this area). For example, Bloch (2007) showed how an adolescent heritage English learner found space for reflection, self-presentation, and personal expression in the class blog, and thereby developed critical literacy.

Similarly, Gebhard, Shin, & Seger (2011) demonstrated how a young English learner's use of a class blog for a range of academic and social purposes expanded her communicative repertoire, developed literacy skills, and built metalinguistic and genre awareness.

Research shows that in formal contexts, agency and autonomy go hand-in-hand with L2 digital literacies development. For example, analyzing the social media activity of learners of Japanese over four years, Pasfield-Neofitou (2011) showed that learners used different social media tools strategically for different purposes, and that language and topic choice indexed identity presentation, conceptions of nationality, and the perceived ownership of online spaces. Analyzing the daily Facebook posts of three learners of Portuguese studying abroad in Brazil, Back (2013) found considerable differences in post features over time. Findings were that social networking site use afforded the development of audience and register awareness, albeit via different pathways, at differing rates, and to different degrees for individual learners. Vandergriff (2016) examined how learners of German exercise considerable agency in educational social networking sites through strategic self-presentation, deployment of multilingual resources, negotiation for supportive space, engagement in play, and management of learning processes.

L2 digital literacies development can be directly addressed in the L2 classroom through culture and language learning tasks, using various digital tools (Kurek & Hauck, 2014). Blogs, wikis, and social media can serve as mediums for projects, spaces for experimentation, and windows onto the cultures and languages of study. For example, Ducate & Lomicka (2008) had nine American university-age learners of French and 20 of German first follow and then present on specific bloggers from the target culture, developing interpretive and presentational skills, and then build and interact through personal blogs, thereby developing interpersonal skills. Lee (2012) had study abroad students interview local informants to create blog-based resources for future students, building critical intercultural awareness. Blattner & Fiori (2009) had university-level French and Spanish learners in the US observe expert speakers informally through Facebook's group function and focus on how the performance of various speech acts differed depending on audience and variety. In a later study, Blattner & Fiori (2011) had advanced Spanish learners participate in guided discourse analysis tasks designed to raise sociopragmatic awareness of various speech acts and discourse functions in Facebook groups whose subjects corresponded to course topics. Mills (2011) had advanced French learners participate in a Facebook-mediated global simulation and develop simulated identities by completing joint narrative authoring tasks, interacting as their characters in wall posts and status updates, and sharing various online resources. In short, social media can serve as windows onto the L2, playgrounds for its practice, and gateways to participation in it.

Social media is an ideal arena for the practice of "social pedagogies", an approach in which the learner is envisioned as a *locuteur/acteur* (speaker/ actor, see Kern & Liddicoat, 2008; Bass & Elmendorf, 2012). It acknowledges the centrality of language form and cultural knowledge in instructed L2 settings while also emphasizing that students are social agents who learn by mobilizing symbolic and linguistic resources to successfully negotiate complex intercultural, transactional, and ideational processes that involve engagement beyond the walls of the classroom. In a recent edited volume, Dubreil & Thorne (2017a, 2017b) bring together a collection of papers that illustrate social pedagogies and the enabling role of technology and media literacies in their implementation. Topics include community-engaged service learning (Brates et al., 2017), spatial and linguistic landscape analysis in multilingual cities (Charitos & Van Deusen-Scholl, 2017), fan interaction and engagement with contemporary literature (Pellet & Myers, 2017), students as producers, curators, and consumers of authentic language-culture resources (Greenfield et al., 2017), and the struggles and breakthroughs associated with the use of online games and communities that were incorporated into classroom instruction (Warner & Richardson, 2017). Social pedagogies, broadly construed, present a diverse array of structured approaches that attempt to bring together social action in the digital and material world with the pedagogical amplification that is possible in instructed learning spaces. The ultimate goal is to support students in developing the translingual and transcultural abilities to participate effectively in complex and diverse communities, both now and in the future.

While classroom studies remain dominant, it is an obvious point that learning outside of instructional contexts is perhaps the primordial human developmental context for our species. Especially over the past few decades, considerable research has focused on cognition and learning "in the wild" (Hutchins, 1995) and on L2 learning and digital literacies development in particular (Reinhardt & Thorne, 2011; Sockett, 2014; Sundqvist & Sylvén, 2016; Thorne & Reinhardt, 2008; Thorne, Sauro, & Smith, 2015; Wagner, 2015). Digital settings have included discussion boards (Hanna & de Nooy, 2009), fan groups (Black, 2008; Thorne & Black, 2011), online gaming environments (Rama et al., 2012; Reinhardt, Warner, & Lange, 2014; Reinhardt, 2017a; Thorne, 2008, 2012, 2013; Thorne & Fischer, 2012), and social networking sites (Reinhardt, 2017b). Some of the earliest work was done by Lam (2000, 2004), who used language socialization frameworks to show how bilingual Chinese immigrant teens developed dynamic, translingual identities in online fan spaces. Also focusing on identity development, Black (2008) explored how adolescents learned and practiced English by networking and sharing interests in fan-fiction communities. More recent research has examined social media; for example, Chen (2013) showed how two L1 Chinese graduate student multilingual writers in the US used Facebook differently according to their perceived audiences and differing socialization purposes. Schreiber (2015) showed how a Serbian adolescent was able to develop and present both local and transnational English-mediated identities in Facebook through a variety of translingual re-entextualization and sharing practices that affiliated him with global hip-hop communities. Solmaz (2015) described how international students in the US exercised a wide variety of social media literacies through Facebook and Twitter to interact online with home and sojourn communities. In an examination of digitally mediated multilingual and multimodal practices, Leppänen, Kytölä, & Westinen (2017) review investigations of informal, interest driven participation in contemporary technology contexts that include issues of heteroglossia, resemiotization, and agentive opportunities for exploration of multiple positionalities. Their review of research critically framed challenges associated with the compatibility of informally acquired competences in relation to formal education, the problem of anglophone centrism, and the need to remain vigilant regarding inequalities of access and participation in geopolitical peripheries (i.e., the global South).

In the sections below, we bring together lessons learned in instructionally located and in the wild L2 language and literacy studies to inform a pedagogical framework and specific activities to advance to the development of L2 digital literacies.

4   A New Pedagogical Framework for Developing L2 Digital Literacies

The aforementioned studies used a variety of frameworks for designing and implementing instruction; for example, situated learning (Lave & Wenger, 1991; Mills, 2011), a multiliteracies framework (New London Group, 1996; Blattner & Fiori, 2011), social pedagogies (Dubreil & Thorne, 2017a, b), and bridging activities (Thorne & Reinhardt, 2008; Reinhardt & Ryu, 2013). In the first version of this chapter (Reinhardt & Thorne, 2011), we surveyed multiple frameworks applicable to literacy development for both L1 and L2 that could be used or adapted for designing and implementing L2 digital literacies in structured, formal learning contexts (see Table 1 for an

Table 1 Frameworks for comparisons-focused digital L2 pedagogies (Reinhardt & Thorne, 2011)

Approach or framework	Sample comparisons-focused activity
Online reading comprehension (Leu et al., 2007)	Using and comparing L1 and L2 portals and search engines to find information
Media literacy education (Buckingham, 2003)	Analyzing multimodal structures of parallel L1 and L2 advertisements and questioning sources and motives
Language awareness (Bolitho et al., 2003; McCarthy & Carter, 1994)	Comparing chat transcripts and transcripts of spoken conversations on the same topic and questioning speaker choices
Genre awareness (Hyland, 2001)	Analyzing and comparing blogs as social text types, across languages and topics
Corpus-informed approaches (O'Keeffe, McCarthy, & Carter, 2007)	Comparing the frequencies of words and structures in parallel L1 and L2 corpora of news discussion board comments
Multiliteracies (New London Group, 1996; Kern, 2000)	Transforming the biography of a well-known historical figure from the target culture into a social network page
Bridging activities (Thorne & Reinhardt, 2008)	Collecting online gaming chat transcripts in the L2, analyzing them, and comparing them with similar transcripts in the L1

overview). We also showed how activities reflecting the principles behind the frameworks could reflect the ACTFL comparisons standard.

In this current fully rewritten contribution to the third edition of this volume, we offer a different approach to designing activities that develop L2 digital literacies by examining "traditional" digital literacies – computer, information, and media literacies – in light of the participatory, multifarious, and everyday qualities that typify "new" digital literacies. Each of these qualities aligns with principles of L2 pedagogical practices informed by SLA research, and offers both opportunities and challenges in implementation.

Participation is a key tenet of social interactionist and constructivist approaches to L2 teaching, as well as Freirean pedagogies grounded in social justice (Larsen-Freeman & Anderson, 2011). Accordingly, digital literacies instruction should integrate opportunities for participation and interaction wherever possible. Since many digital literacies are by design participatory, activities to practice them can leverage the sharing, interaction, and collaborative engagement that new tools and online communities afford. However, since new sorts of participation entail "reprodusage," activities involve copying, mixing, and sharing that may challenge traditional understandings of ownership and authorship. Traditional activities meant only for an audience of the teacher and perhaps classmates are now somewhat anachronistic, and digital activities in particular should consider involving broader audiences and purposes that would help students to engage with the world outside of the classroom. For example, King (2015) had his English learners collaborate on Wikipedia entries on various local subjects and reflect on how the experience impacted their identities as English users. Some students reported feeling a sense of writer responsibility, obligation to a wider Wikipedia community, and satisfaction when their entries were not deleted, while others demonstrated a sense of legitimate participation when discussing with other Wikipedians the status of their contributions. Wikipedia has entries for hundreds of languages that present authentic opportunities for authorship and contribution for most any world language program that would emphasize the development of formal writing and descriptive prose.

Digital literacies are also **multifarious** – in the sense of being both multiple and diverse – which presents additional opportunities and challenges. L2 pedagogical approaches grounded in integrated skills and intercultural competence align well with an open-ended, non-prescriptivist, and emergent characterization of digital literacies. Multimodal composition and digital storytelling projects offer opportunities to integrate various digital skills, media, and modalities, but instructors may need to address issues related to not only copying and mixing, but also code-mixing and use of the L1, which are prevalent among bi- and plurilingual individuals online. Oskoz & Elola (2016) explore how digital stories have been used for L2 learning and explain the procedures for implementation: focus on content development, written text, images, oral text, technology training, and presentation. They argue that digital stories, because they are integrative and multimodal, but are completed through a sheltered and scaffolded process, are an ideal means for learners to develop L2 digital literacies. Stories can be personal or focus on cultural and social issues (see Elola & Oskoz in this volume for more information). Additional possibilities are to incorporate opportunities for fan-fiction authorship. Sauro & Sundmark (2016) have developed pedagogical approaches for interaction within fandom communities and have designed curricula that bring together task-based language teaching with fan-fiction authoring. This approach attempts to unite the educational goal of technically accurate narrative prose with passion-driven storytelling.

That digital literacies are **everyday** also poses opportunities and challenges for L2 educators. Digital literacies are usually learned experientially through immersion, trial-and-error, and tutorials integrated into the site or tool being used. This means digital literacies are vernacular, ad hoc, and often unanalyzed by participants. They become part of our "habitus" – our dispositional "taken-for-granted" understanding of the social world (Bourdieu, 1991). This offers opportunities to "bridge" everyday practice with academic distance and analysis and enables students to see that what they do with technology in their everyday lives is also done by speakers of the L2 – using written language in personally meaningful and purposeful ways, creating videos, posting on social media, playing digital games, etc. (Thorne & Reinhardt, 2008). At the same time, because many digital literacy practices are socially oriented and associated with non-academic contexts, it is possible that L2 learners may not see the value in treating them critically or as an environment that is appropriate in formal L2 learning contexts. Teachers may experience resistance from students who may not want to use their everyday digital identities for formal academic purposes. For example, Reinhardt & Zander (2011) found that some students resisted activities designed to develop critical awareness of Facebook as an interactional genre because they thought they knew how to use it already, and did not see the value of social media activities when the TOEFL was looming. Reinhardt, Warner, & Lange (2014) reported on a project where learners used digital games to learn German both experientially, by playing games reflectively, and analytically, by examining German cultural perspectives on digital gaming. While some students responded positively and developed genre awareness, others were resistant to using games for the serious activity of classroom-based German language learning, including students who identified as "gamers." In short, since students often use social media tools informally outside of school, they may assume they are inappropriate for academic study, and may balk at developing criticality towards them. While student resistance may need to be explicitly addressed, as technology mediation has become ubiquitous across professional, interpersonal, and recreational dimensions of students' lifeworlds, we argue that building critical language awareness of diverse forms of literacy will help to ensure that instructed language learning is ecologically aligned with communication needs outside of school and university settings.

After considering the participatory, multifarious, and everyday qualities that typify "new" digital literacies, the traditional definitions of computer, information, and media literacy are no longer adequate. In the following subsections, we examine how these definitions have been challenged, before presenting newly reconceptualized activities that take into account these new qualities.

4.1   New L2 Computer Literacies

Computer literacy is the proficiency to use computer hardware, software, and associated technologies, but as technology has developed and changed, so have the literacies needed to use it. The participatory aspect of basic computer literacy has become central since many contemporary tools are designed to enhance the sharing of processes and products. For example, authorship once only meant creating a word processing document and saving it to a hard drive, but now it can also involve creating a Google doc to be immediately shared and co-authored through the cloud. Regarding the multifarious quality of new computer literacies, the number and diversity of platforms an individual uses in both their everyday and work lives – desktops, laptops, tablets, smartphones, game consoles, smart televisions – has expanded dramatically. The number of software applications has grown as well, with a greater variety of smaller, more focused apps available for different platforms (e.g., PC vs. mobile) displacing single multifunctional, comprehensive programs. With broadband affording greater bandwidth access, creating and sharing images and videos has become a widespread practice that requires knowledge of a greater range of software and hardware than ever before (although interfaces may be easier to use). Finally, as digital technology has become a regular part of everyday practice, students enter the classroom with established dispositions towards a variety of technologies that 25 or 30 years ago they may have first experienced in educational settings. Students have learned how to use many digital tools through ad hoc trial-and-error, supported by built-in tutorials and informal just-in-time peer networks rather than through explicit instruction. The computers they now find at school, ironically, may be less sophisticated than their own devices. At the same time, students from less privileged backgrounds may have little hands-on experience with the latest tools, and school computers may be all they have. This presents the challenge of providing activities that are both sophisticated and engaging enough for learners at one end of the digital divide, yet accessible for those at the other.

4.2   L2 Information Literacies

The second sort of digital literacy that has changed since the "Web 2.0 turn" is *information literacy*, defined by the American Library Association as the ability "to recognize when information is needed and have the ability to locate, evaluate, and use effectively the needed information" (American Library Association, 2018). Each element of this definition warrants a closer look. First, recognizing when information is needed requires critical awareness, not to mention curiosity and skepticism. Identifying when a belief is asserted as a fact, and whether support is inadequate or not is key. Moreover, in an age when anyone can publish a professional-looking website, it is not adequate to judge reliability and veracity of information by simply examining a URL, a date, or an author's name; critical users should know when and why to question the veracity or reliability of online information regardless of its appearance. Second, locating information may seem to have gotten easier, but the ease may also have a downside in that search engines provide direct access to information without the physical experience of having located it in relation to other information, which bypasses opportunities for developing organizational and taxonomic skills, as well as for serendipitous discovery of related material through browsing. Physically locating books in a library or in information in a reference book, for example, may develop not only alphabeticization skills, but also awareness that information can be organized in, and thus located by means of, hierarchical taxonomies, which themselves form ideological and evaluative frames of reference. Third, evaluation is dependent on scientific, mathematical, and statistical literacy, and requires a basic understanding of what is a fact vs. an opinion, what is causation vs. correlation, why anecdotes or commonsense beliefs may be misleading, and how algorithmically enabled echo chambers and confirmation bias work. Finally, effectively using information is dependent on knowing its value and relationship to other information.

Like computer literacy, information literacy has also become more participatory, multifarious, and everyday. With regards to participation, information literacy now means not only knowing how to find and evaluate information, but also knowing when, with whom, and why it is appropriate to share it. In an L2 context this requires the additional consideration of cultural differences in sharing – what's acceptable and what's considered private or public to other participants. Like computer literacy, information literacy has also become multifarious in terms of the sheer number of tools and resources available. Users now must recognize and compare the many available Internet resources and search tools. For L2 users, this also entails knowing how they compare across languages, populations, and cultures in terms of features, function, and popularity. For example, Chinese learners may not realize that the Chinese language version of Google is less popular than Baidu, and assume they can find the same information through either search engine, but a quick comparison of the search results page of the same term in both shows considerable differences. Finally, since Internet access and web-based information has become ubiquitous, the practice of finding information has become more everyday and taken for granted. However, evaluation skills and criticality lag, as an overabundance of information frequently inculcates users to presume veracity. Critical information literacy means knowing that, and how, everyday activities like reading news reports of world events necessarily inculcate particular perspectives and biases. On a more quotidian level for language learners, finding and following directions, and making plans and meeting friends are intertwined with information seeking and evaluating, which for many people, in many parts of the world, are now dependent on Internet and smartphone access. L2 learners may not be aware of the extent to which this is the case in the culture of study, and how it might impact participation in it.

4.3   L2 Media Literacies

Information literacy usually goes hand in hand with *media literacy*, which involves critical awareness of the role of media in society and the ideological origins of media discourses. The latest definition used by the Center for Media Literacy spans aspects of information literacy and includes creation and participation: "Media literacy provides a framework to access, analyze, evaluate, create and participate with messages in a variety of forms – from print to video to the Internet. Media literacy builds an understanding of the role of media in society as well as essential skills of inquiry and self-expression necessary for citizens of a democracy." (Center for Media Literacy, 2018). Media literacy once entailed recognizing political and social propaganda and being critical of biased perspectives in media and advertising, which in a "read only" world focused on consumer awareness. However, in a world where media consumers are now "reprodusers" of content who must manage their own online identities, media literacy also entails knowing how to use, rather than be used by, media in autonomous and intentional ways.

As social media becomes a, if not the, primary arena of media participation and digital literacy practice for many, media literacy has become intertwined with *social* media literacies. Social media literacies can be equated with the computer literacy needed to use social media tools – Facebook, Twitter, Instagram, YouTube, etc. – knowing how to curate one's profile, how to traverse connections, and how to articulate one's network (Ellison & boyd, 2013). It also entails critical awareness of how social media functions; for example, how "clickbait" works and how algorithms trace user behavior and sell it to sponsors for various purposes. Social media is the primary arena for practice of what Jenkins et al. identify as new media "cultural competencies and social skills" (2006: xiii–xiv):

- Play: the capacity to experiment with the surroundings as a form of problem solving.
- Performance: the ability to adopt alternative identities for the purpose of improvisation and discovery.
- Simulation: the ability to interpret and construct dynamic models of real-world processes.
- Appropriation: the ability to meaningfully sample and remix media content.
- Multitasking: the ability to scan the environment and shift focus onto salient details.
- Distributed cognition: the ability to interact meaningfully with tools that extend mental capacities.
- Collective intelligence: the ability to pool knowledge and compare notes with others toward a common goal.
- Judgment: the ability to evaluate the reliability and credibility of different information sources.
- Transmedia navigation: the ability to follow the flow of stories and information across multiple modalities.
- Networking: the ability to search for, synthesize, and disseminate information.
- Negotiation: the ability to travel across diverse communities, discerning and respecting multiple perspectives, and grasping and following alternative norms.

For L2 learners, there are extra layers of both opportunity and challenge in developing and practicing L2 (social) media literacies, especially in regards to their participatory, multifarious, and everyday qualities. For example, L2 learners now have the opportunity to participate in new media practices associated with the language and culture of study, and face the challenge of integrating that participation into their online identities. Whether and how they might participate is a critical question, as their identities as L2 users/learners are at play (e.g., Klimanova & Dembovskaya, 2013; Pasfield-Neofitou, 2011). In addition, as with computer and information technologies, media technologies have become more numerous and diverse – there are more social networks, more tools with which to create and share content, and more news sources and agencies. Finally, as ubiquitous access and always-on personal digital technology has become commonplace, different aspects of users' lives have become mediatized (Lundby, 2009), including tasks as varied as fitness maintenance, house hunting, vacation planning, entertainment, and shopping. Equivalent mediatized practices in the cultures of study offer possibilities for L2 learners as potential means for both formal and informal learning.

5   Activities to Develop L2 Digital Literacies

With the advent of Web 2.0 and social media practices involving "reprodusage," traditional digital literacies activities – computer, information, and media – should be updated to reflect the participatory, multifarious, and everyday qualities of digital literacy practice. This section describes six activities: web scavenger hunts, web quests, online ad and post analysis, online dictionary and translator activities, app collections, and online role-play and simulation activities, with an eye towards how they might be designed to reflect new digital realities.

5.1   L2 Web Scavenger Hunts

Web scavenger hunts have been around as long as educators have attempted to develop computer and information literacies in their students. Integrated computer literacy skills develop as one uses various browser application features like tabs and bookmarks, and copies and pastes between applications, while information literacy develops as a user composes and tests out search terms, scans and evaluates search results pages, and follows links. Doing these actions in an L2 interface adds to user cognitive load, especially in initial phases of learning.

For the activity, an instructor prepares a list of 10–12 trivia questions, perhaps related thematically, and has students work individually or in dyads to find the answers on the web. For an intermediate Japanese class doing their first hunt, for example, questions might be: "What is the population of Osaka?", "What are the operating hours of the Tsukiji Fish Market?", or "What will the weather be like in Sapporo tomorrow?" Focus can be on the use of particular L2 search tools (including but also extending beyond Google in that language), on particular techniques and search terms specific to the language, and on critical analysis and interpretation of search results pages. Activities can be gamified with points and competition mechanics if desired (e.g., timed races between teams). After searches, successful students can share the terms they used, their search histories, and the reasons for the choices they made while searching. Assessment should focus on the particular objectives of the activity – for example, how fast results were found vs. how accurate they were, or how well evaluation criteria were applied to a particular search results page.

To develop critical awareness of the participatory aspect of web search-ing, there might be discussion of how search behavior is used by search engines to provide predictive results and how top results may be paid for by advertisers. To address the multifarious nature of searching, learners might compare results from different search engines (perhaps from two or three engines in the L2, or from an L1 engine and an L2 one), and discuss which one they prefer, and why. To address the fact that many learners will probably have established search habits already, they might complete pre-activities that survey and critically situate those habits, and reflect after-wards on how the experience of searching in the L2 was different from their expectations.

5.2   L2 Web Quests

Web quests are similar to scavenger hunts but are more appropriate for more advanced students who have higher language proficiency as well as some comfort using L2 search tools already. In comparison to scavenger hunts, they focus more on information and media literacy skills – how to eval-uate sources and identify bias and perspective. Students engage in more complex inquiry-based investigations involving questions and problems that are focused on cultural, political, and historical topics, e.g., "Catalan Independence" or "Immigration in France." A basic web quest should be based on a reading or news story that is rich in ideas and that will allow stu-dents to come up with critical follow-up questions that ask why and how (rather than what). After reading the story, discussing it, and coming up with follow-up questions, students search for answers and derive new questions based on them. Students can write a summary of their findings and reflect on the web-based research project – how easy or hard it was to find answers, what tools they used and why they chose them, and how reliable and trust-worthy they judged their sources to be. A short project can be expanded into larger critical media evaluation projects that can include final products like reports, multimedia presentations, or digital stories, all of which can develop computer literacies. Plagiarism, proper citation, and reliability of sources should be included when discussing products, especially consider-ing the Web 2.0 nature of "reprodusage." Again, assessment should align with the particular objectives of the activity – for example, how many dif-ferent sources were used and how, what critical follow-up questions were generated, or how well the reliability of sources was judged.

5.3   L2 Online Advertisement or Social Media Post Analysis

Similar to a web quest, an ad or post analysis activity develops critical information and media literacies, while the creation of products for the project, like reports or fake ads, can also develop computer literacies. As advertising and propaganda techniques are often culturally specific, they fit well with units on L2 news and entertainment, politics, and history. The basic form of the activity has students analyze online advertisements or social media posts in the L2 for the use of rhetorical (e.g., logos, pathos, or ethos) or propaganda techniques (e.g., bandwagon, testimonials, plain folks, glittering generalities, name calling, etc.), used for commercial products, tourist locations, or for very advanced learners, political campaigns.

For example, an intermediate German instructor might first collect online examples of several different techniques and lead learners through websites, social media pages, video commercials, and apps for various German products (e.g., BMW, Aldi, Der Spiegel) to identify sales techniques and how they imagine their consumer audiences. Dyads or individuals could then choose a company or product to examine more closely and create a presentation or write a report on it; they might choose and compare several companies selling similar products, or compare how one company sells differently to different global consumers. For a longer unit with multiple related activities, students might read about advertisement practices in the target culture, or create fake ads and posts for the product using various techniques in a variety of formats – memes, vlog commentaries, banners, etc. – and discuss and evaluate their perceived effectiveness. Assessment could accordingly focus on how well different techniques were identified in the real ads or posts, or used in the fake ads.

5.4   Online Translator and Dictionary Activities

The unsanctioned use of online translators, especially at lower proficiency levels, is often the bane of L2 instructors. However, the fact that they are ubiquitous, and that their use may in fact be central to the future of L2 use for many learners, makes the case for teaching their critical use explicitly. Online dictionaries vary widely, from extensive suites of tools designed for L2 learners like Linguee, to the basic use of Google search with "define: (word)." Some results or entry pages offer information like pronunciation, invented or authentic examples, related words, and grammatical information, and some do not – students might benefit from comparing results of different resources, including traditional print dictionary entries. Critical language awareness can also be developed through reverse translation activities, e.g., looking up a word, phrase, or prose selection in the L2, then translating it back into English, and speculating why the reverse translation was or was not accurate – poetry and song lyrics are especially useful for this sort of activity. Translator activities can be done alongside web hunts and quests, since they will generate authentically contextualized vocabulary usage examples, and in conjunction with discussion of self-directed vocabulary study, which might include critical discussion and evaluation of various L2 study tools and online apps. Assessment would again depend on the activity's objectives – for example, if an activity asked students to find and analyze mistakes on a reverse translation activity using Google Translate, assessment might score the accuracy and feasibility of their analysis.

5.5   App Collections

The increasing multifariousness of apps and other technological resources for both formal and informal L2 learning warrants direct instruction on how to curate, evaluate, and utilize personalized collections of them, especially in consideration of their widely varying quality. Students may learn of apps through advertisements, word of mouth, or simply by searching for them independently, but may not know how to evaluate their pedagogical value and soundness, or be aware of their diversity, or how to integrate them effectively into study practices. An app collection project could focus on evaluation and be integrated into discussion of study habits and dictionary or translator usage skills. After discussion and deciding on evaluation criteria – for example, ease of use, price, pedagogical approach, skills areas, proficiency level, design, etc. – a class could create a database of evaluations for apps designed not only specifically for L2 learning (e.g., Memrise), but also for self-study generally (e.g., Quizlet), as well as non-educational culture and language-focused apps (e.g., newspapers or search engines). The project could be spread out over a semester, with individuals or pairs of students presenting a new app evaluation every week, and a database could be built over the course of several semesters by different cohorts of learners. Three or four students could test out apps over a few weeks and each offer an evaluation and rating, similar to an app store or shopping website, and the database might be converted to a website and made accessible to a public audience online. Assessment would align with activity objectives, for example, how well an evaluation considered all the various criteria. (See Hubbard's chapter in this volume for more information about evaluating apps.)

5.6　Online Role-Play and Simulation Activities

In online L2 simulation activities (e.g. Levine, 2004; Mills, 2011; Reinhardt & Ryu, 2013), students use Internet tools like social media, blogs, or wikis as mediums for short-term or long-term individual or shared role-play, practicing new identities and perspectives. Projects can span a week to an entire semester, and can be integrated with digital storytelling and the aforementioned web hunts and quests. Students first create a group of characters – friends, colleagues, family, or neighbors – and decide on a setting. They can be real (e.g., movie stars or historical persons), but might be diverse in age, gender, and background. Using various computer and information literacy skills, students then develop the online persona and background stories of the characters and create social media accounts for them. The instructor then presents various events and scenarios, both benign (e.g., asking for a restaurant recommendation) and controversial (e.g., reaction to crises), to which students have characters react, both as individuals and in interaction with the other characters. The class can evaluate whether a character's language use and reaction are appropriate for a given scenario and the character's history, and characters can be switched after a period, to allow practice of different voices and associated varieties and registers. Assessment might focus on whether, and the degree to which, the elements of a particular task were completed, use of focus linguistic elements (e.g., formal pronouns, tenses, or target vocabulary) was accurate, and self or peer editing of classmates' characters' language use took place.

For example, Reinhardt & Ryu (2013) had an intermediate Korean class create several Facebook accounts[4] for famous Korean television drama personalities of various ages living in Seoul and "friend" each other. For two-week spans through the semester, a different dyad of learners took on the role of one character and reacted to scenarios that practiced various functions introduced by the instructor, like "invite another character to dinner and decide on where to go," and "post what you did today and respond to someone elses' post." Without knowing who played whom, the class together evaluated the lexicogrammatical and pragmatic appropriateness of the language used by the characters, and were then given the chance to update their posts.

4　Instructors should first research the restrictions that different social media sites and services have for creating accounts and proving identities. Facebook, for example, is more restrictive than before and requires an email address, while other sites might even require a phone number, and Instagram is less restrictive, although it has fewer features.

6   Conclusion

Examining the "traditional" digital literacies of computer, information, and media literacy through the lens of ontologically "new" participatory, multifarious, and everyday qualities implicates new sorts of L2 learning activities that develop digital literacies. This approach is only one way to imagine new yet principled learning activities situated in L2 learning theory – other approaches like those listed in the first version of this chapter (Reinhardt & Thorne, 2011) offer steps or procedures that can be methodically applied. To a certain extent, traditional digital literacies have always been participatory, multifarious, and informally learned, but in a Web 2.0 era where digital socio-literacy practices involve not only consumption, but production and remix, or "reprodusage" of media, those features take on ontologically new dimensions, not replacing the old skills, but joining them. Because literacy activities so readily involve identity and social interaction, they are also dispositional in that they are tied up with one's self-perception, attitudes, ambitions, and histories, in ways that were not visible in Web 1.0 communities. Moreover, those dispositions are often expressed through language and other forms of self-expression and interaction that are culturally intertwined. L2 learners engage in formal and informal digitally-mediated L2 learning practices that are informed by their histories as technology users, i.e., the cultures-of-use of communication tools that involves both tool and language socialization process (Thorne, 2003, 2016). This includes digital practices that they already do and value, many of which are subconscious and attitudinal. What it takes and means to make, find, evaluate, and share something online has changed over time, as has what it means to be a person online. If L2 learners are to add new linguistic and cultural dimensions to who they are online, these considerations are important. Enhanced digital literacy instruction focused on computer, information, and media literacy, as described above, can be used to recognize and better understand the nuances and complexities of online communication that will help to enable full participation in existing and future communities of practice across the lifespan.

Questions for Reflection

1. How can digital literacies be developed through foreign language study? How can digital literacy development be integrated into other, traditional L2 learning activities that address interpretive, presentational, or interpersonal communication?

2. How can learners' everyday Internet usage habits be leveraged, or used strategically, when it comes to developing L2 digital literacies? For example, a student who loves gaming might play their favorite game in the L2. In contrast, when might those habits get in the way or challenge that development? For example, using a keyboard can be quite a challenge for learners of languages that use non-Roman writing systems.

3. To what extent is it the responsibility of FL educators to address the development of digital literacies in L2 learners? Should computer, information, and media literacies be included as explicit objectives in an L2 course curriculum? Why or why not?

4. In the modern digital world, global, local, and "glocal" cultures coexist online, and everyday Internet use sometimes involves polylingual code meshing and the use of non-standard varieties. With this in mind,

    a. Find and present an example of the meshing of codes, images, or other discourses in the L2 that in some way challenges traditional stereotypes. How might this example be used in the classroom?

    b. Do you think contemporary FL educators should allow or even teach learners to use non-standard Internet language? To code switch and mesh between their L1 and the L2? Why or why not? And if so, how?

Case Study

Teaching

An instructor of intermediate Spanish in the US and an instructor of advanced English in Colombia are designing a telecollaboration/online intercultural exchange project for their two classes about environmental issues. They want students to watch short documentaries about issues in the other country (water in the US West and rainforest destruction in Colombia), read articles about the issues, and write reaction essays on the pieces. They'd like the students to collaborate on multimodal compositions as culminating activities. The US students have a slightly lower Spanish proficiency relative to the Colombian students' English proficiency, but in general they have more advanced computer literacy skills and access to more powerful devices and better broadband.

In a pair or small group, brainstorm and outline the objectives, tools, and basic procedures of one of the tasks for the project. Consider the following questions to evaluate your task designs:

1. How do the task designs reflect and respect the varying needs, proficiencies, and contexts of the two groups, and individual learner differences within them?
2. How do the task designs focus on linguistic and cultural development, at the same time as they develop computer, information, and/or media literacies?
3. How do the task designs take into account the participatory, multifarious, and everyday nature of Internet use?

Ideas for Action Research Projects

A. Adapt one of the activities in section 5 for your current or future L2 teaching situation and conduct an action research project on it. Consider using a framework like the New London Group's multiliteracies cycle (New London Group, 1996; Kern, 2000; Reinhardt & Thorne 2011). For example, an online translator activity using a multiliteracies framework could include phases that focus on situated practice, guided instruction, critical framing, and transformed practice. The first phase would have learners write a reflection about their current online translation practices for homework. In the second phase the instructor would lead the learners through the various features of how to use a particular tool like Linguee. The third would have the learners compare the tool's search results page with a print dictionary entry or the results of another online tool and critically evaluate how useful the tools would be for different purposes, such as looking up a word while conversing with another person, writing an essay, or reading a news article. The fourth would have the learners reflect on how their understanding of the utility of the new tool changed because of the activity.

An action research project based on this intervention would pose the question whether and to what extent online translation literacies can be developed through explicit instruction, and would involve documentation of the intervention and collection and analysis of learner work. Data from phase 1 and phase 4 would be compared to infer whether and to what extent the intervention facilitated learner development or transformation, and all data could be used to evaluate which phases were most or least effective. For example, if several learner phase 4 reflections missed the inclusion of certain key Linguee features, it could be that the phase 2 tour of features missed or underemphasized that feature. If some noted uncritically that the examples provided in Linguee were useful, while others noted critically that the examples are not particularly useful without knowing which ones match their needs, the phase 2 activity might be changed to include not only a tour, but also a discussion to raise awareness of genre and register differences.

B. Research the state of digital literacies among native and expert users of the language of study – start by searching for "technology use statistics in (country)" in both English and the other language. How are digital technologies used in the culture(s) of study, for work, play, and social uses, and how does it compare to similar statistics for the US or the students' home country? What does technology and access cost, and what digital divide issues are there? For example, what social media tools are popular, by which users, and to what degree? What chat tools and online games are popular? A related measure might involve surveying some speakers of that language with regards to technology use and digital literacies. After collecting the data, compare them with L2 learners (your students), and consider how this information informs your instruction. What differences between your students' L1 and L2 with regards to technology usage and digital literacies are relevant? Do your students need to recognize that unfamiliar social media tools are popular in the culture of study, and is access less or more widespread than they might imagine? A related research project would be to investigate digital literacies (computer, information, and media) education in the culture of study. How do these practices compare to your school's practices and the education that your students have received in the area?

C. Conduct a social media discourse analysis to find evidence of digital literacies practices. On a social media platform like Facebook, join a few groups related to your interests and hobbies in your L2 and observe the interactions among members. Into a new document, copy and paste some of the posts with their threaded conversations until you have at least 5 different posts and about 3–5 pages worth of threads. Conduct an analysis of the interactions and ask:

1. What are the topics and the functions (e.g., argumentation, making jokes, requests, inviting, sharing information, etc.) members engage in?
2. What are the varieties of language being used, especially Internet and non-standard varieties and evidence of code-meshing?
3. How are images and videos used in addition to language?
4. How is affect and pragmatic meaning conveyed (e.g., with emojis, non-conventional spellings, etc.)?

5. What are the norms of participation (e.g., what is appropriate, acceptable, and 'well-liked')?
6. What vocabulary and grammatical structures are used? Which are relatively common and uncommon? What patterns of language – greetings, leave taking, collocational patterns, are familiar and which are new to the participants? Consider having students produce a "grammar-of-use" that is visible in the data they collect.

Write a short report that includes the analysis and reflections on the following: What digital literacies are practiced by the participants? How do you think group members learn to interact in this group in these ways? Should, and could, L2 learners be taught these practices explicitly, and if so, how?

References

American Library Association (2018). Information literacy competency standards for higher education. Retrieved from http://www.ala.org/Template.cfm?Section=Home&template=/ContentManagement/ContentDisplay.cfm&ContentID=33553

Barton, D. (2007). *Literacy: An introduction to the ecology of written language.* London: Blackwell.

Back, M. (2013). Using Facebook data to analyze learner interaction during study abroad. *Foreign Language Annals, 46*(3), 377–401. https://doi.org/10.1111/flan.12036

Bass, R., & Elmendorf, H. (2012). *Designing for difficulty: Social pedagogies as a framework for course design.* Retrieved from https://blogs.commons.georgetown.edu/bassr/social-pedagogies/

Bax, S. (2011). Normalisation revisited: The effective use of technology in language education. *International Journal of Computer Assisted Language Learning and Teaching, 1*(2), 1–15. https://doi.org/10.4018/ijcallt.2011040101

Bezemer, J., & Kress, G. (2016). *Multimodality, learning and communication.* London: Routledge.

Black, R. (2008). *Adolescents and online fan fiction.* New York: Peter Lang.

Blattner, G., & Flori, M. (2009). Facebook in the language classroom: Promises and possibilities. *International Journal of Instructional Technology and Distance Learning, 6*(1), 17–29.

Blattner, G., & Fiori, M. (2011). Virtual social network communities: An investigation of language learners' development of sociopragmatic awareness and multiliteracy skills. *CALICO Journal, 29*(1), 24–43. https://doi.org/10.11139/cj.29.1.24-43

Bloch, J. (2007). Abdullah's blogging: A generation 1.5 student enters the blogosphere. *Language Learning & Technology, 11*(2), 128–141.

Blommaert, J. (2010). *The sociolinguistics of globalization.* Cambridge: Cambridge University Press. https://doi.org/10.1017/CBO9780511845307

Bolitho, R., Carter, R., Hughes, R., Ivanic, R., Masuhara, H., & Tomlinson, B. (2003). Ten questions about language awareness. *ELT Journal*, 57(3), 251–259. https://doi.org/10.1093/elt/57.3.251

Bourdieu, P. (1991). *Language and symbolic power*. Cambridge: Polity Press.

Brates, V., Del Carpio, C., Miano, A., Houts, P., Carvajal, I., & Barco, M. (2017). Abriendo Caminos: Breaking new ground in community-engaged language learning. In S. Dubreil & S. L. Thorne (eds.), *Engaging the world: Social pedagogies and language learning* (pp. 87–108). Boston, MA: Cengage.

Buckingham, D. (2003). *Media education: Literacy, learning, and contemporary culture*. London: Blackwell.

Center for Media Literacy (2018). Media literacy: A definition and more. Retrieved from www.medialit.org/media-literacy-definition-and-more.

Charitos, S., & Van Deusen-Scholl, N. (2017). Engaging the city: Language, space, and identity in urban environments. In S. Dubreil & S. L. Thorne (eds.), *Engaging the world: Social pedagogies and language learning* (pp. 15–36). Boston, MA: Cengage.

Chen, H. (2013). Identity practices of multilingual writers in social networking spaces. *Language Learning & Technology*, 17(2), 143–170.

Danet, B. & Herring, S. (2007). *The multilingual Internet: Language, culture, and communication online*. New York: Oxford University Press.

Darvin, R., & Norton, B. (2015). Identity and a model of investment in applied linguistics. *Annual Review of Applied Linguistics*, 35, 36–56. https://doi.org/10.1017/S0267190514000191

Dubreil, S., & Thorne, S. L. (eds.) (2017a). *Engaging the world: Social pedagogies and language learning*. Boston, MA: Cengage.

Dubreil, S., & Thorne, S. L. (2017b). Social pedagogies and entwining language with the world. In *Engaging the world: Social pedagogies and language learning*, pp. 1–11. Boston, MA: Cengage.

Ducate, L., & Lomicka, L. (2008). Adventures in the blogosphere: From blog readers to blog writers. *Computer Assisted Language Learning*, 21(1), 9–28. https://doi.org/10.1080/09588220701865474

Ellison, N., & boyd, D. (2013). Sociality through social network sites. In W. Dutton (ed.), *The Oxford handbook of Internet studies*, pp. 151–172. Oxford: Oxford University Press.

Gebhard, M., Shin, D. & Seger, W. (2011). Blogging and emergent L2 literacy development in an urban elementary school: A functional perspective. *CALICO Journal*, 28(2), 278–307. https://doi.org/10.11139/cj.28.2.278-307

Gee, J. P. (1999). *An introduction to discourse analysis*. London: Routledge.

Gee, J. P. (2004). *Situated language and learning: A critique of traditional schooling*. London: Routledge

Greenfield, J., Finch, V., & Johnson, M. (2017). Networked learning: Students as producers, curators, and consumers of authentic resources on campus and abroad. In S. Dubreil & S. L. Thorne (eds.), *Engaging the world: Social pedagogies and language learning*, pp. 168–198. Boston, MA: Cengage.

Hanna, B., & De Nooy, J. (2009). *Learning language and culture via public Internet discussion forums*. New York: Palgrave Macmillan.

Hutchins, E. (1995). *Cognition in the wild*. Cambridge, MA: MIT Press.

Hyland, K. (2001). *Genre and second language writing.* Ann Arbor, MI: University of Michigan Press.

Ito, M., Baumer, S., Bittanti, M., boyd, d., et al. (2010). *Hanging out, messing around, and geeking out: Kids living and learning with new media.* Cambridge, MA: MIT Press.

Jenkins, H., Purushotma, R., Clinton, K., Weigel, M., & Robinson, A. (2006). *Confronting the challenges of participatory culture: Media education for the 21st century.* Chicago: MacArthur Foundation.

Jewitt, C. (2014). *The Routledge Handbook of Multimodal Analysis.* London: Routledge.

Kern, R. (2000). *Literacy and language teaching.* Oxford: Oxford University Press.

Kern, R., & Liddicoat, A. J. (2008). De l'apprenant au locuteur/acteur. In G. Zarate, D. Lévy, & C. Kramsch (eds.), *Précis du plurilinguisme et du pluriculturalisme,* pp. 25–33. Paris: Éditions des archives contemporaines.

King, B. W. (2015). Wikipedia writing as praxis: Computer-mediated socialization of second-language writers. *Language Learning & Technology,* 19(3), 106–123.

Klimanova, L., & Dembovskaya, S. (2013). L2 identity, discourse, and social networking in Russian. *Language Learning & Technology,* 17(1), 69–88.

Kramsch, C., & Whiteside, A. (2008). Language ecology in multilingual settings: Towards a theory of symbolic competence. *Applied Linguistics,* 29(4), 645–671. https://doi.org/10.1093/applin/amn022

Kress, G. (2010). *Multimodality: A Social semiotic approach to contemporary communication.* London: Routledge.

Kurek, M., & Hauck, M. (2014). Closing the "digital divide" – a framework for multiliteracy training. In G. P. Guikema & L. Williams (eds.), *Digital literacies in foreign and second language education: Research, perspectives, and best practice.* CALICO Monograph Series. San Marcos, TX: CALICO.

Lam, W. (2000). Second language literacy and the design of the self: a case study of a teenager writing on the Internet. *TESOL Quarterly,* 34(3), 457–483. https://doi.org/10.2307/3587739

Lam, W. (2004). Second language socialization in a bilingual chat room: Global and local considerations. *Language Learning & Technology,* 8(3), 44–65.

Lankshear, C., and Knobel, M. (2006). *New literacies: Everyday practices and classroom learning.* New York: Open University Press.

Larsen-Freeman, D., & Anderson, M. (2011). *Techniques and principles in language teaching.* Oxford: Oxford University Press.

Lave, J., & Wenger, E. (1991). *Situated learning: Legitimate peripheral participation.* Cambridge: Cambridge University Press. https://doi.org/10.1017/CBO9780511815355

Lee, L. (2012). Engaging study abroad students in intercultural learning through blogging and ethnographic interviews. *Foreign Language Annals,* 45(1), 7–21.

Leppänen, S., Kytölä, S., & Westinen, E. (2017). Multilingualism and multimodality in language use and literacies in digital environments. In S. L. Thorne & S. May (eds.), *Volume 9: Language, Education, and Technology. Encyclopedia of Language and Education,* 3rd edition, pp. 119–130. Berlin: Springer.

Leu, D., Zawilinski, L., Castek, J., Banerjee, M., Housand, B., Liu, Y., & O'Neil, M. (2007). What is new about the new literacies of online reading comprehension? In L. Rush, A. J. Eakle, and A. Berger (eds.), *Secondary school literacy: What research reveals for classroom practice.* Urbana, IL: NCTE.

Lessig, L. (2008). *Remix: Making art and commerce thrive in the hybrid economy.* London: Bloomsbury. https://doi.org/10.5040/9781849662505

Levine, G. (2004). Global simulation: A student-centered, task-based format for intermediate foreign language courses. *Foreign Language Annals,* 37(1), 26–36. https://doi.org/10.1111/j.1944-9720.2004.tb02170.x

Lundby, K. (2009). *Mediatization: Concept, changes, consequence.* New York: Peter Lang.

May, S. (2014). *The multilingual turn: Implications for SLA, TESOL and bilingual education.* New York: Routledge.

McCarthy, M., & Carter, R. (1994). *Language as discourse: Perspectives for language teaching.* London: Longman.

McLuhan, M. (1964). *Understanding media: The extensions of man.* New York: McGraw-Hill.

Mills, N. (2011). Situated learning through social networking communities: The development of joint enterprise, mutual engagement, and a shared repertoire. *CALICO Journal,* 28(2), 345–368. https://doi.org/10.11139/cj.28.2.345-368

Mitch, D. (2005). Education and economic growth in historical perspective. *EH.Net Encyclopedia,* ed. Robert Whaples. July 26. Downloaded May 2, 2018, from http://eh.net/encyclopedia/education-and-economic-growth-in-historical-perspective/

New London Group (1996). A pedagogy of multiliteracies: Designing social factors. *Harvard Educational Review,* 66(1), 60–92. https://doi.org/10.17763/haer.66.1.17370n67v22j160u

O'Keeffe, A., McCarthy, M., & Carter, R. (2007). *From corpus to classroom: Language use and language teaching.* Cambridge: Cambridge University Press. https://doi.org/10.1017/CBO9780511497650

Oskoz, A., & Elola, I. (2016). Digital stories: Overview. *CALICO Journal,* 33(2), 156–173. https://doi.org/10.1558/cj.v33i2.29295

Pasfield-Neofitou, S. (2011). Second language learners' experiences of virtual community and foreignness. *Language Learning & Technology,* 15(2), 92–108.

Pellet, S., & Myers, L. (2017). Social-pedagogical life imitates art: Scaffolding the voices of L2 fans and critics. In S. Dubreil & S. L. Thorne (eds.), *Engaging the world: Social pedagogies and language learning,* pp. 111–137. Boston, MA: Cengage.

Pennycook, A. (2010). *Language as a local practice.* New York: Routledge.

Pennycook, A., & Otsuji, E. (2015). *Metrolingualism: Language in the city.* New York: Routledge.

Rama, P., Black, R., Es, E., & Warschauer, M. (2012). Affordances for second language learning in World of Warcraft. *ReCALL,* 24(3), 322–338. https://doi.org/10.1017/S0958344012000171

Reinhardt, J. (2017a). Digital gaming. In C. Chapelle and S. Sauro (eds.), *Handbook of technology in second language teaching and learning,* pp. 202–216. Hoboken, NJ: Wiley-Blackwell. https://doi.org/10.1002/9781118914069.ch14

Reinhardt, J. (2017b). "Social network sites and L2 education." In S. L. Thorne & S. May (eds.), *Volume 9: Language, Education, and Technology. Encyclopedia of Language and Education*, 3rd edition, pp. 389–400. Berlin: Springer.

Reinhardt, J., & Ryu, J. (2013). Using social network-mediated bridging activities to develop socio-pragmatic awareness in elementary Korean. *International Journal of Computer Assisted Language Learning and Teaching*, 3(3), 18–33. https://doi.org/10.4018/ijcallt.2013070102

Reinhardt, J., & Thorne, S. (2011). Beyond comparisons: Frameworks for developing digital L2 literacies. In N. Arnold & L. Ducate (eds.), *Present and future promises of CALL: From theory and research to new directions in language teaching*, pp. 257–280. San Marcos, TX: CALICO.

Reinhardt, J., Warner, C., and Lange, K. (2014). Digital game literacies in L2 German. In J. Pettes-Guikema and L. Williams (eds.), *Digital literacies in foreign language education*, pp. 159–177. San Marcos, TX: CALICO.

Reinhardt, J., & Zander, V. (2011). Social networking in an intensive English program classroom: A language socialization perspective. *CALICO Journal*, 28(2), 326–344. https://doi.org/10.11139/cj.28.2.326-344

Sauro, S., & Sundmark, B. (2016). Report from Middle Earth: Fanfiction tasks in the EFL classroom. *ELT Journal*, 70(4), 414–423. https://doi.org/10.1093/elt/ccv075

Schreiber, B. R. (2015). "I am what I am": Multilingual identity and digital translanguaging. *Language Learning & Technology* 19(3), 69–87.

Scribner, S., & Cole, M. (1981). *The psychology of literacy.* Cambridge, MA: Harvard University Press. https://doi.org/10.4159/harvard.9780674433014

Sockett, G. (2014). *The online informal learning of English.* Basingstoke: Palgrave. https://doi.org/10.1057/9781137414885

Sockett, G., & Kusyk, M. (2015). Online informal learning of English: Frequency effects in the uptake of chunks of language from participation in web-based activities. In T. Cadierno & S. W. Eskildson (eds.), *Usage-based perspectives on second language learning*, pp. 153–177. Berlin: deGruyter Mouton. https://doi.org/10.1515/9783110378528-009

Solmaz, O. (2015). *Multilingual students' management of transnational identities in online participatory sites.* Unpublished PhD dissertation, University of Arizona, Tucson, USA.

Standage, T. (2013). *Writing on the wall: Social media – the first 2,000 years.* New York: Bloomsbury.

Street, B. (1984). *Literacy in theory and practice.* Cambridge, MA: Harvard University Press.

Street, B. (1995). *Social literacies: Critical approaches to literacy in development, ethnography and education.* Longman: London.

Sundqvist, P., & Sylvén, L. (2016). *Extramural English in teaching and learning: From theory and research to practice.* London: Palgrave. https://doi.org/10.1057/978-1-137-46048-6

Thorne, S. L. (2003). Artifacts and cultures-of-use in intercultural communication. *Language Learning & Technology*, 7(2), 38–67.

Thorne, S. L. (2008). Transcultural communication in open Internet environments and massively multiplayer online games. In S. Magnan (ed.), *Mediating discourse online*, pp. 305–327. Amsterdam: John Benjamins. https://doi.org/10.1075/aals.3.17tho

Thorne, S. L. (2012). Gaming writing: Supervernaculars, stylization, and semiotic remediation. In G. Kessler, A. Oskoz, & I. Elola (eds.), *Technology across writing contexts and tasks*, pp. 297–316. San Marcos, Texas: CALICO.

Thorne, S. L. (2013). Digital literacies. In M. Hawkins (ed.), *Framing languages and literacies: Socially situated views and perspectives*, pp. 192–218. New York: Routledge.

Thorne, S. L. (2016). Cultures-of-use and morphologies of communicative action. *Language Learning & Technology*, 20(2), 185–191.

Thorne, S. L., & Black, R. (2007). Language and literacy development in computer-mediated contexts and communities. *Annual Review of Applied Linguistics*, 27, 133–160. https://doi.org/10.1017/S0267190508070074

Thorne, S. L., & Ivković, D. (2015). Multilingual Eurovision meets plurilingual YouTube: Linguascaping discursive ontologies. In D. Koike & C. Blyth (eds.), *Dialogue in multilingual and multimodal communities*, pp. 167–192. Amsterdam: John Benjamins. https://doi.org/10.1075/ds.27.06tho

Thorne, S. L., & Fischer, I. (2012). Online gaming as sociable media. *Apprentissage des Langues et Systèmes d'Information et de Communication*, 15(1). https://alsic.revues.org/2450.

Thorne, S. L., & Payne, S. (2005). Evolutionary trajectories, Internet-mediated expression, and language education. *CALICO Journal*, 22(3), 371–397. https://doi.org/10.1558/cj.v22i3.371-397

Thorne, S. L., & Reinhardt, J. (2008). "Bridging activities," new media literacies and advanced foreign language proficiency. *CALICO Journal*, 25(3): 558–572. https://doi.org/10.1558/cj.v25i3.558-572

Thorne, S. L., Sauro, S., & Smith, B. (2015). Technologies, identities, and expressive activity. *Annual Review of Applied Linguistics*, 35, 215–233. https://doi.org/10.1017/S0267190514000257

Tusting, K. (2017). Ecologies of digital literacies: Implications for education. In S. L. Thorne & S. May (eds.), *Volume 9: Language, Education, and Technology. Encyclopedia of Language and Education*, 3rd edition, pp. 3–15. New York: Springer. https://doi.org/10.1007/978-3-319-02237-6_3

Vandergriff, I. (2016). *Second-language discourse in the digital world: Linguistic and social practices in and beyond the networked classroom.* Amsterdam/ Philadelphia: John Benjamins. https://doi.org/10.1075/lllt.46

Wagner, J. (2015). Designing for language learning in the wild: Creating social infrastructures for second language learning. In T. Cadierno & S. W. Eskildsen (eds.), *Usage-based perspectives on second language learning*, pp. 75–101. Berlin: deGruyter Mouton. https://doi.org/10.1515/9783110378528-006

Warner, C., & Richardson, D. (2017). Beyond participation: Symbolic struggles with(in) digital social media in the L2 classroom. In S. Dubreil & S. L. Thorne (eds.), *Engaging the world: Social pedagogies and language learning*, pp. 199–226. Boston, MA: Cengage.

Warschauer, M. (1999). *Electronic literacies: Language, culture, and power in online education.* Mahwah, NJ: Erlbaum.

Warschauer, M., & Grimes, D. (2007). Audience, authorship, and artifact: The emergent semiotics of Web 2.0. *Annual Review of Applied Linguistics,* 27, 1–23. https://doi.org/10.1017/S0267190508070013

About the Authors

Jonathon Reinhardt is Associate Professor of English Applied Linguistics and Second Language Acquisition and Teaching at the University of Arizona.

Steven L. Thorne is Professor of Second Language Acquisition and holds faculty appointments in the Department of World Languages & Literatures at Portland State University and in the Department of Applied Linguistics at the University of Groningen, The Netherlands.

7 Writing between the Lines: Acquiring Writing Skills and Digital Literacies through Social Tools

Idoia Elola and Ana Oskoz[1]

Preview Questions

1. Blogs, Facebook, wikis, and other social tools are now increasingly being used in second language (L2) classrooms to develop writing skills. Have you worked with digitally-mediated writing tasks using these tools? How do the texts produced this way differ in terms of communicative purpose and language use from other types of writing?
2. What are some ways in which L2 courses could use social tools to develop writing skills? To what extent should social tools shape existing curricula?
3. Social tools can be used in a synchronous manner (working together, with real-time exchange of information, as in Skype) or an asynchronous manner (working in turn, with a time delay between exchanges of information, as in wikis). To what extent can these two features be exploited and used in L2 classrooms to develop students' writing processes and help them master writing conventions?
4. The adoption of social tools requires decisions about linguistic features of the target language in conjunction with writing conventions (e.g., the use of the past tense for narration). What language features and which genres do you associate with digital social tools?

---

1   Both authors contributed equally to this chapter.

1 Introduction

The introduction of digital tools, such as wikis, blogs, Twitter, or digital story software has influenced the act of writing in ways unimaginable a few years ago. Writing is no longer seen as primarily a solitary endeavor; rather, it is now a social act, either because the writing happens collaboratively (e.g., via wikis or Google Docs) or because it is directed to an audience of individuals who participate in an exchange of ideas (e.g., via Twitter or Facebook). Further, although a written text is often the selected mode for communication, many of today's digital tools allow for, and even encourage, the inclusion of other semiotic resources, such as images and sound. For instance, learners engaged in digital storytelling can easily combine text, images, and sound to produce a multimodal text.

Yet, despite the ubiquity of social tools in our daily lives, and despite a body of research advocating digital technology-based second language (L2) writing (Arnold, Ducate, & Kost, 2012; Elola & Oskoz, 2016, 2017; Kessler, 2009; Oskoz & Elola, 2016), many L2 instructors remain uncertain about how to integrate digital tools and multimodal texts into L2 curricula and into their classroom practices. To overcome this challenge, instructors must first recognize the paradigmatic shift that digital tools bring to the classroom (Elola & Oskoz, 2017); second, they need to move away from traditional L2 pedagogical principles that value only the textual component of students' assignments (Nelson, 2006; Oskoz & Elola, 2014, 2016; Yang, 2012); and, third, they need to recognize emerging digital genres and add them to their traditional repertoire of genres (Yang, 2012). Therefore, the interesting question now for L2 researchers and educators is how, without disregarding traditional (and still fundamental) literacy skills, they can "orient themselves to the changing qualities, purposes, and contexts of [digitally] mediated language use [...] and toward the issue of which genres and communication tools should be included in L2 curricula" (Thorne & Black, 2007: 134).

In seeking to answer this question, this chapter is intended to guide L2 writing instructors in how to enter the adventurous world of digital written literacies. First we ground our discussion within the theoretical frameworks that inform digital literacy practices, before evaluating a range of digital tools that we believe can be successfully introduced into the L2 class. The chapter then addresses the relevance of multimodal tools in the development of new digital genres, provides specific examples of how to integrate the use of multimodal tools with practical student tasks, and finishes with some questions for further reflection. In addition to educators' training in digital literacies, we also know that today's learners will need to master

digital tools in order to communicate successfully in academic and professional contexts. Indeed, we recognize the need to prepare learners to
understand and value the affordances – actions that individuals are able to
perform because of a particular tool of sharing, communicating, or information discovery (McLoughlin & Lee, 2007) – that digital tools bring to the
writing process itself.

2   Theoretical Approaches to the Use of Social Tools

When we consider theoretical frameworks in the context of digital social
tools, we need to first acknowledge that, as Thorne (2003) points out,
advances in technology have led to major shifts in communicative practices. Not only must we recognize that learners need to acquire multimodal
competence, but we must also exploit the full potential of these new competencies in the language learning process. To date, three theoretical frameworks have informed the implementation of social digital tools in the L2
classroom: sociocultural theory, activity theory, and socio-semiotic theory.

2.1   Sociocultural Theory

Perhaps because of the collaborative nature of digital tools, most studies
of L2 digital writing follow sociocultural theory, which focuses on writers' co-construction of knowledge. Within sociocultural theory, the two
central tenets that have been highly influential in the analysis of L2 writing with digital tools are mediation and scaffolding. With regard to mediation, sociocultural theory argues that higher forms of mental activity, such
as attending, predicting, planning, monitoring, and inferencing, are mediated mental activities whose sources are external to the individual, and in
which the learner participates through dialogue. The mediation of these
cognitive functions occurs using psychological or semiotic tools, such as
numbers, symbols, or language, as well as through exposure to physical
tools or artifacts, such as blogs, wikis, or digital story software. Studies in
technology-assisted L2 writing have examined how, through collaborative
dialogue in wikis and chats, learners assist each other with content development (Arnold et al., 2009; Kessler, 2009) or focus on linguistic forms
(Adams & Ross-Feldman, 2008). With regard to scaffolding, Oskoz & Elola
(2014) found that in the learner–learner dialogic interactions that assist in
the development of more complex meaning in the zone of proximal development (Wood, Bruner, & Ross, 1976), L2 learners noticed discrepancies,

controlled frustration, and pursued identified goals – all features that become visible in the scaffolding process.

2.2 Activity Theory

Activity theory, which holds that cognitive development has cultural and social roots, highlights the dynamic nature of the interrelationships between the various elements of the writing process (author, audience, tools, tasks). *Activity* has been defined as "a collective complex systemic formation that has a complex mediational structure" (Engeström, 2008: 26) and as "a form of doing directed to an *object*" (Kuttii, 1996: 27). The individual's conscious and unconscious actions directed towards a goal occur at the nexus of three factors: the available tools and artifacts (e.g., computers, languages, and tasks), the community and its understood rules (e.g., between the instructor and learners in a classroom), and the division of labor (e.g., among learners). Blin & Appel (2011) studied the essential role of the artifacts used or created by L2 learners and found that the use of the wiki to support a writing task influenced all aspects of the activity, such as the object produced, the set of rules conveyed to the learners, the shared understanding of the task, and the working relationships among participants. However, even when instructors and learners share the same goal – the completion of the writing activity – how they set about achieving that goal might differ and, to some extent, create contradictions or "structural tensions within and between activity systems" (Engeström, 2001: 137). These contradictions manifest as problems, ruptures, breakdowns, clashes (Kutti, 1996: 34), or disturbances, in other words "actions that deviate from the expected course of regular procedure" (Engeström, 2008: 27). However, contradictions generally trigger changes that help learners change their perceptions of the writing act.

2.3 Socio-Semiotic Theory

Perhaps the theoretical approach that best accommodates the complexity of digital tools is social-semiotic theory (Kress, 2010). According to this theory, the multimodal process in which the author is immersed when producing a text is defined as a *design* for which the author makes use of *semiotic resources* to sit within a *frame* (genre) and in which several types of *modes* (e.g., written, oral) are used in the production of a text. This implies that learners become active designers who arrange and rearrange the presentation of their message by selecting and mingling semiotic resources (e.g., images, sounds, text) according to the meanings they intend to convey

(Yang, 2012). When working with multimodality, it is important to integrate resources (such as visuals, audio, or text,) in a process called synesthetic semiosis (Kress, 1998), "within which writers understand not only the role played by the mode of representation as a design element but also the effects of both the absence and the existence of design elements on readers' responses to the multimodal text" (Shin & Cimasko, 2008: 378). In the L2 classroom, learners face two challenges that are pivotal when developing a multimodal text (Kress, 2009): (1) *transformation,* the actions that reorder and reposition semiotic resources within a particular mode (e.g., reconstructing the syntax or structural complexity of sentences from a narrative [written] story into a digital script), and (2) *transduction*, the reorganization of semiotic resources across modes (e.g., the shift of written narration into spoken language). When shifting from traditional academic writing to a multimodal format, learners are faced with the challenge of integrating or manipulating different modes of expression. For example, Yang's (2012) L2 learners used transformation within the oral mode (playing with tone, stress, and intonation), visual mode (orchestrating color and lines of images), and aural mode (arranging tempos, rhythms, melodies). Through a process of transduction across modes, they were then able to convey their intended meanings in their digital stories. Learners need to be guided in these processes of developing their own compelling multimodal texts, in which learners express explicit and implicit meaning by combining text, images, and sounds. Without a doubt, helping L2 learners acquire this kind of digital competency requires a carefully considered plan underpinned by an appropriate pedagogical framework.

3   Digital Tools

When thinking of digital tools for L2 writing classrooms (see Table 1), one approach might be to place them on a continuum, from more traditional tools to more innovative ones. It might be more productive, however, to examine digital tools in terms of those characteristics that might make them suited for developing either local (vocabulary, editing, grammar) or global (content, structure, organization) aspects of learners' writing. This knowledge will help L2 instructors to assess the usefulness of new tools as they arrive in the wake of rapid changes in communicative technology and purposes.

Table 1 Digital tools in the foreign language classroom

Tools	Description	Linguistic components	Modes	Genres
Digital story software	Asynchronous tools that attract the attention of the audience through personal storytelling	Content, grammar, structure and organization	Textual, visual, and aural	Digital storytelling that can include scripts based on narrations
Blogs	Asynchronous tools that encourage the development of lengthier written texts	Creativity, content, skills of persuasion and argumentation	Mostly textual and visual, sometimes aural resources	Blogging (travel blogs, financial blogs, news blogs), fan fiction, etc.
Social networks (e.g., Facebook, NING)	Asynchronous tools that incite fast and immediate responses from users and followers	Vocabulary, grammar, spelling, fluency	Mostly visual and aural with some textual resources	Opinion pieces, summaries, fan fiction Facebooking: amalgam of opinions, commentaries
Twitter	Asynchronous tools that incite fast and immediate responses from users and followers	Vocabulary, grammar	Mostly textual and visual	Tweets
Wikis and Google Docs	Asynchronous and synchronous tools that provide space for collaborative writing	Rhetorical organization, coherence, grammar, content	Textual, sometimes with visual resources	Argumentative or expository essays, reports, Wikipedia entries…

3.1   Digital Story Software

Digital story software is an editing tool that allows users to create a digital story (DS), in other words a storyline that integrates text, images, and sounds in an online environment. When working on a DS, learners generally rely on a mix of traditional skills (e.g., researching, writing, interviewing) and newly acquired skills (e.g., creating/selecting graphics, animation, music), allowing for an expanded definition of storytelling (Lambert, 2012). The visual and audio components of DSs have obvious appeal, especially to a younger generation of learners, but they also promote "deep language acquisition and meaningful practice" (Rance-Roney, 2008: 29). Because of their strong writing component, DSs have been used in the L2 classroom (Castañeda, 2013; Oskoz & Elola, 2014, 2016; Rance-Roney, 2008; Vinogradova, Linville, & Bickel, 2011; Yang, 2012). The DS allows learners to write creatively, organize their thoughts coherently, and construct their own narratives (Gakhar & Thompson, 2007; Robin, 2006). Studies have shown that the DS genre encourages learners to pay attention to grammatical rules (Reyes-Torres, Pich-Ponce, & García-Pastor, 2012) just as much as traditional academic writing (Oskoz & Elola, 2014).

3.2   Blogs

Blogs are online journals where a writer or group of writers post thoughts and ideas in chronological order. Farmer, Yue, & Brookes (2008) point out that bloggers express their own ideas and views while at the same time engaging in social networks of interaction and exchange. Blogs are, therefore, transformational in the sense that they allow users to connect with and become part of an active social community while exercising and legitimizing their personal expressive spaces (Papacharissi, 2006); at the same time text content is enhanced by the opinions, advice, and criticism coming from the audience (Ward, 2004).

Since the early 2000s, L2 educators have seen the possibilities of blogging for intercultural development (Elola & Oskoz, 2008; Lee, 2009); reflection on language learning experiences (Hourigan & Murray, 2010; Murray, Hourigan, & Jeanneau, 2007) and L2 reading and writing practices (Ducate & Lomicka, 2008; Lejas, 2007; Ward, 2004). Blogs place greater emphasis on creativity than on the attainment of perfect grammar or spelling (Lejas, 2007), reflecting that the journalistic nature of blogs enables learners to share and appreciate experiences in a uniquely personal manner (Ducate & Lomicka, 2008).

3.3   Facebook

Facebook, founded in 2004, is a social networking site whose mission is to "give people the power to build community and bring the world closer together" (Facebook, 2018: para. 2). Although there is no length limit on posts, Facebook users, who create a community of friends, usually write and share short messages. In terms of community engagement, users can share news articles or websites of their interest and other users' posts, visually react to others' posts, and/or comment on them.

While engaging with Facebook, learners have reported improvements in multiliteracy and general language skills (Blattner & Fiori, 2011; Kabilan, Ahmad, & Abidin, 2010) as well as sociopragmatic development through grammar and vocabulary analyses (Blattner & Fiori, 2011). In terms of writing development, L2 learners have reported gains in writing fluency (Dizon, 2016; Wang & Vasquez, 2012), spelling, word choice, and overall writing skills when engaged in role-play assignments (Yen, Hou, & Chang, 2015) and in conjunction with blended courses in lower-level courses (Shih, 2011). Recently, however, the use of Facebook has been diminishing among young learners, who now show a preference for Instagram (which allows users to post images, videos, and text with captions), Snapchat, and other tools and so it will be interesting to assess the long-term potential of this social networking application for L2 writing.

3.4   Twitter

Founded in 2006, Twitter is another social networking site which potentially gives "everyone the power to create and share information instantly, without barriers" (Twitter, 2017: para. 1). Communicating using a maximum of only 280 characters, users can also retweet, favorite other people's posts, and use hashtags to connect their tweets to a larger topic or community. Despite its prevalence in the social and political spheres, with an average of 335 million monthly active users in the second quarter of 2018 (Statista, 2018), Twitter is still cautiously employed in L2 language classrooms (even by learners in their own personal lives), making it probably the least examined digital tool for L2 language instruction. The most common use of Twitter is as a source for gaining content knowledge and accessing current external information. Some studies into Twitter's educational uses suggest that it can help with the interpretation of hashtags (Blattner, Dalola, & Lomicka, 2016b), promote collaborative learning (Ullrich, Borau, & Stepanyan, 2010), or increase community building (Pérez-Sabater & Montero-Fleta, 2015). In terms of writing development, Twitter has some uses for vocabulary learning (Pérez-Sabater & Montero-Fleta, 2015) and practicing specific grammatical structures (Hattem, 2012, 2014).

3.5   Wikis and Google Docs

Because of their potential to create, transform, and erase learners' work with built-in accountability (Arnold et al., 2009; Elola & Oskoz, 2010; Kessler, 2009; Kessler & Bikowski, 2010), wikis and Google Docs are perhaps the applications most commonly used for collaborative writing. The difference between them is that the former is asynchronous while the latter is synchronous. In a wiki, learners provide each other with feedback using a comment function (also asynchronous), while in Google Docs, users can communicate with one another using the synchronous chat feature.

Because more than one learner can write and edit the same document, the collaborative nature of these tools seems conducive to content development, whether it involves research into the historical background of a novel (Arnold et al., 2009), discussion of cultural topics (Kessler, 2009; Kessler & Bikowski, 2010), or elaboration on the content of argumentative, expository essays or annotated bibliographies (Elola & Oskoz, 2010; Li & Zhu, 2017). Wiki-supported collaborative work also encourages learners to focus effectively on elements of rhetorical structure and organization (Elola & Oskoz, 2010). At the same time, users have been found to focus on the grammatical accuracy of their own writing (Elola & Oskoz, 2010) or that of their partners (Arnold et al., 2009). However, other studies have found that L2 learners are more concerned with meaning than with form (Kessler, 2009). To exploit the collaborative nature of wiki writing, it is not unusual to combine wikis with other digital tools, such as written or spoken chats (Elola & Oskoz, 2010), blogs (Stickler & Hampel, 2010), or forums and blogs (Miyazoe & Anderson, 2010).

4   From New Digital Tools to New Digital Genres

When planning the use of social tools for writing purposes, it is important to differentiate between tools and genres (see Table 1). A tool has been defined as "the technological means of shaping the ways any message is conveyed and accessed" (Guichon & Cohen, 2016: 510). That is, digital tools are the physical means that we employ to produce meaning (e.g., digital story software, blogs, Twitter). While many tools can potentially include the textual, aural, and visual modes, it is crucial to discriminate between them in terms of which tool works best for which purpose. For example, wikis and Google Docs are predominantly text-based tools, although one could include images to support the content and add voice to the document, in either a synchronous (Google Docs) or asynchronous (wikis) manner (see Table 1). Facebook and Twitter, in contrast, encourage the use of written text (often in abbreviated form) together with the frequent use of emojis, and often as a commentary on an image (visual mode). An interesting aspect of these tools is that both Twitter and Facebook, while asynchronous, support fast and even immediate responses from users. Blogs, however, are asynchronous tools that encourage the development of lengthier written texts (textual mode), often accompanied by images (visual mode) to support the message. Finally, the most sophisticated multimodal tool is perhaps DS software, in which users combine the visual mode (images, videos), the aural mode (the sound, spoken word, music), and the textual mode (subtitles, inserted text).

Genre, on the other hand, is a term that encompasses the "abstract, socially recognized ways of using language" (Hyland, 2007: 149), as well as the recognized and distinctive ways of using language that are related to a specific form of communication (Hyland, 2007). Common written digital genres, used by our L2 learners in their personal lives and sometimes in the classroom, include the following: (1) digital storytelling, multimodal personal narratives (Nelson, 2006; Oskoz & Elola, 2014, Yang, 2012); (2) blogging or online journal writing, usually accompanied by images and used as a valid forum for self-expression and identity exploration (Lee, 2009); and (3) tweeting, short and succinct messages that often include images or links and are comments on a daily news story or personal moment (Blattner, Dalola, & Lomicka,, 2016a, 2016b). Crucially, these multimodal digital genres have shifted our understanding of what constitutes text, moving from an understanding of the written word itself as the totality of text to a more complex understanding of what text might be. Yet, as Elola & Oskoz (2017) pointed out, it is still not unusual to find on digital platforms the replication of classical writing genres, such as descriptions, narratives, argumentations, expositions, and (cultural) reports/summaries (Arnold, Ducate, & Kost, 2012; Elola & Oskoz, 2010; Oskoz & Elola, 2014). The pedagogical expectation however, is that new genres, such as tweets in Twitter become part of the writing repertoires of our students. Digital genres should "no longer [be] solely viewed as pathways to more traditional academic genres" (Vandergriff, 2016: 71), but as genres in their own right.

5   Assessment of Digital Genres

Integrating digital social tools and multimodal genres in the classroom requires the teacher to rethink what type of assessment might be most appropriate – not only in terms of learners' linguistic abilities, but also recognizing and assessing nonlinguistic aspects, such as creative use of images and sounds. When we address both linguistic and nonlinguistic aspects, we assist L2 learners to become successful 21st-century communicators as they become "progressively digitally literate" (Caws & Heift, 2016: 133). Assessing multimodal texts requires us to move away from traditional practices that generally focused on the writing itself and its linguistic characteristics, to also consider many other qualities: for instance, effective collaborative writing, the audience impact of blogs, the use of hashtags in Twitter, and the integration of sound and images in digital stories. Lotherington & Ronda noted that integrating multimodalities into the classroom requires a revised model for assessment that "moves away from standardized measures of individual written performance [...], and towards multimodal, multiplatform, collaborative and socially authentic forms of assessment" (2012: 122).

According to Kalantzis & Cope (2008), in addition to linguistic and often summative assessments, instructors should use more formative assessments, which give credit to multimodality (when possible), and provide learners with ongoing instructor/peer feedback in areas such as content, impact on the audience, and structure. A mixture of formative and summative assessment (see Appendixes A and B), at different stages of the writing activity, triggers learners' engagement with the task and allows for a process approach suitable for dealing with the complexity of multimodal texts. Given the more personal perspectives and diverse forms that multimodal texts take, we recommend co-constructing "a rubric of success alongside students, holding their design perspectives and [the instructor's] as part of the process" (Hessler & Lambert, 2017: 29).

6   Pedagogical Implications

Although we know that students and educators might be familiar with social media, we should not infer that they are digital learning "natives." Students "need to receive adequate and substantial tuition in exploiting [social tools] for learning purposes" (Hourigan & Murray, 2010: 212). In line with this need, we advocate a task-based approach, based on "the principle that language learning will progress most successfully if teaching aims simply to create contexts in which the learner's natural language learning capacity can be nurtured rather than making a systematic attempt to teach the language bit by bit" (Ellis, 2009: 222). A task-based approach breaks learning down into manageable steps that guide learners in the completion of a task. In Oskoz & Elola's (2014) case, this approach divided writing into the stages of planning, drafting, seeking and receiving feedback, revising, and publishing. These stages were carefully sequenced in a series of well-defined writing tasks. Additionally, it is imperative to bear in mind the affordances of the tool itself, the inclusion of semiotic resources, the communicative purpose and the value of each tool to support specific aspects of the writing process. In the following subsection, we present a sample task in which the process of familiarization with social tools and their characteristics help learners familiarize themselves with the new tools without feeling the pressure of being graded.

6.1 Sample Task: Looking for a New Roommate

This section describes one particular learning task – a project resulting from one Spanish instructor's realization that the writing act needed to reflect the practices and experiences of her current class of learners. As part of an introductory Spanish class, learners generally worked on a variety of written texts. However, the instructor felt that students tended to rush through them and were not very receptive to the feedback she provided on their work. To overcome this problem, she decided (a) to introduce a collaborative approach to writing using wikis (Elola & Oskoz, 2010), and (b) to follow a task-based approach (Samuda & Bygate, 2008) in which the final product would be a digital story. This meant that the number of writing assignments in the semester was reduced (i.e., from four to two) and that each writing activity would happen over six weeks, in four distinct phases. Extending the time allocated for the activity helped the students to focus on their writing process during which they improved their grammar and expanded their vocabulary constantly. Importantly, the flow of their creative ideas was increased, as they were building new knowledge in class and at the same time receiving feedback from both their classmates and the instructor.

In the activity presented below, students (in groups of three) were to be the hosts of a Spanish-speaking student who had arrived with a new group of students attending the college that semester. The final product, after learners had developed their written presentations, was to be a digital story in which they described themselves, talked about their daily activities, and shared what they liked or did not like in a quest to find their best roommate.

Phase 1: Learning to understand semiotic resources (week 1) Guided by the instructor, the learners viewed sample digital stories and commented on how well the authors had integrated images, text, and sounds within the digital storytelling genre. While viewing the stories, images were evaluated in terms of their level of explicitness (the literal reflection of the object presented) or implicitness (indirect relationship with the object presented) and assessed for their values or messages. The learners also gained an understanding of the effect that different music styles and sounds have on the audience. When discussing both images and sounds, the instructor emphasized the need to abide by copyright laws. The learners further considered how the authors of digital stories used transitions to express meaning, and how they made use of textual, visual, and aural modes to create a multimodal text. To reduce the anxiety that such a new approach might bring with it, that week learners also received initial training in the use of Final Cut or iMovie, the chosen editing software packages, in the language lab. They were also allowed to use any other software they had available on their own computers.

Phase 2: Starting the introductions (weeks 1–4) After each class, in which learners participated in communicative activities, such as introducing themselves to another person or describing their daily routine, they were asked to incorporate what they were learning in a letter in the wiki for the potential roommate. The following days, in class, the instructor brought some wiki examples to address issues of content, accuracy (grammar and vocabulary), and flow of ideas. They also discussed how to combine all group members' ideas to make a coherent introduction for each of the three roommates who would be sharing the apartment. As part of this process, learners also searched for images that reflected the content of the introduction, both implicitly and explicitly, and for suitable music that could accompany their presentations. After receiving feedback from their instructor and classmates, learners made appropriate changes and improvements to their introductions in the wiki. Writing in the wiki, providing feedback, and searching for images and sound were discussed regularly in the classroom (see Appendix A).

Phase 3: Sharing the first draft (week 5) The learners brought to class the final version of their introduction, together with the images, and soundtracks they had selected, and shared them with their classmates in small groups of learners, who then offered feedback on the story, images, and sounds. Learners read their introductions aloud, providing an opportunity for discussion and the giving and receiving of feedback on content, structure, and organization, and on the kinds of images, music, and sounds to include in the final DS. Reading the scripts aloud also allowed learners to consider the emotions that the script might evoke in listeners. At this point, the instructor made suggestions about how to convert the personal essays into digital story scripts of approximately 500 words, 5 minutes in duration (see Appendix A for assessment). After the group session, learners worked to complete their digital story scripts and to reassess their selected images and music, searching for new ones and discarding others.

Phase 4: Showtime! (Week 6) Upon completing their digital stories, learners uploaded them to the web (either to their own YouTube channel or to the instructor's channel) and presented them to the class in a special event. Before presenting, the learners gave a brief explanation of the process they went through in writing, composing, and creating their digital story. After each presentation, classmates gave an informal evaluation, focusing on the creative integration of visuals and audio as well as the content, following the course rubric (see Appendix B). At the end, learners voted to select the best story.

7   Conclusion

As L2 instructors begin to incorporate digital tools into their instruction, they will realize that the affordances and characteristics of these tools provide a rich amalgam of educational possibilities. Digital tools allow for synchronous and/or asynchronous responses, for individual or collaborative tasks, and they effectively include textual, visual, and aural dimensions. These are new approaches that will change the very act of writing and will also support the acquisition of linguistic knowledge, which still remains an important focus for L2 language learners. Clearly, this new paradigm requires innovative and more radical approaches to teaching and learning, in which learners become aware of the power of the new tools to support their writing and ultimately to form a natural bridge between their classroom assignments and activities in the outside world. Essentially, this chapter provides instructors with holistic perspectives on technology and its potential to make the act of writing an exciting yet meaningful experience. As we have shown in this chapter, the key to success in teaching with digital tools is to integrate them into your classes in a carefully planned manner. Only by integrating your digitally-based-instructional changes with those of your fellow practitioners will we be able to achieve enduring changes in our curricula.

Questions for Reflection

1. An important aim of L2 learning is to investigate how instruction can facilitate the acquisition of a target language. Choose a grammatical feature such as the past tense and think of ways in which the use of multimodal texts (i.e., integrating text, video and sound) could help learners to practice its use (for example in narrations, personal accounts, travel postings, etc.).

2. Earlier in this chapter, you read that the potential of social tools for educational purposes stems from their *affordances* (actions that individuals can perform using a particular tool). Create a table in which you clearly (a) state what the affordances of particular social tools are and (b) suggest specific tasks that L2 instructors could offer their classes to optimize the use of these tools (e.g., Google Docs for writing collaboratively about an event in the past so students can develop the genre of narration and the use of the past tense).

3. Subsection 6.1 provided an example of a learning task that integrates text, images, and sound in the development of digital stories. Considering that your learners are familiar with social tools, think of a task in which the integration of different modes could motivate learners to explore culture in more informal ways. For example, how would you use Facebook or digital stories to develop students' cultural awareness and to reflect on what they see, read, or hear in either personal or more academic formats?

4. Digitally-based collaborative writing can be fostered by using one or more tools for a single task (e.g., Google Docs are already paired with chats). Taking into consideration your learners' proficiency level, the purpose of your L2 (writing) class, and the tools available to you, design a writing task (e.g., story creation, newspaper, letter, digital story) in which learners make use of more than one tool. In order to design an effective task, break the task into different phases (e.g., writing a first draft, selecting images, incorporating music or videos), taking into account different writing processes (e.g., planning, drafting, revising, editing), and indicating which tool(s) could be used in each phase.

Case Study

Ms Yoon teaches an advanced Korean course at the local community college and has long wished to strengthen the connection between the college and the community, while also fostering her students' digital literacy and use of multimodal genres. To mark the Korean community's 20-year anniversary, she wants to compile the stories of members who remember the establishment and early days of the community. Ms Yoon connects her class to the local Korean community, with the idea that the students might help develop a series of digital stories to be included on the center's website.

In order to develop digital stories, students form groups of three and follow these steps: (1) they investigate the history of the establishment of the Korean community in the area and develop a series of questions to ask the early members of the center to draw out their memories; (2) they meet with those who volunteered to participate, and together, they select images either from their own collections or from the community's archives they think could be included in the digital story; and (3) they write a script for the story that includes both the storyline of the Korean community center and excerpts from the personal shared memories of the volunteers.

The instructor, the community, and the students are very excited about the project. After talking with the community members in several interviews, L2 learners feel they have the material to write the digital story. But when the L2 learners begin to write the script, they realize that while they have engaged in very interesting conversations, they have sometimes ended up talking about topics not relevant to the establishment of the Korean community in the area. In terms of language, because English was also used as a strategy to avoid communication breakdowns, the L2 learners do not always have the linguistic knowledge to develop a meaningful script, and the project becomes a daunting challenge for them. When the community members offer feedback to the learners, they find the learners are not always very receptive to their suggestions, preferring to rely on their instructor's feedback. Ms Yoon, her learners, and the community members, although mindful of the project's potential, grow disenchanted with the writing and designing of the digital story. Ms Yoon wonders how to restructure the task to make it more fruitful.

Discussion Questions:
1. How could Ms Yoon have guided students to create more specific questions regarding the establishment of the Korean community? What type of pedagogical considerations could Ms Yoon have taken into account to ensure that the questions were adequate

and well-thought out before the students met with the community members? How could the students have integrated the information from the interviews not related to the establishment of the community to create digital stories still relevant to the community at large?

2. What could Ms Yoon have done differently to ensure the community members and students understood the goal of the digital story and the role that each of them played in its design? That is, how could she have made it clear that the digital story was a collaborative work in which both students and the community had a say? What can kind of digital story examples could have effectively shown both populations how to better integrate the scripts with the images and sounds?

3. How could Ms Yoon have guided both the community members and the students to better integrate the community members' feedback, instead of relying on her as the only source of linguistic and multimodal knowledge? How could she have emphasized the importance of peer feedback provided by the community members as reliable sources of knowledge?

4. What kind of formative assessment criteria (categories of the rubric) could Ms Yoon have shared with the community members and the students to ensure the successful completion of the interviews (e.g., focus on specific and relevant questions) and the digital stories (e.g., include the interviews' information in a digital story that represents the interviewees and their community)?

Ideas for Action Research Projects

Classroom projects, such as the one described in subsection 6.1, present opportunities for the development of the instructor's own research agenda. Here, we outline two ideas for action research using two digital social tools, which could support the design of research projects. The main idea is to reflect on how to develop a language-rich, intercultural research project using these social tools. The researcher will have to think about the nature of the set tasks, the sequencing of tasks, and ways to obtain quality data that can be analyzed later. This can lead to a useful evaluation of the benefits and challenges that flow from the integration of social tools in the language classroom.

1. Use of Blog Journals for Promoting Writing Development
Blogs have multiple uses in the L2 classroom. For example, they are used in the project described here to improve journalistic writing as seen in NGOs'

information platforms. Using blogs as a platform, learners write a set of brief journalistic reports (300 words) about how their target language country (or countries) acts upon diverse topics of social justice (e.g., immigration, water usage, green energy alternatives, and gender inequality). In the process, they will be encouraged to identify which of the measures they have read about could be applied to their own context. Learners are also encouraged to upload images and videos to support their findings. In terms of language, they are expected to learn the conventions of the journalistic genre and to utilize a range of appropriate vocabulary and grammar repertoires.

Ask yourself these questions:
1. In what class would you conduct this research project?
2. How would you prepare your students for this assignment? How might you guide them to be able to apply aspects of the journalistic genre?
3. Which data collection techniques would you use to assess learners' understanding of social justice and the success of the project? Would you use Likert scale questionnaires with space for learners to elaborate upon their answers/analyze the blog entries?
4. What aspects of the blog entries would you assess? Would you look for content or depth of discourse rather than linguistic accuracy, or emerging themes, or all of the above? How would you analyze the journalistic entries in terms of rhetorical components, content, and grammar?

To prepare for class discussion:
1. How would you design your research methodology for your study (e.g., collaborative or task-based data collection techniques) considering what you have learned in this chapter?
2. What specific prompts would you provide the learners to guide them in their blogs?
3. How can blogs be used for observing and measuring their writing development (e.g., genre mastery, language accuracy)? How would you measure and analyze this growth?

2. Google Maps for Community Engagement: What is my local Hispanic community like?
The goal of this project is to help learners discover cultural and historical aspects of their Hispanic communities (or any other community of your choosing), share them with their classmates, and create a linguistic and cultural "mapping." Learners select specific landmarks of interest, which

they mark in Google maps, then upload an image and write a commentary (around 200 words) using the appropriate vocabulary and grammatical structures learned in the course. In doing so, learners uncover the historical migration patterns and settlements that represents different aspects of the community.

Ask yourself these questions:
1. Following a task-based approach, how would you break the project down into specific phases? Think about (a) helping learners understand the purpose of the project; (b) selecting objects or artifacts with linguistic or cultural connotations; and (c) developing ideas for classroom assignments from the sharing of tweets.
2. What features will the Google maps descriptions include? For example, would you use word-count restrictions, text, specific grammar structures, photos, etc.?
3. How can Google Maps be used to represent historical and cultural aspects of your learners' local communities?

To prepare for class discussion:
1. How would you evaluate how the project's potential benefit for learners' writing development? What categories would you use to evaluate the Google Maps descriptions (number of words, photos, etc.)?
2. How would you collect data to capture learners' engagement with the technology used (creating the map, including images, etc.) as well as any cultural and/or linguistic gains? For example, would you use questionnaires, journals, Google Maps entries, etc.?
3. How could you promote peer feedback to help learners improve their descriptions of the cultural and historical landmarks?

References

Adams, R., & Ross-Feldman, L. (2008). Does writing influence learner attention to form? In D. Belcher & A. Hirvela (eds.), *The oral-literate connection*, pp. 243–266. Ann Arbor: University of Michigan Press.

Arnold, N., Ducate, L., & Kost, C. (2012). Collaboration or cooperation? Analyzing group dynamics and revision processes in wikis. *CALICO Journal*, 29(3), 431–448. https://doi.org/10.11139/cj.29.3.431-448

Arnold, N., Ducate, L., Lomicka, L., & Lord, G. (2009). Assessing online collaboration among language teachers: A cross-institutional case study. *Journal of Interactive Online Learning*, 8(2), 121–139.

Blattner, G., Dalola, A., & Lomicka, L. (2016a). Mind your hashtags: A sociopragamatic study of student interpretations of French native speakers' tweets. In L. Winstead & W. Congcong (eds.), *Handbook of research on foreign language education in the digital age*. Hershey, PA: IGI Global.

Blattner, G., Dalola, A., & Lomicka, L. (2016b). Twitter in foreign language classes: Initiating learners into contemporary language variation. In W. Wang (ed.), *Handbook of research on learning outcomes and opportunities in the digital age*, pp. 769–797. Hershey, PA: IGI Global.
https://doi.org/10.4018/978-1-4666-9577-1.ch034

Blattner, G., & Fiori, M. (2011). Virtual social network communities: an investigation of language learners' development of socio-pragmatic awareness and multiliteracy skills. *CALICO Journal*, 29(1), pp. 24–43.
https://doi.org/10.11139/cj.29.1.24-43

Blin, F., & Appel, C. (2011). Computer supported collaborative writing in practice: An activity theoretical study. *CALICO Journal*, 28(2), 473–497.
https://doi.org/10.11139/cj.28.2.473-497

Castañeda, M. E. (2013). "I am proud that I did it and it's a piece of me": Digital storytelling in the foreign language classroom. *CALICO Journal*, 30(1), 44–62. https://doi.org/10.11139/cj.30.1.44-62

Caws, C., & Heift, T. (2016). Evaluation in CALL: Tools, interactions, outcomes. In F. Farr & L. Murray (eds.), *The Routledge handbook of language learning and technology*, pp. 127–140. New York, NY: Routledge

Dizon, G. (2016). A comparative study of Facebook vs. paper-and-pencil writing to improve L2 writing skills. *Computer Assisted Language Learning*, 29(8), 1249–1258. https://doi.org/10.1080/09588221.2016.1266369

Ducate, L., & Lomicka, L. (2008). Adventures in the blogosphere: From blog readers to blog writers. *Computer Assisted Language Learning*, 21(1), 9–28. https://doi.org/10.1080/09588221.2016.1266369

Ellis, R. (2009). Task-based language teaching: Sorting out the misunderstandings. *International Journal of Applied Linguistics*, 19, 222–246.
https://doi.org/10.1111/j.1473-4192.2009.00231.x

Elola, I., & Oskoz, A. (2008). Blogging: Fostering intercultural competence development in foreign language and study abroad contexts. *Foreign Language Annals*, 41(3), 421–444. https://doi.org/10.1111/j.1944-9720.2008.tb03307.x

Elola, I., & Oskoz, A. (2010). Collaborative writing: Fostering foreign language and writing conventions development. *Language Learning & Technology*, 14, 30–49.

Elola, I., & Oskoz, A. (2016). Supporting second language writing using multimodal feedback. *Foreign Language Annals*, 49(1), 58–74.
https://doi.org/10.1111/flan.12183

Elola, I., & Oskoz, A. (2017). Writing with 21st-century social tools in the FL classroom: New literacies, genres, and writing practices. *Journal of Second Language Writing*, 36, 52–60. https://doi.org/10.1016/j.jslw.2017.04.002

Engeström, Y. (2001). Expansive learning at work: Toward an activity theoretical reconceptualization. *Journal of Education and Work*, 14, 133–156.
https://doi.org/10.1080/13639080020028747

Engeström, Y. (2008). *From teams to knots: Activity-theoretical studies of collaboration and learning at work*. Cambridge: Cambridge University Press. https://doi.org/10.1080/13639080020028747

Facebook. (2018). About. Retrieved from https://www.facebook.com/pg/facebook/about/

Farmer, B., Yue, A., & Brookes, C. (2008). Using blogging for higher order learning in large cohort university teaching: A case study. *Australasian Journal of Educational Technology*, 24(2), 123–136. Retrieved from http://www.ascilite.org.au/ajet/ajet24/farmer.pdf; https://doi.org/10.14742/ajet.1215

Gakhar, S., & Thompson, A. (2007). *Digital storytelling: Engaging, communicating, and collaborating.* Paper presented at the Proceedings of the Society for Information Technology & Teacher Education International Conference 2006, Chesapeake.

Guichon, N., & Cohen, C. (2016). Multimodality and CALL. In F. Farr & L. Murray (eds.), *The Routledge handbook of language learning and technology*, pp. 509–521. New York, NY: Routledge.

Hattem, D. (2012). The practice of microblogging. *The Journal of Second Language Teaching and Research*, 1(2), 38–70.

Hattem, D. (2014). Microblogging activities: Language play and tool transformation. *Language Learning & Technology*, 18(2), 151–174.

Hessler, B., & Lambert, J. (2017). Threshold concepts in digital storytelling: Naming what we know about storywork. In G. Jamissen, P. Hardy, Y. Nordkvelle, & H. Pleasants (eds.), *Threshold concepts in digital storytelling: Naming what we know about storywork*, pp. 19–36. Cham, Switzerland: Palgrave Macmillan. https://doi.org/10.1007/978-3-319-51058-3_3

Hourigan, T., & Murray, L. (2010). Using blogs to help language students to develop reflective learning strategies: Towards a pedagogical framework. *Australasian Journal of Educational Technology*, 26(2), 209–225. https://doi.org/10.1007/978-3-319-51058-3_3

Hyland, K. (2007). Genre pedagogy: Language, literacy and L2 writing instruction. *Journal of Second Language Writing*, 16(3), 148–164. https://doi.org/10.1016/j.jslw.2007.07.005

Kabilan, M. K., Ahmad, N., & Abidin, M. J. Z. (2010). Facebook: An online environment for learning of English in institutions of higher education? *Internet and Higher Education*, 13, 179–187. https://doi.org/10.1016/j.iheduc.2010.07.003

Kalantzis, M., & Cope, B. (2008). The assess-as-you-go writing assistant. Transforming student assessment. New learning: Transformational designs for pedagogical and assessment. Available online at http://newleraningonline.com/news/assess-as-you-go

Kessler, G. (2009). Student-initiated attention to form in wiki-based collaborative writing. *Language Learning & Technology*, 13(1), 79–95.

Kessler, G., & Bikowski, D. (2010). Developing collaborative autonomous language learning abilities in computer mediated language learning: Attention to meaning among students in wiki space. *Computer Assisted Language Learning*, 23(1), 41–58. https://doi.org/10.1016/j.iheduc.2010.07.003

Kress, G. (1998). Visual and verbal modes of representation in electronically mediated communication: The potentials of new forms of text. In I. Snyder (ed.), *Page to screen: Taking literacy into the electronic era*, pp. 53–79. London: Routledge. https://doi.org/10.1016/j.iheduc.2010.07.003

Kress, G. (2009). What is a mode? In C. Jewitt (ed.), *The Routledge handbook of multimodal analysis*, pp. 54–67. Abingdon, UK: Routledge.

Kress, G. (2010). *Multimodality: A social semiotic approach to contemporary communication*. New York: Routledge.

Kutti, K. (1996). Activity theory as a potential framework for human-computer interaction research. In B. A. Nardi (ed.), *Context and consciousness: Activity theory and human-computer interaction*, pp. 17–44. Cambridge: MIT Press.

Lambert, J. (2012). *Digital storytelling: Capturing lives, creating community* (4th ed.). Berkeley: Digital Diner.

Lee, L. (2009). Promoting intercultural communication with blogs and podcasting: A study of Spanish-American collaboration. *Computer Assisted Language Learning*, 22(5), 425–443. https://doi.org/10.1080/09588220903345184

Lejas, H. (2007). Improving writing skills in foreign language classes. In M. Camilleri, P. Ford, H. Leja, & V. Sollars (eds.), *Blogs: Web journal in language education*, pp. 27–34. Graz, Austria: European Centre for Modern Languages, Council of Europe. Retrieved from http://www.ecml.at/documents/D1_Blogs_E_web.pdf

Li, M., & Zhu, W. (2017). Explaining dynamic interactions in wiki-based collaborative writing. *Language Learning & Technology*, 21(2), 96–120. Retrieved from http://llt.msu.edu/issues/june2017/lizhu.pdf

Lotherington, H., & Ronda, N. Sinitskaya (2012). Multimodal literacies and assessment: Uncharted challenges in the English classroom. In C. Leung and B. V. Street (eds.), *English: A challenging medium for education*, pp. 104–128. Bristol, UK: Multilingual Matters. https://doi.org/10.21832/9781847697721-008

McLoughlin, C., & Lee, M. J. W. (2007). Social software and participatory learning: Pedagogical choices with technology affordances in the Web 2.0 era. *Proceedings ASCILITE Singapore 2007*, pp. 664–675. Retrieved from http://www.ascilite.org/conferences/singapore07/procs/mcloughlin.pdf

Miyazoe, T., & Anderson, T. (2010). Learning outcomes and students' perceptions of online writing: Simultaneous implementation of a forum, blog, and wiki in an EFL blended learning setting. *System*, 38(2), 185–199. https://doi.org/10.1016/j.system.2010.03.006

Murray, L., Hourigan, T., & Jeanneau, C. (2007). Blog writing integration for academic language learning purposes: Towards an assessment framework. *Iberica*, 14, 9–32. Retrieved from http://www.aelfe.org/documents/14-02_murray.pdf

Nelson, M. E. (2006). Mode, meaning, and synaesthesia in multimedia L2 writing. *Language Learning & Technology*, 10(2), 56–76.

Oskoz, A. & Elola, I. (2014). Promoting FL collaborative writing through the use of Web 2.0 tools. In M. Lloret & L. Ortega (eds.), *Technology and tasks: Exploring technology-mediated TBLT*, pp. 115–147. Philadelphia, PA: John Benjamins.

Oskoz, A., & Elola, I. (2016). Digital stories in L2 education: Overview. *CALICO Journal*, 33(2), 157–173. https://doi.org/10.1558/cj.v33i2.29295

Papacharissi, Z. (2006). Audiences as media producers: Content analysis of 260 blogs. In M. Tremayne (ed.), *Blogging, citizenship, and the future of media*, pp. 21–38. New York, NY: Routledge.

Pérez-Sabater, C., & Montero-Fleta, B. (2015). ESP vocabulary and social networking: The case of Twitter. *Ibério*, 29, 129–154.

Rance-Roney, J. (2008). Digital storytelling for language and culture learning. *Essential Teacher*. Retrieved from http://www.nwp.org/cs/public/download/nwp_file/12189/Judith_Rance-Roney_Digital_Storytelling.pdf?x-r=pcfile_d

Reyes-Torres, A., Pich-Ponce, E., & García-Pastor, M. D. (2012). Digital storytelling as a pedagogical tool within a didactic sequence in foreign language teaching. *Digital Education Review*, 22, 1–18.

Robin, B. (2006). *The educational uses of digital storytelling*. Paper presented at the Proceedings of the Society for Information Technology & Teacher Education International Conference 2006, Chesapeake.

Samuda, V., & Bygate, M. (2008). *Tasks in second language learning*. London: Palgrave Macmillan. https://doi.org/10.1057/9780230596429

Shih, R. (2011). Can Web 2.0 technology assist college students in learning English writing? Integrating Facebook and peer assessment with blended learning. *Australasian Journal of Educational Technology*, 27(5), 829–845. https://doi.org/10.14742/ajet.934

Shin, D.-S., & Cimasko, T. (2008). Multimodal composition in a college ESL class: New tools, traditional norms. *Computers and Composition*, 25(4), 376–395. https://doi.org/10.1016/j.compcom.2008.07.001

Statista. (2018). Number of monthly active Twitter users worldwide from 1st quarter 2010 to 2nd quarter 2018 (in millions). Retrieved from https://www.statista.com/statistics/282087/number-of-monthly-active-twitter-users/

Stickler, U., & Hampel, R. (2010). CyberDeutsch: Language production and user preferences in a Moodle virtual learning environment. *CALICO Journal*, 28(1), 49–73.

Thorne, S. L. (2003). Artifacts and cultures-of-use in intercultural communication. *Language Learning & Technology*, 7(2), 38–67. https://doi.org/10.11139/cj.28.1.49-73

Thorne, S. L., & Black, R. W. (2007). Language and literacy development in computer-mediated contexts and communities. *Annual Review of Applied Linguistics*, 27, 133–160.

Twitter (2017). About. Retrieved from https://about.twitter.com/en_us/company.html

Ullrich, C., Borau, K., & Stepanyan, K. (2010). *Who do students interact with? A social network analysis perspective on student interaction within the Twitter microblogging environment*. Paper presented at the 10th IEEE International Conference on Advanced Learning Technologies (ICALT), Barcelona, Spain.

Vandergriff, I. (2016). *Second-language discourse in the digital world: Linguistic and social practices in and beyond the networked classroom*. Amsterdam, The Netherlands; Philadelphia, PA, USA: John Benjamins Publishing Company. https://doi.org/10.1075/lllt.46

Vinogradova, P., Linville, H. L., & Bickel, B. (2011). "Listen to my story and you will know me": Digital stories as student-centered collaborative projects. *TESOL Journal*, 2(2), 173–202. https://doi.org/10.5054/tj.2011.250380

Wang, S., & Vasquez, C. (2012). Web 2.0 and second language learning: What does the research tell us? *CALICO Journal*, 29(3), 412–430. https://doi.org/10.11139/cj.29.3.412-430

Ward, J. M. (2004). Blog-assisted language learning (BALL): Push button publishing for the pupils. *TEFL Web Journal*, 3(1), 1–16.

Wood, D. J., Bruner, J. S., & Ross, G. (1976). The role of tutoring in problem solving. *Journal of Child Psychiatry and Psychology*, 17, 89–109. http:/dx.doi.org//10.1111/j.1469–7610.1976.tb00381.x

Yang, Y.-F. (2012). Multimodal composing in digital storytelling. *Computers and Composition*, 29(3), 221–238. https://doi.org/10.1016/j.compcom.2012.07.001

Yen, Y.-C., Hou, H.-T., & Chang, K. E. (2015). Applying role-playing strategy to enhance learners' writing and speaking skills in EFL courses using Facebook and Skype as learning tools: A case study in Taiwan. *Computer Assisted Language Learning*, 28(5), 383–406. https://doi.org/10.1080/09588221.2013.839568

Appendix A: Formative Assessment Rubric for the Writing Process in the Wiki and Digital Story

Phase 2		
Writing	Update your personal information based on the material presented in class (e.g., how to write about daily activities).	30%
Feedback	Provide feedback grammar (3 items) and content (3 comments) to your group members using the wiki. Accept or reject (explain why) the feedback provided to you.	30%
Images and sound	Share with your roommates images (implicit and literal) that could be used to introduce yourselves to the potential roommate. Discuss music that could be incorporated in your introduction. (Watch out for copyright issues!)	20%
Phase 3		
Circles	Share with your classmates your own introduction (narrative, images and sounds/music) and be an audience for theirs. Provide feedback on the content of their introductions, the use implicit and literal images, and the selection of the music. Accept or reject (explain why) the feedback provided to you.	20%

Appendix B: Summative Assessment

View your classmates' digital story and evaluate it (following the rubric below). Write also comments on elements that you like or that could be improved. At the end of the presentations, the class will vote on the best digital story.

Category	4 Points	3 Points	2 Points	1 Point
Pacing	The pace suits the story-line and helps engage the audience.	The pacing is occasionally too fast or too slow.	An attempt is made at pacing, but the audience is not fully engaged.	No attempt at pacing is made.
Audio elements	Narration is clear. Soundtrack/effects complement but do not overwhelm the narration.	Narration is fairly clear but is occasionally overwhelmed by soundtrack/effects.	Narration is often hard to discern; the soundtrack is distracting.	There is no soundtrack or sound effects.
Image elements	All images are appropriate and clear and there is a good mix of literal and symbolic use.	A few images are inappropriate and/or unclear, and very few of them are used symbolically.	Many images are inappropriate or unclear, and there is no symbolism.	Images are inappropriate, unclear and literal.
Economy	The story is told with exactly the right amount of detail and is neither too long nor too short.	The storyline is sometimes disjointed or includes unnecessary details; it sometimes seems to drag.	The story needs more editing and is noticeably too long or too short.	The story needs extensive editing; ignores economy.
Credits	The title is included; all images and sounds are cited or credited where necessary.	Title, or some citations or credits are missing.	Title and/or many citations and credits are missing.	There is neither title nor credits.

Language	Wide range of structures with few or insignificant errors.	Adequate range of grammatical structures; overuse of constructions; some minor errors.	Limited range of structures; poor control of grammar.	Frequent and persistent grammatical errors.
Vocabulary	Makes full use of the vocabulary of the topic being presented; little or no evidence of English interference.	Vocabulary accurate but somewhat limited; some errors or interference from English.	Vocabulary limited, with overuse of imprecise and vague terms; English interference is evident.	Very limited vocabulary; overuse of imprecise and vague terms; English interference is evident.
Effects: motion and transitions	Used at least 4 motion effects; transitions are effective.	Used at least 3 motion effects; transitions are mostly effective.	Used at least 1 motion effect; some transitions are distracting.	Used no motion effects; no transitions.
DS completion	Excellent integration of the elements (content, texts, images, and sound).	Good integration of the elements (content, texts, images, and sound).	Poor integration of the elements (content, texts, images, and sound).	Lack of integration of the elements (content, texts, images, and sound).

Notes about the DS to share with your classmates: _____

About the Authors

Idoia Elola is a Professor of Spanish and Applied Linguistics & Second Language Studies at Texas Tech University. Her research focuses mainly on second language writing, such as collaborative and individual writing when using Web 2.0 tools, Spanish heritage language learners' writing processes, and revision and feedback.

Ana Oskoz is an Associate Professor of Spanish at the University of Maryland, Baltimore County (UMBC). Her research focuses on second language and technology, such as the use of synchronous and asynchronous communication tools to enhance second language writing and foster intercultural competence development.

8   Interpersonal Communication in Intracultural CMC[1]

Zsuzsanna Abrams

Preview Questions

1. List the kinds of computer-mediated communication (CMC) you regularly participate in (e.g., WhatsApp, Facebook [Messenger], Skype, Twitter). Who are your fellow participants in these activities? What is the communicative or social purpose of these interactions?
2. What are the strengths of these types of CMC? Can you think of *language learning tasks* that might best take advantage of these strengths, whereby they place the learner at the center of the L2 learning process?
3. What would you expect the linguistic features, language use, and interactional patterns of two non-native speakers to look like in CMC exchanges (e.g., in a chat room, a Skype video chat, a video blog, etc.)?
4. What criteria would you consider important for assessing students' participation in CMC tasks? Once you identify two or three possible criteria, reflect on their relevance for the way *you* use CMC exchanges. In what ways do the criteria match the *authentic* and pedagogical purposes of CMC?
5. How do traditional ways of assessing learners' output and participation need to be modified in order to accommodate the characteristics of modern CMC exchanges?

---

1   This chapter is similar in structure to an earlier iteration (Ducate & Arnold, 2006; Arnold & Ducate 2011) but it has been substantially revised and updated in content.

1   Introduction to the Topic and Definition of Terms

Communication, as Hall rightly points out, "is at the heart of all social life" (1999: 16). This standard comprises a significant portion of the charge set forth by our profession, demanding, in essence, that we make learners' ability to partake in social action a priority in our second/foreign language (L2) courses. Effective social action requires that participants in an interaction be knowledgeable about the setting, the other participants (including their social roles), as well as the goals and purposes of the interaction (Hymes, 1971). Furthermore, Hymes argued, social interaction is meaningful and is situated within contexts of use. This view of what it means to be competent in a language underscores the need for language practice that fulfills similarly purposeful, interpersonal, and meaningful uses of language. Computer-mediated communication (CMC) turned out to be uniquely well-suited for fostering such interpersonal and socially-oriented use of language.

In today's "technologically interconnected, globalized world ... it is not possible to 'opt out' of using technology: It is so pervasive and so interwoven with human activity that to teach language without some form of technology would create a very limited and artificial learning environment – if it were even possible at all" (Chun, Kern, & Smith, 2016: 65). In fact, technology is so ubiquitous that it is difficult to fathom that just a couple of decades ago, CMC was in its infancy, and its use in L2 pedagogy was revolutionary. When it made its debut in L2 learning and teaching in the 1990s, CMC bore no resemblance to today's multimodal, interpersonal computer-mediated communication technologies. At the beginning, electronic networks for interaction (Bruce, Kreeft Peyton, & Batson, 1993) allowed language learners to communicate with their classmates, usually through a local area network (computers set up in the same physical location with computer-to-computer connectivity) and typically in synchronous CMC (i.e., interacting at the same time, without a time-lag between contributions), thus relying on first-generation CMC tools (Blake, 2013). Many early adopters hailed from the University of Texas – Austin, and reported their findings from chats conducted in the *Daedalus Interchange Writing Environment* (Chun, 1994; Kern, 1995). These studies have since developed into an area of inquiry that continues to grow exponentially.

Since it is impossible to review all CMC-related articles in one chapter, this review focuses on a representative sample of studies that illustrate the rich uses and development of CMC in L2 instruction. The chapter further narrows down its focus to *intracultural* CMC (Abrams, 2011). That is, it explores the cognitive, affective, and interpersonal benefits of CMC among learners of second languages, which in most studies means having participants who share a native language and cultural context. *Intercultural CMC*, which typically examines L2 learners' interactions with native speakers (e.g., Belz & Kinginger, 2003), has been addressed in a separate chapter in this volume (see Guth & Helm). The review of early and recent uses of CMC is followed by suggestions for areas of possible future inquiry. The second half of the chapter examines pedagogical implementation and task design, and addresses issues related to effective assessment of CMC activities. Some questions for discussion and reflection follow the concluding remarks, as well as possible research projects that emerge from the current literature on intracultural CMC.

2   A Review of the Literature

2.1   Early CMC Research: Theoretical Perspectives and Empirical Findings

Kern & Warschauer (2000) and Sun (2017) describe the development of the use of computers in language teaching as moving from structuralist, to cognitive/constructivist, and more recently to sociocognitive perspectives of language learning (this last perspective will be dealt with in further detail in subsection 2.2). *Structuralist* perspectives (during the first half of the 20th century) understood language learning as habit formation through practice, with a primary focus on structure. Accordingly, computer-assisted learning tools commonly available in the 1970s through the '90s aimed to foster automaticity through repetition (Chapelle, 2001). Theories of second language acquisition (SLA) in the 1980s, in contrast, were informed by Chomsky's (1957, 1965) *cognitivist* theories of first language acquisition, such as Long's (1996) interaction hypothesis, whose theoretical core is that:

> *negotiation of meaning*, and especially negotiation work that triggers *interactional* adjustments by the [native speaker] or more competent interlocutor, facilitates acquisition because it connects input, internal learner capacities, particularly selective attention, and output in productive ways. (1996: 451–452).

The three pillars of this hypothesis are (a) *input*, which provides positive evidence for learners and serves as a model for building their own utterances in the L2, (b) *output* that learners must produce in order to progress from a semantic processing of the L2, which is used in comprehension, to the grammatical processing required for production, and (c) *interaction* with others, during which learners receive negative evidence, or feedback,[2] that alerts them to gaps in their knowledge compared to L2 patterns (Gass, 2006).

Cognitive approaches to SLA emphasized psycholinguistic processes of individual learners in the development of interlanguage and focused primarily on oral language (Ellis, 1999; Doughty & Pica, 1986; Krashen, 1980, 1985; Long, 1996; Schmidt, 1993; Swain, 1985, 1995; Varonis & Gass, 1985). CMC studies following this paradigm examined the role of interaction and input, opportunities for increased output, as well as lexical and grammatical gains yielded by negotiated interactions.

In a seminal study in 1994, Chun examined first-year German students' communicative competence in CMC discussions and found that participants interacted with each other in ways that they did not in regular, face-to-face (F2F) classroom settings: learners used less of their native language and produced a broader selection of discourse functions than they usually did in classroom interactions. In a related study, Kern's (1995) analysis of discourse patterns among beginning learners of French revealed that participants interacted with each other in genuine exchanges of information without relying on the teacher to provide the typical teacher-question, student-response, teacher-feedback scaffolding. Both studies highlighted CMC's ability to push learners beyond what they would normally learn in more traditional classroom interactions, particularly by facilitating "direct interpersonal communication" (Kern, 1995: 459). A year later, Warschauer analyzed the interactions and language use of 16 advanced learners of English as a Second Language (ESL) and discovered that participants interacted more equally than in F2F conversations, even shyer students becoming quite vocal online. Warschauer also noted that students' language "was both more formal and more complex than [during] the face-to-face discussion" (1996: 21). An important contribution of this study was ways of measuring the quality of student output, in terms of lexical richness and grammatical complexity.

Studies that examined the role of input and interaction remained central in CMC research after the turn of the millennium. Analyzing synchronous

2   Various types of feedback have been considered in SLA research, including positive, negative, implicit, and explicit feedback (Doughty, 2006), in response to L2 learners' mistakes and subsequent uptake of correct forms (Lyster & Ranta, 1997). *The handbook of second language acquisition* (2006) edited by Doughty & Long offers an excellent introduction and thorough overview of psycholinguistic processes in SLA for readers who wish to further their understanding of negotiated interactions and different types of feedback in L2 learning.

CMC (SCMC) exchanges among 25 learners of Spanish, Blake (2000) found that regardless of the task type (information gap, jigsaw, or decision-making task), learners' interactional patterns matched those identified by Varonis & Gass (1985) in F2F interaction: trigger, indicator, response, and reaction. Alleviating an oft-cited concern by teachers, Blake also discovered that participants did not learn incorrect language from each other, but rather collaboratively corrected mistakes to clear up misunderstandings that arose from them. His participants also reported enjoying extended discussions and a freer sense of interaction with their peers than what they typically experienced in the classroom.

Similarly, when Smith (2003) investigated students' interactions, he found that lexical errors triggered the most negotiation of meaning routines, but proposed revising the Varonis & Gass (1985) model for negotiations of meaning in CMC. Specifically, he argued that the time-lag inherent in SCMC interactions necessitates a more complex indication, response/repair routine, which requires that students develop a novel interactive skill for this new communicative environment. A follow-up study (Smith, 2004) revealed that learners who had to participate in extensive negotiations of meaning about unfamiliar lexical items were able to recognize and produce these items on a lexical post-test at much higher levels than words that were simply translated for the learners. The conclusion Smith drew from these findings was that CMC's permanence, the written word that stayed on the screen, helped to reinforce the lexical items, leading to improved learner uptake and subsequent lexical acquisition.

Further delving into the cognitive benefits of CMC, Pelletieri (2000) examined the interactions of pairs of intermediate Spanish learners, who completed a variety of tasks in weekly 30-minute SCMC sessions. Not surprisingly, the author found that lexical, semantic, morphosyntactic, and content problems all triggered negotiations. She also noted, supporting Smith's (2003, 2004) findings, (1) that CMC required longer negotiation sequences (since multiple threads of discussions were taking place simultaneously), and (2) that collaborative composition tasks, in which the participants co-authored an essay, led to improved morphosyntactic awareness, which subsequently brought about improved language output from the participants, possibly as a result of self- and peer-editing.[3]

Another group of studies (Beauvois, 1995; Kelm, 1998; Meunier, 1998) examined the affective benefits of CMC, such as increased motivation, improved attitudes and lower anxiety levels among students. This research

---

3   Slimani-Rolls (2005) argues that the *quality* of negotiation-of-meaning routines matters more than their *quantity*.

was influenced by Krashen's (1985) hypotheses suggesting that stronger learner motivation and lower levels of anxiety contribute to an affective state that facilitates language learning. Sullivan & Pratt (1996), for example, focused on how ESL learners' writing evolved as a result of CMC-based practice. The findings indicated that learners in the CMC group had a more positive attitude towards writing, experienced lower writing apprehension, and wrote better quality texts compared to the control group, which completed the same tasks in a traditional, face-to-face classroom. Similarly, Meunier (1998) investigated French and German learners' anxiety, risk-taking, sociability, and motivation while using CMC. She found that learners experienced lower L2 anxiety, took more risks, became more creative with the L2 in a CMC environment, and – echoing Kern's findings (1995) – participated extensively in learner-to-learner exchanges without instructor prompting. Interestingly, 24% of Meunier's students considered majoring in the L2 as a result of participating in CMC, possibly because they had more control of the interaction and liked the authenticity of the exchanges.

A series of studies conducted by Beauvois (1995, 1998a, 1998b) played a key role in guiding CMC research in the first two decades. Beauvois' participants reported that CMC allowed them more freedom of expression not available to them in typical instructional contexts (i.e., in which teachers ask questions, students provide limited answers, followed by feedback or evaluation from the instructor). Her studies were the first to suggest that CMC-based interaction may positively impact oral communication, helping students focus on communicating ideas rather than just focusing on grammatical and lexical accuracy. The only negative finding, later supported by Arnold (2002), was the fleeting nature of CMC exchanges: students who needed more time to think of an answer, compose a message or type in a response felt that they were left behind in the conversation by students who were faster typists, potentially more fluent in the language or just less concerned about the accuracy of their comments. These cognitively oriented studies suggested that increased motivation and more positive attitudes towards a task may lead to linguistic gains as well (increased time on task, exposure to language input, and output, etc.).

Other studies, informed by linguistic anthropology and sociolinguistics (Goffman, 1974; Gumperz, 2001; Halliday, 1973; Hymes, 1971, 1974), offered analyses of learner-to-learner interactions and explored the interface between individual phenomena and group characteristics, such as how interactive CMC can lead to learners' development of diverse participant roles (Abrams, 2001), interactive competence (Chun, 1994), a wider use of discourse functions (Kern, 1995) or language play (Warner, 2004). Arguably, these studies belong in the cognitivist paradigm because they examine the potential of CMC for individual learners' improvement, even if that improvement takes place in larger, discursive contexts.

This historical overview has covered early studies that relied on what Godwin-Jones (2003) terms first-generation communication systems (i.e., Web 1.0 text-based communication systems) and that made comparisons between F2F and CMC environments or drew on F2F frameworks of analysis (i.e., interaction hypothesis) in a new communicative context. They also examined the affective benefits of CMC exchanges (e.g., attitude, anxiety, or motivation). In addition, some of these studies explored whether CMC may offer cross-modal benefits, such as transferred improvements in L2 writing or speaking. Studies of this nature remain valuable for several reasons. First, they provide an ongoing analysis of CMC's potential effects on specific language phenomena or even on overall L2 ability. Second, we can understand an entity (i.e., CMC or the development of L2 pragmatics) better by comparing and contrasting it to other entities (e.g., face-to-face conversation). Finally, our knowing the benefits (and limitations) of CMC-based activities may be necessary for administrative decisions (e.g., justifying the expense of computer equipment, training of instructors, etc.). In the early 2000s, however, a second cohort of CMC studies shifted the research focus, exploring CMC's power for interaction not for linguistic gain per se, but to foster communities of practice and facilitate interpersonal communication, within the computer-mediated environment as an authentic communicative domain.

2.2 Sociocultural CMC Research: The New Millennium

According to *sociocultural* perspectives, language is dynamic and is used by individuals to create meaning. It is a social and socially constructed event, during which less knowledgeable individuals learn from more competent, knowledgeable counterparts (i.e., experts) through interaction (Lantolf & Appel, 1994; Meskill, 1999; Vygotsky, 1978). The difference between learners' abilities when they are working independently versus when they are assisted by the more expert partner(s) is called the zone of proximal development (Brooks & Donato, 1994; Darhower, 2002; Donato, 1994; Lantolf, 2000). The expert provides scaffolding (both linguistic and social support) for the novice participant, who learns to make sense of new information. In other words, learning – including learning an L2 – is social in nature, collaboratively constructed in dialog with others (Darhower, 2002; Donato & McCormick, 1994).

This sociocollaborative process also requires that participants establish and maintain *intersubjectivity*, which is shared contextual knowledge between them, including "background knowledge of a topic of conversation" or "a shared perspective between an expert and a learner in a problem-solving task in order to sustain the dialog process (Darhower, 2002: 253). If shared expectations are not available a priori, "interlocutors must achieve a new definition of the situation that all participants can share in order for communication to continue. If the attempt to reestablish intersubjectivity fails, then the communicators are faced with switching to some sort of strategic action (e.g., breaking off communication altogether or recommencing action oriented toward reaching understanding at a different level)" (Darhower, 2002: 253–254).

Darhower's article was one of the first studies that used a sociocollaborative framework to examine his participants' language as "a product of social interaction with other individuals" (2002: 251). Specifically, Darhower analyzed students' interactions and found that they used extensive humor, language play,[4] "off-task" behavior, and the L1 in order to create a social space and establish and maintain intersubjectivity vis-à-vis their peers. This finding had been reported by early CMC research as well, noting that discussions and tasks were often "hijacked" by the participants to fulfill emergent social purposes, most often language play, instead of following pedagogically determined objectives (e.g., Beauvois, 1995; Kern, 1995). Darhower's study was innovative in two ways, however. First, his project examined the nature of CMC interactions without looking at how these interactions might lead to other linguistic gains, outside of the CMC context (a key feature of early CMC research). Second, he analyzed the data not with an eye on individual cognitive and/or linguistic development, but rather by looking at how the participants in the entire class created a coherent social sphere through CMC.

Language play in CMC may foster second language awareness and development, as Warner (2004) found. She analyzed the interactions of two German language classes (intermediate and advanced learners). Expanding conceptualizations of language play by Lantolf (1997) and Cook (2000) – who identified form, content, and frame as the primary purposes of playful language use – Warner proposes that it is not merely the referential that is being negotiated by such exchanges, but social relationships "between speakers, their interlocutors, the medium, and the context" as learners play "*within*" [emphasis original] the language (2004: 81). This is a unique feature of CMC, the author argues, because of the flexibility of role-playing and the anonymity that this medium provides.

4   Cook (1997: 227) defines language play as "behaviour not primarily motivated by human need to manipulate the environment (and to share information for this purpose) and to form and maintain social relationships – though it may indirectly serve both of these functions."

In an analysis of SCMC sessions among learners of English at two Japanese universities, Peterson similarly found expanded discourse functions expressed by his students, such as "requests for and provision of assistance, continuers, off-task discussion, task-focused discussion, self- and other-initiated correction" for managing interactions (2009: 318). The author argued that a high level of intersubjectivity allowed participants to maintain a shared context for interaction for an extended period of time, and also pointed to the role that personal and contextual variables may play in CMC. He posited that his participants' exceptionally high level of motivation (they were English majors) and the fact that the task was a good fit with their interests may have led to the higher level of intersubjectivity as well. This hypothesis found further support from a study by Vandergriff & Fuchs, who analyzed learners' use of humorous language in face-to-face and CMC interactions, and examined both form-based language play (playing *with* the language) and pragmatic play ("play *within* the foreign language") (2009: 31, emphasis in original). The data, the authors claimed, suggested that both individual learner characteristics (e.g., proficiency levels, experience with CMC) and shared group history could be factors in leading to more sustainable interactions.

The cognitivist and sociocollaborative studies discussed in the previous subsection mostly used synchronous CMC, establishing both cognitive and sociocollaborative benefits of using this medium: learners' language seemed to exhibit lexical and grammatical gains, and they had positive affective reactions to SCMC interactions, with increased motivation, more positive attitudes towards language practice, for example. Similarly, the social coherence among learners – i.e., intersubjectivity – was very strong, often as a result of language play. Lin found ample evidence to support these observations in CMC research:

> Interaction opportunities in a socio-cultural context provide likelihood for negotiations in that input becomes comprehensible, and learners' attention can be drawn to form and ways of developing discourses (Gass & Varonis, 1994)... [and] online interactions/ communications mediated by computers/technology can generate similar or even superior opportunities for L2 learning than are found in face-to-face settings. (2015: 102)

Recent research, based on new technologies, has focused more on asynchronous CMC (ACMC), such as blogs, Twitter, or wikis. The *affordances* of these new technologies (van Lier, 2000) – the inherent qualities or parameters that define their use in a social context (e.g., time-delay, multimodality, one-to-one or one-to-many participant constellations) – expand both the possibilities of CMC use and pose new challenges for language teaching, as the following subsection examines.

2.3 Recent Developments: Social networking via Blogs and Other Web 2.0 Tools

Stevenson & Liu (2010) and Blake (2013) identify newer social networking systems such as blogs, IM chatting, Skype, video-chatting, and Twitter as Web 2.0 tools (second-generation in interactive computer use). These tools provide a "collaborative environment in which users have the opportunity to contribute to a growing knowledge base ... and participate in online communities" (Stevenson & Liu, 2010: 233) with a higher level of social authenticity. The multimodality of tools such as Facebook, Twitter, or WhatsApp, for example, allows users to include textual, graphic, sound-based, or other visual components to enrich their interactions. Given the emphasis of such tools on developing social networks, it is not surprising that studies that examine L2 learners' performance in socially networked CMC almost exclusively view students' interactions from a sociocollaborative perspective. What is surprising, however, is that while studies analyzing the uses and benefits of blogs abound, there is a relative dearth of studies that focus on spoken language via Web 2.0 tools. Others in this volume (see Elola & Oskoz) offer an in-depth analysis of written Web 2.0 tools (blogs and wikis), therefore these are not discussed here in detail. Yet, several findings from blog-based research are worth mentioning because they may help inform future second-generation CMC studies with L2 learners, and can also offer useful insights into developing effective intracultural tasks.

Weblogs, or blogs, enable self-expression and have pedagogical potential for classroom implementation as well (Horvath, 2009). They are asynchronous personal or news reports, shared with the public or with select audiences (Blake, 2013; Chun, Kern, & Smith, 2016; Ducate & Lomicka, 2005), can be one-to-many (one author, many readers) or collaboratively generated, and can include a variety of images, videos, sound files (Blake, 2013; Godwin-Jones, 2003). Ferdig & Trammell (2004), Lee (2010a), and Murray & Hourigan (2008) note several benefits of student blogging, including (1) increasing student interest and autonomy for learning, (2) developing a community of practice among learners to foster free exchange of ideas, (3) sharing perspectives in- and outside of the classroom, (4) improving learners' fluency in L2 writing, (5) increasing learners' critical thinking as they interact with peers, and (6) improving lexical and grammatical accuracy when the instructor participates.

Sun (2009), who similarly noted scaffolded (i.e., collaboratively generated) interactions among her participants, reported that students also appreciated the increased sense of task-authenticity that blogging afforded them, including an inherent real audience, which "enables meaningful exchanges with oneself, with classmates and with the teacher" (Shaw, 2009: 1278). Murray & Hourigan (2008) offer several reasons for implementing these tools – blogging in particular, which includes microblogging, or Twitter as well – in L2 learning contexts: blogs are easy to set up, hosting sites can be multilingual, while the content is publishable and allows instantaneous comments by other participants (peers and the instructor).

In spite of these positive aspects of second-generation CMC tools (Blake, 2013), research on their optimal uses for L2 learning has been limited, and it remains to be seen how affordances of reflectivity and authenticity can most optimally be incorporated into L2 pedagogical tasks.

2.4   Future Research Directions

In a recent paper, Sun (2017) makes the case for forward-oriented CALL designs that are adaptive to innovative technologies, while keeping learners' needs and learning interests at the forefront. She emphasizes the potential of "*social CALL*," which "is keen on producing authentic language-learning environments utilizing the task-based approach, and… urges that a much more productive rather than passive role be given to the learners" (2017: 578, emphasis original). She adds that social CALL offers "interactive and visually stimulating environments for problem-based learning" (p. 579).

Future research in intracultural CMC should follow these guidelines. Tasks that we design for students must be forward-oriented and adaptive, and offer students agency in their own L2 learning experience. With the final objective of helping learners develop the literacy skills needed in authentic communication with other real-world users of the L2, we can foster these skills in collaboration with other novice learners at earlier stages of L2 development.

Chun, Kern, & Smith (2016) describe several skills unique to second-generation CMC tools (and currently emerging third-generation tools): reading and typing at a fast pace, parsing longer comments into shorter ones (e.g., multiple interconnected Tweets), managing multiple threads of interaction simultaneously, encoding/decoding multimodal information rapidly, and attending to the various social roles inhabited by participants in an exchange. Each text type, regardless of modality, requires genre-specific digital literacies, as writing/reading emails does not draw on the same skill-set as creating multimedia stories or tweeting (Blake, 2013;

Chun, Kern, & Smith, 2016). As well, different types of second-generation CMC may have a dominant modality (e.g., Skype is primarily visual and audio-based), but also utilize secondary, supportive channels of communication; thus, training in navigating multiple channels of interaction in the L2 might require attention in the L2 curriculum.

Interaction with peers or the instructor(s) would help L2 learners become aware of and potentially develop the skills to shift among different registers, since academic forums might promote the use of significantly different language than what we use in more informal settings (Chun, Kern, & Smith, 2016). Such fora can also reveal important insights into the L2 developmental process, which may be obscured by written-only CMC.

The studies discussed above represent a rich body of research that explores both cognitive and sociocognitive benefits of intracultural CMC. They examine issues such as linguistic and affective gains, innovative applications, synchronicity, tasks, task design, and affordances. Empirical studies that build on this disciplinary foundation must continue to identify ways in which new technologies can be best used in L2 instruction. Future studies can draw on the theoretical paradigms presented here or expand to models of learning more broadly defined (Sun, 2017). The following are a few questions or areas of inquiry that could be explored:

1. Considerably more in-depth analyses are necessary for examining what van Lier (2000) terms *affordances*: the parameters which arise from a social context, which influence the choices a learner makes, including tools and resources the specific interaction may offer. What are the affordances of CMC interactions – and within different modalities and task types – at different levels of proficiency? Are there affordances that are particular to communities of L2 learners?

2. *Social presence* is a novel way of looking at communities of practice within CMC, "... specifically affective, interactive, and cohesive indicators as they occur during asynchronous online discussion" (Arnold et al., 2005: 537). How is social presence constructed, negotiated among participants in various learner groups (e.g., different levels of language competence)? How is learning socially mediated and collaboratively co-constructed among L2 learners?

3. Future research should consider CMC's *application to K-12 contexts* as most current studies focus on adult learners. Not only different levels of proficiency but different layers of literacy skills,

maturity levels, or socialization may impact (and should impact) how CMC is incorporated into L2 learning.

4. Projects should explore the challenges and possibilities of *using CMC in non-Latin-based orthographies* (e.g., such as Russian, Arabic, Hindi, or Korean). Most CMC studies look at ESL/EFL (English as a Second/Foreign Language), Spanish or German contexts, and the dearth of studies available in other languages (Lin, 2015; Zhao, 2003) remains unsatisfying.

5. What is *the role of personal or contextual variables in successful CMC interactions* (e.g., motivation, proficiency, task, experience with computers, learner/teacher attitude)?

6. If collaborative learning already *fosters intersubjectivity and interactional management skills*, can these practices be "improved" in CMC? If yes, how? Is there a "ceiling" for what L2 learners can teach each other in terms of interactional competence?

7. *How is language play co-constructed in the non-linear discourse practice of CMC exchanges?*

8. Authentic uses of CMC include social networking, connecting to others, or sharing ideas and information, among other purposes. *How can intracultural CMC tasks remain true to authentic uses of CMC and still lead to linguistic gains?*

9. The role that *personal experience* plays in a broader collaborative learning environment may offer fascinating insights into (a) why pedagogically designed tasks occasionally (often?) result in more "ecologically" developing activities (i.e., the interaction that develops is based on participants' own interests and personalities), and (b) what forces may shape CMC-based interactions in particular ways (see, for example, Wildner-Bassett's [2005] study of American learners of German and issues of power).

10. *Comparative studies between intracultural (L2 learner to L2 learner) and intercultural (L2 learner to native speaker) CMC* are needed, in order to determine what the interactional patterns are (in terms of lexical use, linguistic or content scaffolding, intersubjectivity, language play, the affective responses of both learners and their partners, etc.). Such explorations could elucidate appropriate levels for intra- and intercultural collaboration and optimal ways of incorporating both types of CMC into an effective L2 curriculum.

11. WhatsApp, Instagram, Twitter, or Facebook allow for the inclusion of *multimodal communication* online. This feature can be inherently motivating for learners, can provide visual scaffolding for L2 input (i.e., a meme, image, or sound file that supports a

verbal/textual utterance) and offer important insights into learn-ers' L2 developmental processes. However, as yet, we have little knowledge regarding how learners – especially at lower levels of L2 proficiency, when intracultural CMC might be more useful and comfortable – develop the skills to process and produce such diverse text types and learn to navigate multiple channels and modalities of communication.

12. How can L2 educators create a sustainable and coherent "learn-ing context [that] is increasingly learner-centered, technology-rich and ever evolving," in a way that meets learners' authentic L2 use needs and prioritizes design for learning, without overwhelming the instructor or fragmenting the learning experience too much in terms of technology (Sun, 2017: 583)?

Naturally, as new technologies emerge, we need to continue to exam-ine critically, how "innovative forms of expression … challenge traditional notions of authorship" (Blake, 2013: 114) and how our understanding of CMC and oral versus written forms of communication might change as a result. This would be essential for establishing useful pedagogical objec-tives in light of new digital literacies required of our students (Chun, Kern, & Smith, 2016) and for assessing learner contributions as well. With the rise of Web 3.0 technologies that interact with "a user's previous actions to interpret and make connections with this information" (ibid.: 72) – new questions will emerge regarding optimal pedagogical implementation or revised theories of L2 acquisition. It is essential that incorporating emer-gent CMC technologies into L2 pedagogy be grounded in sound theoretical and pedagogical conceptualization (Blake, 2013; Shaw, 2009).

3   Pedagogical Implications: Task Design, Implementation, Evaluation of Outcomes

As the studies reviewed above suggest, similar tasks can have remarkably different outcomes. One contributor to this difference may be task design. The success of a CMC activity may depend on the instructor's understand-ing of the pedagogical and theoretical foundation of that activity, which should also be designed to ensure smooth integration into other classroom activities. The following guidelines aim to facilitate this integration.

3.1 Task Design and Implementation

Effective language learning tasks are purposeful activities that engage at least learners' comprehension, but preferably also their production of language (Lee, 2000). In traditional classroom-based contexts, tasks have been conceptualized as "activities that teachers assign to attain particular learning objectives" (Richards, 1990: 11). In CMC environments, however, "task" is broadened to include socially motivated uses of learning events, in line with activity theory (cf. Lantolf, 2000), because participants often re-purpose an interaction. In order for a CMC task to be successful, several questions must be answered during preparation:

a. What are the learning objectives of this CMC task? (i.e., what should students be able to do via or as a result of this activity?)
b. Which type of CMC is best suited for achieving these objectives (and is a CMC activity indeed best-suited for these objectives)? Which type of CMC is most authentically used for this type of purpose?
c. What knowledge and skills – for example, language knowledge, technical know-how, digital literacy – do students need in order to participate in the CMC task?

When it comes to task design, it is best to start with expected outcomes, which the first question addresses. A well-designed pedagogical task should have clearly-defined learning objectives, and subtasks should lead clearly to these objectives. Pre-reading or -writing activities should provide important linguistic scaffolding and generate ideas for a following CMC exchange. Alternatively, the CMC exchange may be more productive if it is used for a task that holds students accountable after the online discussion. As Salaberry argues, "the success of a technology-driven activity will likely depend as much, or more, on the successful accomplishment of pre- and post-activities than on the technology activity itself" (2001: 51).

The second question prompts us to ensure a good fit between the learning objectives and the type of CMC task that is implemented. This includes both the synchronicity of computer tools (i.e., synchronous or asynchronous CMC) and the group constellations (one-to-one, small group, or large group exchanges). The task should also make the best use of the application's affordances, including options for video-conferencing, multimedia features, streaming, etc. SCMC seems to foster more playful, social facets of interactions, whereas ACMC perhaps offers more opportunities for in-depth thinking, reflectivity, and collaborative goal-oriented projects. Another consideration, which still needs empirical testing but is suggested by common sense and anecdotal evidence, is that certain types of CMC applications may be better suited for beginning learners than for more advanced learners. Keller-Lally's (2006) participants reported being overwhelmed with many-to-many synchronous CMC discussions because the text appeared and disappeared on the screen at a fast pace; perhaps many-to-many constellations in CMC require more advanced linguistic skills in the L2. In contrast, short blurbs such as tweets may be very effective for beginning and intermediate language learners (see Steckenbiller, 2016, for an example of creative Twitter use in an intermediate German language course). This is still an area in need of research, though.

Third, students should have the necessary background information to be able to complete the content component of the task, as well as the linguistic knowledge required for producing the desired output. Equally importantly, they need to have the technical skills to participate in the CMC activity (e.g., having set up the necessary software, accessed applications, etc.). Using an L2 blog, as Ducate & Lomicka (2005) did, helps improve the quality of students' own products by providing opportunities for linguistic scaffolding and by generating ideas for improved content. Similarly, if the instructor is involved with the project, s/he can also offer linguistic scaffolding, leading to further gains by the learners (Lee, 2010a, 2010b). If learners do not receive adequate and appropriate training, they may produce lower-quality output or may be unable to complete the assigned tasks (Cornelius & Boos, 2003).

There are two further considerations in designing effective CMC tasks, and these are perhaps the greatest challenge of intracultural CMC: *communicative authenticity* and *task authenticity*. While researchers may be excited by studies that illuminate SLA processes or those that examine how language skills gained in CMC can be transferred to other skill areas (e.g., to oral production), the tasks commonly used in these studies (e.g., jigsaw tasks) may be quite uninteresting for students and not particularly well-suited for the actual affordances offered by CMC environments. The real benefits of CMC in L1 non-pedagogical contexts lie in its ability to create socially defined discourse communities and foster social networking, and these authentic purposes of CMC activities need to be incorporated into L2 tasks as well (Antenos-Conforti, 2009; Shaw, 2009). The question we must ask ourselves as educators, is how to make our CMC tasks as similar to the "authentic," non-pedagogic uses as possible, even if our interactants are non-native speakers of the L2, while harnessing the power of CMC for pedagogical purposes.

In order to tackle the first consideration, *communicative authenticity*, one could argue that students spend 22 years in an educational context, which makes classroom-based teacher-student interactions inherently authentic. This does not diminish the fact that our ultimate objective is to prepare students to participate in L2 interactions beyond the classroom, but merely recognizes the reality that students spend hours communicating with us and with their peers, and – even though display questions are still present in classroom discourse – opportunities for genuine exchanges of ideas are plentiful in communicative language teaching. Such open exchanges should be seen as having high *communicative authenticity*, and should simulate the inherent affordances of non-pedagogic CMC interactions. Tasks involving texts or cultural issues that students are interested in make excellent topics for open-ended SCMC chats and debates, can be found in "real-life" online communities and make students genuine interactants, with legitimate communicative purposes. Similarly, class wikis offer opportunities for "authentic" interaction. Students can research complementary aspects of a theme and share their contributions with their classmates. A class blog that allows students to reflect on their individual and collective learning, to set and refine learning objectives for themselves, or to share their study-abroad experience with others in a multimedia format would also offer *communicative authenticity*.

The second consideration is what I call *task authenticity*. The CMC application must fit the task that an instructor wishes to implement in the L2 classroom. Students will enjoy and participate more in CMC tasks if the interactions have real-life relevance and centralize their learning needs and interests (Sun, 2017). To this end, we need to identify the authentic function(s) of CMC applications (IM, chat room, Twitter, Facebook, etc.) and find ways in which that purpose can be harnessed for L2 learning. We must ensure that we take advantage of social and linguistic affordances of CMC tools and not merely use technology "as a substitute vehicle for existing instructional techniques and methodologies" (Weible, 1994: 67). Table 1 offers three illustrations for retooling authentic CMC tasks for L2 learning.

Although classroom-based tweets, blogs, or debate might be culturally semi-authentic – i.e., they have a pedagogical objective and are produced by L2 learners who might not interact with each other in the L2 outside the classroom – these interactions can still be communicatively and task-wise authentic since the learning task imitates real-life uses of the CMC environment. In addition to the challenge of creating authentic interactions in potentially inauthentic contexts, there are other potential pitfalls in using CMC in the L2 classroom, and instructors need to be prepared to meet these challenges, which the next subsection addresses.

Table 1 Retooling authentic CMC tasks for L2 learning

CMC application	Authentic social function of CMC application	Sample implementation of authentic purpose for L2 teaching
Twitter	Twitter allows people in L1 contexts to offer immediate commentaries about what they observe or experience in their environment; can be public or private, has 280 character limit.	*Watching a film:* tweeting reactions to a film that is shown in class can enrich the learners' experience by noticing more details, reacting personally to events and scenes in the film, and offering commentary for follow-up in-class discussions.
Blogging	Blogs allow individuals to stay connected to family and friends, keep a social commentary, among other purposes. A blog can be public or private, has multimedia presentation. In terms of its chronological organization, a blog is similar to a diary.	*Study abroad reporting:* Students share mini-reports with visual (and possibly hyperlinked) support with each other and/or an instructor, engaging in reflection and leading to richer understanding by narrating similar experiences from multiple perspectives.
Synchronous CMC	SCMC allows participants in a chat room to interact, share personal stories, joke, get to know each other, participate in debates, or problem-solve collaboratively, among other purposes.	*Debate:* For the purposes of a debate, SCMC can be used either to brainstorm and generate ideas (as a pre-speaking activity) or for the actual debate itself. Students can be assigned or select sides (if there are diverse opinions) and are asked to defend or argue against certain positions.
Facebook group	Facebook-based ACMC allows participants to contribute shorter or longer texts, include multimedia components, such as images, memes, gifs, or videos, and promotes social cohesion.	*Classroom community:* Students could share favorite meals, movies, reactions to an in-class presentation, newsfeeds, or cartoons from L2 cultural contexts, among other experiences they have already shared or in preparation of in-class discussions. *Note:* If not enough activity occurs on Facebook, interest and participation peters out quickly.
Skype exchange (or other video-based application, such as Facebook Messenger, WhatsApp)	Participants engage in one-to-one or many-to-many video or audio-only chats, with access to supplemental chat function that can be used for clarification or to share hyperlinks, for example. Unfortunately, recording these conversations requires additional software (https://www.cnet.com/how-to/record-skype-calls-for-free/)	*Interviews, oral exams, pragmatics:* Students can use Skype to practice asking and answering questions on a variety of topics. By setting up the exchanges with another, unknown, group of L2 learners, the activity becomes semi-authentic, since there is a real impetus to find out about one's interlocutor whom learners do not know from the class. At advanced levels of L2 proficiency, students can interview one another or discuss ideas in preparation of a subsequent writing or debate assignment.

3.2 Practical Pedagogical Considerations

A few practical issues related to participant behavior and technical matters should be considered before implementing CMC activities. For example, students may exhibit flaming behavior (such as inappropriate or aggressive language; Abrams, 2003b) or they may "lurk" (i.e., they are apparently present in the chat forum, but do not contribute anything). Lack of participation is especially common in ACMC (Abrams, 2003a), where responses may lag so substantially that the communication completely peters out. Such silent behaviors, however, may still lead to linguistic benefits for L2 learners. Either in preparation of public participation or reflecting personal preferences, some learners might engage in lurking (i.e., reading what others write, without contributing comments), an activity that can still foster community-building and provide learners with essential input and modeling in the L2 (Arnold & Paulus, 2010; Dennen, 2008; Nonnecke & Preece, 2003).Another important pedagogical concern might be the low linguistic quality or content of learner contributions, suggesting that CMC interactions may lack intellectual depth (Belz & Kinginger, 2003). Herring (2003), Thomson (2006) and Yates (2001) have also reported gender inequity (male dominance) in CMC interactions, at least in the L1.

While such challenges can be frustrating, many of them can be prevented or fixed. For example, flaming behavior may be managed by the CMC community or guidelines can be set up clearly outlining expectations of language use and consequences for flaunting those expectations (Abrams, 2003b). Similarly, although lurking may be acceptable CMC behavior in L1 contexts, in pedagogical tasks it can hinder or completely break down small-group work. At the very least, the student does not get the intended practice, cannot get feedback, and cannot be evaluated. Once again, clear expectations and consequences can help prevent or ameliorate the situation.

Any potential "low quality" content or language might actually be a function of the learners' level combined with the pace of submissions (especially in SCMC) or with the task they are asked to perform (Lee, 2010b). Perhaps the instructor's expectations need to be modified, viewing SCMC as improving fluency instead of accuracy (Abrams, 2003a). Quality of content and linguistic performance may also benefit from extended preparation: students should read to increase their knowledge about the topic of discussion and to build vocabulary that can provide scaffolding for the learners' own CMC interactions. Additionally, tasks can be repeated to allow learners to focus on content first, then on form. Using chat transcripts to focus on form during subsequent writing tasks can be effectively promote accuracy.

Table 2 Potential pitfalls and solutions in implementing CMC tasks

Potential pitfalls	Potential solutions/pre-emptive measures
1. Partner selection	To the extent possible, students should be paired up with a partner with whom they can work effectively. A student who likes to have things done well before the deadline working with someone who is most creative under pressure at the eleventh hour may find the encounter frustrating. Students who are highly motivated should be able to work with other highly motivated learners. One possible solution is to allow students to pick their own partners or to hand out a needs analysis (what is your interest in learning this language, what experience do you have with CMC?, etc.). Once a task is in progress, student concerns should be addressed quickly, with a solution negotiated among the partners and the instructor (e.g., switching out a passive partner).
2. Topic choice	Topics should be selected in consultation with the learners if possible (be it a research project or a pedagogical task). If topics reflect student interest, participation and motivation may be higher, and task-completion is more likely (Herring, 1993; Sun, 2009; Thomson 2006; Zeiss & Isabelli-García, 2005). A higher level of motivation, in turn, leads to sustainable autonomous learning (Kessler & Bikowski, 2010).
	Provocative topics can also lead to more interaction (instructors may participate themselves in the discussion, moderate them, or they can let the participants do so). Specific questions that may "hook" into students' own experience may also be more effective than vague, overly broad questions.
	If topics are selected in advance, perhaps due to curricular constraints, students can still be asked to identify sub-topics that are of interest to them (e.g., if immigration is a broad topic, students could select two-three sub-issues within immigration they find especially relevant).
3. Communication with learners	Provide in writing the purpose of the activity, tasks, sub-tasks, expectations (in terms of language output and/or rules for participation), as well as the criteria for assessing learners' performance. Clear communication can facilitate successful interaction. Task descriptions should be clear and concise. However, be prepared for completely different outcomes than what you expect. That is a function of CMC tasks (Abrams, 2003b; Kern, 1995) and is a sign that students have taken ownership of the interaction.
	Beginning language learners should get the task description in the L1 (if possible; this is typically not an option in the case of ESL classes); even more advanced learners should have a chance to clarify assignments.

When CMC is used for research purposes, clear communication is crucial. While research protocols often demand that we not offer overly specific information about the language features under study, the more information we can give about the steps involved in a process (research project or pedagogical task), and the reasons behind our decision-making, the more collaborative our students may be.

4. Step-by-step implementation of tasks and task-sets	Specific skills, materials, or information students need *prior* to the task must be provided in advance. If students need to download Skype on their own laptops, make sure they can do it on their own or provide a workshop on setting up the application together. Multi-step activities need to progress logically. Do not ask students to email another L2 learner, then tell them *after* the exchange that they need to submit copies of all email communication.

Provide specific expressions you want students to use during their interactions (e.g., phrases used for agreeing or disagreeing with someone, steering the discussion back on task, or asking for help for themselves).

Especially if you are conducting research, analyze some data after the first iteration of the task, to ensure that you are collecting the right kind of data that really answers your research questions. It is fairly easy to change course midway; it is not easy to retrofit your research questions to fit the bizarre collection of data you end up with, if a task is off.

5. Technical support	Most technical problems are easy to fix by reading the Help menu in any application. You should also not be too proud to ask your students for help; many of them will have more experience with certain applications than the instructor. Utilize their expertise.

Some problems, however, need a bit more planning. Find out, and state clearly for your students too, what technical support is available for them (and for you). If you use a language lab, make sure that the application – and the correct version of the application – is available on all computers in the lab. If you are using audio- or video-chats, make sure that the labs have the necessary additional equipment, such as microphones and/or headsets (especially in PC labs this could be an issue).

If you have experts who specialize in training particular applications (e.g., *Second Life*, which has a relatively steep learning curve), take advantage of their expertise as well. It takes a different set of skills to *use* an application than to *explain* how to use it.

6. Time, effort, and other resources needed	Students – and you – may feel bothered by having to spend an hour in a workshop learning the ins and outs of an application only to use it once for a 20-minute activity. It may be better to keep using the same application throughout the semester, or using 2–3 applications, than trying to get data from or practice on every conceivable CMC-type during one school term. Make your pedagogical decisions carefully, select the appropriate CMC-application, and stay with it (unless you encounter insurmountable technical difficulties). While CMC applications are free of charge, and many students have access to computers, if not personal ones then at least on campus, it behooves us all to remember that textbooks are expensive, and asking learners to purchase other technical components should be pedagogically justifiable.

The list of practical issues can by no means be exhaustive due to space, but technical issues must be mentioned as well. They range from lack of appropriate software and/or bandwidth, to access to computers or even the automaticity of the technology. Instead of viewing the technical difficulty as a negative, creative solutions can allow the task to continue and can even yield pedagogical benefits. In such instances, students can share a computer or alternative technologies can be used by some students (e.g., cell phones). For situations that are unpreventable, having technical support is crucial and should be readily accessible.

Other technical hiccups that instructors can prepare for include discussing email (or other applications) usage explicitly with students; sharing the correct Skype name or email address is essential, as is ensuring that messages arrive in the inbox and not the spam folder (Sadler, 2007). Also, all software and hardware (e.g., having external microphones for Skype on a PC, knowing passwords used in the media lab) should be checked prior to CMC tasks, in cooperation with the instructional technology support team. It is also helpful to familiarize students with different appearances of application across different platforms (i.e., Mac vs. PC), so instructors should be thoroughly familiar with the applications themselves. Table 2 above describes some further potential challenges that might arise and offers possible solution(s) to the problem.

This subsection has offered several guidelines for designing effective CMC tasks with clear learning objectives. Assessment, however, also plays an important role in the success of CMC interactions, since the criteria for evaluation may impact how students perceive the task and how they will participate in it. Assessment may be particularly challenging when the CMC interaction is authentic. How do you evaluate authenticity and global interaction? Yet, cohesion between task design, CMC task, and assessment is essential, as the discussion below suggests.

3.3 Assessment

The evaluation and assessment of what students are learning and how they are learning it is an essential part of any L2 teaching context. Assessment can follow traditional measures (e.g., 5 points for grammatical accuracy, 5 points for lexical accuracy), but can also be qualitative, descriptive, self-reflective (performed by the student), or trajectory-based (i.e., looking at long-term development). Assessment is important because it gives students useful feedback about the content and/or the form of their contributions in CMC environments.

The key to effective assessment is to return to the pedagogical objective of the CMC task: what was it that students were supposed to know/be able to do during this CMC activity or as a result of it? The criteria must match the stated objectives, and the objectives should be as "authentic" as possible. If we ask students, for example, to tweet three times a week, but then grade them on grammar and vocabulary, they are likely not to continue tweeting (negative washback effect, see Bachman & Palmer, 1996). The "authentic" purpose of tweeting is to exchange informal status reports; grammar will likely suffer (not just in the L2 but in the L1 as well), the lexicon will be abbreviated or skeletal, and learners will likely use multiple semiotic systems (e.g., letters, numbers, images, sound). In order to encourage ongoing tweets, the assessment criteria should match the task: points should be included for a certain amount of content, length, frequency, and interactivity (i.e., responding to other people's submissions, not just submitting a tweet). Similarly, CMC-based writing, especially SCMC, is very informal (see Beauvois, 1995; Kern, 1995). Giving students grades, even on an ACMC task, that require subordinate clauses in support of main arguments will be frustrating, both for the instructor and for the learner. Not only should the criteria match the task, they should also be identified and shared with the students *before* the task, ideally, determined in collaboration with the students or at least with their input. Figure 1 offers some suggested criteria for evaluating CMC tasks.

These criteria can be assessed in either analytic or holistic ways (cf. Bachman & Palmer, 1996; Hughes, 1989; Scott, 1996; Weir, 1991). Analytic scoring provides scores for subcategories such as grammar, lexicon, comprehensibility, and content (the categories may vary, depending on learning and task-objectives). Holistic scoring offers a global score for the entire submission. After describing a sample assignment, the creation of a study

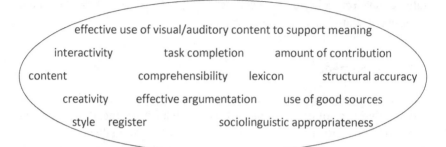

Figure 1 Potential assessment categories for CMC tasks (from Abrams, 2006: 193).

abroad community in Facebook, Table 3 provides a possible example for grading it analytically or holistically.

Pedagogical context and overarching task

- A class of first-year students at a US university compiles an L2-language "menu" of study-abroad opportunities in a country where the L2 is used (e.g., French in France or Senegal), situated in a closed Facebook group, which includes the intact class, more advanced students returning from study abroad programs, and the instructor. The course textbook used at this level includes countries where the L2 is spoken, academic subjects (i.e., possible majors), readings that have touched upon the different educational systems used in some countries that use the L2, comparing similarities and differences to the students' own experiences. This assignment is intended to have students familiarize themselves with different aspects of their potential host institutions, the organization of their websites, course registration, housing information, possible extra-curricular activities at the university and the broader environment (e.g., town, region), as well as other information that the students might encounter and find interesting.

- It is important to keep in mind that pedagogical tasks need to be designed for the specific learning context. The pedagogical orientation of the program (e.g., developing communicative and inter-cultural competence), the level of learners' language knowledge, their motivation for working to achieve the specific learning objectives (i.e.., learning about study abroad programs), the availability of returning students as resources, access to technology (e.g., both for students on their own time and for the class as a whole for collaborative in-class activities), the length and complexity of source texts, and the organization of the host institutions' websites need to be considered carefully. For beginning L2 courses some of the readings could/should be done in class, to allow for questions and provide learners with sufficient background knowledge to understand the text. This could serve as a pre-task for subsequent interviews and writing. Students also need explicit guidance for reading L2 websites, as their organization and content might be very different from what the learners are used to seeing.

Sub-tasks for small groups
- The first-year students work in groups of three or four to collect relevant information about study abroad opportunities in the L2 (host universities and towns) and generate questions for an interview with a study-abroad returnee.
- Students conduct the interview with their more advanced peers, taking notes and posting mini-reports to the closed Facebook website; they can include relevant, supporting images, memes, links to websites or even videos of their interview or ones that their interview participants were willing to share with them from their study abroad sojourn.
- Individual students are expected to engage with the reports of other groups, responding to their posts, asking questions, suggesting links between their and others' comments.

While teacher-student Skype interviews or dyadic chat assignments (i.e., written by a pair of students) may be relatively easy to grade, SCMC can be challenging, because transcripts blend contributions by different participants, and the instructor first needs to identify individual students' output to be able to measure their participation. The participation score also needs to include the interactivity of learners' responses.

It is important to note that a CMC session can be left ungraded if it is used as a preparatory activity for a subsequent graded task. Assessment can be done by the student (e.g., as self-assessment, using a checklist of learning objectives and grading criteria), by peers (feedback or response), by the instructor (for feedback only or for feedback and grade), or a combination of these options. Students could also compile electronic portfolios, including a wiki page, a series of blogs, email exchanges with a peer, or other L2 products. Portfolio assessments are particularly effective for showcasing long-term linguistic gains such as over the course of a semester, and can be very motivating for learners (Wright, 2003).

Table 3 Sample analytic and holistic scoring for a Facebook assignment

Analytic Scoring (20 points) Half of the points are assigned to the group, half for the individual contributions	Holistic Scoring (15 Points) Two-thirds of the points are assigned to the group, one-third for the individual contributions
Comprehensibility: 4 points: little or no difficulty for instructor to follow meaning (2 points for the group, 2 for the individual contributions). 2 points: some difficulty in following meaning (1 point for the group contribution, 1 point for the individual).	*9–10 points (group) + 5 points (individual posts)* Original post (summary of interview) is of sufficient length and depth. Relevant support is included from the host university's website, with meaningful images and/or video. Rich lexicon draws on classroom discussions and readings; it is also mostly accurate both in form and register. Grammar is effective, fairly accurate; sentences vary in structure; signs of pragmatic awareness (e.g., register). Effective use of visual, auditory and / or hyperlinked material in the original post; some also used in individual responses to peers.
Content: 4 points: extensive original post; meaningful link to relevant websites, images, videos; sufficient follow-up contributions (sufficient length & number). 2 points: minimal original post, with marginally relevant linking of websites, images, or other supportive material; minimal follow-up contributions (few, short and/or inaccurate/irrelevant). 0 points: insufficient or missing original post, little evidence of relevant supporting materials; insufficient follow-up contributions (either in content or number).	*7–8 points (group) + 4 points (individual posts)* Original post (summary of interview) is focused, but somewhat short. Some minimal supporting materials is included (links to websites, few images and/or video). The lexicon draws mostly from vocabulary already learned. Regular lexical mistakes, even with learned material. Mostly effective grammar, although more inaccuracies than in the higher category. Varied sentence structure; some pragmatic awareness. Effective use of visual, auditory and/or hyperlinked material.

Vocabulary and expression:
4 points: rich, extensive vocabulary, varied expression, incorporates new phrases and lexical items from course-work, readings and class discussions.
2 points: some difficulties with newly learned vocabulary, some misspellings, lacks idiomatic expression, relies on for-mulaic phrases.
0 points: mistakes in vocabulary already covered, very few new lexical items incorporated, limited lexical richness (variety of lexical items used).

5–6 points (group) + 3 points (individual posts)
While the original post is well-focused, it is quite short, with limited information included; there might be some difficul-ties with coherence. Limited supportive information is provided only, and the multimodal environment is not utilized. Some of the information may be incor-rect. The lexicon draws mostly from vocabulary already learned. Several lexical mistakes are present. Grammar is only partially accurate or is very "safe." Limited variation in sentence structure; no sign of contextually appropriate pragmatic language use. Relevance of comments to others' posts is unclear, and no visual or hyperlinked material is included in individual responses.

Grammatical accuracy:
4 points: (mostly) accurate use of cov-ered grammatical structures – with allowances for CMC's more relaxed grammar use.
2 points: partially accurate use of gram-matical structures already covered, no variety in syntactic expression.
0 points: many grammatical mistakes (make contributions incomprehensible).

3 – 4 points (group) + 2 points (individual posts)
The original post is insufficient or not related to the assigned topic; it may include irrelevant or inaccurate mate-rial. Limited lexical richness, problems with register and accuracy. Little varia-tion in sentence structure, many gram-matical mistakes make posts difficult to understand. No evidence of pragmatic awareness or contextually inappropri-ate pragmatic language use. Responses to peers' posts are minimal and/or irrelevant.

Creativity and presentation:
4 points: original post is very creative, with effective use of multimedia (images, videos, links, etc); individual comments are detail-rich, relevant and indicate engagement with others' posts.
2 points: original post is somewhat creative, with some relevant, supportive sources; comments to peers are ade-quate, some engagement with peers' contributions.
0 points: very limited original post, with irrelevant or missing supportive materi-als; comments to peers are inadequate, showing a lack of engagement with others' posts.

1–2 points (group) + 1 point (individual posts)
The original post is missing or inad-equate; completely irrelevant, inaccu-rate or missing supportive information. Little variety in lexicon, many inaccura-cies interfere with comprehensibility. Many grammatical mistakes (also inter-fere with communication). No prag-matic awareness evident. Responses to peers inappropriate, inaccurate, com-pletely irrelevant or absent.

More research is needed on effective and appropriate ways of evaluating learners' performance on CMC tasks. In the meantime, instructors should ensure that criteria for evaluation (1) are formulated clearly, (2) match the learning objectives of the task and the tool being used, and (3) are shared with students prior to the activity to foster more valuable CMC exchanges, because, ideally, they highlight expected optimal language use.

4   Conclusions

This chapter has provided a brief overview of key themes in the rapidly growing body of scholarship on synchronous and asynchronous CMC. Research shows that intracultural CMC offers L2 learners several linguistic and affective benefits, such as (a) gains in lexical richness and grammatical accuracy (Smith, 2004; Warschauer, 1996), (b) a wider array of discourse functions and participant roles learners can adopt (Abrams, 2001; Chun, 1994), not in small part due to the lower "asymmetric power relationship between the teacher, the all-knowing expert, and the L2 beginner" (Blake, 2013: 105), (c) increased social coherence and opportunities for language play (Darhower, 2002), (d) improved opportunities for shared contexts of learning and intersubjectivity (Lee, 2010b), and (e) an intermediate stepping stone before learners enter into intercultural CMC (i.e., with native speakers), which they may find overwhelming at the beginning of their L2 journey (Blake, 2013). These observations can be complemented by Lin's (2015) meta-analysis of 59 studies, in which she summarized systematic findings regarding the impact of CMC on L2 development:

1. CMC benefits L2 writing primarily, although this may be due to the fact that most studies employed primarily, or at least some, written components of CMC;
2. students working in pairs saw the greatest increases in L2 development, with somewhat lower effectiveness seen in small groups, and none in large group interactions (this is especially the case in voice-based chat, where overlapping comments make conversations disjointed and incomprehensible);
3. CMC in class was more effective than assigned outside of it, possibly because students are more focused and task-oriented during class-time;
4. CMC projects of less than 10 weeks in duration were the most effective, with benefits dropping off significantly after 11 weeks, and almost completely by 24 weeks; and

5. CMC done in English as a foreign or second language was most impactful, possibly due to the high level of motivation these students bring with them to the learning context.

Drawing on the studies reviewed in this chapter, several guidelines emerge for designing effective CMC tasks, calling special attention to the notion of *authenticity*. This is a significant challenge for intracultural CMC assignments, but not insurmountable, as long as instructors attempt to connect pedagogical objectives to real-life purposes of CMC applications, even if the activity itself may lack cultural authenticity. Real-world relevance is essential if we want to design learner-centered and stimulating CMC tasks (Sun, 2017). Inherently linked to the classroom use of intracultural CMC is how students are assessed when they participate in computer-mediated exchanges. Just as the task(s) should match authentic purposes of CMC applications, the criteria by which students are assessed should reflect the way that the application is used in real life (what gets evaluated, how and why).

Computer-mediated communication is a component of our everyday lives, and has earned a rightful place in the toolkit of L2 instructors as well. As novel technologies emerge, however, we need to examine continually the way we design CMC tasks and how we assess CMC interactions in a way that reflects the affordances inherent in these technologies. Ongoing research will continue to refine our understanding of optimal uses of CMC among L2 learners and will continue to inform us about both the cognitive processes that take place within the individual and the social practices among L2 learners. It is useful to remind ourselves that "each [CMC tool] has its own appropriate time and place" (Blake, 2013: 110). Therefore, instructors need to identify the most effective ways of implementing intracultural communication in the L2 classroom, taking into consideration the pedagogical objectives, the educational and social contexts, and the L2 learners' goals and needs.

Questions for Reflection[5]

1. What are the inherent strengths of different kinds of CMC real-life communication, and what types of language learning tasks take full advantage of these strengths the best?

---

5   These questions are similar to the ones at the beginning of the chapter, to foster deeper reflection.

2.   What kinds of CMC tasks can learners at different levels of L2 proficiency complete? Should they participate in different types of CMC tasks? Which ones and why these?
3.   How would CMC activities and assessment need to change, if at all, for languages that have an orthography that few interpersonal communication tools might support (e.g., for teaching Russian, Arabic, or Chinese in the US)?
4.   Think of a CMC activity that you regularly participate in. How would you create an L2 teaching activity that utilizes the affordances of the *authentic* CMC interaction? What kind of language output and interactive behavior do you expect students to produce in this CMC task? What criteria can you identify for assessment that would best reflect the original aspects of participation in social-networking and interpersonal communication (i.e., the purposes you would use this type of CMC for)?

Key Terms

affordances	intracultural CMC
assessment	(extended) negotiation of meaning
asynchronous CMC	sociocultural theory
blogging	synchronous CMC
communicative authenticity	task authenticity
interaction hypothesis	Web 1.0, 2.0 and 3.0 technologies

Case Studies

While you read the following two case studies, keep the following questions in mind:

*   What is the situation – what do you actually know about it from reading the case? *(Distinguishes between fact and assumptions & critical understanding)*
*   What issues are at stake? *(Opportunity for linking to theoretical readings)*
*   What questions do you have – what information do you still need? Where/how could you find it?
*   What problem(s) need to be solved? *(Opportunity to discuss communication versus conflict, gaps between assumptions, sides of the argument)*

- What are all the possible options? What are the pros/cons of each option?
- What are the underlying assumptions for [person X] in the case – where do you see them?
- What criteria should you use when choosing an option? What does that mean about *your* assumptions?

Case Study One: Research

You and a colleague are teaching first-semester German and decide to incorporate Skype sessions into your syllabus every second week, both the voice protocol and the text messaging options. You are both comfortable with using Skype, and talk on Skype at least once or twice a week with other friends who speak German. Neither of you is a native speaker of German.

After three sessions (i.e., during week 6) your colleague comes to complain to you that she is ready to quit because her students (a) do not seem to be enjoying the task, (b) forgot to record some of their interactions and cannot earn grades for the assignments, and (c) produce language that is of considerably lower quality than your colleague had expected. You are surprised, because your students (a) participate with enthusiasm in the Skype activities, (b) remember to record all interactions with one or two exceptions, and (c) produce language that is not very formal, but – you feel – reflects language play and engagement in the language.

Obviously, you and your colleague are curious. You decide to collect empirical evidence, so you can understand better what is going on and write a research project based on your findings.

Discussion Questions:
1. What are the specific affordances for Skype-based voice and text chatting?
2. What are the apparent differences between your class and your colleague's class?
3. What linguistic, affective, and/or pedagogical factors may lead to these differences?
4. If you have identified three-four possible variables, what kind of research questions could you formulate to learn more about them? What kind of data would you want to collect to answer your questions?

potentially problematic variable	possible question(s) to examine what is going on with this issue	type of data needed to answer the research question

5. With a partner, select one of the variables you identified in question 4 and prepare a working definition of the variable, formulate/ revise the research question, brainstorm further the type of data you would collect to analyze this variable, and the data analyses you are planning to use. Is your research innovative? Can you expect to find out *new* information about language learning or CMC-based interactions? Be prepared to explain and justify your selection to your peers.

Case Study Two: Teaching

A teacher, who has been teaching Italian in the US for about ten years, has decided to implement regular SCMC discussions in her fourth-semester intermediate class to brainstorm and elaborate ideas for in-class discussions. She also wants to use these exchanges to help students explore their thinking so that they can write more formal follow-up essays on topics of discussion throughout the semester. Furthermore, she prides herself in being a supporter of authentic or plausible opportunities for language practice, and sees great value in learner-to-learner interaction even beyond pedagogical reasons. The class will use the course management website's synchronous CMC tool, in order to have a record of the interactions that students and the instructor can refer to as they write their essays.

The first synchronous CMC session takes place on the second Friday of the semester. The students have their own computers, with the technological tools already set up. The assignment asks students to "Discuss the changing role of men and women in society and the family" (the first thematic unit in the class is men's and women's roles in today's Italy). The instructions are intentionally vague, because the teacher wants to delimit the sub-topics students choose and does not want to be too authoritative in this novel environment.

The students are excited about using CMC in the classroom, and begin chatting online even before the bell rings. The instructor does not partici- pate, so that she can walk around the room to make sure all students are on-task. She also wants to be there as a resource in case someone does not know a word or phrase. There is a lot of typing, many comments flowing in, and the instructor is very enthusiastic about this idea, until she sees the transcript at the end of the class. Of the 22 students in class, only about 10 people contributed significantly. The language is very informal, to say the least ("bad" grammar, L1 interspersed with L2 comments), and the con- versation has gone off-task more often than stayed on-task. A few students offered excellent ideas that are worthy of follow-up essays, but some of these ideas were not developed further by other students. It also appears that 4–5 students self-selected themselves into a mini-conversation and included rather inane – or possibly even offensive – jokes in their "deliberations." The last 5 minutes of the CMC exchange consists of leave-taking turns "Ciao, ciao!" "Ciao, bella."

The teacher is disappointed, and is wondering how to restructure the next CMC session so it is more productive, meeting the pedagogical objective of generating, elaborating on, and developing ideas in depth.

Discussion Questions:
1. What was the pedagogical objective for this task? What were the conditions of this activity (group constellation, specifics of the assignment)? Would you consider this activity disappointing? In what way? In what way could this transcript be used for positive pedagogical purposes?
2. What do you think the teacher needs to do to restructure the CMC task and make it productive? How would you devise the specifics of the activity? What would the students do before participating in this task? What would their specific assignment for the activ- ity itself be, and what would they do afterwards (e.g., a follow-up task)?
3. What kind of assessment tool would you perhaps implement? What criteria would you establish to evaluate students' performance on this activity? What would be the advantages or disadvantages of sharing these criteria with the students *before* the next SCMC ses- sion? (You may find the module on assessment at the following website: http://tltc.la.utexas.edu/tltc/projects/pprojects.html very helpful.)

Ideas for Action Research Projects

You may want to read the article in the reference section by de Almeida Soares (2008), who uses *Exploratory Practice*, a concept promoted by Dick Allwright (2003). EP is related to action research (i.e., where the practitioner is also the researcher) but offers an alternative to a "problem" approach to examining one's own teaching (i.e., the basic assumption is not that there is something "wrong" with one's teaching, rather, EP asks: what is going on with my teaching?).

1. While some educators feel that they support innovative teaching practices, when push comes to shove, the activities they design and the assessment criteria they use for their students reveal that their practice is a bit out of sync with their perceived beliefs. Keep a teaching journal for a semester, every week identify one CMC activity (chat, Twitter, Instagram, anything) that (a) you use yourself in everyday life, and (b) you can incorporate into your lesson plans (either in class or as a homework assignment). As soon as you think of the activity, jot down quickly (without too much reflection) what language phenomena you would expect to see from your students, and how you would evaluate their performance on this activity. Then put the journal down, and come back to it 24 hours later. What would you change (a) in your activity design and/or (b) in your plans for evaluating the students' work after reflecting upon the points raised in this chapter (if anything)?

2. You want to encourage your students' use of free discussions and set up a bi-weekly synchronous computer-mediated communication activity in class. The students enjoy it, you are seeing the type of language use you were hoping for (language play, humor, joking, even ribbing, but in good faith, extended language use). However, not everybody participates (at all or at least not as much as you had hoped to see). In order to prevent burn-out, you also want to change the activities a little bit (but want to keep the same CMC application to avoid technical overload). What could you change on the activities? How would you collect information about the way the students experience the different activities? What would you do with the information? What other data would you want to collect to contextualize the students' (self-reported) experiences better? How might you be able to use a CMC tool to collect, analyze and reflect on, and share with other your interpretive processes?

References

Abrams, Zs. (2001). Computer-mediated communication and group journals: Expanding the repertoire of participant roles. *System*, 29(4), 489–503. https://doi.org/10.1016/S0346-251X(01)00041-0

Abrams, Zs. (2003a). The effects of synchronous and asynchronous CMC on oral performance in German. *The Modern Language Journal*, 87(2), 157–167. https://doi.org/10.1111/1540-4781.00184

Abrams, Zs. (2003b). Flaming in CMC: Prometheus' fire or Inferno's? *CALICO Journal*, 20 (2), 245–260. https://doi.org/10.1558/cj.v20i2.245-260

Abrams, Zs. (2006). From theory to practice: Intracultural CMC in the L2 classroom. In L. Ducate & N. Arnold (eds.), *Calling on CALL: From theory and research to new directions in foreign language teaching*, pp. 181–209. CALICO Monograph Series 5. San Marcos, TX: Computer Assisted Language Instruction Consortium.

Abrams, Zs. (2011). Interpersonal Communication in Intercultural CMC. In N. Arnold, N., & L. Ducate (eds.) *Present and future promises of CALL: From theory and research to new directions in language teaching*, pp. 61–92. CALICO Monograph Series 5 (2nd ed.). San Marcos, TX: Computer Assisted Language Instruction Consortium.

Allwright, D. (2003). Exploratory practice: Rethinking practitioner research in language teaching. *Language Teaching Research*, 7(2), 113–141. https://doi.org/10.1191/1362168803lr118oa

Antenos-Conforti, E. (2009). Microblogging on Twitter: Social networking in intermediate Italian classes. In L. Lomicka & G. Lord (eds.), *The next generation: Social networking and online collaboration in foreign language learning*, pp. 59–90. CALICO Monograph Series No 9.

Arnold, M. N. (2002). *Computer-mediated communication: Writing to speak without foreign language anxiety?* Unpublished doctoral dissertation, University of Texas – Austin.

Arnold, M. N., & Paulus, T. (2010). Using a social networking site for experiential learning: Appropriating, lurking, modeling and community building. *Internet and Higher Education*, 13, 188–196. https://doi.org/10.1016/j.iheduc.2010.04.002

Arnold, M. N., & Ducate, L. (eds.). (2011). *Present and future promises of CALL: From theory and research to new directions in language teaching*. CALICO Monograph Series 5 (2nd ed.). San Marcos, TX: Computer Assisted Language Instruction Consortium.

Arnold, M. N., Ducate, L., Lomicka, L., & Lord, G. (2005). Using computer-mediated communication to establish social and supportive environments in teacher education. *CALICO Journal*, 22(3), 537–566. https://doi.org/10.1558/cj.v22i3.537-566

Bachman, L. F., & Palmer, A. S. (1996). *Language testing in practice.* Oxford, UK: Oxford University Press.

Beauvois, M. H. (1995). E-talk: Attitudes and motivation in computer-assisted classroom discussion. *Computers and the Humanities*, 28(2), 177–190.

Beauvois, M. H. (1998a). Write to speak: The effects of electronic communication on the oral achievement of fourth semester French students. In J. A. Muyskens (ed.), *New ways of learning and teaching*, pp. 93–115. Boston: Heinle & Heinle.

Beauvois, M. H. (1998b). Conversations in slow motion: Computer-mediated communication in the foreign language classroom. *The Canadian Modern Language Review*, 54(2), 198–217. https://doi.org/10.3138/cmlr.54.2.198

Belz, J. A., & Kinginger, C. (2003). Discourse options and the development of pragmatic competence by classroom learners of German: The case of address forms. *Language Learning*, 53(4), 591–647. https://doi.org/10.1046/j.1467-9922.2003.00238.x

Blake, R. (2000). Computer-mediated communication: A window on L2 Spanish interlanguage. *Language Learning & Technology*, 4(1), 120–136.

Blake, R. (2013). *Brave new digital classroom: Technology and foreign language learning.* Georgetown University Press.

Brooks, F., & Donato, R. (1994). Vygotskan approaches to understanding foreign language learner discourse. *Hispania*, 77(2), 262–274. https://doi.org/10.2307/344508

Bruce, B. C., Kreeft Peyton, J., & Batson, T. (eds.). (1993). *Network-based classrooms: Promises and realities.* New York: Cambridge University Press.

Chapelle, C. A. (2001). *Computer applications in second language acquisition.* New York: Cambridge University Press. https://doi.org/10.1017/CBO9781139524681

Chomsky, N. (1957). *Syntactic structures.* The Hague: Mouton.

Chomsky, N. (1965). *Aspects of the theory of syntax.* Cambridge, MA: MIT Press.

Chun, D. M. (1994). Using computer networking to facilitate the acquisition of interactive competence. *System*, 22(1), 17–31. https://doi.org/10.1017/CBO9781139524681

Chun, D. M., Kern, R., & Smith, B. (2016). Technology in language use, language teaching, and language learning. *The Modern Language Journal*, 16, 64–80. https://doi.org/10.1111/modl.12302

Cook, G. (1997). Language play, language learning. *ELT Journal*, 51(3), 224–231. https://doi.org/10.1093/elt/51.3.224

Cook, G. (2000). *Language play, language learning.* New York: Oxford University Press.

Cornelius, C., & Boos, M. (2003). Enhancing mutual understanding in synchronous computer-mediate communication by training. *Communication Research*, 30(2), 147–177. https://doi.org/10.1177/0093650202250874

Darhower, M. (2002). Interactional features of synchronous computer-mediated communication in the intermediate L2 class: A sociocultural case study. *CALICO Journal*, 19, 249–277. https://doi.org/10.1558/cj.v19i2.249-277

de Almeida Soares, D. (2008). Understanding class blogs as a tool for language development. *Language Teaching Research*, 12(4), 517–533. https://doi.org/10.1177/1362168808097165

Dennen, V. P. (2008). Pedagogical lurking: Student engagement in non-posting discussion behavior. *Computers in Human Behavior*, 24, 1624–1633. https://doi.org/10.1016/j.chb.2007.06.003

Donato, R. (1994). Collective scaffolding in second language learning. In J. Lantolf & G. Appel (eds.), *Vygotskian approaches to second language research*, pp. 33–56. Norwood, NJ: Ablex.

Donato, R., & McCormick, D. (1994). A sociocultural perspective on language learning strategies: The role of mediation. *Modern Language Journal*, 78(4), 453–464. https://doi.org/10.1016/j.chb.2007.06.003

Doughty, C. J. (2006). Instructed SLA. In C. J. Doughty & M. H. Long (eds.), *The handbook of second language acquisition*, pp. 256–310. Malden, MA: Blackwell.

Doughty, C. J., & Long, M. H. (2006). *The handbook of second language acquisition*. Malden, MA: Blackwell.

Doughty, C. J., & Pica, T. (1986). "Information gap" tasks: Do they facilitate second language acquisition? *TESOL Quarterly*, 20, 305–325. https://doi.org/10.2307/3586546

Ducate, L., & Arnold, N. (eds.). (2006). *Calling on CALL: From theory and research to new directions in foreign language teaching*. CALICO Monograph Series 5. San Marcos, TX: Computer Assisted Language Instruction Consortium.

Ducate, L., & Lomicka, L. (2005). Exploring the blogosphere: Use of web logs in the foreign language classroom. *Foreign Language Annals*, 38(3), 410–422. https://doi.org/10.1111/j.1944-9720.2005.tb02227.x

Ellis, R. (1999). Theoretical perspectives on interaction and language learning. In R. Ellis (ed.), *Learning a second language through interaction*, pp. 3–30. Amsterdam: John Benjamins. https://doi.org/10.1075/sibil.17.04ell

Ferdig, R., & Trammell, K. (2004). Content delivery in the "blogosphere." *T.H.E. Journal*, February, 12–20.

Gass, S. M. (2006). Input and interaction. In C. J. Doughty & M. H. Long (eds.), *The handbook of second language acquisition*, pp. 224–255. Malden, MA: Blackwell.

Gass, S. M., & Varonis, E. M. (1994). Input, interaction, and second language production. *Studies in Second Language Acquisition*, 16, 283–302. https://doi.org/10.1017/S0272263100013097

Godwin-Jones, R. (2003). Blogs and wikis: Environments for on-line collaboration. *Language Learning & Technology*, 7(2), 12–16.

Goffman, E. (1974). *Frame analysis: An essay on the organization of experience*. Boston, MA: Northeastern University Press.

Gumperz, J. J. (2001). Interactional sociolinguistics: A personal perspective. In D. Schiffrin, D. Tannen, & H. E. Hamilton (eds.), *The handbook of discourse analysis*, pp. 215–228. Malden, MA: Blackwell.

Hall, J. K. (1999). The communication standards. In J. K. Phillips & R. M. Terry (eds.), *Foreign language standards: Linking research, theories, and practices*, pp. 15–56. Lincolnwood, IL: National Textbook Company.

Halliday, M. A. K. (1973). *Explorations in the functions of language.* London: Edward Arnold.

Herring, S. (1993). Gender and democracy in computer mediated communication. *Electronic Journal of Communication*, 3(2). Retrieved from http://www.cios.org/EJCPUBLIC/003/2/00328.HTML

Herring, S. C. (2003). Gender and power in online communication. In J. Holmes and M. Meyerhoff (eds.), *The handbook of language and gender*, pp. 202–228. Oxford: Blackwell. https://doi.org/10.1002/9780470756942.ch9

Horvath, J. (2009). Hungarian university students' blogs in EFL: Shaping language and social connections. *TESL-EJ*, 12(4), 1–9.

Hughes, A. (1989). *Testing for language teachers*. New York: Cambridge University Press.

Hymes, D. H. (1971). *On communicative competence*. Philadelphia: University of Pennsylvania Press.

Hymes, D. (1974). *Foundations in sociolinguistics: An ethnographic approach*. Philadelphia: University of Pennsylvania Press.

Keller-Lally, A. M. (2006). *Effect of task-type and group size on foreign language learner output in synchronous computer-mediated communication*. Unpublished doctoral dissertation, University of Texas – Austin.

Kelm, O. R. (1998). The use of electronic mail in foreign language classes. In J. Swaffar, S. Romano, P. Markley, & K. Arens (eds.), *Language learning online: Theory and practice in the ESL and L2 computer classroom*, pp. 1–15. Austin, TX: Daedalus.

Kern, R. (1995). Restructuring classroom interaction with networked computers: Effects on quantity and quality of language production. *Modern Language Journal*, 79, 457–476. https://doi.org/10.1111/j.1540-4781.1995.tb05445.x

Kern, R., & Warschauer, M. (2000). Introduction. Theory and practice of network-based language teaching. In M. Warschauer & R. Kern (eds.), *Network-based language teaching; Concepts and practice*, pp. 1–19. New York: Cambridge University Press. https://doi.org/10.1017/CBO9781139524735.003

Kessler, G., & Bikowski, D. (2010). Developing collaborative autonomous learning abilities in computer mediated language learning: Attention to meaning among students in wiki space. *Computer Assisted Language Learning*, 23(1), 41–58. https://doi.org/10.1080/09588220903467335

Krashen, S. (1980). *Second language acquisition and second language learning*. Oxford: Pergamon.

Krashen, S. (1985). *The input hypothesis: Issues and implications*. New York: Longman.

Lantolf, J. P. (1997). The function of language play in the acquisition of L2 Spanish. In A. Pérez-Leroux & W. R. Glass (eds.), *Contemporary perspectives on the acquisition of Spanish*, pp. 3–24. Somerville, MA: Cascadilla Press.

Lantolf, J. P. (2000). Introducing sociocultural theory. In J. P. Lantolf (ed.), *Sociocultural theory and second language learning*, pp. 1–26. New York: Oxford University Press.

Lantolf, J., & Appel, G. (1994). Theoretical framework: An introduction to Vygotskian perspectives on second language research. In J. Lantolf & G. Appel (eds.), *Vygotskian approaches to second language research*, pp. 1–32. Norwood, NJ: Ablex.

Lee, J. F. (2000). *Tasks and communicating in language classrooms*. Boston, MA: McGraw-Hill.

Lee, L. (2010a). Fostering reflective writing and interactive exchange through blogging in an advanced language course. *ReCALL*, 22(2), 212–227. https://doi.org/10.1017/S095834401000008X

Lee, L. (2010b). Exploring wiki-mediated collaborative writing: A case study in an elementary Spanish course. *CALICO Journal*, 27(2), 260–276. https://doi.org/10.11139/cj.27.2.260-276

Lin, H. (2015). A meta-synthesis of empirical research on the effectiveness of computer-mediated communication (CMC) in SLA. *Language Learning & Technology*, 19(2), 85–117. Retrieved from http://llt.msu.edu/issues/june2015/lin.pdf.

Long, M. (1996). The role of the linguistic environment in second language acquisition. In W. Ritchie & T. Bhatia (eds.), *Handbook of research on second language acquisition*, pp. 413–468. New York: Academic Press. https://doi.org/10.1016/B978-012589042-7/50015-3

Lyster, R., & Ranta, L. (1997). Corrective feedback and learner uptake: Negotiation of form in communicative classrooms. *Studies in Second Language Acquisition*, 20, 37–66. Available at https://www.cambridge.org/core/journals/studies-in-second-language-acquisition/article/corrective-feedback-and-learner-uptake/59229F0CA2F085F5F5016FB4674877BF

Meskill, C. (1999). Computers as tools for sociocollaborative language learning. In K. Cameron (ed.), *CALL: Media, design and applications*, pp. 141–164. Lisse, The Netherlands: Swets & Zeitlinger.

Meunier, L. E. (1998). Personality and motivational factors in computer-mediated foreign language communication. In J. A. Muyskens (ed.), *New ways of learning and teaching*, pp. 145–197. Boston: Heinle & Heinle.

Murray, L., & Hourigan, T. (2008) Blogs for specific purposes: Expressivist or socio-cognitivist approach? *ReCALL*, 20(1): 82–97. https://doi.org/10.1017/S0958344008000719

Nonnecke, B., & Preece, J. (2003). Silent participants: Getting to know lurkers better. In C. Leug & D. Fisher (eds.), *From Usenet to CoWebs: Interacting with social information spaces*, pp. 110–132. London: Springer-Verlag. https://doi.org/10.1007/978-1-4471-0057-7_6

Pelletieri, J. (2000). Negotiation in cyberspace. In M. Warschauer & R. Kern (eds.), *Network-based language teaching: Concepts and practice*, pp. 59–86. New York: Cambridge University Press. https://doi.org/10.1017/CBO9781139524735.006

Peterson, M. (2009). Learner interaction in synchronous CMC: A sociocultural perspective. *Computer Assisted Language Learning*, 22(4), 303–321. https://doi.org/10.1017/CBO9781139524735.006

Richards, J. C. (1990). The dilemma of teacher education in second language teaching. In J. C. Richards & D. Nunan (eds.), *Second language teacher education*, pp. 3–15. New York: Cambridge University Press.

Sadler, R. (2007). Computer-mediated communication and a cautionary tale of two cities. *CALICO Journal*, 25(1), 11–30. Available at https://calico.org/journalTOC.php

Salaberry, M. R. (2001). The use of technology for second language learning and teaching: A retrospective. *The Modern Language Journal*, 85(1), 39–56. https://doi.org/10.1111/0026-7902.00096

Schmidt, R. (1993). Awareness and second language acquisition. *Annual Review of Applied Linguistics*, 13, 206–226. https://doi.org/10.1111/0026-7902.00096

Scott, V. M. (1996). *Rethinking foreign language writing.* Boston, MA: Heinle & Heinle.

Shaw, P. A. (2009). The syllabus is dead, long live the syllabus: Thoughts on the state of the language curriculum, content, language, tasks, projects, materials, wikis, blogs and the world wide web. *Language & Linguistics Compass*, 3(5), 1266–83. https://doi.org/10.1111/j.1749-818X.2009.00154.x

Slimani-Rolls, A. (2005). Rethinking task-based language learning: What we can learn from the learners. *Language Teaching Research*, 9, 195–218. https://doi.org/10.1191/1362168805lr163oa

Smith, B. (2003). Computer-mediated negotiated interaction: An expanded model. *The Modern Language Journal*, 87(1), 38–57. https://doi.org/10.1111/1540-4781.00177

Smith, B. (2004). Computer-mediated negotiated interaction and lexical acquisition. *Studies in Second Language Acquisition*, 26(3), 365–398. https://doi.org/10.2307/3588451

Steckenbiller, C. (2016). *Am kürzeren Ende der Sonnenallee* in 140 characters or less: Using Twitter as a creative approach to literature in the intermediate German classroom. *Unterrichtspraxis*, 49(2), 147–160. https://doi.org/10.1111/tger.12008

Stevenson, M. P., & Liu, M. (2010). Learning a language with Web 2.0: Exploring the use of social networking features of foreign language learning websites. *CALICO Journal*, 27(2), 233–259. https://doi.org/10.11139/cj.27.2.233-259

Sullivan, N., & Pratt, E. (1996). A comparative study of two ESL writing environments: A computer-assisted classroom and a traditional oral classroom. *System*, 29(4), 491–501. https://doi.org/10.1016/S0346-251X(96)00044-9

Sun, S. Y. H. (2017). Design for CALL – Possible synergies between CALL and design for learning. *Computer Assisted Language Learning*, 30(6), 575–599. https://doi.org/10.1080/09588221.2017.1329216

Sun, Y. (2009). Voice blog: An exploratory study of language learning. *Language Learning & Technology*, 13(2), 88–103.

Swain, M. (1985). Communicative competence: Some roles of comprehensible input and comprehensible output in its development. In S. Gass & C. Madden (eds.), *Input and second language acquisition*, pp. 235–253. Rowley, MA: Newbury House.

Swain, M. (1995). Three functions of output in second language learning. In G. Cook & B. Seidlhofer (eds.), *Principle and practice in applied linguistics: Studies in honor of H.G. Widdowson*, pp. 125–144. Oxford: Oxford University Press.

Thomson, R. (2006). The effect of topic of discussion on gendered language in computer-mediated communication discussion. *Journal of Language and Social Psychology*, 25, 167. https://doi.org/10.1177/0261927X06286452

van Lier, L. (2000). From input to affordance: Social-interactive learning from an ecological perspective. In J. Lantolf (ed.), *Sociocultural theory and second language learning*, pp. 245–260. New York: Oxford University Press.

Vandergriff, I., & Fuchs, C. (2009). Does CMC promote language play? Exploring humor in two modalities. *CALICO Journal*, 27(1), 26–47. https://doi.org/10.11139/cj.27.1.26-47

Varonis, E. M., & Gass, S. (1985). Non-native/non-native conversations: A model for negotiation of meaning. *Applied Linguistics*, 6(1), 71–90. https://doi.org/10.11139/cj.27.1.26-47

Vygotsky, L. S. (1978). *Mind in society: The development of higher psychological processes*. Cambridge, MA: Harvard University Press.

Warner, C. (2004). It's just a game, right? Types of play in foreign language CMC. *Language Learning & Technology*, 8(2), 69–87. Retrieved from http://llt.msu.edu/vol8num2/warner/

Warschauer, M. (1996). Comparing face-to-face and electronic discussion in the second language class-room. *CALICO Journal*, 13(2&3), 7–26.

Weible, D. M. (1994). Towards a media-specific methodology for CALL. In W. F. Smith (ed.) *Modern media in foreign language education: Theory and implementation*, pp. 67–83. Lincolnwood, IL: National Textbook Company.

Weir, C. J. (1991). *Communicative language testing.* Engelwood Cliffs, NJ: Prentice Hall.

Wildner-Bassett, M. E. (2005). CMC as written conversation: A critical social-constructivist view of multiple identities and cultural positioning in the L2/C2. *CALICO Journal*, 22(3), 635–656. https://doi.org/10.1558/cj.v22i3.635-656

Wright, D. A. (2003). Asynchronous negotiations: Introducing electronic portfolios to promote professional development in foreign language business class-rooms. *Global Business Languages*, 8, 88–107.

Yates, S. J. (2001). Gender, language and CMC for education. *Learning and Instruction*, 11, 21–34. https://doi.org/10.1016/S0959-4752(00)00012-8

Zeiss, E., & Isabelli-García, C. L. (2005). The role of asynchronous computer mediated communication on enhancing cultural awareness. *Computer Assisted Language Learning*, 18(3), 151–169. https://doi.org/10.1080/09588220500173310

Zhao, Y. (2003). Recent developments in technology and language learning: A literature review and meta-analysis. *CALICO Journal*, 21, 7–28. https://doi.org/10.1558/cj.v21i1.7-27

Useful Resources

1. All Blackboard, Canvas or WebCT course management systems have built-in and user-friendly synchronous and asynchronous CMC tools. If, however, you do not have access to these educational applications, Google has Google Talk, Facebook has Messenger and WhatsApp has its own internal capabilities for voice as well as text-based interactions. All of these applications

allow for one-to-one, one-to-many, or many-to-many chats and support audio and visual content as well (make sure you check the individual applications for the availability of written transcripts for SCMC – not all hosts provide this service). They are also free and readily available.

Facebook Messenger:	https://www.messenger.com/
Google Talk:	http://www.google.com/talk/
WhatsApp:	https://www.whatsapp.com/

2. Skype allows both written and audio-video interactions. The former can be synchronous or asynchronous, the latter only synchronous. Text-based interactions can be many-to-many, and most often audio- and video-content can be done in conference format among multiple participants. However, video quality can depend on your available bandwidth and may be limited to two interactants per group. The Skype application is free and can be downloaded in the United States at http://www.skype.com/intl/en-us/home.

3. Blogspot offers free and very user-friendly blog sites at https://www.blogger.com. Instructors can also set up easy-to-use and free blogs at http://www.blog-city.com.

4. For classroom wiki sites, PB Wiki is a good resource, although both instructors and language learners have found wikis to have somewhat of a steep learning curve. The peer-editing processes are especially cumbersome; if you do not save your comments and accidentally navigate away from a page, none of your comments are saved and there is no reminder to save them before you leave a page. However, once users are familiar with the application, http://pbworks.com is a good resource for L2 classrooms.

About the Author

Zsuzsanna Abrams is a Professor at the University of California Santa Cruz. Her research focuses on computer-mediated communication, second language development, computer-supported L2 writing, and language pedagogy, with a particular interest in helping learners develop the ability to use the L2 in real-world communicative situations.

9　Targeting Pronunciation (and Perception) with Technology

Mary Grantham O'Brien

Preview Questions

1. Second language learners often report wanting to sound like native speakers when they speak a second language. What does a "native speaker" sound like, and do you think that it is a realistic goal?
2. Is speaking with a "foreign accent" always a problem? What should be our goal when it comes to targeting pronunciation in the language classroom?
3. Think about your language learning experience. Were you explicitly taught pronunciation? If so, were you taught the sounds of the language, or were you taught additional aspects like word stress, sentence rhythm, and intonation? Which of these aspects play an important role in being understood in a second language?
4. How does perceptual training fit into pronunciation teaching?
5. What might be some reasons teachers give for not teaching pronunciation to their students?
6. What are some aspects surrounding the teaching of pronunciation in a second language that might make pronunciation training an ideal candidate for CALL?

1　Introduction

One of the first things we notice when speaking with someone is his or her accent, or pronunciation that differs from an expected norm. Even native speakers produce *speech segments* (i.e., individual sounds) and *prosody* (i.e., word and sentence stress, intonation, and rhythm) that are highly salient and mark them as being from a particular place. When we interact with non-native speakers, we encounter pronunciation that is influenced by the other language(s) they speak. We refer to this as a *foreign accent* (i.e., speech that deviates from native norms). Research has demonstrated that speaking with a foreign accent can lead to stigmatization (Bresnahan et al., 2002; Gluszek, Newheiser, & Dovidio, 2011; Munro, 2003; Oyama, 1976), and Duppenthaler posits that pronunciation is used "to rank the overall mental ability and degree of sophistication of the non-native speaker in question" (1991: 33).

Work in the field of second language (L2) pronunciation has revealed that most post-pubescent learners speak their L2s with a noticeable foreign accent in most instances (e.g., Derwing & Munro, 2009), and non-native speech can be differentiated from native speech even when very short (i.e., 30 milliseconds) samples are played for listeners (Flege, 1984), when the individual speech sounds are removed, leaving only the speech melody (e.g., Trofimovich & Baker, 2006), and when the speech is played backwards (Munro, Derwing, & Burgess, 2010). In fact, Major (2007) found that even listeners who do not speak a particular language are able to detect foreign accents. In spite of what may seem to be the inescapable fate of language learners (i.e., that they will always speak with an accent), research has shown that targeted pronunciation training can be effective, especially when it comes to ensuring that L2 learners are better understood (e.g., Brinton, 2014).

Although listeners usually quickly tune in to foreign accents, research has demonstrated that they can often understand accented speech quite well (e.g., Derwing & Munro, 2009). Recent approaches to L2 pronunciation have emphasized the notion of *intelligible* (i.e., understood), as opposed to native-like, L2 pronunciation (e.g., Derwing & Munro, 2009; Grant, 2014; Levis, 2005; Thomson & Derwing, 2015). Within this framework, our goal should therefore not be flawless, unaccented pronunciation, but rather intelligible pronunciation that enables our students to make themselves understood in the L2. Therefore, although certain aspects of L2 speech may be salient (i.e., easily noticed) to native listeners (e.g., German <r> and <ch> produced by English native speakers; see O'Brien, 2004 and Ducate & Lomicka, 2009), pronunciation training should focus on aspects that negatively influence the effectiveness of overall communication (i.e., those that most affect intelligibility).

Learners highly value pronunciation and report that they wish to receive pronunciation training (e.g., Foote, Holtby, & Derwing, 2011), but language teachers often do not focus on pronunciation in their classrooms. They offer a number of reasons for not including pronunciation training in their curricula. Among these are a lack of classroom instructional time, a perceived lack of student interest and/or motivation (e.g., Hedgcock & Lefkowitz,

2000), a dearth of engaging pronunciation exercises (Baker, 2014), and the general view that pronunciation training is futile given the general lack of success shown by post-pubescent learners (Scovel, 1969). More importantly, though, teacher education programs provide teachers with relatively little, if any, instruction in how to adequately target pronunciation in their language classes (e.g., Murphy, 2014).

When classroom pronunciation training does occur, it tends to involve one-size-fits-all, controlled activities (e.g., repetition, reading aloud) and correction of salient student errors (e.g., Baker, 2014; Derwing & Munro, 2015). Therefore, a major concern of language instructors regards the fit of pronunciation training in communicative language classrooms. Teachers report finding it difficult to reconcile what are often form-based pronunciation activities with communicative language tasks (e.g., Isaacs, 2009). While research has demonstrated that targeted pronunciation activities can be quite effective (e.g., Lee, Jang, & Plonsky, 2014; Thomson & Derwing, 2015), it is important to note that controlled tasks are not enough. Pronunciation instruction should progress to guided (i.e., semi-structured) and eventually free (i.e., highly communicative, open-ended) tasks that enable learners to apply what they have learned to situations that they are likely to encounter in the real world (i.e., Baker, 2014; Levis & Pickering, 2004).

Given the constraints on classroom time and teacher training as well as the likelihood that our learners have different pronunciation needs, computer-assisted pronunciation training (CAPT) is an ideal solution. Reasons for this include the potential for learner autonomy, capabilities to enable differentiation (i.e., individualized instruction and assessment), repeatability, and potential to include a large database of speech samples, to name a few. Within CAPT, it is important to distinguish between software designed for research purposes and *courseware*, in other words "CALL-mediated curricula-based" software specifically designed for L2 learners (O'Connor & Gatton, 2004: 199). In recent years, a large quantity of courseware has been released as apps (Foote & Smith, 2013).

The focus of some courseware is the *speech segment* (i.e., the individual speech sound) within individual words. At the word level and beyond, it is also possible to focus on *prosody*, that is, aspects of pronunciation larger than the segment: learners can focus on producing correct word or sentence *stress* (i.e., prominence given to a particular syllable) or segmental *duration* (i.e., the length of time it takes to produce a particular sound in relation to others around it). For example, some languages such as German and Dutch make a distinction between long and short vowels, and certain words in Japanese, for instance, are distinguished from one another by the duration of their consonants. Some courseware takes the sentence or even *discourse* (i.e., longer, unified chunks of speech involving reactions to and/or from an interlocutor) as its level of analysis, thereby allowing learners to focus on their pronunciation in a larger communicative context. When the focus of pronunciation moves to the sentence level and beyond, prosodic aspects of *rhythm* (i.e., the timing of stressed vs. unstressed units within speech) and *intonation* (i.e., the tune of an utterance) come into play.

There are various means employed by the developers of courseware to enable learners to focus on their pronunciation. Some technology focuses primarily on developing learners' perception of segments and prosodic features. A popular and, by many accounts, successful means of targeting pronunciation is the use of *visualization* techniques that allow learners to view representations of speech stream characteristics and analyze their own productions, often in comparison with those produced by a native speaker. In addition, *automatic speech recognition* (ASR) is gaining in popularity and effectiveness in its ability to recognize and analyze learners' speech. These technologies will be discussed in further detail in the sections that follow.

2   Review of the Literature

2.1   A Brief History of Pronunciation Training

With the advent of Audiolingualism and its focus on accurate production in the L2, pronunciation became an important aspect of language pedagogy. Pronunciation training focused on the speech segment as the locus of pronunciation practice. This was primarily done through the use of *minimal pair drills* (e.g., Larsen-Freeman, 2000). That is, learners were given a pair of words that differed in only one speech segment (e.g., "bat" vs. "cat", "boot" vs. "boat") and were expected to learn the differences in pronunciation as a reflection of meaning differences. From the late 1960s to the 1980s, however, pronunciation instruction fell out of favor (Isaacs, 2009). Beginning in the late '80s, researchers and practitioners (e.g., Chun, 1998, 2002; Kaltenböck, 2001; Morley, 1991; Pennington & Richards, 1986; Teich et al., 1997) demonstrated a renewed interest in pronunciation, and the focus of training began to move away from the individual segment. These researchers called for top-down pronunciation training with a focus on prosody. It has been found that prosodic training is indeed effective. For example, the participants in Derwing, Munro, & Wiebe's (1998) study who received prosodic training were rated as more *comprehensible* (i.e., perceived as being easier to understand) than those who received only segmental training. Eskenazi, who refers to intonation as the "glue" that holds together messages (1999b: 64), claims that "(e)arly prosody instruction, starting in the first year of language study, could be a boon to learning both syntax and phone articulation" (1999a: 462).

Today many researchers (e.g., Derwing & Munro, 2015; Field, 2014; Gilbert, 2014) call for a focus on all levels of pronunciation including individual speech segments, stress patterns in words and phrases, pauses, and the function and contrastive nature of intonation. Pronunciation instruction also focuses on the development of *fluency* (i.e., fluidity or smoothness of speech [e.g., Derwing et al., 2004]).

2.2 Current Research in Computer-Assisted Pronunciation Training (CAPT)

CAPT is an ideal use of computer technology for a number of reasons. According to Pennington (1999), it is, among other things, motivating, quick, repeatable, reliable, and it raises awareness, fosters precision, builds confidence, and develops learners' skills. On the other hand, researchers warn that some commercial CAPT systems that make use of novel technology may not be very helpful to users and may even be pedagogically unsound (e.g., Munro, Derwing, & Thomson, 2015; Neri, Cucchiarini, & Strik, 2004). Incorrect feedback is also a possibility (e.g., Eskenazi 1999b). Pennington cautions that "most software is not based on any particular theory or model of pronunciation which differentiates variation from (true) error" (1999: 431). Moreover, because not all pronunciation errors contribute equally to comprehensibility (e.g., Brinton, 2014), a great deal of pronunciation technology promotes accuracy (i.e., accent reduction) over intelligibility (e.g., Levis, 2007).

Many studies have demonstrated at least a moderate improvement among L2 learners who engage in CAPT (Lee, Jang, & Plonsky, 2014; Thomson & Derwing, 2015). For example, Hardison (2004) found that learners trained in L2 prosody were able to extend the training to L2 segments and to generalize their skills to new utterances. Importantly, a number of recent studies have demonstrated that students who use CAPT improve similarly in their pronunciation to those learners who receive traditional, in-class pronunciation instruction (e.g., Martin, 2018). Taken together with the benefits mentioned at the beginning of this subsection, this means that technology may be especially well suited for individualized pronunciation training both inside and outside of the classroom. For example, Liakin, Cardoso, & Liakina (2017) found that the learners who used text-to-speech technology as well as those who met with the teacher to do similar, non-CAPT pronunciation activities, improved in their production of French liaison (i.e., the production of word-final consonants before vowels in certain contexts like *les amis* [lez ami]). But research has also demonstrated that not all students may benefit equally from the training. Beginner-level learners may benefit to a greater extent from pronunciation instruction than more advanced students, as less proficient learners have the most to gain from instruction (e.g., Derwing & Munro, 2015; Zielinski & Yates, 2014).

2.3   Research Approaches to Pronunciation Training

Research investigating the effectiveness of a particular type of pronunciation training usually either involves some sort of rating of learners' speech or learner evaluations of the training. The former commonly entails the collection of speech samples before and after training. Most often native or advanced non-native speakers are then asked to rate the speech for accentedness, fluency, or comprehensibility or to perform an intelligibility task (e.g., Ducate & Lomicka, 2009; Foote & McDonough, 2017; Lord, 2008; Tanner & Landon, 2009; Warren, Elgort, & Crabbe, 2009). In order to attribute changes in pronunciation to training, studies investigating the effectiveness of CAPT technology should compare the pronunciation of learners who have received CAPT to those who have received either no training (i.e., a control group) or to those who have received some other sort of pronunciation training (i.e., a comparison group [Thomson & Derwing, 2015]).

Studies involving learner evaluation of training can make use of self-report data on attitudes toward pronunciation (e.g., through the use of Elliott's 1995 Pronunciation Attitude Inventory) and perceived improvements in pronunciation over the course of the training, assessments of the effectiveness and usability of the particular technology, or a combination thereof. Many recent studies have provided evidence that students appreciate the training that they receive (e.g., Hincks & Edlund, 2009; Levy & Steel, 2015; Lord & Harrington, 2013; McCrocklin, 2016; Motohashi-Soto & Hardison, 2009). Nonetheless, a great deal of research into the effectiveness of CAPT carried out in a university setting points to the relatively short length of training. Most pronunciation training studies take place over the course of one university semester, and researchers often conclude that this length of time is most likely insufficient to observe real improvements in learners' pronunciation (e.g., Ducate & Lomicka, 2009; Tanner & Landon, 2009).

The results of studies into various forms of pronunciation training also point to the important role played by learner awareness. Whereas the students in Lord's (2008) study showed improved pronunciation after making use of podcasting technology over the course of one semester, those in Ducate & Lomicka's (2009) study did not. A major difference between these two studies was that the students in Lord (2008) created podcasts as part of a Spanish phonetics class that focused specifically on pronunciation, and those in Ducate & Lomicka (2009) received no focused pronunciation training. Although the learners in Martin & Jackson's (2016) study, like those in Ducate & Lomicka (2009), also performed their tasks outside of class time in a course that did not focus only on phonetics, the tasks they carried out focused specifically targeted on pronunciation. The accuracy of learners' use of word stress to indicate meaning in Martin & Jackson (2016) improved as a result of the pronunciation training they received. These results as well as those of additional studies (e.g., Hincks & Edlund, 2009; Mora & Levkina, 2017) point to a need to focus specifically on pronunciation, since it is unlikely that students will acquire better pronunciation in exclusively meaning-based tasks.

2.4   Connection to Pedagogy

Classroom pronunciation training falls into the debate surrounding form-focused instruction (FFI). According to Ellis (2001), FFI is any planned or incidental instructional activity that is intended to induce language learners to pay attention to linguistic forms. Ellis (2009) argues that the term "form" not only applies to discrete grammatical points such as verb conjugations or the gender of nouns, but that pronunciation is a prime candidate for FFI. Spada & Lightbown (2008) mention that isolated FFI that makes salient potentially problematic yet subtle differences between a learner's first language (L1) and the L2 may prove helpful, especially when it is designed to specifically target errors that are the result of transfer, that is, they can be traced back to learners' L1s.

In addition to the learner-specific FFI that is possible in CAPT, it fulfills a number of pedagogical goals, perhaps the most important of which is the promotion of learner autonomy (e.g., Wallace, 2016). CAPT software and apps, especially those that promote differentiation by allowing students to individualize their instruction and assessment and track their success, may be especially beneficial to students wishing to improve their L2 pronunciation (e.g., Derwing & Munro, 2015; Thomson & Derwing, 2015). While meeting the needs of every student is a major challenge in any classroom, CAPT may enable learners to focus on the issues that most impede the comprehensibility of their own speech, at the rate and with the intensity they desire.

Although learners who speak the same L1s often experience similar problems with L2 pronunciation, individuals also differ in the specific areas in which they need the most improvement. A computerized pronunciation tutor has a number of benefits over a human teacher. Engwall et al. (2004) argue that CAPT allows for more practice time, patience, and flexibility, and that learners are less concerned about making errors when interacting with a computer than when interacting with human interlocutors. In addition, learners are able to hear large quantities of speech from a variety of speakers (e.g., Levis, 2007). Although the type of input varies – from individual words to scripted sentences to more natural utterances and even dialogues from a variety of speakers – the best CAPT products provide learners with comprehensible and often enhanced input, thereby making salient those aspects of pronunciation that they are to practice. The enhancement of input may be typographical (e.g., through the highlighting or underlying of particular sounds or via visualization techniques, as in Whipple et al., 2015) or in the speech stream itself (e.g., with extra emphasis added to the aspects on which learners are to focus, as demonstrated in Leeman, 2003 and Sagarra & Abbuhl, 2013). Such textual (e.g., Whipple et al., 2015) and auditory (e.g., Martin & Jackson, 2016) enhancement may promote noticing, which is believed to be an important prerequisite for learning (e.g., Schmidt, 2001).

A number of products focus on the skills of perception and production, thereby allowing learners to hone these two mutually dependent skills. Because we lose our ability to distinguish sounds that do not occur in our native languages between 6 and 12 months of age (Werker & Tees, 1984) and because of the close relationship between perception and production (e.g., Brinton, 2014; Derwing & Munro, 2015), it is essential that pronunciation training also focus on improving learners' perceptual skills.

Corrective feedback plays an important role in pronunciation instruction, as it has been shown to positively correlate with learner improvement (e.g., Lee & Lyster, 2016; Liakin, Cordoso, & Liakina, 2015; White, Gananathan, & Mok, 2017). Some courseware does not provide any feedback and instead relies on self-evaluation, which may prove difficult for some learners (e.g., Dlaska & Krekeler, 2008). Although some CAPT technologies provide feedback, it is often not explicit enough for it to be helpful to learners (e.g., Chun, 2013).

As illustrated above, CAPT technology holds great promise for aiding learners in attaining more accurate pronunciation, and both researchers and software designers are interested in developing new resources. Nonetheless, they come to the task from different angles. Whereas researchers are interested in determining the effectiveness of software in improving pronunciation, software designers are often focused on technological innovations. The review that follows mostly takes a research-first approach. That is, pedagogical soundness and demonstrated effectiveness of a particular type of training are given priority over technological innovations for their own sake. The products that are available range greatly in their goals, quality, and functionality. It is therefore essential to set forth evaluation guidelines to assist instructors and students alike in determining which software provides the best fit in a given situation.

3 Pedagogical Implications: Evaluating CAPT Software and Apps

When we evaluate the effectiveness of CAPT software and apps, we need to consider a number of factors. Rosell-Aguilar (2017) provides four main categories for assessing apps: pedagogy, technology, user experience, and specific aspect of language learning being targeted. CAPT technology should also be assessed in terms of the quality of input and levels of learner autonomy. While it may not be possible for any piece of software to fulfill the most stringent requirements in all categories, it is important to keep all of them in mind when assessing software for implementation. In addition, certain criteria may be prioritized over others depending on the learning context.

The pedagogical value of software should be central in the decision-making process. Pedagogy can be divided into teaching and learning on the one hand and assessment and feedback on the other. As Rosell-Aguilar (2017) notes, good courseware should not only test, but also explain and model, language. Learner autonomy and differentiation are essential, and learners should have direct access to different levels within a given program depending on ability and their precise pronunciation needs (e.g., Derwing, 2010). Learners should be able to measure their improvement and receive support as they advance (e.g., Levis, 2007) as well as control the recording of their speech (Atwell et al., 1999).

The quality of assessment of and feedback provided on learner speech is another essential component in the evaluation of any CAPT software. This first involves the ability of the system to diagnose learner errors. When diagnosing errors, it is important to remember the realistic goal of pronunciation teaching: intelligibility rather than native-like pronunciation. Therefore, those errors that have been shown to lead to a breakdown in communication (e.g., Atwell et al. 1999; Derwing, 2010; Thomson & Derwing, 2015) or be potentially humiliating (Derwing & Munro, 2015) should be brought to the attention of learners. Moreover, learners should be made aware of both where the error is (Engwall et al., 2004) and what they can do to improve their pronunciation (e.g., Atwell et al., 1999; Engwall et al., 2004). As Menzel et al. (2001) found, without explicit feedback, learners often cannot locate or determine the nature of the problem. The quantity, quality, and type (e.g., implicit or explicit) of feedback given to students is an additional aspect that should be evaluated (e.g., Brinton, 2014; Chun, 2013). In order for feedback to be effective and for learners' pronunciation to improve, it must be clear and easily interpretable (e.g., Eskenazi, 1999b; Neri, Cucchiarini, & Strik, 2004). Eskenazi (1999b) reminds us that feedback that is too frequent or too verbose may lose its effectiveness. Relevant feedback indicating the type of error that was made is essential (e.g., articulatory feedback for articulatory errors [Engwall et al., 2004]), and learners should be able to compare their own voices with target stimuli multiple times. Perhaps most importantly, learners should receive explicit tips for improving those aspects of pronunciation that affect the intelligibility of their speech (e.g., Atwell et al., 1999; Engwall et al., 2004).

At least as important as the pedagogy employed is the second of Rosell-Aguilar's (2017) factors: technology. This means that a system should not needlessly make use of the latest technological advances, but it should, at a minimum, have an intuitive interface and menus, (clear) instructions, and a help menu. Good systems should be stable and should operate smoothly without crashing (e.g., O'Brien et al., 2018). Learners should be able to use the technology easily and effectively without requiring expert knowledge of phonetics (Fouz-González, 2015). Finally, gamified software may motivate learners and encourage them to engage more fully with the technology (e.g., Levy & Steel, 2015).

According to Rosell-Aguilar (2017), the third factor, user experience, involves that ability of users to interact with a given technology and to share content. The ability to share responses with an instructor is especially beneficial for classroom-instructed L2 learners (McCrocklin, 2016). The appropriate price of a tool, a smooth registration process, and the absence of advertising while engaging with it also play important roles in users' experience.

In terms of the final factor, language learning goals, Rosell-Aguilar (2017) only makes one comment about CAPT: effective software should focus on both segments and prosody. As such, activities should consist of controlled perceptual activities (e.g. Shport, 2016; Thomson, 2011, 2012), production activities including minimal pair and reading activities (Delmonte, 2009), and the imitation of model speakers (e.g., Lima, 2015; Zając & Rojczyk, 2014). Software that engages the learner and allows for guided and free communication in the L2 is certainly beneficial, but few systems are adaptive enough to allow for this. Neri et al. (2002) recommend moving beyond decontextualized minimal pair activities and instead allowing learners to engage in language learning tasks that require them to answer simple questions and to participate in dialogues with native speakers while working on their pronunciation. They also argue that, when possible, tasks should be contextualized so that learners have the opportunity to practice their pronunciation in situations that most closely represent real-world interactions. In order for CAPT to be truly communicative, Menzel et al. argue that learners must have "at least a minimal degree of choice" in the production of their responses (2001: 68). The Dutch ASR-based "Development and Integration of Speech Technology into Courseware for Language Learning" (DISCO) system (Strik et al., 2012) and Walker et al.'s (2011) system that relies on videoclips and a speech recognition system represent meaningful steps in this direction. Learners have the opportunity for limited interaction with an onscreen character, and the systems provide learners with feedback on their productions.

In order for learners to be able to produce comprehensible speech, it is essential that they be exposed to high-quality input from a variety of native speakers (Eskenazi, 1999a; Fouz-Gonzáles, 2015; Levis, 2016). Chun points to the importance of input "to represent the diversity of speech sounds and the great variation that exists within a language" (1998: 66). High Variability Phonetic Training, described in Thomson (forthcoming) and discussed in more detail below, is one example of training that has as its starting point high-quality and highly variable input.

4   CAPT Courseware and Apps

CAPT courseware and apps tend to fall into one of four main categories: (1) perceptual training, (2) basic pronunciation courseware that relies on the computer for speech recording and on the learner for the analysis of pronunciation, (3) that which makes use of ASR technology to draw attention to learner errors, and (4) visualization courseware that provides learners with images to assist them in analyzing their speech. There has been an explosion in CAPT resources, especially apps, in recent years. Many of the resources focus only on English pronunciation, however, and, as Foote & Smith (2013) note, they are of variable quality, and some are even pedagogically unsound.

In the subsections that follow, I provide a short overview of each type of training and focus primarily on tools whose underlying methodology has been empirically tested. Where courseware exists, I highlight a few examples and provide an evaluation according to the criteria set forth in section 3 above. It is essential to note that the selection courseware presented below is by no means exhaustive, and the inclusion of one product over another is not based upon value judgments. Instead, the products below are included to provide a sampling of the types of products that are available with an emphasis on those whose effectiveness has been tested.

4.1   Perceptual Training

Research points to a close connection between perception and production (e.g., Brinton, 2014), and a number of studies have demonstrated that L2 learners are able to develop more accurate pronunciation after engaging in purely perceptual training (e.g., Bradlow et al., 1999; Lee & Lyster, 2016; Thomson, 2011).

A simple way for learners to engage in perceptual training is by listening to new vocabulary items. Many online dictionaries as well as the dictionaries that are components of many current course materials have a built-in pronunciation feature that enables learners to hear how a word sounds, thereby encouraging them to establish correspondences between a word's spelling, its meaning, its use, and its pronunciation (e.g., Levy & Steel, 2015). In their study investigating the extent to which including a pronunciation feature encourages more robust Chinese vocabulary learning, Zhu, Fung, & Wang (2012) demonstrated that learners who made use of digital flashcards with both audio and visual input demonstrated better vocabulary learning than those who did not receive the auditory input. Given the usefulness of talking dictionaries, classroom teachers may encourage their students to listen to and practice pronouncing new vocabulary as homework before they practice it in class.

Simply drawing learners' attention to various pronunciation features by presenting them with spoken real-world examples in context may be an effective way to teach pronunciation. Mompean & Fouz-González (2016) tested the effectiveness of Twitter for pronunciation teaching among English language learners in Spain. Participants received daily tweets that focused on a difficult word and that provided learners with a link to the word in an authentic context (e.g., an interview, a song, or a video clip). The researchers found that participants' pronunciation improved over time, and Fouz-González (2017) demonstrated both that participants maintained their improvement over time and that there was a correlation between student engagement levels and pronunciation improvement. Classroom teachers may wish to consider providing learners with contextualized pronunciation practice in the form of weekly tweets or emails that contain specific speech segments, difficult words, or specific intonation patterns in context.

A number of courseware apps focus on developing perceptual skills through high variability phonetic training (HVPT), perceptual training based on the premise that exposure to speech segments produced in a range of voices in various phonetic contexts enables learners to develop more robust perceptual categories (e.g., Logan, Lively, & Pisoni, 1991; Thomson, forthcoming), and that this exposure often leads to gains in both perception and production (e.g., Levis, 2016). Thomson (2011) carried out a three-week HVPT with Mandarin learners of English who were trained to perceive English vowels as produced by 21 speakers. The participants' intelligibility as assessed by five native listeners of Canadian English improved. Thomson's (2017) *English Accent Coach*, available online and as an app, is a gamified version of HVPT for English vowels and consonants whose effectiveness has been demonstrated in teaching the perception and production of English segments (Thomson & Derwing, 2016).

A further option for exposing L2 learners to pronunciation models is text-to-speech (TTS) systems, which convert written texts into spoken language. Although originally designed for other audiences including the hard-of-hearing, L2 researchers have demonstrated the usefulness of TTS in providing learners with high-quality pronunciation models of words, sentences, or longer texts. Liakin, Cardoso, & Liakina (2017) demonstrated that the L2 learners of French who relied on a TTS system on mobile devices to learn French liaison improved in its use over time. They note that some of the benefits include increased opportunities for input and the development of grapheme-phoneme correspondence. Moreover, learners report that they find TTS beneficial for learning pronunciation features (e.g., Cardoso, Collins, & White, 2012; Cardoso, Smith & Garcia Fuentes, 2015). Fouz-González (2015) and O'Brien et al. (2018) predict that the usefulness of TTS technology for pronunciation training will grow in the coming years. TTS offers an advantage over talking dictionaries in that it can provide learners with models of scripted dialogues or other stretches of speech longer than individual words.

A final option for providing learners with high-quality pronunciation models is the use of applications that slow down speech samples while maintaining the segmental and prosodic features of the original sound file. Chan (2017) indicates that these have the built-in option of enabling learners to speed up playback incrementally as they become more proficient. This feature can be especially helpful when learners listen to authentic texts like songs or podcasts.

Software that can be used for training in perceptual skills is provided in Table 1.

Table 1 Selected technology that can be utilized to develop L2 perceptual skills

Software	Training type	Teaching and assessment	Technology	User experience	Input quality	Learner autonomy
Forvo www.forvo.com, iOS, Android 349 languages	talking dictionary	N/A	clear and easy to use	free, large number of ads	words recorded by individuals vary in quality, no translations	learners can look up any word, create personal dictionary, download mp3 recordings
English Accent Coach www.englishaccentcoach.com, iOS devices English	HVPT game	ability to assess skills and measure improvement, clear feedback	intuitive, clear instructions	inexpensive, no ads, report card after lessons	high-quality recordings from a large range of speakers	learners choose segments to focus on
NaturalReader Software https://www.naturalreaders.com/software.html Mac and Windows, iOS devices, Android 45 languages (e.g., Czech, Danish, Latvian, Ukrainian)	TTS	N/A	clear and easy to use	free web version works well, no ads	natural sounding TTS, ability to change speaker and speech rate and download sound files	learners can choose any file with text (documents, websites, books) to have read aloud
Anytune https://anytune.us/, iOS devices, Mac any language	slowdown	N/A	intuitive, clear menu	inexpensive, no ads, trial version works well	ability to change tempo without affecting pitch	learners choose any sound file in iTunes library to slow down

4.2　Basic Pronunciation Training

The most basic CAPT resources replicate in many ways classic language laboratories in that learners hear a native speaker model and record themselves as they repeat what was said. The activities are not communicative, as learners rarely engage in true communication with the computer. The focus of the practice varies, from the production of individual sounds to words and sentences.

Perfect English Pronunciation (Victoria Productions, 2017) provides learners a chance to practice English sounds and words, and it also provides training in rhythm and lexical stress, while *American Speechsounds* (English Talk Shop, 2015) focuses on prosody (including word and sentence stress, intonation, and linking). The activities in the most basic pronunciation courseware are often limited to the imitation of native speaker models and minimal pair exercises that learners are expected to judge on their own. This can be problematic, however, since it has been shown that learners are often unable to diagnose their own pronunciation errors (Dlaska & Krekeler, 2008).

Learner autonomy is also restricted in the most basic pronunciation software, as learners are able to record single words and basic utterances and are not encouraged to produce sentences on their own. Moreover, without guidance, learners may focus on salient sounds that may not affect the comprehensibility of their speech. Nonetheless, directed pronunciation practice of this sort may be useful in certain situations such as teaching students about the basic segments and major intonation contours (e.g., statements vs. yes-/no-questions).

Researchers have found that shadowing, a task in which learners are presented with a speech sample and are expected to repeat it word-for-word "as closely and as quickly as possible" (Luo et al., 2008: 5), is a relatively easy and effective form of listen-and-repeat practice. The effectiveness of shadowing has been demonstrated in the production of segments (Zając & Rojczyk, 2014) and prosodic features (Lima, 2015). Foote & McDonough (2017) found that their English learners' comprehensibility and fluency improved after eight weeks of shadowing practice. Hamada (2016) demonstrated that shadowing may also improve beginner and intermediate learners' phoneme perception and listening comprehension. Given its relative ease of implementation and overall effectiveness, teachers are encouraged to implement shadowing tasks in their classes. Those who wish to have students practice shadowing require little more than access to sound files and digital recording software. Lima (2015) provides clear guidelines for

Table 2 Selected technology that can be used for shadowing tasks in a range of languages

Software	Teaching and assessment	Technology	User experience	Input quality	Learner autonomy
Multi Track Song Recorder http://mtsr-app.com/ iOS app	N/A	simple recording interface	free, no advertising	possible to play/ shadow any sound file	learners can choose file to shadow and record according to interest
Audacity www.audacityteam.org/	N/A	intuitive interface, good help menu	free, no advertising	possible to play/ shadow any sound file	learners can choose file to shadow and record according to interest
VoiceTube https://www.voicetube.com/ iOS devices, Android	organized according to proficiency (TOEIC, TOEFL, IELTS) levels, opportunity to quiz for listening comprehension	easy to use, sub-titles aligned with video	free with a large number of ads	over 40,000 videos organized by topic	learners can choose proficiency level and topic, adjust speed, turn sub-titles on or off

using *Audacity* (Audacity Team, 2018) for shadowing. Software that has been tested for shadowing is provided in Table 2.

4.3   Automatic Speech Recognition (ASR)

ASR technology, that is, software that captures, recognizes, and reacts in some way to human speech, is gaining in popularity and functionality as speech recognizers become more advanced (e.g., Chun, 2013; Wu, Su, & Liu, 2013). A general use of ASR technology can be found in software such as *Dragon Naturally Speaking* (Nuance Communications, 2017), a popular speech-to-text conversion (i.e., dictation) tool created for native speakers. Sustaric (2003) advocates for the use of off-the-shelf speech recognition software like *Dragon Naturally Speaking* in pronunciation teaching, and recently a number of researchers have demonstrated that using dictation apps like *Siri*, *Sounds*, built-in software like *Windows Speech Recognition*, and Internet-based software *Google Web Speech* and *Google Cloud Speech* technology may enable L2 learners to identify intelligibility errors and increase their autonomy (McCrocklin, 2014, 2016; Wallace, 2016). Liakin, Cordoso, & Liakina (2015) demonstrated that French L2 learners who made use of a free dictation app improved significantly in their production of /y/ after using the technology.

A number of researchers, however, caution against using commercial dictation software with L2 learners, as even native speakers of a given language produce speech with great variability (e.g., Coniam, 1999; Derwing & Munro, 2015; Derwing, Munro, & Carbonaro, 2000; Saraçlar & Khudanpur, 2004). Therefore, L2 learners making use of dictation systems may experience great frustration with the systems' inability to recognize their accented speech samples. Dictation systems differ from CAPT, since the primary goal of dictation systems is speech recognition. CAPT that makes use of ASR technology starts at recognition and moves to error detection, often providing learners with feedback on their utterances that aligns with the type of feedback a human could provide (e.g., Cox & Davies, 2012). Recent research has demonstrated that ASR systems designed for a particular group of learners who share an L1 and are learning a common L2 may be most effective (e.g., Atwell et al., 1999; Hussein et al., 2011; Neri, Cucchiarini, & Strik, 2008; Ohkawa et al., 2009).

ASR holds the promise of allowing for more real-world interactions with the computer. In the L2 setting, the hope is that learners will eventually be able to communicate with and receive feedback from the computer (Egan & LaRocca, 2000). Currently, ASR technology is not advanced enough to allow for completely free interactions between language learner and computer. Although there has been some movement toward less controlled interactions, ASR is still most successful at recognizing and providing feedback in controlled contexts (e.g., Atwell et al., 1999; Walker et al., 2011). Therefore, activities usually constrain the learner's answer to one of a limited number of possible answers. Learners may be required to choose from and read aloud a number of potential responses to questions, provide answers to pointed questions about pictures (e.g., learners see a picture of a woman wearing a red shirt and are asked "Who is wearing the red shirt?"), and produce formulaic expressions (e.g., answers to questions such as "How are you?").

In recent years, a number of advances in ASR technology have expanded the usefulness of speech recognition in L2 pronunciation learning. Walker et al. (2011) created an ASR solution that enables learners to interact with their computers. These researchers made use of the *EduSpeak* (SRI International, 2016) speech recognition system in conjunction with videos of virtual patients to simulate nurse-patient medical history interviews. Healthcare professionals who were non-native speakers of English asked questions to the system and received helpful feedback from the recognizer. The researchers demonstrated that a virtual dialogue, albeit rather limited, is indeed possible.

Perhaps the most promising aspect of ASR-based courseware lies in its assessment capabilities. Strik et al. (2009) found, however, that most CALL software that uses ASR provides learners with some sort of global score instead of actually pinpointing errors and providing learners with the feedback on how to improve incorrect pronunciation. Bajorek (2017b) reviewed the feedback provided by a range of courseware using ASR, and found overall that the feedback provided by most (i.e., *Rosetta Stone*, *Babbel*, and *Duolingo*) is binary. Thus, learners know that their speech is not recognized, but they do not get feedback on how to make it more intelligible. Erroneous, unreliable feedback is often a problem (e.g., Eskenazi, 1999b; Hincks, 2003; Menzel et al., 2001; Neri, Cucchiarini, & Strik, 2004; Neri et al., 2002; Saraçlar & Khudanpur, 2004). Moreover, the software is designed to focus on recognition, and not always on the meaning, of learners' speech. In addition, one of the main issues with ASR is that most systems are trained to target salient errors and not those that affect intelligibility and comprehensibility (O'Brien et al., 2018). In spite of these issues, however, ASR technology may be beneficial for pronunciation training in limited contexts.

4.4   Visualization Techniques

Visualization techniques allow learners to see how they deviate from native speaker norms in their L2 pronunciation, for example, through the use of notations relating to stress and rhythm, talking heads that provide learners with facial movements, ultrasound images that provide learners with dynamic representations of the articulatory process, and acoustic displays including pitch contours, waveforms, and spectrograms.

Inceoglu (2015) demonstrated the value of providing learners access to multimodal information that includes both auditory (i.e., sound files) and visual information (e.g., videos that show how the teeth and lips are used in the production of various sounds). The French learners in her study who received audiovisual training improved significantly more in the production of French nasal vowels than those who only received audio-only training.

Recent studies have demonstrated that ultrasound technology may promote more accurate L2 pronunciation (e.g., White, Gananathan, & Mok, 2017). Bliss et al. (2017) demonstrated that even the use of ultrasound overlay videos that show where in the mouth various segments are produced – and not the costly ultrasound hardware – may encourage learners to produce more accurate vowels and consonants.

Free software designed for acoustic analysis such as *Praat* (Boersma & Weenink, 2018) and *Audacity* (Audacity Team, 2018) may be used to provide learners with information about their productions. Waveform displays such as that in Figure 1 can provide learners with visual information about a number of aspects including segmental duration and aspiration.

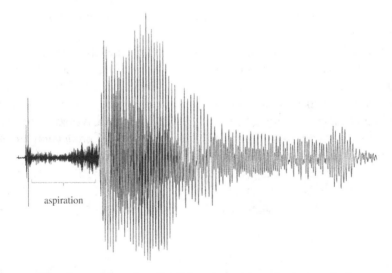

aspiration

Figure 1 Waveform of American English <pin> with aspiration marked.

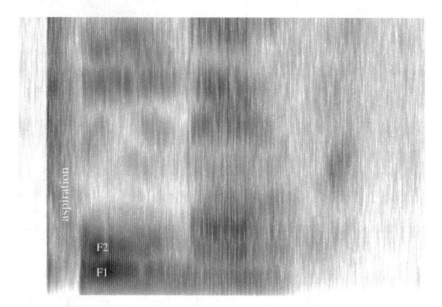

Figure 2 Speech spectrogram of German <Thomas>.

Motohashi-Saigo & Hardison (2009) demonstrated that providing L2 Japanese learners with waveform displays of geminates vs. singleton (i.e., long vs. short) consonants resulted in significant improvement in their ability to both identify and produce them. Visualization in the form of speech spectrograms such as that in Figure 2 can be useful in teaching learners about segmental aspects including aspiration, tongue height, and lip rounding in vowel production and voicing.

Pearson, Pickering, & Da Silva (2011) demonstrated that native speakers of Vietnamese improved in their production of English syllable-final consonants through the use of spectrograms, and Quintana-Lara (2014) showed that providing spectrographic displays resulted in improved pronunciation of English /i/ and /ɪ/ among Spanish speakers of English. A number of additional studies have shown improvements in segmental production among learners who make use of spectrograms (e.g., vowel duration in Okuno & Hardison, 2016; intervocalic stops in L2 Spanish in Olson, 2014a; American English <r> in Patten & Edmonds, 2015). Olson (2014b) reports that even beginner-level learners appreciate using *Praat* and that they find it easy to use.

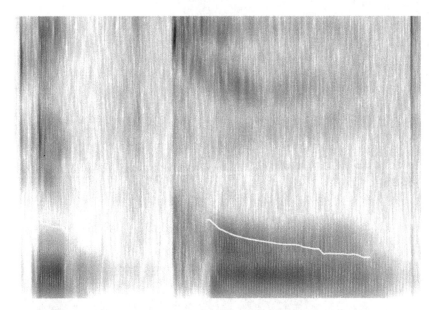

Figure 3 Falling pitch contour in the declarative sentence "It's cold."

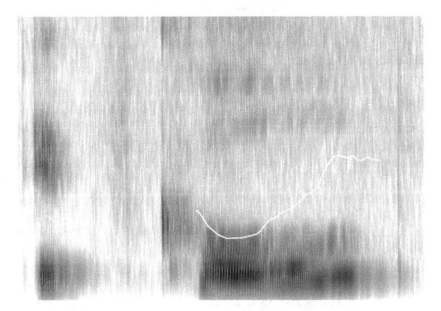

Figure 4 Rising pitch contour in the interrogative "It's cold?"

High intonation at end of clause

Pause at end of clause

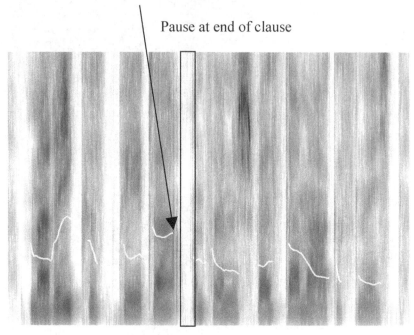

Figure 5 Coordination sentence ("Marie küsst Peter und seine Schwester mag es nicht." / "Marie kisses Peter, and his sister doesn't like it.") produced by a German native speaker.

Pitch contours such as those provided in Figures 3 and 4 can be used to demonstrate the contrastive use of pitch that native speakers make use of when they interact. In spite of the fact that the words in the two utterances are identical, the pitch contours, shown in white, vary greatly. Learners' attention can easily be drawn to the different patterns, and they can attempt to replicate the intonation patterns in utterances such as these. Similarly, more advanced learners can make use of software for more complex sentences. In an example like the one in Figure 5, instructors could point out the level (and relatively high) intonation and pause produced at the end of an independent clause before a coordinating conjunction.

Researchers have demonstrated that acoustic displays may be especially beneficial for training learners in the production of pitch contours such as those in Figures 3, 4, and 5 (e.g., Chun, 2013; Chun, Jiang, & Ávila, 2013; Chun et al., 2015; Levis, 2007; Levis & Pickering, 2004). Using them can contribute to learners' success in producing intonation patterns in the L2 at a variety of levels of proficiency and in a range of languages (e.g.,

Anderson-Hsieh, 1996; Hirata, 2004; Molholt, 1988; Spaai & Hermes, 1993).

4.4.1 Visualization software Visualization software allows teachers of any language to create activities for their students that fit their own needs and the needs of the students. However, many of the products that allow for visualization were designed for performing speech analysis for research and not for pedagogical purposes. The effectiveness of visualization software depends a great deal on the teacher's willingness and organization in planning student activities as well as his or her ability to both understand the results of phonetic analyses performed and to impart this understanding to the learners in the class. In addition, the expenditure of time and energy necessary in creating exercises for students with visualization software can be considerable.

Instructors should proceed with caution before encouraging learners to engage in acoustic analysis, given the variability that speakers exhibit in their productions. For example, males' and females' formant values differ greatly. Thus, at the very least, teachers should make themselves familiar with the technology before asking their students to analyze their vowel formant values. Learners should be encouraged to compare their productions with a speaker of their own gender. In addition, the goal should not be to match a native speaker's formant values, but instead to approximate the pattern of formant values exhibited by a native speaker.

Finally, Chun posits that "(p)itch-tracking software can certainly be used to teach [...] basic intonation contours, but for the future, in accordance with the current emphasis on *communicative* and *sociocultural* competence, more attention should be paid to discourse-level communication" (2002: 126). Therefore, we should avoid the tendency to provide students with only the basic sounds and quintessential intonation contours for various syntactic patterns (e.g., falling intonation for statements, commands, imperatives, and wh-questions; and rising intonation for yes-/no- and echo questions and unfinished sentences) and should strive for including a more complete view of the phonological systems.

Praat (Boersma & Weenink, 2018) and *Audacity* (Audacity Team, 2018) were designed specifically for phonetic speech analysis. Their research functions are quite impressive, and yet they are easy enough to use to be a viable option for teachers who are willing to invest the time to learn about their functionality as well as implement them in class. They are also well supported by the online community. Learners may find that waveforms are difficult to interpret, although they are usually able to compare their waveforms and actual productions to those of native speakers. This may be especially helpful when working on issues related to timing (e.g., overall speech rate and vowel length). It may be beneficial in the earliest phases of software use to provide learners with extensive training in the interpretation of the images so that learners are able to diagnose their errors and ultimately produce more comprehensible speech. Imber, Maynard, & Parker (2017) found that learners may develop autonomy by making use of acoustic analysis software, and they provide a series of steps for teaching students to use *Praat*.

While visualization software allows little room for creative, contextualized utterances – especially at lower proficiency levels – learners may come to produce more comprehensible speech with proper guidance. But we must be aware of several potential problems including perhaps most importantly the relatively steep learning curve on the part of both the instructor and the students. Nonetheless, like Lord (2005), I have found through personal experience that this software can be very effective with advanced L2 students enrolled in phonetics classes.

4.4.2 Visualization courseware Courseware that utilizes visualization techniques can provide learners with the objective feedback that may be helpful as they seek to improve their pronunciation. It can address a variety of aspects of L2 pronunciation ranging from sounds to words to sentences. Some visualization courseware includes front views of speakers' faces and drawn sagittal sections of the head to demonstrate the articulation of sounds. Other software enables learners to record utterances and compare their waveforms to those of native speakers. An assessment of visualization courseware is provided in Table 3.

Perhaps the most important thing to remember about the feedback provided in the courseware listed in Table 3 is that its effectiveness depends essentially on the ease of interpretation as well as on the tips that learners are given for improvement of their pronunciation. The front and side views of a real person's face may be especially helpful for learners who need to work on developing those articulatory movements that are visible from the outside such as lip rounding and jaw position. Learners who need to work on those articulatory features that cannot be seen by looking at a speaker's face (e.g., tongue position) may find that the sagittal view of the face is more helpful.

Table 3 Selected visualization courseware

Software	Visualization type	Teaching and assessment	Technology	User experience	Input quality	Learner autonomy
Saundz http://saundz.com/ American English	animated front and sagittal views	sounds presented in words, learners record and compare words to native speaker productions	intuitive, clear instructions	affordable ($19.99)	four native speakers	learners can focus on the perception and production of their most problematic sounds
Easy Pronunciation https://easypronunciation.com/ en/ (Windows, Mac, and Linux) American English, French, Russian	side and front views of a real person's face	ability to choose problematic sounds	clear playback and speed buttons, requires Java	affordable ($19.99)	learners can hear words at various speech rates and in questions	learners can choose which sounds and which words to practice
English Pronunciation App for iOS devices American English	waveforms of sentences	three scores: overall, pronunciation and timing	clear and easy to use	free, no ads	sentences recorded by single native speaker	learners can choose topic of training (e.g., job interview, sales, socializing, travel)

5   Evaluation

Thomson & Derwing (2015) note the importance of individualized instruction that focuses on developing learners' comprehensibility, and Derwing & Munro (2015) recommend that pronunciation training be preceded by a needs assessment (i.e., a diagnostic test at the beginning of a course) in order to determine the areas in which each student needs improvement. They note that the assessment should include a few different types of tasks (i.e., both read and extemporaneous speech samples) that target those aspects of pronunciation (i.e., both segmental and prosodic) that play a role in comprehensibility. The assessments should include both perception and production. Importantly, the production instrument should be a relatively brief and easy-to-implement recording (e.g., via *Praat* or *Audacity*) that is saved for analysis and comparison over time. Formative assessments (i.e., progress testing) throughout a course enable learners to track their development, and summative assessments at the end of the semester allow learners to determine what they have attained in a course (Derwing & Munro, 2015).

Learners' perception and production should be evaluated regularly as they progress through their CAPT experience. Lee & Lyster (2016) demonstrated that the combination of corrective feedback and encouraging listeners to listen to the target item again resulted in an improvement of both perceptual and production skills. Thus, a learner's accuracy in perceiving segments and prosody can be relatively straightforward, for example, "correct" vs. "incorrect" responses along with the opportunity to hear the target word and try again, as in *English Accent Coach* (Thompson, 2017). Instructors teaching languages other than English may consider assessing students' perceptual skills by creating similar sorts of perception tasks in their course management systems (e.g., Blackboard or D2L).

Fully automated assessment of pronunciation is possible with ASR systems. As noted above, however, most often these systems are not entirely reliable. Most assessment, therefore, is still carried out by humans. Teachers rarely have the opportunity to provide thorough analyses of their students' pronunciation on a regular basis. Thus, fellow students are often a good source of formative assessment. Lord (2008) and Lord & Harrington (2013) demonstrated that recorded feedback from fellow learners (especially those with advanced levels of proficiency and phonetic training) on recordings posted online may be beneficial for pronunciation development. An effective way for learners to assess their own pronunciation is through the use of visualization software (e.g., through the use of spectrograms and pitch contours) as described in subsection 4.4 above.

Although feedback is important, Martin (2017) demonstrated that it is not essential. The participants in her study completed for homework Innovative Cued Pronunciation Readings (iCPRs). In short, teachers choose a set of pronunciation features – both segmental and suprasegmental – and create PowerPoint presentations that focus on the development of perceptual and productive skills. Learners who engaged in these self-directed perception and pronunciation activities improved as much as students who received similar in-class instruction. Importantly, however, Martin (2017) demonstrated that this improvement (both accentedness and comprehensibility) took place without providing learners with feedback. At the same time, learners in the study expressed a desire for feedback on their productions. It is possible to imagine the negative effect that a complete lack of feedback might have on learners' motivation.

Derwing (2010) points to what might be perhaps the most important reason for assessing pronunciation: if pronunciation is included among those aspects of the L2 to be tested, it will be taught. Because the results of a host of L2 pronunciation studies demonstrate the benefits of pronunciation instruction and targeted feedback (e.g., Lee, Jang, and Plonsky, 2014; Thomson & Derwing, 2015), when providing pronunciation feedback, instructors should be clear in what they are assessing (i.e., a given feature or set of features), which mistakes learners have made, and how learners can go about improving the intelligibility of their pronunciation.

6 Conclusion

Once marginalized within second language research and teaching, pronunciation is now receiving long-overdue attention (Levis, 2016; O'Brien & Levis, 2017). The establishment of conferences and journals dedicated to L2 pronunciation in recent years has enabled researchers to share their findings, and the explosion of pronunciation software and apps allows language learners to practice their pronunciation almost anywhere. CAPT resources offer a number of advantages over traditional classroom listen-and-repeat pronunciation training. Learners are able to individualize their training to focus on the areas of L2 pronunciation that cause them the greatest difficulty, and seeing themselves improve can have a motivating effect. Moreover, learners have control over their learning, and they can repeat specific activities that they find most beneficial. A number of options that range in price and effectiveness are available to teachers and students. Table 4 presents the categories of software and describes them according to general evaluation criteria.

Table 4 Evaluation of categories of CAPT courseware/software

	Pedagogy	Input	Diagnosis/assessment	Autonomy	Learner age
Perceptual training	auditory training	high quality, variety of native speakers	clear feedback on accuracy of perception	limited	all
General CAPT courseware	listen-and-repeat, minimal pairs, reading, shadowing (not communicative)	high quality, variety of native speakers	at discretion of learner	limited	all
Dictation software utilizing ASR technology	not designed for pedagogical purposes; learners can produce any utterance	N/A	based on native speech, which may result in frustration	high level	adults only
Courseware utilizing ASR technology	communication limited to a small number of possible responses	high quality, variety of native speakers	depends on accuracy of the speech recognizer	limited	adults only
Visualization software	not designed for pedagogical purposes; success depends on teacher preparation; learners can visualize any utterance	at the discretion of the instructor	limited by technological knowledge of student and teacher	moderate	teenagers and adults only
Visualization courseware	not communicative, but can be useful for communication	high quality, native speaker input varies	depends on familiarity with visualization techniques and ease of interpretation of images	limited	all

The research summarized above has demonstrated that each type of training may be beneficial for L2 learners. In deciding on the appropriateness of a broad category of CAPT technology, teachers should consider these general criteria, and when choosing particular software or apps, teachers should rely on the specific criteria outlined in section 3.

7   The Future of CAPT

Five issues remain to be addressed by those working in CAPT. A first step involves a coordinated effort by researchers to determine which pronunciation features have the greatest impact on intelligibility when a specific group of L2 learners speaks a given L2 (O'Brien et al., 2018). The development of L2 corpora like that developed by Yoon et al. (2009) is an important first step toward collecting enough L2 speech samples necessary to make generalizations. Next, teachers, researchers, and software developers should coordinate to create engaging and pedagogically sound software that focuses on the development of intelligibility (O'Brien et al., 2018). Much of the software that exists still focuses on shibboleth sounds that, although they may mark a learner as a non-native speaker of a given language, do not play a role in the effectiveness of the speaker to communicate. Derwing & Munro (2009) assert that accented speech is not a disorder, that pronunciation training can be effective, and that it should focus on the areas that enable L2 learners to be understood, thereby promoting more successful communication. The third issue that remains has to do with the disconnect that exists between sound communicative classroom pedagogy and the often technical nature of pronunciation training. Current CAPT courseware does not provide learners with many opportunities for true communication. An additional issue is that many of the CAPT resources that exist focus only on the development of pronunciation skills and not on the integral connection between perception and production. As Levis (2016) notes, it is essential that pronunciation training materials train learners to both perceive and produce the target language. The final issue has to do with the technological shortcomings of current software. ASR, which clearly holds promise, is currently less powerful than many expect it to be. Learners are unable to produce creative utterances (Eskenazi, 1999a), and often the software is unable to decode highly accented learner speech (Menzel et al., 2001). Similarly, the effectiveness of visualization courseware is often limited by the users' ability to interpret the images. More generally, problems with varying technological requirements and unstable software continue to plague the field.

It is easy for L2 learners, practitioners, and researchers to get caught up in the negative aspects of CAPT. In spite of the limitations, CAPT is indeed effective for a variety of reasons. Neri et al. (2002) remind us that pronunciation software allows for individual problems to be addressed, learners can train at their own pace for as long as they like, anxiety is reduced, learners may save profiles and monitor problems/improvements, and they receive feedback.

Unintelligible L2 speech makes communication impossible. Many language learners express their desire to practice pronunciation, while teachers often express their frustration at teaching pronunciation in the classroom. Teachers owe their students the opportunity to improve their L2 pronunciation, and they must make learners aware that (in)comprehensible pronunciation affects their interactions with native speakers. CAPT courseware offers the potential to enhance a central aspect of students' communication skills while at the same time saving class time for interpersonal communicative tasks.

Questions for Reflection

1. One reason given for not focusing on pronunciation in the language classroom is that pronunciation is intertwined with identity. How do you feel about this statement? How can you back up your position in terms of the research that has been done into L2 pronunciation?
2. What is the role of language varieties in pronunciation teaching? Should students be taught the dialects of the L2 or should the "standard language" be the focus of pronunciation training?
3. Should courseware that employs ASR technology be relied upon for pronunciation assessment and training in spite of its technological shortcomings? Why or why not? Consider the potential benefits and drawbacks of (a) dictation software designed for native speakers and (b) ASR courseware in your own teaching context.
4. Which target language features could you imagine training via visualization software for your students? Why?
5. Are teachers justified in testing pronunciation? Please provide at least one situation in which you feel teachers are justified and one in which you feel they are not.
6. In recent years, a number of "pronunciation professionals" have come onto the scene, claiming to rid non-native speakers of their accents by promising to eradicate highly salient sounds. Would you recommend this sort of training to your learners? Why or why not?

Case Study

Joanna has been teaching the pronunciation class at the local ESL school for five years now and has grown increasingly frustrated as time has gone by. She started out teaching the class from a book that addressed various aspects of pronunciation. The book she used had always been used at the school, and the activities in it focused on speech segments, word and sentence stress, and complex intonation patterns. She noticed moderate improvement in some of her students' pronunciation at the end of her first semester. Beginning with her second semester of teaching the course, she decided to ask the students what they believed they need the most work on, and the overwhelming answer was difficult segments in English (<l> and <r> distinctions for native speakers of Japanese, <th> for native speakers of German, consonant clusters for native speakers of Spanish, just to name a few), and so she decided to restructure her class to focus on the segmental aspects of their speech in the classroom lessons. She assigned computerized pronunciation exercises for the students to work on during their free time. The app she chose promised "perfect pronunciation." Since she made the switch, however, she has noticed very little improvement in her students' pronunciation. Why do you think that Joanna's students would like her to help them improve their pronunciation of these highly salient segments? Why might focusing on these problematic sounds not lead to learners' improved intelligibility? How would you help Joanna solve her problem?

Ideas for Action Research Projects

1. To test the salience (accentedness) vs. intelligibility hypothesis, ask a group of native speakers of the language you teach to let you know what makes native speakers of a specific L1 group stand out (e.g., the American English <r> in most other languages). After gaining ethics approval, which is required if you hope to present or publish your results, record samples of L2 speech (e.g., a picture description task) from four or five L2 speakers. As a first task, have a group of 8–10 raters orthographically transcribe (i.e., write down) what they have heard (a test of intelligibility), marking aspects that gave them difficulty in their determination of what was being said. Then ask a new group of 8–10 raters to provide accent ratings (e.g., on a scale from 1 [native-like, no foreign accent] to 9 [strong foreign accent]) of the speech. Ask them to also point out which aspects of the learners' speech most made them stand

out as accented. How do the results of your research align with what we know about the differences between intelligibility and accentedness?

2. Based on the results of what you found in (1) above or your own intuitions, design a series of basic word- or sentence-level perceptual and basic pronunciation tasks for learners of the language you teach: one that focuses on salient sounds (leading to the perception of a foreign accent) and one that focuses on a particular prosodic aspect of speech that played a role in intelligibility. To do this, ask a male and female native speaker of the target language to record a series of words and/or sentences with the "problem" (salient) sounds and with the prosodic aspect that affected learners' intelligibility. Before starting the training, have the students perform a pre-test (e.g., a storytelling task). Divide the students taking part in the study into two groups: salience and intelligibility, depending on the type of training they will complete. Once a week for four weeks, have them complete the perceptual and production tasks assigned to their group. In the fifth and sixth weeks, have them come up with their own activities that target the appropriate topic. In week 7 have them complete a post-test that is identical to the pre-test. Refer to subsection 2.3 above to test the effectiveness of the training.

3. To determine the effectiveness of ASR for L2 speech, test various programs that have been developed. Begin, for example, with a dictation system designed for native speakers, such as *Dragon Naturally Speaking.* Then test some of the commercial ASR courseware that has been designed to handle non-native speech. Which aspects of speech can it handle best, and which does it not deal at all well with? In the courseware designed specifically for non-native speakers, how would you rate the ability of the software to evaluate your speech? Does this differ from its ability to diagnose your errors? What are the various roles played by segmental vs. prosodic errors? Are you ever able to "trick the system" so that it determines that an incorrect utterance is actually correct?

References

Anderson-Hsieh, J. (1996). Teaching suprasegmentals to Japanese learners of English through electronic visual feedback. *JALT Journal*, 18(2), 315–325.

Anytune. (2015). *Anytune*. https://anytune.us/

Atwell, E., Herron, D., Howarth, P., Morton, R., & Wick, H. (1999). Pronunciation training: requirements and solutions. *ISLE deliverable.* Available at http://nats-www.informatik.uni-hamburg.de/~isle/public/D14/D14.pdf

Audacity Team. (2018). *Audacity.* http://www.audacityteam.org/

Bajorek, J. P. (2017a). Pronunciation technology: Global community and innovative tools in *Forvo* and *NetProF* pronunciation feedback. *FLTMAG.* http://fltmag.com/pronunciation-technology/

Bajorek, J. P. (2017b, September). French and Spanish pronunciation in CALL software. Poster presented at the 5th Pronunciation in Second Language Learning and Teaching Conference, University of Utah.

Baker, A. (2014). Exploring teachers' knowledge of second language pronunciation techniques: Teacher cognitions, observed classroom practices, and student perceptions. *TESOL Quarterly*, 48(1), 136–163. https://doi.org/10.1002/tesq.99

Bliss, H., Cheng, L., Schellenburg, M., Lam, Z., Pai, R., & Gick, B. (2017). Ultrasound technology and its role in Cantonese pronunciation teaching and learning. In M. O'Brien & J. Levis (eds.), *Proceedings of the 8th Pronunciation in Second Language Learning and Teaching Conference*. Calgary, AB, August 2016, pp. 33–46. Ames, IA: Iowa State University. https://apling.engl.iastate.edu/alt-content/uploads/2017/05/PSLLT_2016_Proceedings_finalB.pdf

Boersma, P., & Weenink, D. (2018). *Praat: Doing phonetics by computer.* Available at http://www.praat.org

Bongaerts, T., Mennen, S., & van der Slik, F. (2000). Authenticity of pronunciation in naturalistic second language acquisition: The case of very advanced learners of Dutch as a second language. *Studia Linguistica*, 54(2), 298–308. https://doi.org/10.1111/1467-9582.00069

Bradlow, A. R., Akahane-Yamada, R., Pisoni, D. B., & Tohkura, Y. I. (1999). Training Japanese listeners to identify English /r/ and /l/: Long-term retention of learning in perception and production. *Attention, Perception, & Psychophysics*, 61(5), 977–985. https://doi.org/10.3758/BF03206911

Bresnahan, M. J., Ohashi, R., Nebashi, R., Ying Liu, W., & Morinage Shearman, S. (2002). Attitudinal and affective response toward accented English. *Language and Communication*, 22, 171–185. https://doi.org/10.1016/S0271-5309(01)00025-8

Brinton, D. M. (2014). Epilogue to the myths: Best practices for teachers. In Grant, L. J. (ed.), *Pronunciation myths: Applying second language research to classroom teaching,* pp. 235–242. Ann Arbor: University of Michigan Press.

Cardoso, W., Collins, L., & White, J. (2012). Phonological input enhancement via text-to-speech synthesizers: The L2 acquisition of English simple past allomorphy. Paper presented at the American Association of Applied Linguistics Conference, Boston, MA: Researchpublishing.net.

Cardoso, W., Smith, G., & Garcia Fuentes, C. (2015). Evaluating text-to-speech synthesizers. In F. Helm, L. Bradley, M. Guarda, & S. Thouësny (eds.), *Critical CALL – Proceedings of EUROCALL*, pp. 108–113. Padova: Cambridge University Press. https://doi.org/10.14705/rpnet.2015.000318

Chan, M. J. (2017). *Anytune* slows down sound tracks for language practice. In M. O'Brien & J. Levis (eds.), *Proceedings of the 8th Pronunciation in Second Language Learning and Teaching Conference*, Calgary, AB, August 2016, pp. 191–194. Ames, IA: Iowa State University. https://apling.engl.iastate.edu/alt-content/uploads/2017/05/PSLLT_2016_ Proceedings_finalB.pdf

Chen, M. (2017). *Saundz* (Review). In M. O'Brien & J. Levis (eds.), *Proceedings of the 8th Pronunciation in Second Language Learning and Teaching Conference*. Calgary, AB, August 2016, pp. 228–235. Ames, IA: Iowa State University. https://apling.engl.iastate.edu/alt-content/uploads/2017/05/PSLLT_2016_ Proceedings_finalB.pdf

Chun, D. (1998). Signal analysis software for teaching discourse intonation. *Language Learning & Technology*, 2(1), 61–77.

Chun, D. (2002). *Discourse intonation in L2: From theory and research to practice.* Amsterdam/Philadelphia: John Benjamins. https://doi.org/10.1075/lllt.1

Chun, D. M. (2013). Computer-assisted pronunciation teaching. In C. A. Chapelle (ed.), *Encyclopedia of applied linguistics*, pp. 823–834. Oxford: Wiley-Blackwell.

Chun, D. M., Jiang, Y., & Ávila, N. (2013). Visualization of tone for learning Mandarin Chinese. In J. Levis & K. LeVelle (eds.), *Proceedings of the 4th Pronunciation in Second Language Learning and Teaching Conference.* pp. 77–89. Ames, IA: Iowa State University. https://apling.engl.iastate.edu/alt-content/uploads/2015/05/PSLLT_4th_ Proceedings_2012.pdf

Chun, D. M., Jiang, Y., Meyr, J., & Yang, R. (2015). Acquisition of L2 Mandarin Chinese tones with learner-created tone visualizations. *Journal of Second Language Pronunciation*, 1(1), 86–114. https://doi.org/10.1075/jslp.1.1.04chu

Coniam, D. (1999). Voice recognition software accuracy with second language speakers of English. *System*, 27, 49–64. https://doi.org/10.1016/S0346-251X(98)00049-9

Cox, T., & Davies, R. S. (2012). Using automatic speech recognition technology with elicited oral response testing. *CALICO Journal*, 29(4), 601–618. http://www.jstor.org/stable/calicojournal.29.4.601; https://doi.org/10.11139/cj.29.4.601-618

Defense Language Institute MIT Lincoln Library. (2017). *NetProF* https://np.ll.mit.edu/

Delmonte, R. (2009). Prosodic tools for language learning. *International Journal of Speech Technology*, 12, 161–184. https://doi.org/10.1007/s10772-010-9065-1

Derwing, T. M. (2010). Utopian goals for pronunciation teaching. In J. Levis and K. LeVelle (eds.), *Proceedings of the 1st Pronunciation in Second Language Learning and Teaching Conference*, pp. 24–37. Ames, IA, Iowa State University.

Derwing, Tracey M., & Munro, Murray J. (2009). Putting accent in its place: Rethinking obstacles to communication. *Language Teaching*, 42(4), 476–490. https://doi.org/10.1017/S026144480800551X

Derwing, T. M., & Munro, M. J. (2015). *Pronunciation fundamentals: Evidence-based perspectives for L2 teaching and research.* Amsterdam/Philadelphia: John Benjamins. https://doi.org/10.1075/lllt.42

Derwing, T., Munro, M., & Carbonaro, M. (2000). Does popular speech recognition software work with ESL speech? *TESOL Quarterly*, 34 (3), 59–603. https://doi.org/10.2307/3587748

Derwing, T. M., Munro, M. J., & Wiebe, G. E. (1998). Evidence in favor of a broad framework for pronunciation instruction. *Language Learning*, 48, 393–410. https://doi.org/10.1111/0023-8333.00047

Derwing, T. M., Rossiter, M. J., Munro, M. J., & Thomson, R. I. (2004). Second language fluency: Judgments on different tasks. *Language Learning*, 54, 655–679. https://doi.org/10.1111/j.1467-9922.2004.00282.x

Dlaska, A. & Krekeler C., (2008). Self-assessment of pronunciation, *System*, 36, 506–516. https://doi.org/10.1016/j.system.2008.03.003

Ducate, L., & Lomicka, L. (2009). Podcasting: An effective tool for hone language students' pronunciation? *Language Learning & Technology*, 13(3), 66–86.

Duppenthaler, P. (1991). What about pronunciation? *English Today*, 27, 32–36. https://doi.org/10.1017/S0266078400005721

Egan, K, &. LaRocca, S. (2000). Speech recognition in language learning: A must. *Proceedings of InStill 2000*, pp. 4–7. Dundee: University of Abertay.

Elliott, A. R. (1995). Foreign language phonology: Field independence, attitude, and the success of formal instruction in Spanish pronunciation. *Modern Language Journal*, 79, 530–542. https://doi.org/10.1111/j.1540-4781.1995.tb05456.x

Ellis, R. (2001). Investigating form-focused instruction. *Language Learning*, 51 Suppl. 1, 1–46. https://doi.org/10.1111/j.1467-1770.2001.tb00013.x

Ellis, R. (2009). Task-based language teaching: Sorting out the misunderstandings. *International Journal of Applied Linguistics*, 19(3), 221–246. https://doi.org/10.1111/j.1473-4192.2009.00231.x

English Talk Shop (2015). *American Speechsounds.* Available at https://www.englishtalkshop.com/etswebapp

Engwall, O., Wik, P., Beskow, J., & Granström, B. (2004). Design strategies for a virtual language tutor. Paper presented at the ICSLP 2004 Conference. Available at http://www.speech.kth.se/ctt/publications/papers04/icslp2004_tutor.pdf

Eskenazi, M. (1999a). Using a computer in foreign language pronunciation training: What advantage? *CALICO Journal*, 16(3), 447–469.

Eskenazi, M. (1999b). Using automatic speech processing for foreign language pronunciation tutoring: Some issues and a prototype. *Language Learning & Technology*, 2(2), 62–76. Available at http://llt.msu.edu/vol2num2/article3/

Evove Limited. (2016). *Saundz.* http://saundz.com/

Field, J. (2014). Pronunciation teaching has to establish in the minds of language learners a set of distinct consonant and vowel sounds. In L. J. Grant (ed.), *Pronunciation myths: Applying second language research to classroom teaching.* Ann Arbor: University of Michigan Press, pp. 80–106.

Flege, J. E. (1984). The detection of French accent by American listeners. *Journal of the Acoustical Society of America*, 76, 692–707. https://doi.org/10.1121/1.391256

Foote, J. A., Holtby, A. K., & Derwing, T. M. (2011). Survey of the teaching of pronunciation in adult ESL programs in Canada, 2010. *TESL Canada Journal*, 29(1), 1–22. https://doi.org/10.18806/tesl.v29i1.1086

Foote, J., & Smith, G. (2013, September). Is there an app for that? Paper presented at the 5th Pronunciation in Second Language Learning and Teaching Conference, Ames, Iowa.

Foote, J., & McDonough, K. (2017). Using shadowing with mobile technology to improve L2 pronunciation. *Journal of Second Language Pronunciation*, 3(1), 34–56. https://doi.org/10.1075/jslp.3.1.02foo

Forvo Media SL (2017). *Forvo.* www.forvo.com

Fouz-González, J. (2015). Trends and directions in computer-assisted pronunciation training. In J. A. Mompean & J. Fouz-González (eds.), *Investigating English Pronunciation: Trends and Directions*, pp. 314–342. Basingstoke & New York: Palgrave Macmillan. https://doi.org/10.1057/9781137509437_14

Fouz-González, J. (2017). Pronunciation instruction through Twitter: the case of commonly mispronounced words. *Computer Assisted Language Learning*, 30(7), 631–633. https://doi.org/10.1080/09588221.2017.1340309

Gilbert, J. (2014). Intonation is hard to teach. In L. J. Grant (ed.), *Pronunciation myths: Applying second language research to classroom teaching.* Ann Arbor: University of Michigan Press, pp. 107–136.

Gluszek, A., Newheiser. A.-K., & Dovidio, J. F. (2011). Social psychological orientations and accent strength. *Journal of Language and Social Psychology*, 30, 28–45. https://doi.org/10.1177/0261927X10387100

Google. (2017). *Google Web Speech.* https://www.google.com/intl/en/chrome/demos/speech.html

Google. (2017). *Google Cloud Speech.* https://cloud.google.com/speech/

Grant, L. (ed.) (2014). *Pronunciation myths: Applying second language research to classroom teaching.* Ann Arbor: University of Michigan Press. https://doi.org/10.3998/mpub.4584330

Hamada, Y. (2016). Shadowing: Who benefits and how? Uncovering a booming EFL teaching technique for listening comprehension. *Language Teaching Research*, 20(1), 35–52. https://doi.org/10.1177/1362168815597504

Hardison, D. M. (2004). Generalization of computer-assisted prosody training: Quantitative and qualitative findings. *Language Learning & Technology*, 8(1), 34–52.

Hedgcock, J., & Lefkowitz, N. (2000). Overt and covert prestige in the French language classroom: When is it good to sound bad? *Applied Language Learning*, 11(1), 75–97.

Hincks, R. (2003). Speech technologies for pronunciation feedback and evaluation. *ReCALL*, 15(1), 3–20. https://doi.org/10.1017/S0958344003000211

Hincks, R., & Edlund, J. (2009). Promoting increased pitch variation in oral presentations with transient visual feedback. *Language Learning & Technology*, 13(3), 32–50.

Hirata, Y. (2004). Computer assisted pronunciation training for native English speakers learning Japanese pitch and durational contrasts. *Computer Assisted Language Learning*, 17(3–4), 357–376. https://doi.org/10.1080/0958822042000319629

Hussein, H., Do, H. S., Mixdorff, H., Ding, H., Gao, Q., Hu, G., Wei, S., & Chao, Z. (2011). Mandarin tone perception and production by German learners. *Proceedings of the Workshop on Speech and Language Technology in Education (SLaTE)*, Venice, Italy.

Imber, B., Maynard, C., Parker, M. (2017). Using Praat to increase intelligibility through visual feedback. In M. O'Brien & J. Levis (eds.), *Proceedings of the 8th Pronunciation in Second Language Learning and Teaching Conference*, Calgary, AB, August 2016, pp. 195–213. Ames, IA: Iowa State University. https://apling.engl.iastate.edu/alt-content/uploads/2017/05/PSLLT_2016_Proceedings_finalB.pdf

Inceoglu, S. (2015). Audiovisual and auditory-only perceptual training: Effects on the pronunciation of French nasal vowels. In J. Levis, R. Mohammed, M. Qian, & Z. Zhou (eds.), *Proceedings of the 6th Pronunciation in Second Language Learning and Teaching Conference*, Santa Barbara, CA, pp. 104–114. Ames, IA: Iowa State University. https://apling.engl.iastate.edu/alt-content/uploads/2015/05/PSLLT_6th_Proceedings_2014.pdf

Isaacs, T. (2009). Integrating form and meaning in L2 pronunciation instruction. *TESL Canada Journal*, 2, (1), 1–12. https://doi.org/10.18806/tesl.v27i1.1034

Jin, H. (2017). *VoiceTube* (Review). In M. O'Brien & J. Levis (eds.), *Proceedings of the 8th Pronunciation in Second Language Learning and Teaching Conference*, Calgary, AB, August 2016, pp. 248–253. Ames, IA: Iowa State University. https://apling.engl.iastate.edu/alt-content/uploads/2017/05/PSLLT_2016_Proceedings_finalB.pdf

Kaltenböck, G. (2001). Learner autonomy: A guiding principle in designing a CD-ROM for intonation practice. *ReCALL*, 13(2), 179–190. https://doi.org/10.1017/S0958344001000428a

Language Arts Press. (2017). *English Pronunciation Tutor.* https://itunes.apple.com/us/app/english-pronunciation-tutor/id975040866?mt=8

Larsen-Freeman, D. (2000). *Techniques and principles in language teaching* (2nd ed.). Oxford: Oxford University Press.

Lee, A. H., & Lyster, R. (2016). Can corrective feedback on second language speech perception errors affect production accuracy? *Applied Psycholinguistics*, 38(2), 371–393. https://doi.org/10.1017/S0142716416000254

Lee, J., Jang, J., & Plonsky, L. (2014). The effectiveness of second language pronunciation instruction: A meta-analysis. *Applied Linguistics*, 36(3), 1–23.

Leeman, J. (2003). Recasts and second language development. *Studies in Second Language Acquisition*, 25, 37–63. https://doi.org/10.1017/S0272263103000020

Levis, J. M. (2005). Changing contexts and shifting paradigms in pronunciation teaching. *TESOL Quarterly*, 39, 369–377. https://doi.org/10.2307/3588485

Levis, J. (2007). Computer technology in teaching and researching. *Annual Review of Applied Linguistics*, 27, 184–202. https://doi.org/10.1017/S0267190508070098

Levis, J. M. (2016). Research into practice: How research appears in pronunciation teaching materials. *Language Teaching*, 49(3), 423–437. https://doi.org/10.1017/S0261444816000045

Levis, J., & Pickering, L. (2004). Teaching intonation in discourse using speech visualization technology. *System*, 32, 505–524. https://doi.org/10.1016/j.system.2004.09.009

Levy, M., & Steel, C. (2015). Language learner perspectives on the functionality and use of electronic language dictionaries. *ReCALL: The Journal of EUROCALL*, 27(2), 177–196. https://doi.org/10.1017/S095834401400038X

Liakin, D., Cardoso, W., & Liakina, N. (2015). Learning L2 pronunciation with a mobile speech recognizer: French /y/. *CALICO Journal*, 32(1), 1–25. https://doi.org/10.1558/cj.v32i1.25962

Liakin, D., Cardoso, W., & Liakina, N. (2017). The pedagogical use of mobile speech synthesis (TTS): Focus on French liaison. *Computer Assisted Language Learning*, 30(3–4), 348–365. https://doi.org/10.1080/09588221.2017.1312463

Lima, E. F. (2015). Feel the rhythm! Fun and effective pronunciation practice using Audacity and sitcom scenes (Teaching Tip). In J. Levis, R. Mohammed, M. Qian, & Z. Zhou (eds.), *Proceedings of the 6th Pronunciation in Second Language Learning and Teaching Conference*, Santa Barbara, CA, pp. 277–284. Ames, IA: Iowa State University. https://apling.engl.iastate.edu/alt-content/uploads/2015/05/PSLLT_6th_Proceedings_2014.pdf

Logan, J. S., Lively, S. E., & Pisoni, D. B. (1991). Training Japanese listeners to identify English /r/ and / l /: A first report. *Journal of the Acoustical Society of America*, 89, 874–886. https://doi.org/10.1121/1.1894649

Lord, G. (2005). (How) Can we teach foreign language pronunciation? On the effects of a Spanish phonetics course. *Hispania*, 88(3), 557–567. https://doi.org/10.2307/20063159

Lord, G. (2008). Podcasting communities and second language pronunciation. *Foreign Language Annals*, 41(2), 364–379. https://doi.org/10.1111/j.1944-9720.2008.tb03297.x

Lord, G., & Harrington, S. (2013). Online communities of practice and second language phonological acquisition. *International Journal of Computer Assisted Language Learning and Teaching*, 3(3), 34–55. https://doi.org/10.4018/ijcallt.2013070103

Luo, D., Shimomura, N., Minematsu, N., Yamauchi, Y., & Hirose, K. (2008). Automatic pronunciation evaluation of language learners' utterances generated through shadowing. *Interspeech 2008*, 2807–2810.

Macmillan Education. (2017). *Sounds*. http://www.macmillaneducationapps.com/soundspron/

Major, R. C. (2007). Identifying a foreign accent in an unfamiliar language. *Studies in Second Language Acquisition*, 29, 539–556. https://doi.org/10.1017/S0272263107070428

Martin, I. A. (2017). Teaching pronunciation through homework assignments: The method of iCPRS. In M. O'Brien & J. Levis (eds.), *Proceedings of the 8th Pronunciation in Second Language Learning and Teaching Conference*, Calgary, AB, August 2016, pp. 214–221. Ames, IA: Iowa State University. https://apling.engl.iastate.edu/alt-content/uploads/2017/05/PSLLT_2016_Proceedings_finalB.pdf

Martin, I. A. (2018). *Bridging the gap between L2 pronunciation research and teaching: Using iCPRs to improve novice German learners' pronunciation in online and face-to-face classes.* Unpublished PhD dissertation, Penn State University, Philadelphia.

Martin, I. A., & Jackson, C. N. (2016). Pronunciation training facilitates the learning and retention of L2 grammatical structures. *Foreign Language Annals*, 49(4), 658–676. https://doi.org/10.1111/flan.12224

McCrocklin, S. (2014). Dictation programs for pronunciation learner empowerment. In J. Levis & S. McCrocklin (eds.), *Proceedings of the 5th Pronunciation in Second Language Learning and Teaching Conference*, pp. 30–39. Ames, IA: Iowa State University.
https://apling.engl.iastate.edu/alt-content/uploads/2015/05/PSLLT_5th_Proceedings_2013.pdf

McCrocklin, S. (2016). Pronunciation learner autonomy: The potential of automatic speech recognition. *System*, 57, 25–42.
https://doi.org/10.1016/j.system.2015.12.013

Menzel, W., Herron, D., Morton, R., Pezzotta, D., Bonaventura, P., & Howarth, P. (2001). Interactive pronunciation training. *ReCALL*, 13(1), 67–78.
https://doi.org/10.1017/S0958344001000714

Molholt, G. (1988). Computer-assisted instruction in pronunciation for Chinese speakers of American English. *TESOL Quarterly*, 22(1), 91–111.
https://doi.org/10.2307/3587063

Mompean, J. A., & Fouz-González, J. (2016). Twitter-based EFL pronunciation instruction. *Language Learning & Technology*, 20(1), 166–190.
http://llt.msu.edu/issues/february2016/mompeanfouzgonzalez.pdf

Mora, J. C., & Levkina, M. (2017). Task-based pronunciation teaching and research. *Studies in Second Language Acquisition*, 39(2), 381–399.
https://doi.org/10.1017/S0272263117000183

Morley, J. (1991). The pronunciation component in teaching English to speakers of other languages. *TESOL Quarterly*, 25(3), 481–520.
https://doi.org/10.2307/3586981

Motohashi-Saigo, M., & Hardison, D. M. (2009). Acquisition of L2 Japanese geminates: Training with waveform displays. *Language Learning & Technology*, 13(2), 29–47.

Moyer, A. 1999. Ultimate attainment in L2 phonology. *Studies in Second Language Acquisition*, 21, 81–108.

Munro, M. J. (2003). A primer on accent discrimination in the Canadian context. *TESL Canada Journal*, 20(2), 38–51. https://doi.org/10.18806/tesl.v20i2.947

Munro, M. J., Derwing, T. M., & Burgess, C. (2010). Detection of nonnative speaker status from content-masked speech. *Speech Communication*, 52, 626–637. https://doi.org/10.1016/j.specom.2010.02.013

Munro, M. J., Derwing, T. M., & Thomson, R. I. (2015). Setting segmental priorities for English learners: Evidence from a longitudinal study. *International Review of Applied Linguistics in Language Teaching*, 53, 39–60.
https://doi.org/10.1515/iral-2015-0002

Murphy, J. (2014). Teacher training programs provide adequate preparation in how to teach pronunciation. In Grant, L. J. (ed.), *Pronunciation myths: Applying second language research to classroom teaching,* pp. 188–234. Ann Arbor: University of Michigan Press.

Natural Soft Limited (2017). *NaturalReader.* https://www.naturalreaders.com/

Neri, A., Cucchuarini, C., & Strik, H. (2004). Segmental errors in Dutch as a second language: How to establish priorities for CAPT. *Proceedings of InSTIL/ICALL 2004-NLP and Speech Technologies in Advanced Language Learning Systems,* Venice, June 17–19, 2004.

Neri, A., Cucchiarini, C., & Strik, H. (2008). The effectiveness of computer-based corrective feedback for improving segmental quality in L2 Dutch. *ReCALL,* 20(2), 225–243. https://doi.org/10.1017/S0958344008000724

Neri, A., Cucchiarini, C., Strik, H., & Boves, L. (2002). The pedagogy-technology interface in computer assisted pronunciation training. *Computer Assisted Language Learning,* 15(5), 441–467. https://doi.org/10.1076/call.15.5.441.13473

Nuance Communications. (2017). *Dragon Naturally Speaking.* Burlington, MA.

O'Brien, M. G. (2004). Pronunciation matters. *Die Unterrichtspraxis: Teaching German,* 37(1), 1–9. https://doi.org/10.1111/j.1756-1221.2004.tb00068.x

O'Brien, M. G. & Levis, J. M. (2017). Pronunciation and technology. In M. O'Brien & J. Levis (eds.), *Proceedings of the 8th Pronunciation in Second Language Learning and Teaching Conference,* Calgary, AB, August 2016, pp. 1–9. Ames, IA: Iowa State University. https://apling.engl.iastate.edu/alt-content/uploads/2017/05/PSLLT_2016_Proceedings_finalB.pdf

O'Brien, M. G., Derwing, T. M., Cucchiarini, C., Hardison, D. M., Mixdorff, H., Thomson, R., Strik, H., Levis, J. M., Munro, M. J., Foote, J. A., & Muller Levis, G. (2018). Directions for the future of technology in pronunciation research and teaching. *Journal of Second Language Pronunciation,* 4(2), 182–206. https://doi.org/10.1075/jslp.17001.obr

O'Connor, P., & Gatton, W. (2004). Implementing multimedia in a university EFL program: A case study in CALL. In Fotos, S. & Browne, C. M. (eds.), *New perspectives on CALL for second language classrooms,* pp. 199–224. Mahwah, NJ: Lawrence Erlbaum Associates.

Ohkawa, Y., Suzuki, M., Ogasawara, H., Ito, A., & Makino, S. (2009). A speaker adaptation method for non-native speech using learners' native utterances for computer-assisted language learning systems. *Speech Communication,* 51, 875–882. https://doi.org/10.1016/j.specom.2009.05.005

Okuno, T., & Hardison, D. M. (2016). Perception-production link in L2 Japanese vowel duration: Training with technology. *Language Learning & Technology,* 20(2), 61–80. http://llt.msu.edu/issues/june2016/okunohardison.pdf

Olson, D. J. (2014a). Benefits of visual feedback on segmental production in the L2 classroom. *Language Learning & Technology,* 18(3), 173–192. http://llt.msu.edu/issues/october2014/olson.pdf

Olson, D. J. (2014b). Phonetics and technology in the classroom: A practical approach to using speech analysis software in second-language pronunciation instruction. *Hispania,* 97(1), 47–68. https://doi.org/10.1353/hpn.2014.0030

Otterwave. (2014). *English Pronunciation.*

https://itunes.apple.com/ca/app/english-pronunciation-otterwave/id540959652?mt=8

Oyama, S. (1976). A sensitive period for the acquisition of a nonnative phonological system. *Journal of Psycholinguistic Research*, 5(3), 261–283. https://doi.org/10.1007/BF01067377

Patten, I., & Edmonds, L. A. (2015). Effect of training Japanese L1 speakers in the production of American English /r/ using spectrographic visual feedback. *Computer Assisted Language Learning*, 28(3), 241–259. https://doi.org/10.1080/09588221.2013.839570

Pearson, P., Pickering, L., & Da Silva, R. (2011). The impact of computer assisted pronunciation training on the improvement of Vietnamese learner production of English syllable margins. In. J. Levis & K. LeVelle (eds.), *Proceedings of the 2nd Pronunciation in Second Language Learning and Teaching Conference*, September 2010, pp. 169–180. Ames, IA: Iowa State University. https://apling.engl.iastate.edu/alt-content/uploads/2016/06/Proceedings_3rd_PSLLT.pdf

Pennington, M. C. (1999). Computer-aided pronunciation pedagogy: Promise, limitations, directions. *Computer Assisted Language Learning*, 12(5), 427–440. https://doi.org/10.1076/call.12.5.427.5693

Pennington, M. C., & Richards, J. C. (1986). Pronunciation revisited. *TESOL Quarterly*, 20, 207–225. https://doi.org/10.2307/3586541

Quintana-Lara, M. (2014). Effect of acoustic spectrographic instruction on production of English /i/ and /ɪ/ by Spanish pre-service English teachers. *Computer Assisted Language Learning*, 27(3), 207–227. https://doi.org/10.1080/09588221.2012.724424

REDIdea Co. (2017). *VoiceTube.* https://www.voicetube.com/

Rosell-Aguilar, F. (2017). State of the app: A taxonomy and framework for evaluating language learning mobile applications. *CALICO Journal*, 34(2), 243–258.

Rosetta Stone. (2017). *Rosetta Stone.* https://www.rosettastone.com/

Sagarra, N., & Abbuhl, R. (2013). Optimizing the noticing of recasts via computer-delivered feedback: Evidence that oral input enhancement and working memory help second language learning. *Modern Language Journal*, 97, 196–216. https://doi.org/10.1111/j.1540-4781.2013.01427.x

Saraçlar, M., & Khudanpur, S. (2004). Pronunciation change in conversational speech and its implications for automatic speech recognition. *Computer Speech and Language*, 18, 375–395. https://doi.org/10.1016/j.csl.2003.09.005

Schmidt, R. (2001). Attention. In P. Robinson (ed.), *Cognition and second language instruction*, pp. 3–32. Cambridge,: Cambridge University Press. https://doi.org/10.1017/CBO9781139524780.003

Scovel, T. (1969). Foreign accents, language acquisition and cerebral dominance. *Language Learning*, 19(3/4), 245–254. https://doi.org/10.1111/j.1467-1770.1969.tb00466.x

Shport, I. A. (2016). Identifying pitch-accent patterns in Tokyo Japanese. *Studies in Second Language Acquisition*, 38, 739–769. https://doi.org/10.1017/S027226311500039X

Spaai, G. W., & Hermes, D. J. (1993). A visual display for the teaching of intonation. *CALICO Journal*, 10(3), 19–30.

Spada, N., & Lightbown, P. M. (2008). Form-focused instruction: Isolated or inte-grated? *TESOL Quarterly*, 42(2), 181–207.
https://doi.org/10.1002/j.1545-7249.2008.tb00115.x

SRI International. (2016). *EduSpeak*.

Strik, H., Colpaert, J., Van Doremalen, J., & Cucchiarini, C. (2012). The DISCO ASR-based CALL system: practicing L2 oral skills and beyond. *Proceedings of the Conference on International Language Resources and Evaluation (LREC 2012)*, Istanbul, May 2012.

Strik, H., Truong, K., de Wet, F., & Cucchiarini, C. (2009). Comparing different approaches for automatic error detection. *Speech Communication*, 51, 845–852. https://doi.org/10.1016/j.specom.2009.05.007

Sustaric, R. (2003). Speech recognition can be applied in phonetics (or more precisely in pronunciation) teaching. In M. J. Solé, D. Recasens, and J. Romero (eds.), *Proceedings of the 15th ICPhS Barcelona*. Available at https://www.internationalphoneticassociation.org/icphs-proceedings/ICPhS2003/papers/p15_2841.pdf

Tanner, M. W., & Landon, M. M. (2009). The effects of computer-assisted pro-nunciation readings on ESL learners' use of pausing, stress, intonation, and overall comprehensibility. *Language Learning & Technology*, 13(3), 51–65. http://llt.msu.edu/vol13num3/tannerlandon.pdf

Teich, E., Hagen, E., Grote, B., & Bateman, J. (1997). From communicative context to speech: Integrating dialogue processing, speech production and natural lan-guage generation. *Speech Communication*, 21, 73–99.
https://doi.org/10.1016/S0167-6393(96)00070-2

Thomson, R. I. (2011). Computer assisted pronunciation training: Targeting second language vowel perception improves pronunciation. *CALICO Journal*, 28(3), 744–765. https://doi.org/10.11139/cj.28.3.744-765

Thomson, R. I. (2012). Improving L2 listeners' perception of English vowels: A computer-mediated approach. *Language Learning*, 62(4), 1231–1258. https://doi.org/10.1111/j.1467-9922.2012.00724.x

Thomson, R. I. (2017). *English Accent Coach*. https://www.englishaccentcoach.com/

Thomson, R. I. (forthcoming). High variability [pronunciation] training (HVPT): A proven technique that every language teacher and learner should know about. *Journal of Second Language Pronunciation*.

Thomson, R. I. & Derwing, T. M. (2015). The effectiveness of L2 pronuncia-tion instruction: A Narrative Review. *Applied Linguistics*, 36(3), 326–344. https://doi.org/10.1093/applin/amu076

Thomson, R. I., & Derwing, T. M. (2016). Is phonemic training using nonsense or real words more effective? In J. Levis, H. Le., I. Lucic, E. Simpson, & S. Vo (eds.), *Proceedings of the 7th Pronunciation in Second Language Learning and Teaching Conference*, October 2015, pp. 88–97. Ames, IA: Iowa State University.

Trofimovich, P., & Baker, W. (2006). Learning second language suprasegmentals: Effect of L2 experience on prosody and fluency characteristics of L2 speech. *Studies in Second Language Acquisition*, 28, 1–30.
https://doi.org/10.1017/S0272263106060013

University of Iowa Research Foundation. (2016). *Sounds of Speech* app.

Victoria Productions. (2017). *Perfect English Pronunciation.*
http://www.apppep.com/

Walker, D. (2017) *Multi Track Song Recorder.* http://mtsr-app.com/

Walker, N. R., Cedergren, H., Trofimovich, P., & Gatbonton, E. (2011). Automatic speech recognition for CALL: A task-specific application for training nurses. *The Canadian Modern Language Review/La Revue Canadienne Des Langues Vivantes,* 67(4), 459–479. https://doi.org/10.3138/cmlr.67.4.459

Wallace, L. (2016). Using Google web speech as a springboard for identifying personal pronunciation problems. In J. Levis, H. Le, I. Lucic, E. Simpson, & S. Vo (eds.), *Proceedings of the 7th Pronunciation in Second Language Learning and Teaching Conference,* Dallas, TX, October 2015, pp. 180–186. Ames, IA: Iowa State University.
https://apling.engl.iastate.edu/alt-content/uploads/2016/08/PSLLT7_July29_2016_B.pdf

Warren, P., Elgort, I., & Crabbe, D. (2009). Comprehensibility and prosody ratings for pronunciation software development. *Language Learning & Technology,* 13(3), 87–102. http://llt.msu.edu/vol13num3/warrenelgortcrabbe.pdf

Werker, J. F., & Tees, R. C. (1984). Cross-language speech perception: Evidence for perceptual reorganization during the first year of life. *Infant Behavior and Development,* 7, 49–63. https://doi.org/10.1016/S0163-6383(84)80022-3

Whipple, J., Cullen, C., Gardiner, K., & Savage, T. (2015). Syllable Circles for pronunciation learning and teaching. *ELT Journal,* 69(2), 151–164. https://doi.org/10.1093/elt/ccu094

White, D., Gananathan, R., Mok, P. (2017) Teaching dark /l/ with ultrasound technology. In M. O'Brien & J. Levis (eds.), *Proceedings of the 8th Pronunciation in Second Language Learning and Teaching Conference,* Calgary, AB, August 2016, pp. 155–175. Ames, IA: Iowa State University.
https://apling.engl.iastate.edu/alt-content/uploads/2017/05/PSLLT_2016_Proceedings_finalB.pdf

Wu, C., Su, H., & Liu, C. (2013). Efficient personalized mispronunciation detection of Taiwanese-accented English speech based on unsupervised model adaptation and dynamic sentence selection. *Computer Assisted Language Learning,* 26(5), 446–467. https://doi.org/10.1080/09588221.2012.687383

Yoon, S-Y., Pierce, L., Huensch, A., Juul, E., Perkins, S., Sproat, R., & Hasegawa-Johnson, M. (2009). Construction of a rated speech corpus of L2 learners' spontaneous speech. *CALICO Journal,* 26(3), 662–673.
https://doi.org/10.1558/cj.v26i3.662-673

Zielinski, B., & Yates, L. (2014). Pronunciation instruction is not appropriate for beginning-level learners. In Grant, L. J. (ed.), *Pronunciation myths: Applying second language research to classroom teaching,* pp. 56–79. Ann Arbor: University of Michigan Press.

Zając, M., & Rojczyk. (2014). Imitation of English vowel duration upon exposure to native and non-native speech. *Poznań Studies in Contemporary Linguistics,* 50(4), 495–514. https://doi.org/10.1515/psicl-2014-0025

Zhu, Y., Fung, A. S. L., & Wang, H. (2012). Spotlight: Memorization effects of pronunciation and stroke order animation in digital flashcards. *CALICO Journal,* 29(3), 563–577. https://doi.org/10.11139/cj.29.3.563-577

Useful Resources

Please note that this list is by no means meant to be exhaustive.

Books Focusing on Teaching Pronunciation

Derwing, T. M., and Munro, M. J. (2015). *Pronunciation fundamentals: Evidence-based perspectives for L2 teaching and research.* Amsterdam/Philadelphia: John Benjamins. https://doi.org/10.1075/lllt.42

Grant, L. (ed.) (2014). *Pronunciation myths: Applying second language research to classroom teaching.* Ann Arbor: University of Michigan Press. https://doi.org/10.3998/mpub.4584330

Celce-Murcia, M., Brinton, D., & Goodwin, J. M. (2010). *Teaching pronunciation: A course book and reference guide.* Cambridge: Cambridge University Press.

Chun, D. (2002). *Discourse intonation in L2: From theory and research to practice.* Amsterdam/Philadelphia: John Benjamins. https://doi.org/10.1075/lllt.1

Jones, T. (ed.) (2016). *Pronunciation in the classroom: The overlooked essential.* Alexandria: TESOL Press.

Reed, M., & Levis, J. M. (eds.) (2015). *The handbook of English pronunciation.* Malden, MA: Wiley Blackwell. https://doi.org/10.1002/9781118346952

Trouvain, J. (2007). *Non-native prosody phonetic description and teaching practice.* Berlin, New York: Mouton de Gruyter. https://doi.org/10.1515/9783110198751

Conference Proceedings

The Pronunciation in Second Language Learning and Teaching (PSLLT) Proceedings. https://apling.engl.iastate.edu/psllt-archive/

Websites Focusing on Teaching Pronunciation

Cauldwell, R. (2017). *Speech in action.* http://www.speechinaction.org/

Hancock, M., & McDonald, A. (2017). *Hancock McDonald English language teaching.* http://hancockmcdonald.com/

Levis, J. (2017). *Pronunciation for teachers.* http://www.pronunciationforteachers.com/john-levis.html

About the Author

Mary Grantham O'Brien (PhD, University of Wisconsin) is a Professor of German at the University of Calgary. She is the co-author (with Sarah M. B. Fagan, University of Iowa) of the 2016 textbook *German phonetics and phonology: Theory and practice.* Her research focuses on L2 pronunciation, and she primarily investigates listeners' reactions of non-native speech as well as how L2 learners perceive and produce L2 prosody.

10 Communities: Exploring Digital Games and Social Networking

Julie M. Sykes, Christopher L. Holden, and
Stephanie W. P. Knight

Preview Questions

1. What communities, digital and/or analog, have you been a part of?
   What are some features of these communities that make them similar or different?
2. How would you define "community" in relation to second language learning? What existing communities would be especially
   useful for language learners? Are you, or your students, members
   of any of these communities?
3. How can mediated spaces, such as digital games and social networking sites, be used to facilitate second language learners' participation in target communities?
4. To what extent are actions or activities in one's community and/or
   mediated space self-directed? Other-directed? Reciprocal?

1   Introduction

The term *community* is both slippery and powerful in the context of second
language (L2) learning. It is a broad, inherently complex term that represents
heterogeneous, dynamic groups with varying behavior and language patterns. Though understandably daunting, unearthing and incorporating one's
self into L2 communities is inextricable from L2 learning. Contemporary
national approaches to language learning rightly encode this connection.
For example, the promise of engagement with "multilingual communities at home and around the world" (ACTFL, n.d.) is explicitly mentioned
in the general goals set forth by the five C's of the *World-readiness standards for learning language*. Additionally, the 2017 NCSSFL-ACTFL

Can-do statements for intercultural communication purport the importance of interaction with members of various communities through a focus on intercultural communicative competence (ICC), or "the ability to interact effectively and appropriately with people from other language and cultural backgrounds" which is "essential for establishing effective, positive relationships across boundaries" (NCSSFL-ACTFL, 2017: 5). This nod toward communities via an emphasis on communication and collaboration is even echoed in additional, multidisciplinary frameworks for learning such as Partnership for 21st Century Learning's *Framework for 21st century learning* (P21, 2016). Clearly, learning in the 21st century involves integration with others.

The aforementioned frameworks, standards, and learning targets provide laudable goals. They attempt to move a (language) learner's experience away from the isolated, community-agnostic textbook and classroom to a more relevant, meaningful, and connected experience. At the same time, they reflect an area in which world language instruction is most notably falling short (Belz & Thorne, 2005; Kramsch 2002; MLA, 2007; Train, 2005). The use of the term *community* connotes meaningful social interaction, collaboration, and an assumption of L2 activity outside classroom contexts. Furthermore, as a general idea, community suggests membership and influence within an identifiable group in which needs (emotional or physical) are met and experiences (space, time, and history) are shared (McMillan & Chavis 1986). However, communities are not simple, monolithic entities, especially as digitally-mediated activity increases, thereby decreasing the limitations of physical locations and increasing the remix and overlap possibilities (Thorne, Sauro, & Smith, 2015). In a discussion of community and digitally mediated activities, Thorne (2009) problematizes the use of the homogeneous term to reflect a complex reality, while at the same time pointing out the strengths the concept provides for understanding social activity. He states,

> while "community" is minimally a polysemous, and potentially a reductive, unit of social analysis, it is also an evocative term with an illocutionary force of pronouncement that has the potential to galvanize individuals into collective action. (2009: 92)

He further cautions against viewing a community as an ideal target or model of behavior that universally indicates sameness (i.e. shared-culture) without consideration of the often-divergent perceptions and behaviors that are inherently part of any group with a collective identity. The widely used term *communities of practice* (CoPs) (Lave & Wenger, 1991) gives the concept of community some internal specificity for L2 contexts. Construed as a group in which practices (i.e., ways of doing things, beliefs, values, and power-relations) emerge as the result of a mutual endeavor, a CoP is defined both by its membership and constitutive practices (Lave & Wenger, 1991). As newcomers assimilate through interactions with established members, they become part of the community, contributing to both its membership and practices. In terms of pedagogical goals, CoP assimilation is a useful environment for aiding second language acquisition: through social learning, students implicitly receive input (linguistic, pragmatic, social, and professional) that is of direct relevance for the accomplishment of mutual endeavors.

Despite this usefulness, CoPs are traditionally bound by a model of "long-term apprenticeship within stable social formations" (Thorne, 2009: 83). Along with a reliance on narrow definitions of membership and belonging, CoPs are critiqued for their inherent hierarchical nature which, in some cases, can limit participation (Zuengler & Miller, 2006). Minimally, they may simply not be descriptive of many modern communal sites of language use, or of a learner's place within these language contexts, especially the collective groupings found in the complex digital spaces under consideration here – digital games and social networks. For example, the concept of identity as it relates to (and is inextricably bound to) community is inherently complex in these contexts. In these spaces, learners are free to use language to carefully cultivate the identity they have (Chun, Smith, & Kern, 2016; Sykes, 2016; Sykes & Reinhardt, 2012). Identity projection in digital contexts, called *projective identities* by Gee (2007) in gaming spaces, may not directly reflect their face-to-face identity representation, but do impact decision making and interaction significantly. In fact, if they are successful, extended identities can facilitate robust community involvement, and are perhaps even an expected community norm. Even in social networking sites (SNSs) in which users accurately display their identifying characteristics (name, photos, and the like), researchers recognize that multimodal language use facilitated by digital technologies enables users to heavily curate their online identity presentation (see Thorne, Sauro, & Smith, 2015 for a detailed review).

Beyond the complications rendered by the internal constitution of any given community, we also recognize that, to an even greater extent, participation and membership in communities is plural and contingent, and not necessarily characterized by novice–expert relationships. It is in this spirit that the current chapter explores communities related to digital games (specifically, massively multiplayer online games and place-based mobile games) and social networking sites for L2 learning. More than mediated contexts in which learners can become part of *a community*, digital games and social networks have the potential to aid learners in gaining the necessary skills (e.g., linguistic, pragmatic, social, professional) to successfully make choices about their involvement in *a variety of communities* through a myriad of social behaviors. Both digital games and social networks offer means for attaining the original goals inspired by community as part of the L2 experience and, in doing so, afford new means of connecting with people both locally and globally.

Why Massively Multiplayer Online Games, Social Networking Sites, and Place-Based Augmented Reality Mobile Games?
Each of the three mediated spaces chosen as the focus of this chapter provides distinct insight for leveraging mediated spaces to empower L2 learners to move beyond the language classroom towards lifelong, multilingual membership in a variety of communities. Together, they represent a breadth of realities which require us to rethink what language and L2 learning means in light of the changing social and cultural practices associated with emerging mediated spaces (Chun, Smith, & Kern, 2016; Thorne, 2003; Thorne & Payne, 2005; Warschauer, 2007). Furthermore, they are especially useful for discussing the multiple ways in which emergent, mediated contexts can help us move away from research and practice where the focus is not community oriented or, alternatively, is focused on a "one culture" version of community.[1]

Massively multiplayer online games (MMOGs) are commercially designed and avatar-based multiplayer virtual worlds within which thousands of people simultaneously interact, compete, and collaborate with one another (Steinkuehler, 2008). This includes games such as *Fortnight, Guild Wars, World of Warcraft, Starwars Galaxies, Lineage 2*, and *Final Fantasy 11*, to name a few. MMOGs are distinct from open social virtualities[2] (e.g., *Second Life, Minecraft*), due to the interplay between designed in-game goals and objectives and the user-driven behavior (Sykes, Oskoz, & Thorne, 2008; Sykes & Reinhardt, 2012), which often creates the complex communities to be discussed here. While the behaviors and designed dynamics are unique in each MMOG, they share common practices such as leveling (i.e.,

---

1   For further discussion of the problematic notion of a single native speaker model and an assumed singular target culture, see Train (2005) and the chapter by Abrams in this volume.
2   Despite their prominence in education, further discussion of open social virtualities and other designed virtual eality spaces is beyond the scope of this work. See, for example, deFreitas (2006), Deutschmann, Panichi, & Molka-Danielson (2009), O'Brien & Levy (2008), and O'Brien, Levy, & Orich (2009).

advancing to more difficult play experiences), asset building (i.e., collecting items, money, skills), and required collaboration (i.e., shared resources, distributed skills and abilities) that are often not central to participation in open social virtualities.[3] MMOGs were chosen for this chapter because they are prominent digital spaces which foster intense, complex, multilingual interaction based on designed, fictional objectives and a textual reality that "transcends the actual reality of individuals sitting in front of keyboards and luminescent screens" (Chun, Smith, & Kern, 2016: 66).

Key to our understanding of communities for L2 learning are ways in which learners can become part of these ever-changing, evolving social spaces (Squire & Steinkuehler, 2006) associated with meaningful gameplay in MMOGs. They offer broader terms of participation and membership than those typically assumed as part of CoPs and foment meaningful language acquisition. As noted by Sykes & Reinhardt (2012), MMOGs align learners' experiences with five fundamental areas of L2 teaching and learning – goal-orientation, interaction, just-in-time feedback, meaningful context construction, and motivation. Most relevant here are the notions of goal-orientation and interaction in the game, through the game, and around the game to achieve said goals. These complex interactions occur frequently in-game, but also take place through a variety of attendant discourses (such as strategy forums and fan-fiction sites) centered around the game.

Social networking sites are:

> web-based services that allow individuals to (1) construct a public or semi-public profile within a bounded system, (2) articulate a list of other users with whom they share a connection, and (3) view and traverse their list of connections and those made by others within the system. (boyd & Ellison, 2008: 211)

Despite stated shifts in purposes and use and purported decreasing day-to-day interaction, the most popular SNS in the United States is *Facebook*; however, many other prominent sites are in existence around the world (i.e., *Reddit, Instagram, High5, Twitter, YouTube*), many of which have distinct user populations and objectives.[4] For example, although not extremely popular in the United States, *Orkut*, an SNS created by Google, is especially popular in Brazil and would be a significant SNS for learners of Portuguese.

3   For a detailed discussion of each of these features related to L2 learning, see
     Sykes, Reinhardt, & Thorne (2010) and Thorne, Black, & Sykes (2009).
4   See the following for more information about social networking sites
     in the United States: http://www.pewinternet.org/fact-sheet/social-
     media/ around the world https://www.statista.com/statistics/265773/
     market-share-of-the-most-popular-social-media-websites-in-the-us

SNSs present an interesting contrast to MMOGs, perhaps mostly due to their ubiquity of use. They represent the most pervasive mediated contexts of those discussed here and are the most closely assimilated into the daily practices of the everyday population for both social and commercial purposes. Take, for example, the notable increase in *Twitter* usage since 2016 due to political events in the United States (Pew Research Center, 2018). We see evidence of this in the noticeably prolific number of available fan sites for news stations, television shows, and commercial products, as well as the ever-increasing number of informal offline conversations related to social networking status updates, photos, and practices. Of important relevance to L2 learners are the various ways to negotiate these spaces in order to build, maintain, and terminate relationships as they expand their own networks to include friends and fan groups from multilingual communities.

Our discussion of SNSs focuses on L2 learners' engagement with very real SNS experiences, as opposed to proxy communities and profiles created for strictly classroom purposes. While we acknowledge the common concerns educators have with SNSs (e.g., privacy, security), we are leery of ignoring the actual practices of SNSs in favor of artificial, simulated, proxy spaces. Without real-life, meaningful connections, the simulated practice of social networking becomes increasingly artificial in contrast to the very real social behavior prevalent today (Blattner & Fiori, 2011; Reinhardt & Zander, 2011). Therefore, our focus remains on ways to engage learners with authentic communities via SNSs.

Place-based, augmented reality mobile games take advantage of the affordances offered by mobile devices (i.e., sociability, portability, location sensitivity, personalization, and connectivity) to deeply engage learners with a place and its associated communities (Holden & Sykes, 2011; Klopfer, 2008; Mathews, 2010; Squire, 2009). These games are played on mobile devices (e.g., smart phone), typically in a particular location (e.g., a nearby neighborhood) using locative sensitivity of the mobile device (e.g., GPS) and/or emulation of that place (e.g., an interactive map on the mobile device). The term *place-based* then refers to the actual gameplay taking place in a certain location of interest (rather than where the computers happen to be) as well as an overall design that seeks to leverage the particulars of that place for desired learning goals. For example, in *Pokémon Go!* players use GPS-enabled mobile devices to seek and capture creatures (Pokémon) that appear randomly at specific locations, battle the creatures captured by opponents at "gyms," locations of community saliency like churches, schools, and statues, and work collaboratively in "raids" to capture particularly strong and usually rare creatures at gyms. While engaging in this game, and others like it, community engagement is characterized by a specific duality; players experience the physical community in that they explore new places and have the potential to build and maintain a gaming community with other players. There is incredible potential for language development in these gaming communities given the robust nature of the emergent and attendant discourses involved.

Augmented reality (AR) refers to the ability of mobile devices to add information and context, in the field, to what we can perceive with our senses (Squire & Klopfer, 2007). This is to be distinguished from virtual reality, where users' sense perceptions of reality are replaced with sense perceptions of a designed world. Think of a museum, where a plaque near a painting tells you the name of the painter, and perhaps a couple of other basic details. While virtual reality may seek to replace the viewing of that painting with a virtual gallery accessed through goggles and gloves, augmented reality would retain the use of the museum, and provide a desired context (e.g., a short video featuring the various stages of the artists' process or music intended to enhance the experience of viewing the art) for the viewer beyond what is possible with a plaque. The distinction is not binary, but overall, the goal of augmented reality is to complement rather than replace the perceived world.

Ludic aspects of AR games (e.g., distributed resources, distinct gameplay experiences) are designed to leverage social behaviors among learners themselves, similar to what we see organized around the accomplishment of shared goals in MMOGs (Squire et al., 2007). Their ability to establish connections between place, community, culture, and language compels their use in L2 learning contexts and makes them especially relevant for this chapter. Local places, both current and historic, present not only a specific relevant occurrence of functional language use for learners in the classroom, but a starting point for their continued investigation and participation in language communities at their doorstep. Places are capable of:

- Motivating community participation among learners by design of gameplay and through openness to interpretation (like MMOGs),
- Leveraging a natural or naturalistic context connected with existing language communities, giving access to certain kinds of texts and interpretations and creating opportunities for participation, and
- Making the game software itself a site of participation, affording learners and language community members access to the academic design community (a feature distinct from MMOGs and SNSs).

Place-based mobile games are currently minor in scope compared to the overwhelmingly larger examples of MMOGs and SNSs that precede them. However, the release of *Pokémon Go!* proliferated place-based, augmented reality games as a record 21 million users were reported in the first week of the game's release. In the educational arena, researchers and practitioners have developed, tested, and implemented place-based, augmented games for learning purposes with several games specifically focused on language learning – *Mentira, Ecopod: Survival, Ecopod: Quake Response, Paris Occupé*, and *CronoOps* (all available on the ARIS platform (https://fielddaylab.org/make/aris/), to name a few. They are important to mention because of the explosive growth of mobile technology and the continually shifting behaviors around human interactions in communities all over the world (e.g., Johnson et al., 2010; Roschelle & Pea, 2002; Norris & Soloway, 2009; Squire, 2009; Thorne, Sauro, & Smith, 2015).

Place-based, augmented reality games also speak to tensions between fictional experiences and mediated gameplay (delivered on a mobile device), and interaction in and association with existing physical places and communities. Regarding MMOGs and SNSs, the fiction of the former and actuality of the latter are often pitted against one another in attempting to leverage community features among L2 learners. How is slaying dragons any more real than a fake *Facebook* profile? Yet, it is precisely in the consideration of community that both MMOGs and SNSs can unproblematically be labeled as "real" contexts of activity. Place-based mobile games play with these tensions because they use fictional or designed play, as well as existing aspects of local communities, to help students realize roles in a variety of language community contexts (Holden and Sykes, 2011).

The remainder of this chapter draws from these perspectives to explore how MMOGs, SNSs, and place-based, augmented reality mobile games can help educators foster community participation for their learners. The next section explores relevant background information, including an overview of research relating to innovation and social practices as well as each of the three mediated contexts under consideration. We then discuss research approaches specifically related to second language acquisition (SLA). The fourth section of the chapter focuses on pedagogical implications in terms of both task design and evaluation of outcomes.

2   Literature Review

Despite their often-stigmatized position within formal educational contexts, digital games and SNSs are reflective of prominent social practices whose impact is difficult to ignore in everyday life. For example, in a study by the Pew Internet and American Life Project, Duggan (2015) reported that 67%

of Americans ages 18–29 played digital games on a multitude of platforms (e.g., gaming consoles, computers, and mobile devices). Additionally, 69% of the American public was reported to use social media to connect with others, up from 5% in 2005 (Pew Research Center, 2018). Based on these trends, we can assume that the numbers are already higher than they were at the time of printing and will continue to grow.

Becoming an adept multilingual speaker involves not only being able to use the target language in academic contexts, but these prominent social spaces as well (Thorne, Black, & Sykes, 2009; Thorne, Sauro, & Smith, 2015; Warschauer, 2007). As educators, it is our responsibility to, at the very least, recognize these spaces as valid communicative contexts, but, more importantly, provide learners with the necessary skills to become active, engaged participants in their associated communities. Detailed historical accounts of MMOGs (deFreitas, 2006), place-based mobile games (Klopfer, 2008), and SNSs (boyd & Ellison, 2008) highlight their emergence, rapid rate of growth and use, impact on everyday social practices, and potential in education. To document their relevance to L2 community interaction, in the subsection that follows we first discuss the nature of interplay between technological innovation and social practices, and then move to an exploration of L2 research related to MMOGs, SNSs, and place-based mobile games.

2.1 Technological Innovation and Social Practices

The underlying theme that guides our discussion of technological innovation and social practice is that of *interpretive flexibility* (Kline & Pinch, 1996). Using the introduction of the automobile in rural communities as an example, the authors dismiss technological determinism in favor of a model where both producer and consumer participate in the contingent process of determining how a tool is (or is not) integrated into social practice. When the automobile was first introduced in rural communities, residents were skeptical about its intended use and frustrated by the negative impact it had on their communities (e.g., noise, speed). Initially, instead of adapting it only as a form of transportation, many rural citizens used components of the automobile to more efficiently perform other tasks, such as powering a mill, turning a saw, or running a washing machine. Corporations soon picked up on these adaptations that moved beyond their own intentions for the automobile and began to build and market separate tools for these functions. As a result, powered appliances and farm machinery came into existence. By repurposing the technology of the automobile and using it in interesting ways, the residents themselves shaped the industry to create new products and innovations. It is not just the tools that change practices, but also the ways in which these tools are used, that shape their creation.

Thus, in our discussion of the emergence of mediated communities in different digital spaces – MMOGs, SNSs, and place-based mobile games – we must not only consider their creation as tools, but also the practices which have shaped, and been shaped by, their use, as well as the complex dynamics of their associated communities. As noted by Thorne, Black, & Sykes, "what occurs online, and often outside of instructed educational settings, involves extended periods of language socialization, adaptation, and creative semiotic work that illustrate vibrant communicative practices" (2009: 815). As educators, we can take advantage of the principles of interpretive flexibility to move learners beyond the role of observers of multilingual social practices to be creators themselves.

In the case of MMOGs, this might mean multilingual participation in highly successful guilds[5] on international servers or prominent participation in online forums which, ultimately, encourage game designers to rethink the designed components of gameplay. Moreover, successful participation in a variety of social networking communities (in the L1 [first language], L2, and maybe even L3 [third language]) connects learners with others of similar interests and ideas (e.g., multilingual fan pages, language learning sites) and can enhance the maintenance of offline relationships with those they have met and are unable to connect with in other ways. Through their use, SNSs not only influence the ways in which people connect and relate, but also shape the tools that make this connection possible.

Likewise, place-based mobile games might serve as the catalyst for learners becoming involved with local issues in a community, as well as multilingual collaboration with residents for the creation of additional game experiences related to current and historical issues affecting the community. Through this involvement, learners move beyond roles as passive visitors or "tourists" to integrated members of the local community with agency and the ability to make decisions that have an impact. Ultimately, by becoming active participants in communities via mediated contexts, learners are empowered to make decisions and contribute to the communities in significant ways.

2.2   Overview of Current Research

In recent years, CALL research has witnessed an increased interest in the areas of both digital games and SNSs for L2 learning. Nevertheless, the

5   Guilds are organized, hierarchical groups that play together in order to accomplish high-level tasks in a game.

availability of empirical work is still limited, making it ill advised to suggest concrete conclusions about when, how, and in what ways each can best be adapted for L2 learning. Instead, many of the conclusions presented here should be viewed as catalysts for continued work in this area.

2.2.1 Massively multiplayer online games Of the three mediated contexts explored here, MMOGs have received the most attention by CALL researchers. Additional related work in other areas includes the exploration of social virtualities, such as *Second Life* (Lee & Hoadley, 2007; Sadler, 2012) and Synthetic Immersive Environments (Sykes, 2009, 2010, 2013, 2014; Sykes, Oskoz, & Thorne, 2008; Zheng et al., 2009);[6] however, our focus here remains on studies specifically examining MMOGs for L2 learning.

While the existence of MMOGs is relatively recent, interest in games for language learning is not (see, Hubbard, 1991; Phillips, 1987). Even with this initial interest, it is not until recently that empirical work specifically examining MMOGs has emerged in the field. While reviews and research overviews can be found elsewhere (see, for example, Cornillie, Thorne, & Desmet, 2012; Sykes & Reinhardt, 2012), the focus of this chapter remains our discussion of how communities are conceived and maintained as social consequences of the collaborative behaviors inherent in MMOG gameplay, as well as the surrounding attendant discourses (e.g., discussion forums, machinima groups, and modding communities)[7] relevant to their use. This work includes evidence of established learning communities (e.g., Bryant, 2006; Peterson, 2013; Reinhardt & Zander, 2011), as well as access to diversity and complexity of written and spoken discourse and authentic texts through MMOG communities (e.g., Liang, 2012; Reinhardt, 2013; Thorne, Fischer, & Lu, 2012). Furthermore, as players advance to higher levels of the game, they develop the social behaviors and communication skills to become more prominent, dynamic, and meaningful members of a variety of game-related communities (e.g., Peña & Hancock, 2006; Thorne, Black, & Sykes, 2009). We see evidence of this through authentic socio-literacy practice (Steinkuehler, 2008; Thorne, Black, & Sykes, 2009) and language socialization (e.g., Piiranen-Marsh & Tainio, 2009; Zheng et al., 2009).

6   For a detailed description of work in these related areas see Thorne, Black, & Sykes (2009) and Sykes & Reinhardt (2012).

7   Machinima groups create cinema with computer graphics engines, oftentimes from video games. Modding communities alter video game content in a way not originally intended by the game designer and utilize the Internet to share their creations.

Table 1 Summary of characteristics of MMOGs for L2 learning (adapted from Sykes & Reinhardt, 2012: 10–11)

Characteristic	Description	References
Goal orientation & goal-directed activity	Parallel to a task-based approach to language learning, quest completion forms the underlying architecture of gameplay in MMOGs. By completing quests, players are rewarded with experience and items in the game. Players have choices from among hundreds of quests and, often, must work with others who have complementary skills for successful completion.	Gee (2003); Purushotma, Thorne, & Wheatley (2008); Sykes, Reinhardt, & Thorne (2010).
Social consequence & interconnectedness	MMOGs are high-stakes, meaningful spaces with social consequences for the players and their relationships with others. Although the tasks themselves have little "real"-world impact outside of the fantasy space of the game, the collaborative behaviors and social relationships are very real and meaningful.	Nardi, Ly, & Harris (2007); Purushotma, Thorne, & Wheatley (2008); Squire & Steinkuehler (2006); Sykes, Reinhardt, & Thorne (2010); Thorne & Black (2007); Thorne, Black, & Sykes (2009).
Language socialization	Gameplay and participation in MMOG communities lead learners towards increasingly complex, dynamic, and intimate relationships related to both in-game and about-game contexts. In becoming more adept at these interactions, learners are socialized to the community, moving from outsiders to insiders.	Nardi, Ly, & Harris (2007); Squire & Steinkuehler (2006); Thorne & Black (2007); Thorne, Black, & Sykes (2009).
Complex, meaningful feedback	Feedback is given to players at multiple levels in meaningful ways, making experimentation and fail-states critical to successful advancement and skill-building.	Gee (2003); Purushotma, Thorne, & Wheatley (2008); Sykes, Reinhardt, & Thorne (2010)
Engagement	Players are immersed in the gameplay activity and, although challenging, find the experiences to be rewarding long-term.	Purushotma, Thorne, & Wheatley (2008).

Players have the opportunity to build relationships with others that traverse international boundaries and languages, an especially important advantage for L2 learning.

In a case study of L2 intercultural communication in the MMOG *World of Warcraft*, Thorne (2008) describes a trilingual interaction (Russian and English, with one Latin proverb) in which two players (Meme and Zomn) engage in a variety of strategies encouraged in L2 learning environments. Utilizing data from a recorded chat log, observation, and personal interaction with one of the participants, Thorne analyzes MMOGs as a site for L2 intercultural communication. During a collaborative questing activity, Meme and Zomn exhibit behaviors that ultimately lead to further inclusion in the in-game and associated communities. These include:

- negotiation of meaning,
- explicit feedback,
- drawing on external resources,
- translation, and
- reciprocal interaction between expert and novice.

Each of these strategies leads the learner towards more intimate relationships with his or her fellow players and is exhibited as they are engaging in a common task within the game itself.

Soares (2010) further confirms the usefulness of *World of Warcraft* as a space for L2 socialization and pragmatic development. Data was collected over the course of eight months via ethnographic observation of two language learners, the researcher and one other focal participant. Special attention was given to pragmatic development and language socialization. This ethnographic study of these two learners of Spanish reveals that they do indeed adopt pragmatic conventions of the online space and, through game advancement, develop some, although not all, L2 pragmatic abilities related to complex, in-game social interactions (e.g., refusals, humor). Although both studies are small-scale examples of the complex relationships and communities possible in MMOGs, they document meaningful intercultural communication via this mediated context.

Additional empirical research specifically related to MMOGs is undoubtedly emerging. While much remains focused on lexical development (deHaan, Reed, & Kuwada, 2010; Hitosugi, Schmidt, & Hayashi, 2014; Neville, 2010; Purushotma, 2005; Sundqvist & Sylvén, 2012), other critical aspects of MMOGs for community engagement are also emerging (e.g., see Sykes, 2016). The few explored here suggest the benefits of MMOG exploration for integration in target communities via mediated contexts.

2.2.2 Social networking sites While general inquiry is prominent in the fields of sociology, computer science, and business, there remains a paucity of empirical research specifically examining SNSs related to L2 learning. In a review of SNSs for language learning, McBride (2009) explores ways in which SNSs might be both beneficial and challenging in L2 classrooms. The proposed benefits include identity performance and self-authorship, student agency in learning, and pragmatic development. Disadvantages include difficulty in implementation, privacy concerns, superficial inter-action, narcissism, technical problems, and challenges in bridging educa-tional and social domains. She concludes with suggestions for classroom implementation including the creation of alternative, classroom-only SNSs, fake or simulated profiles, group profiles, global simulations, media shar-ing (e.g., photos, videos), and themed responses. These suggestions seek to make interactive aspects of SNSs available in the L2 classroom; yet, they do not fundamentally shift the learners' social networking behavior beyond the classroom to meaningful experiences as part of existing communities. In fact, the simulated nature of the activities themselves may be resented by students in SNSs, more so than in other simulated activities, since social networking is so familiar and integrated in their everyday lives, a caution also pointed out by McBride (2009). The pedagogical implications section suggests ways in which alternative classroom activities might take advan-tage of the very personal nature of SNSs to engage L2 learners with target communities.

In a study beginning to address ways to take advantage of SNSs for building classroom community and sociopragmatic competence, Blattner & Fiori (2009) describe the use of the "Groups" feature of Facebook. Through observation and reflection on authentic Facebook groups from the target culture, they suggest learners can be exposed to a multiplicity of pragmatic behaviors and language varieties which will be useful for further involve-ment beyond mere observation, such as posting and interacting in the groups themselves or commenting on others' posts. While formal experi-mental results are not given, anecdotal evidence suggests this has been a positive addition to their learners' classroom experience and parallels what we suggest below as the first pedagogical stage for integrating new medi-ated contexts in the language classroom. Extending their work to include sociopragmatic competence, Blattner & Fiori (2011) present findings from a study of 13 intermediate learners of Spanish via Facebook. Results indicate a positive impact on learners' sociopragmatic competence as reflected by a qualitative analysis of a series of thematically-directed posts in Facebook. In this case, these learners demonstrated improved understanding of greet-ings and leave-takings and benefited from exposure to a variety of language and colloquialisms. As such, SNSs can serve as a meaningful site for developing the language skills needed for successful engagement.

Other recent studies have examined SNSs in intensive English programs in universities in the United States with varying outcomes. Mitchell (2009) describes a qualitative case study of nine participants with different levels of involvement in the Facebook community. Analysis entailed a dataset consisting of initial and final interviews, as well as detailed participant observation. Although it was not their purpose for joining the Facebook community, six of the seven learners who used Facebook felt they had improved their English based on their experience. For these learners, Facebook also served as a productive site for cultural exchange (i.e., learning about US culture or displaying pride in one's own culture) and a place to strengthen existing ties and friendships in both English and their native language.

However, other studies in the same context reveal less promising outcomes. With the intention of "introducing SNS practice as a means for socialization, English use, and IEP community practice," Reinhardt & Zander (2011: 334) present the in-class Facebook experiences of 11 learners of English who engaged in two experiential and three critical awareness activities over the course of two weeks. Results demonstrate general interest and learning on the part of the participants in combination with a notable resistance to Facebook activities in light of the need to pass high stakes tests such as the TOEFL. Of similar note are Zárate & Cisterna's (2017) findings related to the use of Instagram as a classroom intervention for writing. In their small action research study, nine L2 English learners were required to post stories to the SNS. All learners reported that they did not have any sociopragmatic gains from their experience, and almost half (n=4) reported a general frustration with the platform itself. While the frustration experienced by learners is certainly not ideal, it indicates, when taken in concert with the aforementioned frustrations in Reinhardt & Zander (2011), that forcing learner presence in a SNS space does not necessarily yield sociopragmatic gains or the assimilation of community behaviors and practices. Learners must be given the space to notice these behaviors before they can adopt them, as in Blattner & Fiori (2011), and some degree of learner agency in choosing the SNS and/or the community behaviors and norms they wish to observe and evaluate is likely critical to success in formal classroom contexts.

Mixed empirical results point to a continued need for investigating SNSs for L2 learning. As outlined here, early research speaks to their potential for engaging learners with the target language and other speakers as well as the challenges of integrating them into a formal instructional context.

2.2.3 Place-based, augmented reality games Much of the promising research done around place-based mobile games centers on science and social studies (Holden et al., 2015; Mathews, 2010; Klopfer, 2008; Klopfer & Squire, 2008; Squire et al., 2007), but even there, the aim is to produce learning aligned with community-oriented goals similar to those cited above. They seek to enable active learning, relevant to outside groups of people in a way that extends beyond the classroom experience. The place, interest in it and its issues, and the continuing impact of this reality on students motivate a deep and ongoing connection to local community as a purpose and an extension of classroom study.

In the first project examining the development of place-based mobile games for language learning, we see similar promise (Holden & Sykes, 2011). *Mentira* is a place-based, augmented reality mobile game specifically created for L2 language learning. It is a historically-situated Spanish-language mystery where players must work together to solve a local murder.[8] Set in a Spanish-speaking neighborhood in Albuquerque, NM, it plays out much like a historical novel in which fact and fiction combine to set the context and social conditions for meaningful interaction (in Spanish) with simulated characters, other players, and local citizens. While playing *Mentira*, learners must investigate clues and talk to various non-player characters to absolve their own family, proving they are not responsible for a murder in a local neighborhood. In a core component of the game, players are required to visit the local neighborhood in order to collect additional clues and, ultimately, solve the mystery by determining the responsible party.

Participation in the game itself involves the players in the particularities of the neighborhood where the narrative is set; Spanish is not a generic language of exposition here, but rather used specifically to create characters who embody local culture and history. The choices in the game require players to both navigate the personalities and situations involved and to literally decode text. Interpretation of clues to the murder requires understanding of their context. The trip to the local neighborhood as a part of gameplay reveals the setting not as some imaginary or far-off place, but serves to

---

8   The game software runs on Apple iOS devices running iOS version 4 or later, and is available for review at mentira.org. It is not intended to be used alone and outside the larger instructional and local context, but can be run for demonstration purposes. ARIS, the open-source software on which *Mentira* is based, is a general purpose AR app and authoring tool. ARIS can be downloaded free at the iTunes App Store, and the authoring tool is a web-based, drag-and-drop interface. More information on ARIS can be found at arisgames.org.

uncover for learners an aspect of their lived experience that has likely been hidden from them, an area of life penetrated by the use of Spanish.

Students learn to rely on each other to understand their own participation in the narrative, as information is spread out across players in a classic jigsaw. We also see emergent development of communal activity around gameplay whether by ad hoc differentiation of player roles (such as the designation of a vocabulary person in a group), or by groups deciding to adopt different styles of gameplay as it relates to Spanish (such as a group agreeing to only talk in Spanish among themselves during the neighborhood visit part of the game). Thus, we see groups of students acting more like a CoP in their pursuit of a foreign language than a room full of individual and isolated learners.

Interviews with players after the game also suggest that *Mentira* provides a connection between local place and culture and their interest in and pursuit of the Spanish language. Excerpts (1) and (2) are reflective of this practice:

Excerpt (1)
> *Going somewhere else, having somewhere actually ... at a place set in around Los Griegos ... was a difference, it was a breath of fresh air, and I enjoyed it...immensely.* (R1, lines 53–56, Fall 2009)

Excerpt (2)
> *... I feel that one of the hardest things in my ... Spanish classes, is interaction and getting to interact with other students and um to interact with something that feels more like a real world language situation than the classroom ... I think the game provided that real world interface where I didn't feel like I was just learning Spanish in some kind of ... I think it's awesome way to learn.* (A1, lines 28–33, Fall 2009)

Beyond players' interactions with the game as designed, Squire et al.'s (2007) and Mathews' (2010) investigations of teacher and student design suggest that significant local research and game design opportunities could provide more meaningful and lasting interactions among students themselves, as well as between students and outside language community members.

More recent work has also yielded meaningful insights about the nature of learning communities as facilitated by a place-based, augmented reality game. Findings from a set of microanalyses of gameplay discourse indicate a meaningful facilitative role of the place-based, augmented reality game *ChronoOps* for language learners (Hellermann, Thorne, & Fodor, 2017;

Thorne & Hellermann, 2017). As such, the game in which learners are tasked with coming back from the future to save the environment through sustainability serves as an affordance for social and embodied reading experiences within the language learning community. Furthermore, it adds significant context to the experience while catalyzing community learning behaviors essential to action taking. Furthermore, utilizing a pro-social stance common to place-based games, *ChronoOps* adds a strong overlay of community integration and collective responsibility for the sustainability efforts (e.g., bike commuting, rainwater collection), that can lead to reduced effect of climate change. As a result, their participation connects learners, not only to their micro-learning group, but also the larger surrounding community as well.

3   Research Approaches

As can be seen from the sparse literature on each of these topics, empirical research in these areas is both critical and timely as MMOGs, SNSs, and mobile devices become more prevalent in everyday life, and educators look for ways to create designed experiences, such as place-based mobile games, to leverage community in L2 learning environments. Language socialization via community involvement in MMOGs, SNSs, and place-based mobile games is key for second language acquisition, especially in the areas of pragmatic acquisition, literacy skills, and intercultural competence (Reinhardt & Zander, 2011; Thorne, Black, & Sykes, 2009; Thorne, Sauro, & Smith, 2015). Furthermore, the benefits derived from task-based learning (e.g., Ellis, 2003; González-Lloret & Ortega, 2014; Van den Branden, Bygate, & Norris, 2009), negotiation of meaning (e.g., Pica, Kanagy, & Falodun, 1993), and scaffolded feedback (e.g., Lantolf & Thorne, 2006) in each of these spaces affords opportunities for meaningful linguistic development at the lexical, syntactic, pragmatic, and discourse analytic levels.[9]

Currently, two evident trends emerge in research involving digital technologies – one which focuses on mediated contexts as practice spaces that build skills with the intention of transfer to the "real" world, and another which situates mediated contexts as relevant spaces themselves that have an impact on other contexts of language use. Any empirical data adds to our insight of how to best use these spaces; however, the second approach, by entertaining a more comprehensive perspective, moves us to unite classroom and real-world experiences. It "allows for the analysis of, not only

9   For a detailed discussion of SLA theory in each of these areas see Sykes & Reinhardt (2012).

mediated activity, but also the scope, scale, and communities of practice that construct, and are constructed by, the use of emerging technological tools." (Sykes, Reinhardt, & Thorne, 2010). This is critical for our ongoing discussion of how mediated spaces can be used to enhance learners' participation in a variety of communities. In terms of MMOGs and SNSs, this means research addressing a variety of questions.[10] These might include, for example:

- How can MMOGs and SNSs best be used to facilitate learners' assimilation into a variety of communities of practice?
- Are there specific MMOGs and SNSs better suited to L2 development than others? If so, why is this the case? What are other contextual factors that may (or may not) have an impact on learners' community involvement?
- How can learners themselves construct these learning experiences to make their own L2 experience more personal, relevant, and authentic?

Furthermore, in the case of place-based, augmented reality games, we must also focus attention on the design and implementation of games specifically directed towards enhancing L2 learners' experiences in the target communities. This includes questions related to gameplay experiences, community involvement, learner game design, and curricular integration.

4   Pedagogical Implications

Much of the research described above, and, in many cases, the lack of such research in these areas, remarks on the significant distance between digitally-mediated spaces and current classroom practices. Nonetheless, movement has been made in addressing the use of these spaces in practical pedagogy. Drawing on principles from the New London Group's (1996) pedagogical model for multiliteracies as well as Thorne & Reinhardt's (2008) more recent proposal of *bridging activities,* this section includes pedagogical implications for considering digital games, SNSs, and place-based mobile games in terms of successful maneuvering among various communities of practice. Both models advocate the use of new media (i.e., mediated contexts) with rigorous analytic and reflection techniques to expand learners' repertoires in terms of language comprehension, use, and creation. As with

10   For research suggestions related to other areas of language learning see
Sykes, Reinhardt, & Thorne (2010) and Thorne, Black, & Sykes (2009).

any pedagogical innovation, tool selection and implementation consideration must be guided by target learning outcomes prior to task design and curricular decisions. Most importantly, these choices should be guided by pedagogical and learning needs and not the desire to use a specific technological tool. Digital games, SNSs, and place-based mobile games offer significant potential for addressing complex discourse features critical to meaningful membership and participation in communities. The suggestions presented here are by no means comprehensive, but rather ideas educators can use to help students transition their target language use beyond the traditional classroom.

4.1 Task Design

When designing tasks intended to aid L2 learners in becoming part of a community, it is critical to move away from activities that function as merely practice activities for the classroom towards potentially meaningful experiences that prepare learners for active participation in a variety of communities. In this subsection, we examine three stages of task design and the contexts through which the task design would likely be most effectively realized.

The first stage in this process, as outlined by both the New London Group (1996) and Thorne & Reinhardt (2008), is awareness of social practices, discourses, and products related to the communities being considered. This stage is accomplished through the observation of one's own practices in a variety of mediated contexts, as well as passive participation in the target CoPs to collect general observations about the practices of other members of said communities. Table 2 provides activity suggestions for facilitating this stage in the classroom. These activities are likely best realized with a 1:1 device-to-user ratio to promote learner-driven exploration, but teachers will find collaborative (co)construction of meaning in small groups or as a class to be a necessary scaffolding mechanism to promote purely autonomous behavior and to increase instances of noticing community behaviors and norms. Given these affordances, teachers with less technological infrastructure should not shy away from the activities below, but rather think creatively about how to facilitate maximum learner authentication of the learning tasks.

While the emphasis of activities at this stage is to encourage learners to reflect on their own practices as members of communities in different mediated contexts, learners should collect various artifacts (e.g., transcripts, observations, chat logs, photographs) as they observe. These artifacts are critical to the the next phase, using collected artifacts for guided exploration

(Thorne & Reinhardt, 2008), overt instruction, and critical framing (New London Group, 1996). Learners move from data collection to inquiry and scrutiny, engaging in detailed analyses of target language community practices to develop skills and understanding that will enable them to appropriately participate in target communities (or to consciously flout community norms). Table 3 provides activity suggestions for engaging learners in deep thought and thorough analysis.

At this stage explicit discussion and examples from mediated contexts should be used to guide learners towards a greater understanding of language and social practices in the contexts being considered.

In the final and most important stage, learners are encouraged to actively participate in a variety of communities via the mediated contexts they previously analyzed. This stage should promote learner agency in the type, context, and level of participation related to the communities being considered (not all learners want to be part of all communities and can be given choices as to their type of participation), and even documentation of that experience for classroom purposes (for this reason, we do not identify how learners should document their engagement in Table 3). In language acquisition contexts, all learners should be encouraged to focus on participation in communities related to the target language and culture. Given the learner-driven

Table 2 Observation activities

	Self-reflection	Reflection of others
MMOG activity	Comparative analysis of one's own behaviors in the game space with one's behaviors in an offline community.	Observational notebook that documents how others participate in MMOG communities. This notebook may be open-ended or scaffolded with the use of templates to guide observation.
SNS activity	Log that documents students' SNS activities (how many times they log in, what they do in the SNSs, and the communities they interact with in that space).	Journal of recorded observations of interactions on various SNS communities (fan pages, corporate and commercial sites, and personal pages).
Place-based mobile games	List of behaviors provided by teacher. Learners check off those they engage in when acting as an individual and those they engage in when acting as part of a CoP and compare the lists.	Visit to a selected local community to observe abstract concepts (e.g., beauty, systems, and change), pragmatic aspects of language use, or community issues tangibly in real time.

Table 3 Guided exploration activities

	Discourse analysis	Research and experimentation
MMOGs	Lexicon analysis to identify language use to establish expert membership in a targeted community, the appropriate pragmatic features of language used to perform specific language functions, and/or the appropriate tone and level of formality of interactions.	Writing predictions in a journal about how flouting a specific pattern of language use or behavior might impact ultimate success in gameplay. Verifying predictions with gameplay.
SNSs	Small-group analysis of how language is used to construct communities, sustain membership, and form community identity.	Class discussion to identify behaviors (e.g., using hashtags or reposting) that appear to impact community development in SNSs. Learners imagine and verify how/if alternative behaviors might impact community building and how/if a person's degree of proximity in their social spheres (e.g., their friends are very proximate, while the general public is not) influences said impact.
Place-based mobile games	Individual analysis of recorded game interactions (emergent discourses) to discover one's own behavior and language patterns and consider the extent to which those are reflective of community norms.	Class discussion regarding dichotomous relationship between individuality and community, behaviors that instantiate inclusion or exclusion in communities, and target language use in specific contexts. This discussion is validated through behavior and language pattern experimentation during gameplay in a targeted local community.

nature, it is ideal for learners to have access to individual devices or shared devices they are allowed to direct with autonomy for a particular period of time. However, learners wishing to participate in the same community could ostensibly share devices for accessing and interacting within that community. Table 4 provides activity examples for this stage that can easily be adapted to one's existing technological infrastructure.

Table 4 Community participation activities

	Experience	Extend
MMOGs	Immersion in a community associated with the MMOG gameplay,	Participation in attendant discourse communities through the creation of fan-fiction, collaborating as part of a machinima group, or modding.
SNSs	Participation in an existing group with shared experiences or interests in the target language on a SNS.	Creation of a group for others to join and recruitment of members in a manner that is appropriate to the given SNS context.
Place-based mobile games	Formation of a design-based CoP with teachers, students, and/or researchers that is responsible for producing place-based content.	Collaboration with local communities to develop games that promote community exploration and engagement in a way that is sensitive to community practices.

Though this stage is presented as distinct from the analysis phase, it is important to note that success in this stage will require ongoing analysis and awareness of behavioral and language patterns and how those patterns impact community development. Yet, this analysis is not the central crux of these activities. Ultimately, the goal of all of these activities is to transition learners' L2 use and community involvement beyond L1 monolingual experiences and L2 classroom experiences towards multilingual experiences in all areas of their social and professional lives. Intentioned exploration of prominent mediated contexts (i.e., MMOGs, SNSs, and place-based mobile games) is one way, though certainly not the only way, to do this.

4.2 Assessment and Evaluation of Outcomes

Evaluating learning outcomes of the activities above is both a complex and staged process. It is not enough to merely examine products learners create or to count the number of communities in which they participate. The process of analysis and integration must also be considered.

In formal classroom contexts, assessment can be handled in a number of ways. The first, as advocated by Thorne & Reinhardt (2008), is the creation of a portfolio in which the learners collect artifacts, include various analyses of different discourse practices, and self-reflect on their own behaviors. This can be an especially powerful tool for learners' own analysis of their progress throughout the course and can serve as documentation of their enhanced participation in different online communities. Another form of evaluation that would include specific examples as well as self-reflection on the socialization process could be a classroom lesson delivered by students regarding a targeted language function that details examples of what they have observed and analyzed in a targeted mediated space. These lessons could be used to foster a classroom comparison of language functions across online platforms or even the creation of a classroom website for language learners in which they provide sociopragmatic tips to other learners. An additional form of evaluation would be keeping a field notebook to document observation and analysis and using that information to ultimately deliver an artifact that is meaningful for the community, either created by learners (likely in social media platforms) or by adding to the community in some tangible way (e.g., the creation and participation in attendant discourses such as fan fiction related to MMOG play or the development of a place-based experience used by community members).

The choice of evaluation measures is highly dependent upon the target learning objectives as well as the level of the learners. In fact, many of the activities presented in the previous section are most appropriate for intermediate or advanced learners, and the highest levels of achievement on the rubrics provided below necessitate such a proficiency level. However, there is great potential for novice learners to begin the analysis of macro-level discourse features, especially if the L1 is used for analysis and reflection. Yet, no matter the proficiency level, evaluating the success of learners at each of the three stages previously provided is necessary. Since language-specific rubrics are highly dependent on the proficiency level of learners at hand and the functional language goals identified by the practitioner (or more ideally, by the learners with the practitioner's guidance), a series of mastery rubrics, or rubrics that capture the capacity of learners to move beyond collection of knowledge to application of that knowledge in meaningful contexts (Ambrose et al., 2010), is provided below. These rubrics could be used by themselves as a way of evaluating *21st century skills* or incorporated into another rubric as a separate criterion. Words in brackets should be updated by practitioners and/or learners to reflect their specific learning targets and contexts of exploration and interaction.

Awareness The rubric in Table 5 offers an approach to evaluating learners engaged in observation of digitally-mediated target communities and self-reflection regarding their own behaviors as members of communities.

Table 5 Observation rubric

Score	Description
0	Learner's work does not reflect any of the descriptors below.
1	Learner documents observations of [the targeted community] in [a mediated context].
2	Learner documents observations of [the targeted community] in [a mediated context] and supports those observations with [a variety of artifacts] collected during observation.
3	Learner documents observations of [the target community] in [a mediated context] and supports those observations with [a variety of artifacts] collected during observation. Learner offers some reflection about personal engagement in [relevant mediated communities].
4	Learner documents observations of [the target community] in [a mediated context] and supports those observations with [a variety of artifacts] collected during observation. Learner offers in-depth, supported reflection about personal engagement in [relevant mediated communities].

Guided exploration The rubric in Table 6 offers an approach to evaluating the extent to which learners are able to scrutinize and evaluate the artifacts collected in the awareness stage.

Table 6 Awareness rubric

Score	Descriptor
0	Learner's work does not reflect any of the descriptors below.
1	Learner identifies language and behavioral patterns associated with [a targeted community] in [a mediated context].
2	Learner identifies language and behavioral patterns associated with [a targeted community] in [a mediated context]. These language and behavioral patterns are supported with artifacts collected from observation.
3	Learner develops product(s) (e.g., a list of norms, hypotheses) related to [sociopragmatic behavior] in [a targeted community] in [a mediated context] that is based on observed and documented language and behavioral patterns.
4	Learner develops product(s) (e.g., a list of norms, hypotheses) related to [sociopragmatic behavior] in [a targeted community] in [a mediated context] that is based on observed and documented language and behavioral patterns. Learner demonstrates clear, supported understanding of the consequences of flouting [targeted community] norms.

Active participation The rubric in Table 7 offers an approach to evaluating the extent to which learners demonstrate evidence of being able to actively participate in targeted communities in mediated contexts, effectively moving toward multilingual experiences in all areas of their lives.

Table 7 Community participation rubric

Score	Descriptor
0	Learner's work does not reflect any of the descriptors below.
1	Learner provides evidence of engagement with [the targeted community] in [a mediated context].
2	Learner provides evidence of self-reflection related to personal engagement with [the targeted community] in [a mediated context]. This self-reflection is centered on successes and failures related to emulating [targeted language and/or behavioral patterns].
3	Learner provides evidence of self-reflection related to personal engagement with [the targeted community] in [a mediated context]. Successes and failures are identified related to emulating [targeted language and/or behavioral patterns], and intentionality in behavioral and language choices is evident in the artifacts collected to document the experience.
4	Learner provides evidence of self-reflection related to personal engagement with [the targeted community] in [a mediated context]. Successes and failures are identified related to emulating [targeted language and/or behavioral patterns], and intentionality in behavioral and language choices is evident in the artifacts collected to document the experience.
	Learner provides evidence of movement away from classroom-centered or motivated community engagement toward integration with target language communities in his or her life beyond the classroom.

Ultimately, as we have already mentioned, the goal to enable learners to use language beyond the school setting, where the evaluation of outcomes would be long-term and move away from conventional classroom evaluation, is relevant to learners of all proficiency levels. Essentially, to get learners to engage meaningfully with L2 communities is to spark the potential to contribute to lifelong engagement with the target language and culture.

5   Conclusion

The need for educators to connect L2 learners to target communities, to produce life-long, meaningful participation in these spaces, is clear. However, just what a language community is, is not a simple or fixed matter, nor is the constitution of membership or participation. There are new forms of social grouping around language being created every day, many of which are not accounted for in traditional notions of shared-community around a target language. We have presented here some of these new interaction spaces introduced by innovations in technology, what it might mean to participate in them within a vein of attaining intercultural competence, and how it might be possible to structure such participation within a classroom, or leverage it in connection to classroom activities. This is merely a beginning. The only thing we know for sure is that there is a lot of work yet to be done.

Questions for Reflection

1. The concept of "community" encompasses a wide variety of different meanings and practices, particularly when considering MMOGs, SNSs, place-based mobile games. What are some of the consequences of these differences for teachers and learners? How are learners aware of any similarities or differences?
2. Have you created any activities to use in your classroom that encourage students to act as a community of practice? Do they have a common goal? Why would such a goal be desirable?
3. Are students aware of communities that they could engage with that are connected to their L2 learning? In what ways are they aware of or able to participate in these practices? How can you facilitate exploration and participation in these practices?
4. What are some sources of conflict or tension between the pedagogical models integrated here (i.e., New London Group, 1996; Thorne & Reinhardt, 2008) and those that are more commonly present in a second language classroom?
5. What directions for additional research would be especially relevant for your own interest in understanding communities and MMOGs, SNSs, place-based mobile games?
6. Pretend you created an online course that uses SNSs and place-based mobile experiences to encourage learners to leverage their experiences in the community as vehicles to improve language acquisition. The teacher chosen to pilot the course is hesitant to have learners develop their place-based mobile experiences. Craft an explanation of the unique affordances to learning of designing place-based mobile experiences.

Key Terms

communities communities of practice

massively multiplayer online games

place-based augmented reality mobile games

social networking sites

Case Studies

Teaching (A)

Allison has expressed interest in learning language in your class for the primary purpose of playing a MMOG with native speakers. She is tired of playing on her L1 servers and is interested in becoming a prominent member of a guild in the L2. You have been considering incorporating digital games in your classroom in some way, but want to be sure they meet the needs of all your students. You begin by talking with Allison about her interests in MMOGs and ways in which they might be meaningful L2 communities. Together you come up with a list of possible advantages and ways in which MMOGs might be made useful. This includes the potential for authentic interaction(s), multilayer feedback and participation progresses, literacy development, and various opportunities to collect artifacts for evaluation and assessment (e.g., chat logs, screen capture, and forum participation). After talking with Allison, you work with MMOGs to incorporate them in your class.

Discussion Questions:

1. Create a list of three class-related activities that prepare Allison and your other students for community membership in the target MMOG community. For each of the three activities, be sure to describe the learning objective, the activity, and the outcomes assessment.

Activity	Learning Objective	Assessment of Outcomes
(1)		
(2)		
(3)		

2. How would you integrate the activities created above with the rest of your foreign language classroom experience?

3. What are some potential drawbacks and obstacles you might face in implementing these activities? How will you overcome them? Be sure to consider issues of technological access as well as those that concern integrating gameplay into language learning (e.g., the extent to which learners are able to direct their own gameplay may impact their ability to integrate within the targeted community/ies).

4. How you will evaluate the overall success (or failure) of your students' MMOG experience in the target language? How do you analyze separately concept and implementation?

Teaching (B)

A colleague of yours has just created a place-based mobile scavenger hunt with the purpose of learning Chinese in the local Chinatown community close to his university. He put a great deal of effort into making the game. At first, his students seemed really excited about it. However, at the end of the experience, they reported to have not enjoyed the experience. He received the following feedback from his students.

(A) "I liked the idea and love the food and history I saw, but didn't really get a feel for the people in the community. I wish we could have been more involved and talked to more people."

(B) "The game was great at first, but was too spread out and didn't allow us to really get to know one place."

(C) "It was cool to observe the community, but I always felt like an outsider rather than a participant."

Help your colleague improve his game by answering the following questions.

Discussion Questions:

1. What are three techniques your colleague could use to engage learners with the local community via your place-based mobile game on a deeper level?

2. What involvement should/could your colleague have with the members of the Chinatown experience to enhance the game?

3. What could your colleague do to address comment (C) and focus more on interaction than local cultural artifacts?

4. How could learners themselves be more a part of the design process? How would you build this design work into your colleague's curriculum?

Ideas for Action Research Projects

- Spend 1–2 hours participating in an MMOG (e.g., playing the first 2–3 levels), observing an *Instagram* (e.g., reading comments, observing posting conventions), and/or playing a place-based mobile game that involves interaction in the community and then brainstorm ways in which the various spaces might be useful for L2 learning.
- Survey learners on their current use of MMOGs, SNSs, and place-based mobile games in general and for language learning. What are the pedagogical implications of the results? To what extent do learners value these sources for their potential to teach more than vocabulary?
- Investigate how MMOGs and SNSs can best facilitate learners' assimilation into a variety of communities of practice using online data collection and classroom integration of a variety of analysis and reflection practices.
- Have learners play and build place-based mobile games or other place-based experiences using augmented reality tools such as QR codes or *Aurasma* to better understand ways in which they themselves are able to construct authentic learning experiences and engagement with the local community.
- Track learners' participation in multilingual communities beyond their participation in a foreign language course to determine the ways in which lifelong engagement may or may not be attained.
- Design a study in which you specifically address community assimilation through SNSs in a university classroom context. Consider factors such as limited access to mobile devices and consider how the teacher or researcher's involvement in the community might promote or discourage authentic interactions by students.

References

ACTFL. (n.d). *World-readiness standards for learning languages*. Retrieved from https://www.actfl.org/sites/default/files/publications/standards/World-Readine ssStandardsforLearningLanguages.pdf

Ambrose, S. A., Bridges, M., DiPietro, M., Lovett, M. C., Norman, M. K. & Mayer, R. E. (2010). How do students develop mastery? In *How learning works: Seven research-based principles for smart teaching*, pp. 91–120. San Francisco: Jossey Bass.

Belz, J., and Thorne, S.L. (2005). *Internet-mediated intercultural foreign language education.* Boston: Thomson Heinle.

Blattner, G., & Fiori, M. (2009). Facebook in the language classroom: Promises and possibilities. *International Journal of Instructional Technology & Distance Learning,* 6(1). Retrieved from http://www.itdl.org/journal/jan_09/article02.htm

Blattner, G., & Fiori, M. (2011). Virtual social network communities: An investigation of language learners' development of sociopragmatic awareness and multiliteracy skills. *CALICO Journal,* 29(1), 24–43. https://doi.org/10.11139/cj.29.1.24-43

boyd, S., & Ellison, N. (2008). Social network sites: Definition, history, and scholarship. *Journal of Computer-Mediated Communication,* 13(1), 210–230. https://doi.org/10.1111/j.1083-6101.2007.00393.x

Bryant, T. (2006). Using World of Warcraft and other MMORPGs to foster a targeted, social, and cooperative approach toward language learning. *Academic Commons, The Library.* Retrieved from http://www.academiccommons.org/commons/essay/bryant-MMORPGs-for-SLA

Chun, D., Smith, B., & Kern, R. (2016). Technology in language use, language teaching, and language learning. *The Modern Language Journal.* 100, 64–80. https://doi.org/10.1111/modl.12302

Cornillie, F., Thorne, S. L., & Desmet, P. (eds.). (2012). Digital games for language learning: Challenges and opportunities. *ReCALL* [Special issue], 24, 243–380.

deFreitas, S. (2006). Learning in immersive worlds: A review of game-based learning. JISCE-Learning Programme.

deHaan, J., Reed, W. M., & Kuwada, K. (2010). The effect of interactivity with a music video game on second language vocabulary recall. *Language Learning & Technology,* 14, 74–94. Retrieved October 1, 2017, from http://llt.msu.edu/ vol14num2/dehaanreedkuwada.pdf

Deutschman, M., Panichi, L., & Molka-Danielsen, J. M. (2009). Designing oral participation in Second Life: A comparative study of two language proficiency courses. *ReCALL,* 21(2), 206–226.

Duggan, M. (2015). Games and gamers. *Pew Internet American Life Project.* http://www.pewinternet.org/2015/12/15/gaming-and-gamers/

Ellis, R. (2003). *Task-based language learning and teaching.* Oxford: Oxford University Press.

Gee, J. P. (2003). *What video games have to teach us about learning and literacy.* New York: Palgrave Macmillan.

Gee, J. P. (2007). *What video games have to teach us about learning and literacy* (2nd ed.). New York: St. Martin's Griffin.

González-Lloret, M., & Ortega, L. (2014). *Technology-mediated TBLT: Researching technology and tasks.* UK: John Benjamins. https://doi.org/10.1075/tblt.6

Hellermann, J., Thorne, S. L., & Fodor, P. (2017). Mobile reading as social and embodied practice. *Classroom Discourse,* 8(2), 99–121. https://doi.org/10.1080/19463014.2017.1328703

Hitosugi, C. I., Schmidt, M., & Hayashi, K. (2014). Digital game-based learning in the L2 classroom: The impact of the UN's off-the-shelf videogame, Food

Force, on learner affect and vocabulary retention. *CALICO Journal*, 31(1), 19–39. https://doi.org/10.11139/cj.31.1.19-39

Holden, C., Dikkers, S., Martin, J., & Litts, B. (2015). *Mobile media learning: Innovation and inspiration*. Philadelphia, PA: ETC Press.

Holden, C., & Sykes, J. (2011). Leveraging mobile games for place-based language learning. *International Journal of Game-Based Learning*, 1(2), 1–18. https://doi.org/10.4018/ijgbl.2011040101

Hubbard, P. (1991). Evaluating computer games for language learning. *Simulation and Gaming*, 22, 220–223.

Johnson, L., Levine, A., Smith, R., & Stone, S. (2010). *The 2010 Horizon Report*. Austin, Texas: The New Media Consortium.

Kline, R., & Pinch, T. (1996). Users as agents of technological change: The social construction of the automobile in the rural United States. *Technology and Culture*, 37(4), 763–795. https://doi.org/10.2307/3107097

Klopfer, E. (2008). *Augmented learning: Research and design of mobile educational games*. Cambridge. MA: MIT Press. https://doi.org/10.7551/mitpress/9780262113151.001.0001

Klopfer, E., & Squire, K. (2008), Environmental detectives – the development of an augmented reality platform for environmental simulations. *Educational Technology Research and Development*, 56(2), 203–228.

Kramsch, C. (ed.) (2002). *Language acquisition and language socialization. Ecological perspectives*. London: Continuum. https://doi.org/10.1007/s11423-007-9037-6

Lantolf, J., & Thorne, S. L. (2006). *Sociocultural theory and the genesis of second language development*. Oxford: Oxford University Press.

Lave, J., & Wenger, E. (1991). *Situated learning: Legitimate peripheral participation*. New York: Cambridge University Press. https://doi.org/10.1017/CBO9780511815355

Lee, J., & Hoadley, C. (2007). Leveraging identity to make learning fun: Possible selves and experiential learning in massively multiplayer online games (MMOGs). *Innovate*, 3(6). http://innovateonline.info/index.php?view=article%id=348

Liang, M. (2012). Foreign lucidity in online role-playing games. *Computer Assisted Language Learning*, 25, 455–473.

Mathews, J. (2010). Using a studio-based pedagogy to engage students in the design of mobile-based media. *English Teaching: Practice and Critique*, 9(1), 87–102.

McBride, K. (2009). Social networking sites in foreign language classes: Opportunities for recreation. In L. Lomika & G. Lord (eds.), *The second generation: Online collaboration and social networking in CALL*, pp. 35–58. CALICO Monograph Series. San Marcos, TX: CALICO.

McMillan, D. W. & Chavis, D.M. (1986). Sense of community: A definition and theory. *Journal of Community Psychology*, 14(1), 6–23.

Mitchell, K. (2009). *ESOL students on Facebook*. Unpublished MA thesis, Portland State University.

MLA. (2007). *Foreign languages in higher education: New structures for a changing world*. New York: Modern Language Association (MLA).

Nardi, B., Ly, S., & Harris, J. (2007). Learning conversations in World of Warcraft. In *Proceedings of the 2007 Hawaii international conference on systems science*, pp. 1–10. New York: IEEE Press. https://doi.org/10.1109/HICSS.2007.321

NCSSFL-ACTFL. (2017). *Can-do statements for intercultural communication*. Washington DC: American Council on the Teaching of Foreign Languages. Retrieved June 15, 2018, from https://www.actfl.org/publications/guidelines-and-manuals/ncssfl-actfl-can-do-statements

Neville, D. (2010). Structuring narrative in 3D digital game-based learning environments to support second language acquisition. *Foreign Language Annals*, 43, 446–469.

New London Group (1996). A pedagogy of multiliteracies. *Harvard Educational Review*, 66(1), 60–92. https://doi.org/10.17763/haer.66.1.17370n67v22j160u

Norris, C., & Soloway, E. (2009). A disruption is coming: A primer for educators on the mobile technology revolution. In A. Durin (ed.), *Mobile technology for children: Designing for interaction and learning*, pp. 83–98. Burlington, MA: Morgan Kaufman. https://doi.org/10.1016/B978-0-12-374900-0.00005-3

O'Brien, M. G., & Levy, R. M. (2008). Exploration through virtual reality: Encounters with the target culture. *Canadian Modern Language Review*, 64(4), 663–691.

O'Brien, M. G., Levy, R., & Orich, A. (2009). Virtual immersion: The role of CAVE and PC technology. *CALICO Journal*, 26(2), 337–362.

P21 (Partnership for 21st Century Learning). (2016). *Framework for 21st century learning*. Retrieved from http://www.p21.org/storage/documents/docs/P21_framework_0816.pdf

Peña, J., & Hancock, J. (2006). An analysis of socioemotional and task communication in online multiplayer video games. *Communication Research*, 33(1), 92–109. https://doi.org/10.1177/0093650205283103

Peterson, M. (2013). *Computer games and language learning*. New York: Palgrave Macmillan. https://doi.org/10.1057/9781137005175

Pew Research Center. (2018). *Social media fact sheet*. Retrieved from http://www.pewinternet.org/fact-sheet/social-media/

Phillips, M. (1987). Potential paradigms and possible problems for CALL. *System*, 15, 275–287.

Pica, T., Kanagy, R., & Falodun, J. (1993). Choosing and using communication tasks for second language research and instruction. In S. Gass and G. Crookes (eds.), *Task-based learning in a second language*. Clevedon: Multilingual Matters.

Piiranen-Marsh, A., & Tainio, L. (2009). Other-repetition as a resource for participation in the activity of playing a video game. *Modern Language Journal*, 93, 153–169.

Purushotma, R. (2005). Commentary: You're not studying, you're just.... *Language Learning & Technology*, 9(1), 80–96.

Purushotma, R., Thorne, S. L., & Wheatley, J. (2008). *Language learning and video games*. Paper produced for the Open Language & Learning Games Project,

Massachusetts Institute of Technology, funded by the William and Flora Hewlett Foundation. Retrieved from http://knol.google.com/k/ravi-purushotma/10-key-principles-for-designing-video/27mkxqba7b13/2

Reinhardt, J. (2013). Digital game-mediated foreign language teaching and learning: Myths, realities and opportunities. In M. Derivry-Plard, P. Faure, & C. Brudermann (eds.), *Apprendre les langues à l'université au 21ème siècle*, pp. 161–178. Paris: Riveneuve.

Reinhardt, J., and Zander, V. (2011). Social networking in an intensive English program classroom: A language socialization perspective. *CALICO Journal*, 28(2), 326–344. https://doi.org/10.11139/cj.28.2.326-344

Roschelle, J. and Pea, R. (2002). *A walk on the WILD side: how wireless handhelds may change CSCL*. Proceedings of CSCL 2002, pp. 51–60. https://doi.org/10.3115/1658616.1658624

Sadler, R. (2012). *Virtual worlds for language learning*. Peter Lang Publishing. https://doi.org/10.3726/978-3-0351-0406-6

Soares, D. (2010). Second language pragmatic socialization in World of Warcraft. Unpublished doctoral dissertation. University of California Davis.

Squire, K. (2009). Mobile media learning: multiplicities of place. *On the Horizon*, 17(1), 70–80. https://doi.org/10.1108/10748120910936162

Squire, K. D., Jan, M., Mathews, J., Wagler, M., Martin, J., Devane, B., & Holden, C. (2007). Wherever you go, there you are: The design of local games for learning. In B. Sheldon & D. Wiley (eds.), *The design and use of simulation computer games in education*, pp. 265–296. Rotterdam, Netherlands: Sense Publishing.

Squire, K., & Klopfer, E. (2007). Augmented reality simulations on handheld computers. *Journal of the Learning Sciences*, 16(3), 371–413. https://doi.org/10.1080/10508400701413435

Squire, K. D., & Steinkuehler, C. A. (2006). Generating cyber culture/s: The case of Star Wars Galaxies. In D. Gibbs & K. L. Krause (eds.), *Cyberlines 2.0 languages and cultures of the internet*, pp. 177–198. London: Wiley.

Steinkuehler, C. (2008). Massively multiplayer online games as an educational technology: An outline for research. *Educational Technology*, 48(1), 10–21.

Sundqvist, P., & Kerstin Sylvén, L. (2012). World of VocCraft: Computer games and Swedish learners' L2 English vocabulary. In H. Reinders (ed.), *Digital games in language learning and teaching*, pp. 189–208. New York: Palgrave Macmillan. https://doi.org/10.1057/9781137005267_10

Sykes, J. (2009). Learner requests in Spanish: Examining the potential of multiuser virtual environments for L2 pragmatic acquisition. In L. Lomika & G. Lord (eds.), *The second generation: Online collaboration and social networking in CALL*, pp. 199–234. CALICO Monograph Series. San Marcos, TX: CALICO.

Sykes, J. (2010). Multi-user virtual environments: User-driven design and implementation for language learning. In G. Vincenti & J. Braman (eds.), *Teaching through multi-user virtual environments: Applying dynamic elements to the modern classroom*, pp. 283–305.Hershey, PA: IGI Global.

Sykes, J. M. (2013). Multiuser virtual environments: Learner apologies in Spanish. In N. Taguchi & J. M. Sykes (eds.), *Technology in interlanguage pragmatics research and teaching*, pp. 71–100. Amsterdam: John Benjamins. https://doi.org/10.1075/lllt.36.05syk

Sykes, J. M. (2014). TBLT and synthetic immersive environments: What can in-game task restarts tell us about design and implementation? In M. González-Lloret & L. Ortega (eds.), *Technology-mediated TBLT: Researching technology and tasks*, pp. 149–182. Amsterdam: John Benjamins. https://doi.org/10.1075/tblt.6.06syk

Sykes, J. (2016). Technologies for teaching and learning intercultural competence and interlanguage pragmatics. In S. Sauro & C. Chapelle (eds.), *Handbook of technology and second language teaching and learning*, pp. 119–133. New York: Wiley.

Sykes, J., Oskoz, A., & Thorne, S. L. (2008). Web 2.0, synthetic immersive environments, and the future of language education. *CALICO Journal*, 25, 528–546. https://doi.org/10.1558/cj.v25i3.528-546

Sykes, J., & Reinhardt, J. (2012). Language at play: Digital games in second and foreign language teaching and learning. In J. Liskin-Gasparro & M. Lacorte (series eds.), *Second language classroom instruction*, Series on Theory and Practice. New York: Pearson-Prentice Hall.

Sykes, J., Reinhardt, J., & Thorne, S. (2010). Multiplayer digital games as sites for research and practice. In F. Hult (ed.) *Directions and prospects for educational linguistics*, pp. 117–136. New York: Springer. https://doi.org/10.1007/978-90-481-9136-9_8

Thorne, S. L. (2003). Artifacts and cultures-of-use in intercultural communication. *Language Learning & Technology*, 7(2): 38–67.

Thorne, S. L. (2008). Transcultural communication in open internet environments and massively multiplayer online games. In S. Magnan (ed.), *Mediating discourse online*, pp. 305–327. Amsterdam: Benjamins. https://doi.org/10.1075/aals.3.17tho

Thorne, S. L. (2009). "Community," semiotic flows, and mediated contribution to activity. *Language Teaching*, 42, 81–94. https://doi.org/10.1017/S0261444808005429

Thorne, S. L., & Black, R. (2007). Language and literacy development in computer-mediated contexts and communities. *Annual Review of Applied Linguistics*, 27, 133–160. https://doi.org/10.1017/S0267190508070074

Thorne, S. L., Black, R. W., and Sykes, J. M. (2009). Second language use, socialization, and learning in Internet communities and online games. *Modern Language Journal*, 93, 802–821. https://doi.org/10.1111/j.1540-4781.2009.00974.x

Thorne, S. L., Fischer, I., & Lu, X. (2012). The semiotic ecology and linguistic complexity of an online game world. *ReCALL*, 24, 279–301.

Thorne, S. L., & Hellermann, J. (2017). Mobile augmented reality: Hyper contextualization and situated language usage events. *Proceedings of the XVIII international CALL conference: CALL in context*, pp. 721–730. Portland State University.

Thorne, S. L., & Payne, J. S. (2005). Evolutionary trajectories, Internet-mediated expression, and language education. *CALICO Journal*, 22, 371–397. https://doi.org/10.1558/cj.v22i3.371-397

Thorne, S. L., & Reinhardt, J. (2008). Bridging activities, new media literacies and advanced foreign language proficiency. *CALICO Journal*, 25, 558–572. https://doi.org/10.1558/cj.v25i3.558-572

Thorne, S. L., Sauro, S. & Smith, B. (2015). Technologies, identities and expressive activity. *Annual Review of Applied Linguistics*, 35, 215–233. https://doi.org/10.1017/S0267190514000257

Train, R. (2005). A critical look at technologies and ideologies in internet-mediated intercultural foreign language education. In J. Belz and S. Thorne (eds.), *Internet-mediated intercultural foreign language education*, pp. 247–284. Boston: Thomson Heinle.

Van den Branden, K., Bygate, M., & Norris, J. M. (eds.). (2009). *Task-based language teaching: A reader*. Amsterdam: John Benjamins. https://doi.org/10.1075/tblt.1

Warschauer, M. (2007). The paradoxical future of digital learning. *Learning Inquiry*, 1, 41–49. https://doi.org/10.1007/s11519-007-0001-5

Zárate, P., & Cisterna, C. (2017). Action research: The use of Instagram as an interactive tool for developing the writing of short stories. *European Journal of Education Studies*, 2(8), 527–543.

Zheng, D., Young, M., Wagner, M., & Brewer, B. (2009). Negotiation for action: English language learning in game-based virtual worlds. *Modern Language Journal*, 93, 489–511. https://doi.org/10.1111/j.1540-4781.2009.00927.x

Zuengler, J., & Miller, E. (2006). Cognitive and sociocultural perspectives: Two parallel SLA worlds? *TESOL Quarterly*, 40(1), 35–58.

About the Authors

Julie M. Sykes is an Associate Professor in the Department of Linguistics and the Director of the Center for Applied Second Language Studies at the University of Oregon. She earned her PhD from the University of Minnesota with a focus on applied linguistics and second language acquisition. Her research focuses on the use of digital technologies for language acquisition with a specific focus on inter-language pragmatic development and intercultural competence. She has also presented and published on lexical development and web-based, self-access instruction for learners in addition to L1 Spanish research in the areas of phonology and translation.

Christopher L. Holden is an Associate Professor in the University Honors Program at the University of New Mexico in his hometown of Albuquerque. He received his PhD in Mathematics from the University of Wisconsin-Madison in 2008. While there, he spent two years designing augmented reality games with the Local Games Lab. At UNM, his research focuses on the design and implementation of place-based mobile games, mostly using ARIS (arisgames.org). In collaboration with Dr Sykes, he has designed and implemented *Mentira*, an ARIS game for Spanish language learning that is played as part of the UNM 202 Spanish curriculum. He also uses ARIS as a design tool for students in some of the classes he teaches and more generally to convert the masses. While not taking over the world with place-based mobile games, he cares for his 3 cats, 5 chickens, and 3 little boys. His favorite games are still *DDR* and *Katamari Damacy*.

Stephanie W. P. Knight is the Assistant Director at the Center for Applied Second Language Studies at the University of Oregon. Her research focuses on initiatives designed to increase educational access for underrepresented populations of students in advanced secondary and post-secondary contexts and the intentional use of digital tools to advance language acquisition outcomes.

11 Evaluation of Courseware/Tutorial Apps and Online Resource Websites

Philip Hubbard

Preview Questions

1. Think of some language apps or websites you have used or visited recently (or find one now). What are some features or design aspects that you found particularly frustrating or beneficial? Why?
2. Have you ever studied a language using an app or a website? If so, what was your experience? What did you find useful? What might have improved it?
3. Have you ever taught a language class using language learning apps or online resources? If so, how did you decide what to use and how to use it?
4. What do you think are some of the special challenges for finding appropriate language resources online?
5. Some online resources are designed by publishers to go with a particular textbook, while others are independent of any text. What are some of the advantages and disadvantages of each?
6. Based on your knowledge of theory and research along with your experience, how would you characterize your language teaching approach? What are some characteristics of apps and web-based resources that would be consistent with that approach?

1   Introduction and Definition of Terms

The assumption underlying this chapter is that evaluation in the digital age is a specialized skill that differs from evaluating traditional textbooks and other static materials. When teachers evaluate a textbook for possible adoption in a language course, they are working in familiar territory. They have used textbooks for years as students and may already have significant experience teaching with them. Although teachers can profit from receiving instruction in how to approach textbook evaluation more analytically (see Byrd, 2001, for example), textbooks are relatively straightforward to evaluate because they tend to have a transparent structure allowing teachers to skim through them to get an overview of the organization and content. However, even when teachers have access to full versions of interactive digital materials, they can often not be "skimmed" in the same way. Also, although this profile is changing, current language teachers may have limited experience with CALL (computer-assisted language learning) from the learner's perspective and may be novices as well at using a range of technology for teaching. Even those with years of experience with technology can find the evaluation experience daunting. Finally, as Bradin notes, "...language teachers who are not accustomed to looking at CALL software may perceive its purpose very differently than those who are more experienced" (1999: 159). Some may expect the software to take on more of the role of a teacher than it is capable of; others may focus disproportionately on what the software cannot do rather than what it can.

Central to the content of this chapter is a distinction made by Levy (1997) between tutor and tool-oriented computer software. A large part of the discussion here focuses on evaluating tutorial applications – those meant in some way to teach or provide structured or guided language practice. Such software applications were referred to in the previous versions of this chapter from the book's first and second editions as *courseware*, a term well established in CALL literature. However, as the chapter title reflects, the term *tutorial apps* will be used when the context seems to call for it, as this is more familiar and current, especially in the domain of mobile assisted language learning (MALL).

The truth is there are some fuzzy boundaries involved here. At one level, there are *mobile apps* (residing on the smartphone or tablet as independent programs, each represented by its own icon) and *web apps* (residing on web servers and interacted with through browsers). In some cases, the same program may be available in both forms, such as the popular flashcard program *Quizlet*, which can be used either through a browser or through an Android or Apple iOS app. Web apps can be used by laptops and desktop computers, but they can also be used through browsers on smartphones and tablets. Add to this the fact that CD-ROM and DVD-ROM versions of some software still exist, especially in the libraries and language labs of educational institutions, and we thus have a good reason to keep the cover term *courseware* for now.

A second fuzzy area involves the notion of *tutorial*, a key to the difference between courseware and other types of resources (like the video content of

YouTube) and tools (like Google Docs). Following Levy (1997), this chapter uses *tutorial* primarily to refer to computer programs and accompanying content that have a recognizable instructional purpose, or a "teaching presence" (Hubbard & Bradin Siskin, 2004: 457) and language learning objective. Such applications have also been called "dedicated CALL" by Colpaert (2006) among others. Both the degree and quality of the teaching presence vary considerably across CALL courseware, and as with a live teacher, the teaching presence can come in different forms. As we will see, one of the keys in evaluation is to determine whether the teaching presence in a piece of courseware in combination with the content is effective for the given language learning objective.

Some popular courseware like *Duolingo* is clearly tutorial, but the degree of teaching presence in other software is less clear. For example, the previously mentioned *Quizlet* could be perceived as just a tool that learners use for producing their own electronic flashcards to support second language (L2) vocabulary learning (see https://quizlet.com/ for an overview). However, teachers can produce sets of cards for their students with specific target items, supports and linkages, in which case the tutorial nature – the teaching presence – becomes more prominent. Teachers can also select from among the many publicly available sets those that are appropriate to their students' needs. I leave it up to the user to determine the degree of "tutoriality" in a given application, but the guidelines and frameworks provided in this chapter are sufficiently flexible to accommodate a wide range.

In addition to courseware and tutorial apps, this chapter covers evaluation of online resources supported by tutorial elements either dedicated to or exploitable for language learning. As mentioned above, the distinction between supported and unsupported content is a subtle one – back in 1997, Levy noted that a spellchecker integrated into a word processing program, for instance, had elements of both tutor and tool. Here, I simply acknowledge that so-called "rich" content/media can be seen as having tutorial value and thus be co-opted for that role by either teachers or learners regardless of the intention of the developers.

Importantly, this chapter assumes that teaching and learning a language is fundamentally different in some ways from teaching and learning other types of subjects. Evaluation procedures, frameworks, and forms are sometimes borrowed wholesale from general education sources and fail to address important questions related to integrating the CALL materials and resources into language teaching methodology. Although these more general evaluation resources can help inform decisions for language teaching, they are often more useful in looking at the technical rather than the pedagogical dimensions of evaluation in many language education settings.

Other chapters in this volume provide a foundation in a wide range of applications of technology for CALL. Many of these include tasks and activities supported by technological tools for language production, comprehension, communication, and collaboration, what Reinders & Pegrum (2016) call "generic apps," such as Skype, WhatsApp, or Google Docs. González-Lloret (2015) provides a practical overview of integrating these and other technologies into tasks that support language learning. Rather than discussing how to evaluate language learning tasks and activities based on such tools, this chapter focuses on the more limited domain of how to evaluate courseware/tutorial apps, touching when relevant on activities and tasks that may accompany implementing such apps for language learning. Given that tutorial courseware/apps to date typically do not incorporate communicative interactions directly (though they may model them), teachers need to be thinking of how to design follow-up activities that leverage what is learned and/or practiced through the courseware/apps to support such interactions.

The remainder of the chapter proceeds as follows. Section 2 briefly defines evaluation in this context and introduces the different purposes of evaluation, such as selection of courseware or websites for an individual course or for learner self-access. Section 3 describes and compares three major approaches to CALL evaluation: checklists, methodological frameworks, and SLA research-based approaches. Section 4 offers an extended example of a methodological framework similar to the one that informs reviews in the *CALICO Journal* and shows how the framework can be expanded to include evaluation of online resources with tutorial elements. Section 5 discusses implementation considerations, including the importance of learner training. Section 6 concludes with suggestions for evaluating courseware and website appropriateness and effectiveness during and after student use, along with some final comments.

2   Evaluation and Its Purposes

Because *evaluation* can have various interpretations in CALL and other domains of language teaching, this section begins by clarifying the meaning of the term as it used here. Evaluation refers to the process of (1) investigating a piece of CALL courseware or a website to judge its appropriateness for a given language learning setting, (2) identifying ways it may be effectively implemented in that setting, and (3) assessing its degree of success and determining whether to continue use or to make adjustments in implementation for future use. We may think of these three stages respectively as selection, implementation, and assessment. Historically, CALL evaluation has been primarily concerned with the first of these stages and much of this chapter is devoted to that area. However, as we will see, considerations of implementation can and arguably should be an integral part of the selection process. Due to space limitations, assessment during and after implementation is only touched on and its value emphasized in the hopes of encouraging readers to engage in further study.

There are four major purposes for engaging in CALL evaluation: selection for a course, selection for independent student use (self-access), published reviews, and provision of feedback for development and continued use.

2.1   Selection for a Course

The most common reason for doing an evaluation is for a teacher or coordinator to select appropriate courseware for a specific class. In this situation, there is a lot of known information that can be brought to bear on the evaluation process. Such information includes (1) an understanding of the technical infrastructure of the institution and/or the computers or other digital devices and courseware available to the students if they are using their own equipment, (2) relevant data about other course materials, the student characteristics, and the structure and specific objectives of the course, and (3) the teacher's/evaluator's knowledge and assumptions about how language is learned and the role technology can play in that process.

2.2   Selection for Independent Student Use

In an era of increasing learner autonomy, students need and may actively solicit advice from their teachers on tutorial apps and websites to use to complement or supplement their learning. Similarly, teachers or other language professionals may be asked to recommend courseware/tutorial app selections for a self-access lab or resource list for a language program. In this case, the same considerations of technology infrastructure will presumably be made, but the information about student characteristics, course objectives and materials, and teacher assumptions may be less readily available. In addition, there can be a great deal of variability in student and course characteristics that can make the selection process more challenging. An evaluator in this context would do well to begin with some investigation of these factors.

2.3 Reviews

Reviews differ from other forms of evaluation in that they typically focus on the courseware itself rather than on a particular environment the courseware will be used in. Published reviews such as those found in the *CALICO Journal* and other professional periodicals, for example, are aimed at a broad audience of potentially interested parties. As a form of evaluation, a review is an important source of information that others can use both in making the initial identification of possible candidates and in informing their own evaluations.

2.4 Providing Feedback for Development

If a teacher or other language professional is developing CALL materials individually or as part of a team, then the same types of questions one asks of others' work should be addressed. In the case of a large-scale courseware development project, this means recognizing a cycle of development, implementation (piloting and beta testing), and evaluation followed by revisions based on the outcome of the evaluation. Even for individual classroom purposes, there is value in revisiting CALL exercises and activities (online or otherwise) and evaluating them, especially with respect to outcome (see section 6). The point is that evaluation is not a task solely conducted prior to the use of the courseware or website. Information from evaluation after use can inform (1) decisions about changing aspects of a project under development, (2) selection decisions for future use, and (3) changes in implementation both to accommodate the revealed weaknesses of the courseware or website and in some cases to exploit its use beyond its original design intentions.

3   Literature Review: Three Approaches to CALL Evaluation

Evaluation has been a part of CALL almost since its inception (see Hubbard, 1988 for a discussion and critique of some early approaches). Levy & Stockwell (2006) identified three major types of CALL courseware evaluation: evaluation driven by checklists or forms, evaluation guided by methodological frameworks for language teaching, and evaluation linked to second language acquisition (SLA) theory and research-based criteria. Each of these is discussed briefly below.[1]

1   For a more comprehensive contemporary treatment of these three approaches covering not only courseware use but also other CALL tasks, see the evaluation chapter of Levy & Stockwell (2006).

3.1   Checklists

Checklists have been present from the earliest stages of CALL and remain widespread. Section 4.10, for instance, offers two examples of checklists recently developed for mobile learning (Reinders & Pegrum, 2016; Rosell-Aguilar, 2017). Typically, a checklist presents a series of questions or categories for judgment and the evaluator is expected to make a response based on information gathered through the reviewing process. Many checklists simply ask for a yes/no indication (see Figure 1) or a response along a Likert scale. Others, despite the "checklist" label, also include space for short answers or open-ended commentary following specific prompts (e.g., How many hours does it take to complete the activities in the software? What cultural topics or themes does the software discuss?).

Published checklists have been criticized for a number of reasons, including focusing too heavily on technology at the expense of pedagogy and for being biased and restrictive (Hubbard, 1988). However, Susser (2001) provides a rebuttal to such criticisms and builds a convincing case for the value of CALL evaluation checklists. The thrust of his argument is that the problem is not with the concept of checklists but rather with particular instantiations of them.

There are a number of evaluation checklists available online for those interested in pursuing this option for different types of courseware and resources.

- NFLRC (National Foreign Language Resource Center): designed specifically for multimedia language learning software, includes general criteria as well as specific criteria for individual skills like listening and reading (see Figure 1).
- ICT4LT (Information and Communication Technologies for Language Teachers) (Davies, 2009): has a downloadable form for both language software and website evaluation.
- Reinders & Pegrum (2016: 228–229): designed for evaluating mobile learning, focuses on "learning resources" broadly, but accommodates tutorial applications – see subsection 4.10 for more details.
- Son (2005): includes a website evaluation checklist with 15 criteria (see also subsection 4.9).
- The California Language Teachers' Association (CLTA): provides a form that evaluates websites in terms of ACTFL's Five C's (see https://www.actfl.org/sites/default/files/publications/standards/World-ReadinessStandardsforLearningLanguages.pdf). Note that at the time of this writing the CLTA form was not actively available, but a link to it through the Internet Archive is provided in the reference list.

Checklist for listening software (excerpt)

Listening input

Audio
__ conditions against which the audio is played authentic
__ tempo of the sound track natural
__ variety of voices and dialects
__ sound track supported by video or graphics

Listening passages
__ passages authentic
__ topics of interest to intended users
__ variety of topics
__ users can choose among several passages on the same topic
__ variety of genres
__ passages of an appropriate length for intended users
__ vocabulary appropriate for the intended level
__ syntax appropriate for the intended level

Figure 1 Excerpt from the checklist for multimedia language learning software (National Foreign Language Resource Center).

Checklists, especially those produced collaboratively by professionals in the field as part of formal projects (as was the case with the NFLRC–Hawaii list), have value as standard formats. However, caution should be taken in applying them wholesale without taking into account the specifics of the situation in which they will be applied, in particular the teachers, learners, and goals of learning. As Susser (2001) notes, checklists do not have to be accepted as is but can be adapted and updated for particular purposes. They have the capacity to provide teachers with a useful tool for recognizing the variety of elements that make up a courseware application and for triggering reflection on some of their own assumptions about CALL. Finally, in addition to other sources such as general education, items on a checklist may be generated on the basis of *methodological frameworks* and *SLA research*, as discussed in the following two subsections.

3.2 Methodological Frameworks

Methodological frameworks differ from checklists in that such frameworks are largely descriptive rather than judgmental in their form, with the judgment element in the hands of the user rather than being prescriptively integrated into the form. As noted by Hubbard:

> ... A *framework* in this context means an integrated description of the components of something – in this case CALL materials – with respect to a particular goal – in this case evaluation. Rather than asking a specific set of questions, a framework provides a tool through which an evaluator can create his or her own questions or develop some other evaluation scheme. (1988: 52)

Phillips (1985) offered the first such framework explicitly linked to language teaching methodology. It included categories for the CALL program types of its era, but also described dimensions such as language difficulty, learner focus (i.e., skill area – listening, speaking, reading, writing), and language focus (lexis, grammar, discourse) that were important to the language learning character of the program. Hubbard (1988) expanded Phillips' system and integrated it with one developed independently by Richards & Rodgers (1982) for describing and analyzing language teaching methods. They characterized these methods in terms of three descriptive categories: (1) *approach*, or the underlying theories of linguistics and language learning assumed by the method; (2) *design*, consistent with the assumptions of the approach and including the syllabus model, general and specific objectives of the method, and the roles of the students, teacher, and materials; and (3) *procedure*, or the classroom techniques and activities through which the design is realized. Hubbard (1988) adapted the approach, design, and procedure constructs into categories describing key elements of evaluation and renamed them *teacher fit*, *learner fit*, and *operational description*, respectively, to accommodate the technological dimension of language instruction.

The resulting framework became the evaluation module in a comprehensive methodological framework that also included modules for courseware development and implementation (Hubbard, 1996). A version of this framework remains at the core of the procedure used for reviews in the *CALICO Journal*: for details, see Burston (2003) and *CALICO Journal* (2018). Although originally designed to evaluate courseware, most of the considerations embedded in it are relevant for evaluating websites and even CALL activities or tasks that either do not involve courseware or that represent blends of tutorial and tool-oriented applications.

3.3   SLA-Based Approaches

Given that teaching languages with computers *is* a form of language teaching, another reasonable procedure for developing evaluation rubrics is to build directly on recommendations from theory or research in instructed second language acquisition (SLA). Underwood (1984) and Egbert & Hanson-Smith (1999) offered some SLA-based generalizations connected to CALL that were useful for evaluation, but the most ambitious project in this vein is represented by the work of Carol Chapelle in the field she dubbed CASLA – computer applications in second language acquisition. CASLA includes not only CALL but also computer-based language testing and computer-based SLA research. Although parts of the model were developed in earlier articles, the work comes together in Chapelle (2001), which represents a significant advance for (1) its characterization of evaluation on the basis of principles and (2) its specific SLA-based criteria. With respect to the first point, Chapelle offered a set of five principles for evaluating CALL summarized as follows: (1) CALL evaluation is situation-specific; (2) CALL should be evaluated both judgmentally and empirically; (3) CALL evaluation criteria should come from instructed SLA theory and research; (4) the criteria should be applied relative to the purpose of the CALL task; (5) the central consideration should be language learning potential.

In line with the preceding principles, Chapelle proposed a set of six general evaluation criteria useful in determining the appropriateness of a given CALL task for supporting language acquisition. Note that these criteria are relevant for "both the aspects of the task defined by the software and those defined by the teacher" (Chapelle, 2001: 58). As they are targeted to CALL tasks rather than solely to courseware, they have direct relevance to website evaluation as well.

These criteria appeared initially in Chapelle (2001) and were reprised and applied in an evaluation study by Jamieson, Chapelle, & Preiss (2005: 94).

- *Language learning potential:* The degree of opportunity present for beneficial focus on form
- *Learner fit:* The amount of opportunity for engagement with language under appropriate conditions given learner characteristics
- *Meaning focus:* The extent to which learners' attention is directed toward the meaning of the language
- *Authenticity:* The degree of correspondence between the learning activity and target language activities of interest to learners out of the classroom
- *Positive impact:* The positive effects of the CALL activity on those who participate in it
- *Practicality:* The adequacy of resources to support the use of the CALL activity.

Jamieson, Chapelle, & Preiss (2004) show how these criteria can be operationalized for a judgmental analysis of a major courseware project, *Longman English Online (LEO)*.[2] In a follow-up study (Jamieson, Chapelle, & Preiss, 2005), they again build on these criteria to create a rubric for evaluating *LEO* empirically, eliciting data from the courseware developers, a teacher using the courseware, and a set of student users. Table 1 shows an example of their entry for "language learning potential."

It is worth noting that Chapelle's framework, though quite different in structure and in underlying assumptions, is in many respects compatible with the methodological framework and checklist approaches described earlier. For instance, Chapelle's concept of learner fit can be related to that of Hubbard (1988) and Burston (2003). Most of her other criteria are representative of a task-based, interactionist language teaching approach that is likely to provide a good "teacher fit" for many current language instructors, especially those who have been recently trained in such an approach. However, it is less clearly oriented toward sociocultural views of SLA. Finally, as Table 1 illustrates, the result of an SLA-based approach can be a principled checklist, and a given SLA framework can be expanded and adapted to meet other, related conceptualizations of language teaching. Leakey (2011) for example, builds on Chapelle's framework by synthesizing elements from other evaluation models. While keeping Chapelle's

Table 1 Example of CALL criteria and operationalization from the Chapelle (2001) framework (excerpted from Table 2 of Jamieson, Chapelle, & Preiss, 2005: 99)

Criteria	Operationalizations	Desired responses to support claims for quality
Language learning potential Sufficient opportunity for beneficial focus on form	• Will the grammar, vocabulary, and pronunciation that was studied during the week be remembered?	• Yes
	• Were the explanations clear?	• Yes
	• Were there enough exercises?	• Yes
	• Will the students' English improve as a result of *LEO 3*?	• Yes
	• Will the students' quiz scores indicate mastery of the material?	• Yes

2   As Jamieson, Chapelle, & Preiss (2005) note, the *Longman English Online* product was dropped by Longman and much of its content was released on CD-ROM as *Longman English Interactive*. It has subsequently reappeared online as *Longman English Interactive*: see http://www.longmanenglishinteractive.com/home.html

original six categories in his "platform/program/pedagogy" framework, he adds six more: *language skills and combinations of skills, learner control, error correction and feedback, collaborative CALL, teacher factor,* and *tuition delivery modes.* The notion of collaborative CALL in particular provides a nod to the socio-cultural camp within SLA.

This section has outlined approaches to evaluation based on checklists, methodological frameworks, and SLA research. While all three have their merits, the remainder of this chapter will focus on presenting the methodological framework in more detail since it is the most neutral and flexible in terms of accommodating a range of language teaching approaches.

4   A General Evaluation Framework for Courseware/ Tutorial Apps and Websites

The following description is based on the assumption that evaluation is being done for the most common purpose, namely a single teacher or supervisor selecting courseware or websites for integration into a particular course. However, the framework outlined in this section can be readily extended to any of the domains mentioned previously, i.e., selection for self-access or evaluation for a published review. Note also that courseware packages, apps, and websites can be complex, incorporating a number of different types of presentations, activities, exercises, and quizzes. In a thorough evaluation it will be necessary to cover examples of each type.

4.1   Rationale

Two of the articles noted above (Hubbard, 1988, 1996) outlined a methodological framework for CALL combining elements of development, evaluation, and implementation viewed primarily through the lens of language teaching approach and design considerations. The description that follows remains true to the assumption that language teaching and learning judgments are at the core of evaluation rather than, or at most in addition to, generic principles from instructional design or other areas of education. This is both because of the unique nature of language learning and because many teachers performing these evaluations do not have direct experience in these other areas. Also, by linking CALL courseware evaluation to language teaching methodology, the connections necessary for integration can be much more readily made.

This chapter focuses on a methodological framework rather than the alternatives primarily because of the methodological framework's descriptive and more comprehensive nature. Theory and research-based approaches such as Chapelle's (2001) are prescriptive, at least in terms of approach, because they are based on a particular conception of language teaching and learning (even one as well-established as that underlying Chapelle's). A specific checklist procedure is avoided here for the same reason: any checklist selected is likely to be biased toward the particular conception of language learning held by its developer. As noted previously, both checklists and SLA-based evaluation criteria can be largely accommodated by starting with a descriptive methodological framework. Further, a type of checklist – a list of considerations – can be generated directly from the categories and elements in the following framework. In fact, the methodological framework considerations can even be applied to an existing checklist (if the teacher shares the checklist's assumptions about learning) to identify areas that might be incompletely covered or missing altogether.

4.2   Preliminaries – Identification of Potential Courseware and Websites

Before beginning any evaluation, a teacher needs to identify candidates to evaluate. The first step is to have a basic understanding of what characteristics to look for in candidates. While a formal needs analysis is ideal, even a brief look at one's existing course structure will help in identifying programs with potential. Healey & Johnson (1997/1998) offer a useful set of guiding questions for this step as follows:

1.   Who are the users you are targeting?
2.   What are the goals of the students you are targeting?
3.   What setting will the software be used in: independent study lab with no teacher available, lab associated with a class, a teacher-led class with one or a few computers?
4.   How much do the teachers/lab assistants who will work with the students know?
5.   What do you have now in the way of hardware and technical assistance?
6.   How much money do you have to spend?

Robb & Susser conducted a survey of language teachers to explore their courseware selection process, focusing on 11 possible "sources of information potentially affecting purchase decisions" (2000: 45). They found that many practicing teachers use a variety of information sources (not just a checklist-based review) to select courseware and that colleagues are particularly popular as sources information, despite potential questions as to the reliability of their judgments. In fact, when asked about the source of information for courseware they *continued to use* on a regular basis (rather than just purchasing), the largest group (78%) reported relying on a recommendation from a colleague. It is likely that if such a study were done today, it would also include web searches and recommendations through social media as resources.

4.3 Overview of Basic Structure

We begin by assuming that there has been a "pre-evaluation" and that the courseware/app or website under scrutiny is at least superficially a reasonable candidate for ultimate selection. Figure 2 presents the basic structure of the evaluation framework, adapted from Hubbard (1988, 1996) and Burston (2003). At this level, even without further analysis, it reflects a simple evaluation procedure embodying the following stages:

1. *Technical preview.* Make sure that the courseware will run the way you want it to on the equipment that you or the students have available.
2. *Operational description.* Go through the main parts of the courseware or website as a cooperative user (you can try to be less cooperative later). Get an understanding of the flow of lessons and items within them *before* making judgments. You can record your first impressions, but try to withhold judgment until you understand how the courseware or website actually operates and what range of materials and applications it may offer.
3. *Teacher fit.* In the case of courseware, infer the language teaching approach or approaches that it is consistent with (which may be different from what the designers claim) and determine the degree to which it is compatible or incompatible with your own. For websites, try to determine the assumptions about language learning underlying the selection of the content (if relevant) and the types and formats of help options, including what you and students will need to know in order to use them effectively.
4. *Learner fit.* Note how well the content, skills, and language level correspond to your students' needs, especially as determined by the objectives in the course syllabus. Note also how well the courseware fits the students' interests and preferred learning styles. Following Thorne (2003), you may also consider how it fits the students' existing "cultures of use", that is, the way they currently

select and utilize digital devices and apps for personal and social purposes.

5. *Implementation schemes.* Reflect on how the courseware or website material might be integrated into the course or a curriculum, including what students will need to know in order to use it effectively and how much time that may take.

6. *Appropriateness judgments.* Ultimately, make a decision to use or not, based on the quality and degree of teacher fit and learner fit, along with considerations of the costs and benefits of implementation. Keep in mind that no courseware will be a perfect fit. It may be helpful to think of judging a program's teaching presence the way you would judge a human teacher. Ultimately, one or more humans created the materials and in the case of courseware/tutorial apps, structured the program's actions for learning purposes. Do you want that person or persons teaching your students with the material and procedure they provided? In the case of some courseware and websites, parts may be judged more useful or appropriate than others and students can be informed accordingly.

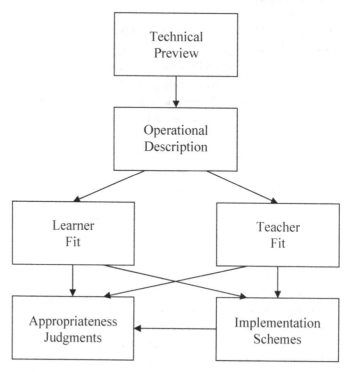

Figure 2 Courseware evaluation framework: core components.

The remainder of this section explores the preceding components in more detail, concluding with a discussion of special considerations in evaluating mobile apps based on two recent frameworks: Reinders & Pegrum (2016) and Rosell-Aguilar (2017).

4.4   Technical Preview

Considerations in the technical preview are of several types. The most basic one is: Will it run on the devices the teacher and students will be using? The primary split for computers continues to be between Microsoft Windows-based PCs and Apple Macintoshes (though Google Chrome devices seem to be gaining some ground, especially in schools). Some courseware runs on all platforms, particularly web-based applications, and some on just one. For apps developed for mobile computing, the primary split is between iOS, for iPhones and iPads, and Android for other smartphones and tablets, although other proprietary formats remain, especially on older devices. The operating system version, memory requirements, and other hardware and software issues are often significant as well. If online materials are being used, how accessible are they? Can students only use them in a lab, or are they available on a larger institutional network, an app, or the web? Additionally, for online materials in some settings there are issues of bandwidth and server access – the speed at which data is transferred and the impact of multiple users tapping into a single application. This is a particularly important point when using video files, which may be delayed or degraded over inherently slow or heavily used connections.

In the case of material resources, courseware, or other applications on websites, this can often be tested on the instructor's computer or mobile device. If the material is going to be used by the instructor in a classroom or on machines in a dedicated learning lab, then those settings can also be tested prior to presenting them to students. If a site is to be used by students independently on either their own devices or those outside of the control of the instructor or his or her support team, then some additional scrutiny is required. Especially for mobile apps, it is important to be aware of how they may differ for Android and iOS devices. For example, at the time of this writing, the Android app for the popular open-source rich flashcard system Anki was free while the iOS version was $24.95.

A description of all the technical issues is well beyond the scope of this chapter. Evaluators who have concerns about their ability to make the preliminary judgments at the technical level are encouraged to seek assistance from others who are more knowledgeable.

4.5   Operational Description

We will begin by outlining the operational description categories for course-ware in line with the conception as outlined in Hubbard (1988, 1996) and refined in Burston (2003). In subsection 4.9 below, we will see how this part of the framework can be adapted to accommodate a description of web-based resource materials and applications.

The operational description is a review of the components of the course-ware and how they operate under control of either the program or the user. Importantly, it is meant to be an *objective* description that can then be used to feed the judgmental aspects of the framework. In earlier versions of the framework, the operational description was presented as a set of more or less independent central and peripheral descriptive categories, and this remains a useful classification.

The peripheral categories include any accompanying text, documenta-tion, tutorial (on how to use the courseware), record keeping features out-side of the main program, and any other utilities, such as teacher authoring capabilities. The central categories include the general *activity type* (e.g., presentation, task, game, drill, quiz, text reconstruction, exploration, sim-ulation, etc.) and the *presentational scheme*, which describes the way a CALL activity is presented to the learners. The reason for this distinction is that a given activity type may have a number of diverse presentational schemes. For example the activity type *text reconstruction* would have different presentational schemes for a gap-filling exercise and a scrambled sentence one.

Some Web resources, such as materials placed on websites dedicated to teaching and learning the target language or adaptable for that pur-pose, are not by themselves activities, but a common type of activity that emerges from them would be simply *comprehension-based*, perhaps fol-lowed by additional production tasks. The category of resources on web-sites can represent a wide range of disparate materials, including text with links to glossaries or e-dictionaries, audio and video materials with text support (transcripts and/or captions), and so on. There is in practice a rather fuzzy boundary between some of these resources and courseware. A video clip with a transcript and captions, for example, could be seen as tutorial material if designed and presented specifically for the purposes of language practice, but those exact same features could be present on a site with no language learning agenda frequented by native speakers of the target lan-guage – e.g., the website hosting presentations from TED (Technology, Entertainment, and Design) conferences: http://www.ted.com.

Presentational schemes are defined by a number of subcategories:

- The *screen layout* or *interface* is concerned with all aspects of the basic appearance on screen, including fonts, color schemes, controls, as well as presence, placement and quality of graphics, video and audio. This is a major area of investigation in the broader field of HCI (human computer interaction) and may involve cultural factors in addition to the more obvious cognitive and esthetic aspects.
- *Timing* is a relevant category for some courseware, for instance, by limiting the time that content material or a prompt is on screen, by limiting the time allowed for a response, or by recording the time a student takes to perform some action.
- The category of *control options* describes what is under learner vs. program control as well as the physical nature of those controls. For example, does the learner have the ability to go to any desired lesson through a menu, or does the program require the student to complete one lesson before moving on to another in a predetermined order? Can the learner call up text support for an audio or video exercise, or is it always present? This is an arena of some debate within CALL and CAI (computer-assisted instruction) in general. A study by Boling & Soo (1999) for instance, found that novice language learners tend to prefer more structured CALL courseware while advanced learners are more comfortable with taking control themselves.
- *User input* (a category missing from earlier versions of the framework) characterizes how the learner responds to implicit or explicit prompts from the program (speaking, typing, clicking a button or hotspot, etc.).
- *Input judging* describes the program's procedure for handling the user input, which can involve such actions as recording a mouse click, various types of pattern matching, speech analysis, or linguistic parsing.
- *Feedback* is provided to the user by the program as the result of the input judging. It is a key part of the description of the presentational scheme as there are a number of options, some of which clearly represent a more active teaching presence than others. Feedback can be either implicit (as when an incorrect answer simply disappears as a choice when it is selected) or explicit. For a typical quiz or practice exercise, feedback can simply indicate a correct or incorrect response, or it can provide additional information in the form of hints or explanations. For other types of programs, such

as simulations, feedback can take other forms (e.g., in a simulated dialogue a character in the program might respond orally to the student's input or perform some requested action). Feedback may also be cumulative, as when the program saves scores and other performance data for the student to review. Finally, in the case of some web-based applications, feedback can be provided by a human through the mediation of the computer, as in commenting on blogs or student work submitted to an instructor online.

- *Help options* represent the final element to consider in the presentational scheme: in addition to a description of the content of the help, the key points here are whether any assistance that is provided is contextualized and targeted for a given item rather than being global and whether help is available at all times or only under certain conditions.

As noted above, the operational description in previous versions of this framework did not directly portray the connections among the various elements, especially those in the presentational scheme (see Hubbard, 1988 for details). An alternative way to conceive of these elements is to model their operation more dynamically at the micro level as an *interactional sequence*: a set of exchanges between a program and a user on a single point or topic, such as a question in a tutorial exercise. An interactional sequence involves one or more turns by each party (the computer and the user) prior to shifting the topic (for example, moving to the next question or item) or ending the interaction. Consider the following example of an interactional sequence: Assume a novice ESL learner is using a program to learn vocabulary through picture identification. In this lesson the focus is on verbs associated with particular animals. The activity is set up on the screen as four pictures: a fish, a lion, a snake, and a bird. These represent the response domain (what the learner can click on).

Computer: Which of these can fly? [prompt]
Learner: (clicks on the fish) [input]
Computer: Sorry, that's not right. Fish can't fly. Fish swim. (fish swims off-screen) [feedback]
            Which of these can fly? [prompt]
Learner: (clicks on the bird) [input]
Computer: That's right. Birds can fly. (bird flies off-screen) [feedback]
            (the screen refreshes and a new set of pictures appears ...)

Hubbard (2001) offers an initial model for such sequences that covers three common modes: presentation, exploration, and interrogation. Presentation mode is found not only in courseware but in websites where text, audio, or video content is available to the user. The controls in such cases include those for display (e.g., a media player for audio and video) and those for activating various language support options like transcripts for audio and video or links from text to online dictionaries. Exploration mode is typically embedded in certain types of courseware activities (e.g., click on an item in a picture to find out the word for it), but may also be seen as the mode used by learners when trying out various links on a web page.

The preceding example, however, is in the interrogation mode because the computer is doing the asking, prompting the student for a response and then providing feedback on the accuracy of that response. This is the primary mode for tutorial courseware such as *Duolingo* or *Rosetta Stone*. If we consider the same type of example, namely teaching vocabulary through pictures, we can see how the other two modes differ from interrogation. In presentation mode, the program would simply be providing information in the target language, for example, highlighting each of the pictures (fish, lion, snake, and bird) one by one and displaying an appropriate description ("This is a bird. A bird can fly"). As with an audio or video tape recording, the student's interaction with the program would be limited to such actions as pausing, repeating, adjusting the volume, and so on. In exploration mode,

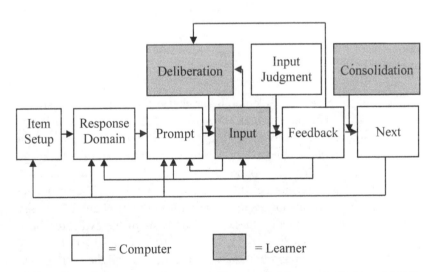

Figure 3 Interactional sequence model for interrogation mode (Hubbard, 2001). The white boxes indicate what the computer does, and the gray boxes, what the learner does.

the learner is the one doing the asking, in this case by clicking on pictures as desired to get information about them, with the option of ignoring those he or she already knows.

The interactional sequence model for possible paths in interrogation mode is shown in Figure 3, though of course not all paths will be open to every item – the richness of the options in an interactional sequence is determined by the program designer. Concepts of particular importance here are *deliberation* and *consolidation*. Deliberation refers to the cognitive operations by the learner prior to taking a physical action (inputting something: a mouse click, text, speech, etc.). It is the largely invisible activity of reflecting and accessing the relevant information to either answer the prompt correctly, make an educated or random guess, ask for help or a hint, or give up. It is fed not only by all that precedes the initial input but also by the feedback from the computer after the first "round" of the interactional sequence. Consolidation is a similar cognitive activity that involves taking whatever bits of information were "learned" from that interaction and taking a moment to reflect on them in the hopes of promoting retention and integration with existing knowledge. It is precisely these cognitive steps that allow such activities to be more than just the mechanistic stimulus-response-reinforcement cycle of behaviorism (see Hubbard & Bradin Siskin, 2004).

How much a given program supports or even interferes with deliberation and consolidation is thus another key consideration. The degree to which learner training (see subsection 5.2) can encourage deliberation and consolidation and the possible cost in time and resources of providing that training are additional points to ponder.

4.6   Teacher Fit

Teacher fit represents considerations largely at the level of Richards & Rodgers' (1982) characterization of *approach*. This begins with the evaluator's assumptions, ideally supported by theory and research, about two areas. The first of these concerns assumptions about the nature of language, including issues such as the relationship between language and communication and the relationship between language and culture. The second set of assumptions (presumably compatible with the first) is about how languages are learned. Together these form the basis of the evaluator's *language teaching approach*.

Depending on when and how they were educated and their subsequent classroom and professional development experiences, teachers will differ in their approaches. For those who find it challenging to characterize them, one place to start in this process would be Lightbown & Spada's (2013) six proposals for second and foreign language teaching. These are summarized below:

1. Get it right from the beginning. This is consistent with structure-based approaches including audio-lingual and grammar-translation methods. The underlying assumptions include that language form is important even at early stages and that language patterns and rules are taught and mastered one by one. Errors need to be corrected in forms that are currently being learned or those that have been previously learned.

2. Just listen ... and read. This is compatible with comprehension-based approaches where meaning rather than form is foregrounded. The role of production is minimized, and interaction is a tool that learners use primarily for getting more comprehensible input.

3. Let's talk. This proposal states that language is fundamentally communication and acquiring it is driven through interaction and negotiation of meaning. Opportunities for both comprehensible input and output are important.

4. Get two for one. This is the proposal that underlies content-based instruction. In the pursuit of acquiring the targeted content, language acquisition also occurs. A manifestation of this is CLIL (Content and Language Integrated Learning), which is widespread in Europe.

5. Teach what is teachable. This is based on the notion that language structures (unlike vocabulary) are acquired in a relatively fixed order, and that more complex ones like question formation, negation, and relative clause formation are acquired in developmental stages. Instruction, practice, and expectations of accuracy should be consistent with those stages.

6. Get it right in the end. This proposal is consistent with the position that language learning is a developmental process, and that errors along the way are natural and expected. While some forms seem to be acquired through language use, others must be focused on explicitly.

It is important to realize that these proposals vary considerably in terms of the quantity and recency of research in support of them as well as the contexts in which they might be more or less effective. In addition to these positions, there are other teaching approaches that have a more sociocultural orientation, ones that focus more on the role of collaborative learning and co-construction of language (Lightbown & Spada, 2013: 118–120),

A further set of considerations emerges from the evaluator's understanding of the capacities of the *computer as a delivery system* for both content and pedagogy. Combined with the language teaching approach, these considerations yield *approach-based evaluation criteria*. In practice, these criteria can remain at a somewhat holistic level (assuming we can recognize when a language learning activity is at odds with our approach), or they can be operationalized into a checklist or some other form. For example, Hubbard (1988: 63) gives the following partial set of evaluation criteria for what were referred to in that work as "explicit learning" approaches:

1. Gives meaningful rather than mechanical practice, contextualized in a coherent discourse larger than a single sentence;
2. Provides hints of various types to lead students to correct answers;
3. Accepts alternative correct answers within a given context;
4. Offers the option of explanations for why correct answers are correct;
5. Anticipates incorrect answers and offers explanations for why they are incorrect.

Regardless of whether they are used directly in the evaluation process, it is an instructive exercise for any evaluator to experiment with producing some approach-based evaluation criteria since this necessitates reflecting on one's own beliefs about language, language learning, and the capacity of the computer to support that learning as well as the foundation on which those beliefs rest.

Having identified one's approach-based evaluation criteria, applying them to the courseware is the final stage, and this is not an easy task. As noted in the *CALICO Journal* Learning technology review guidelines (2018: 4):

> Not surprisingly, the assessment of teacher fit is the most difficult parameter to determine. Partly, this is because developers do not always explicitly state the theoretical/methodological assumptions underlying their program/tool/resource, thereby obliging a reviewer to extract them by implication. On the other side of the coin, producers are very much aware of what methodological approaches are currently in favor (e.g., communicative, learner centered, constructivist, experiential, post-method) and label their products accordingly, whatever the truth of the matter may be.

There is one final point to note in determining teacher fit: the fit does not need to be perfect – it just needs to be compatible. Language learning is a complex process and the more structured activities and exercises often found in tutorial courseware/apps could still be of value within a generally communicative approach.

Beyond tutorial courseware/apps with their own content, authoring programs or systems can represent an interesting challenge for determining teacher fit. They typically provide templates for a restricted set of activity types and presentation schemes (presentation, multiple-choice, matching, gap-filling, glossing, etc.). There is, however, some flexibility in the use of such templates. For example, multiple-choice can be used for discrete-point testing of grammatical forms or vocabulary, or for checking general comprehension or even inference. In such cases, teacher fit is a product of both the design of the program and the individual author. The question then becomes the extent to which a program is consistent with certain learning theories and can accommodate certain methodological approaches.[3]

Moving from courseware to web resources and applications, the considerations in the teacher fit category remain relevant. Resources should be consistent with the teacher's assumptions about language and language learning. For example, if authenticity is a central criterion (as in Chapelle's framework), then resources that lack authenticity are not a good fit. Applications similarly should stay consistent with teacher fit. If a teacher's assumptions about language learning, for example, allow for the L1 to play a role, then websites or apps that include either a translation application or bilingual dictionaries or glossaries will be acceptable. If the teacher is more strongly influenced by a direct approach, where use of the L1 is forbidden, then such a website or app would not meet the requirements for a good teacher fit.

4.7   Learner Fit

Learner fit covers many of the same topics as Richards & Rodgers' (1982) concept of *design*. The two central areas in which we are looking for compatibility are *learner variables* (age, native language, proficiency level, sex, learner needs, learner interests) and the *syllabus*, which describes the learning objectives and paths to achieve them. Each of these variables is fed by a number of other elements, some of which influence both. It should be noted that learner variables are by their nature individual and in some cases not obvious to the teacher. However, if a class or group of students within it can be identified as having similar attributes, these variables become important in the evaluation process. *Learning style* (taken here broadly to subsume

---

3   The author would like to thank an anonymous reviewer for this insight into the special status of authoring systems.

cognitive style, preferred learning strategies, and motivational orientations) and *classroom management* (such as whether the courseware is to be used individually, in pairs or groups, or as a whole class activity, and the degree to which the learners must be monitored) represent considerations associated with learner variables, in particular age and native language and culture. The *linguistic objectives* ("program focus" in earlier versions of the framework and in Phillips, 1985), are discourse/text, syntax, lexis, morphology, and phonology/graphology: these are part of learner fit because they are related to the syllabus, as are the *language skills* targeted by the courseware (previously "learner focus"): listening, speaking, reading, and writing. In line with the *Common European framework* (Council of Europe, 2001: 74–82) and other modern conceptions of language proficiency, a category of *spoken interaction* could be added to language skills as well.

The three remaining elements are connected to both learner variables and the syllabus. *Language difficulty* represents the level of linguistic challenge along several dimensions, such as grammar, lexicon, and speed of presentation and clarity of pronunciation (for audio or video). *Program difficulty* has to do with the learning curve to operate the program (because of inherent complexity or technical design issues) and in the case of games and tasks, the level of extra-linguistic challenge with which the user is faced. In both cases, the time spent in pursuits not directly tied to language learning as well as the potential for frustration are factors to weigh against the likely language learning achievements and any positive impacts on motivation. Finally, *content* is an issue for both the syllabus and learner variables. The content should be considered with respect to its consistency with course objectives (for example, if the target culture is an element of the syllabus, the cultural content should be authentic and appropriate), and the content should also be considered with respect to student interests and existing knowledge.

4.8   Appropriateness Judgments

Teacher-fit and learner-fit considerations combine to yield judgments of the appropriateness of a piece of CALL courseware for a given setting. Although the process of getting to this point appears linear in Figure 2, decisions to reject a program can be made at any point: for instance, if either teacher or learner fit is noted to be poor early on, there is no need to continue. The result of this process is a decision of whether or not to procure the courseware, or if it is free, whether or not to use it. However, a teacher evaluating a promising website or piece of courseware must determine not just whether but also *how* and *when* to use it: this is the domain of implementation, discussed in section 5.

4.9   Additional Considerations for Website Evaluation

Although the methodological framework above was developed initially for computer-based courseware evaluation, the essential elements presented in the model in Figure 2 have relevance for evaluating resource websites as well. The recommended procedure of surveying the technical considerations and the operational description prior to making judgments of teacher and learner fit remains, though obvious lack of fit noted early on can lead to a website being removed from further consideration. The technical considerations and operational description for resources and tool-oriented web applications may differ somewhat from those of courseware. Teacher fit and learner fit, however, can be judged in more or less the same way as with courseware, leading to the appropriateness judgments for all or part of a site. Implementation schemes may differ as well, as most websites have the added flexibility of being accessible outside of the classroom and learning lab on the students' own computers, at Internet cafes, and so on.

For technical considerations and operational descriptions, it is useful to look at published evaluation criteria for direction to supplement the discussion in subsections 4.4 and 4.5 above. Several website review sources (e.g., Davies, 2009; Son, 2005) note that *authorship* or *authority* is a particularly relevant category. This is especially the case for the plethora of online material presented on personal and commercial websites without the benefit of any peer review. Sites found via a Web search may not even have an author (or any significant information about the author).

In addition to *authority*, Son (2005: 217) lists 14 additional judgmental criteria, many of which were derived from a review of seven previous website evaluation models. Son (2010) provides example reviews of websites evaluated using these criteria. In all but one case the criteria can be associated at least roughly to categories in the methodological framework. A number of them, including *purpose, accuracy, currency,* and *authenticity* relate to the category of content in the preceding methodological framework and simply provide a narrower specification of this construct. *Loading speed* and *reliability* refer to technical considerations, while *organization, navigation, feedback,* and *multimedia* are all part of the presentational scheme category. Finally, *usefulness* and *integration* are judgments made at the level of learner fit. Interestingly, only Son's criterion of *communication* seems to be completely outside the previous courseware review framework, perhaps not surprising since as noted in the introduction communication activities are not typically embedded in courseware.

Finally, it is increasingly common for websites to include a wide variety of resources and applications. While these may be integrated as they typically are in dedicated courseware products, they can also just be collections of loosely related items the website developer has determined would be useful. This means that even more so than with traditional courseware, instructors need to select and evaluate the various parts of such websites independently. In such cases, it is likely that some parts will represent better teacher and learner fits than others, so that appropriateness judgments may not be uniform across the site.

4.10   Evaluation Frameworks for Mobile Learning

This subsection looks briefly at two recent evaluation frameworks aimed at mobile learning apps and environments, both demonstrating that there is still appeal in checklists and their like. The first, Reinders & Pegrum (2016), is based on an idealized target (a top score of 150) for mobile language learning manifested in a fairly comprehensive checklist. The paper begins with an important division between materials and activities. They observe that mobile materials can be either dedicated to language learning or generic, and they can be either web-based or app-based. Mobile activities aimed at language learning may use one or a combination of dedicated or generic and web-based or app-based materials.

Their checklist uses a scoring system favoring contemporary views of SLA supported by research. There is a 150-point maximum score encompassing five categories, each with two to 10 subcategories: educational affordances exploited in learning design (50 points), general pedagogical design (50), L2 pedagogical design (15), SLA design (25), and affective design (10). In each case, the points are scored on a Likert scale based on the subcategories. Of the 26 subcategories, 24 are worth up to 5 points, *mobility* is worth up to 20 (highest score for devices, students, and learning experiences all mobile), and *constructivist learning* is worth up to 10 (highest score for social-constructivist, lowest for behaviorist). They recommend application of the framework, before, during, and after implementation. They further acknowledge that the scores are advisory and need to be interpreted relative to the context in which the mobile learning takes place.

The second framework from Rosell-Aguilar (2017) considers more explicitly the realities of current mobile apps, offering both a taxonomy and evaluation criteria. Though the taxonomy includes interaction through computer-mediated communication (CMC), it acknowledges that the majority of these apps focus on the four skills, along with grammar and vocabulary. He also distinguishes between dedicated apps and those that can be exploited for language learning purposes but maintains a separate category for dictionaries and translators. Unlike Reinders & Pegrum, his system explicitly does not rely on scores and claims not to be a rubric; instead it provides lists of yes/no questions across the categories of language learning, pedagogy, user experience, and technology. That it still has the character of a checklist, though, is evident in questions such as these: Does the app provide recognition that can be shared on social media? Does the app include pop-up ads? It is worth noting that although this checklist is designed around mobile learning, most of its questions are directly applicable to web resource evaluation as well.

4.11   Putting it All Together: An Example from a Published Review

In this subsection, I summarize key elements from a courseware review published in the *CALICO Journal*, showing the journal's version of the preceding methodological framework in action. The goal is to give teachers an example of how such a framework can be employed so that they can consider adapting it for their own use.

Torres (2015) provides an evaluation of the web-based tutorial courseware *Hello-hello: Language on the go!* The review begins with an overview of the technological features of the courseware, noting that it is available to support learning in 13 languages (Dutch was the language selected for the review) and that it is usable on any device with a web browser.

Under the Activities (procedure) section (corresponding roughly to the operational description in subsection 4.5 above), the review notes that the program consists of 30 lessons divided into three groups of 10. Each lesson has 8 steps:

1. An animated video of a situational dialogue
2. Dutch subtitles beneath the video
3. Both English and Dutch subtitles beneath the video (for comprehension)
4. Line by line presentation of the dialogue with the option to record a repetition of them
5. Line by line transcription of the dialogue
6. A sentence completion task for the lines
7. Listening comprehension (multiple-choice)
8. Vocabulary building, based on sentences similar to those in the dialogue but with new words added.

Next, there is a vocabulary training course that expands vocabulary through nine major categories (e.g., travel) with each having seven to 7–10 subcategories (e.g. airport). This part has both learning and practice options. For learning, the user can select lists, flashcards, or images. For practice, there are listening, speaking, reading, and writing activities.

Under Teacher Fit (approach), the reviewer notes that the courseware fits a notional-functional approach, including conceptual categories like time and functional categories like describing. The content "is based on situations and functions frequently encountered in everyday life" (Torres 2015: 605). The courseware provides comprehensible input, and incremental noticing opportunities important for language learning. However, the reviewer notes it does not provide for any creative output or opportunities for negotiation of meaning. The reviewer also notes that the program lacks cultural and pragmatic information.

In the Learner Fit (design) section of the review, the reviewer suggests that it is suited in some ways to learners working autonomously because it allows them to select to choose the topics and activities most relevant to them. It is also consistent with a more inductive learning style as it provides "no explicit instruction of linguistic structures" (Torres 2015: 607–608) and that it should appeal to visual and auditory learners. The reviewer concludes that "the ideal learner for this program would be a highly motivated adult in a self-paced learning environment" (ibid.: 607) but that the program can also be used as a supplement for extra practice with useful vocabulary and dialogue material.

Being a review, the preceding example offers *guidance* toward teacher fit and learner fit for this courseware rather than making the judgment that a teacher or coordinator would make for a specific class. Beyond its status as an example here, reviews like this one can be read and reflected upon to help teachers and coordinators in developing a clearer sense of their own notions of teacher and learner fit.[4]

5   Pedagogical Implications: Implementation Schemes

5.1   General Considerations

Although implementation logically occurs after the selection stage in evaluation, looking at the way in which a piece of CALL courseware or a website

---

4   The full review is available at https://journals.equinoxpub.com/index.php/ CALICO/article/view/27070/24456

may be implemented is important for determining how to use it effectively and may influence whether or not it is purchased (see also Chapelle's [2001] criterion of *practicality*). In the common situation where an institution has limited funds for procuring courseware, implementation issues may clearly favor one program over another when the two may otherwise be equally good candidates in terms of teacher and learner fit. This is especially true with websites and mobile apps, which so often are free. The implementation module in Hubbard (1996) provides several points of consideration in developing schemes for learner use. These include accessibility and preparatory and follow-up activities, especially when linked to other course materials such as a textbook. Depending on the features in the courseware or website, implementation may also involve a number of teacher-controlled variables such as classroom management, site monitoring, teacher program control, access to student records, and teacher authoring possibilities. As noted in Reinders & Pegrum (2016), implementations for mobile activities can go beyond those mentioned above, especially when the activity itself is mobile.

5.2   Learner Training

The teacher's job is not complete when the courseware has been selected, procured, and integrated into the syllabus. In most cases, students need time and training to learn how to use the courseware effectively from a pedagogical as well as a technical perspective. In particular, they need to learn how to connect their actions with the courseware to desired language learning objectives. For instance, they need to understand that the primary purpose of a computer reading or listening lesson is not to answer the comprehension questions correctly but rather to engage with the language and content to improve their reading or listening proficiency – comprehension questions are just the most visible part of that process.

Hubbard (2013) provides a series of arguments for why learner training should be a significant part of CALL courseware implementation, echoing previous models that distinguish technical, strategic, and pedagogical training, building on five guiding principles: (1) experience CALL yourself from the learner's perspective; (2) provide learners with some teacher training so that they can make better decisions when working independently – for example, introducing students to notions like top-down vs. bottom-up processing for reading and listening; (3) employ a cyclical approach, making training ongoing rather than relying on one-time training sessions when the courseware is first introduced; (4) use collaborative debriefings to encourage students to reflect as a group on their learning process after using the courseware and to promote finding out about effective procedures from one another; and (5) teach general exploitation strategies so that they can take greater control of the courseware and adapt it in ways that go beyond the designer's vision.

Kolaitis et al. (2006) report on a project that implemented these learner training principles into an ESL program at a community college. They found that while some of the learner training principles were helpful, others, such as giving learners teacher training and finding time for collaborative debriefings, proved much more of a challenge for teachers. They noted, however, that developing the materials and procedures for training their students allowed them to have a clearer view of the need to link courseware and website use to learning objectives and to teach specific CALL strategies to promote that linkage.

6   Pedagogical Implications: Evaluating Student Outcomes

A final area of the evaluation process that needs to be touched on is determining the degree to which the courseware/app or website has been effective in meeting learning objectives. This assessment process helps the teacher decide whether to use the courseware or website in the future, and if so, whether to use it in the same way or differently. It may also add to the teacher's general understanding of what students do when they are in the lab or online, which can influence future evaluations and implementation decisions. It is of course rarely possible to establish a definitive cause and effect relationship between the use of a particular piece of software or website and gains in language proficiency given the other variables present in a language class. Nevertheless, it is instructive to look for evidence of a positive impact of the use of the software or website.

To this end Chapelle (2001) provides a set of questions for determining the results of student use empirically, tied to the six criteria presented previously for judgmental evaluation. For example, for the criterion of learner fit, she offers the following: "What evidence suggests that the targeted linguistic forms are at an appropriate level of difficulty for the learners? What evidence suggests that the task is appropriate to learners' individual characteristics (e.g., age, learning style, computer experience)?" (2001: 68). A more elaborated version appears in Jamieson, Chapelle, & Preiss (2005). As noted above, Leakey (2011) has expanded on Chapelle's assessment model, making it more comprehensive and more compatible with sociocultural approaches.

Although important in principle, this sort of evaluation can be quite challenging and time consuming to accomplish well in practice. Even *some* empirical information is better than none, however, so the use of one or more of the following methods is highly recommended. It should also be noted that this kind of empirical study with students can be done at a "pilot" level during the selection stage if a trial version of the courseware is available. In fact, Robb & Susser report that 56% of their survey respondents during the selection process "obtained a copy/demo and had some students try it" while 52% "used it under class conditions" (2000: 46).

6.1 Observation

A direct way to get information on whether the courseware is having a positive effect on learning is by watching the students as they use it. In a lab situation or even in class when students are on their own mobile devices, the teacher can walk around, notice how they are moving through the learning task, and interact with them as they are interacting with the courseware or other materials. Information gleaned in this manner can be used both to evaluate the courseware or website and to inform ongoing learner training.

6.2 Tracking Systems

Perhaps the best way to get objective information on student use is to select applications that include tracking of student actions. Depending on the type of tracking system used and the nature of the data collected, this can allow for either a superficial overview, for example, student quiz scores or time on the activity (as done by the tracking system in the learning management system *Canvas*), or a dataset that is rich in detail but may be time-consuming to analyze.

6.3 Student Surveys

Another common approach to gathering information on student perceptions of success or failure with the courseware is to ask them by using a survey or questionnaire. While such information can be valuable, there are two concerns. First, if students know their responses are tied to a grade or other assessment, or if they believe (even erroneously) that this is the case, the results will be compromised. Thus, it can be important to insure anonymity if feasible. Second, even when students are trying to be completely honest, their reports may not correspond to their actions. Fischer (2004) reported on a study of French reading courseware in which the student accounts of their use of program features were quite different from what was observed in the objective data in the tracking logs. If surveys are to be used, then, it is advisable to administer them either during or immediately after completion of a CALL activity to tap into fresh memories as much as possible and to supplement them with one or more of the other data sources noted in this section.

6.4   Pre- and Post-Testing

Evaluating student outcomes is a form of research, especially when it is done with software that is untried for a particular setting. Certain types of CALL instruction, particularly those which can be assessed with some degree of validity with discrete point tests such as vocabulary development, may be empirically evaluated using a pre- and post-test regime. Note that while this may give useful information on the outcome, it does not provide the data about the learning process that most of these other options do. It does, however, often have strong face validity with students and school administrations, especially when results are positive.

6.5   Student Journals and Reports

Kolaitis et al. (2006) report success having students keep a "CALL journal" in which they include not only the time and description of the courseware worked on but also reflections on why they believe they got certain answers wrong in exercises. Although this is mainly done for the students' benefit to promote reflective learning, such a journal also provides teachers with useful information on how their students are progressing and using the courseware. Romeo & Hubbard (2010) similarly use student reflective reports and combine them with individual conferences to understand which web-based materials students are using in an advanced listening course are most effective. Note, however, that like questionnaires, the data in student journals and reports may not be fully reliable and should be interpreted accordingly.

7   Conclusion

This chapter has focused on courseware and website evaluation, discussing the three options of checklists, methodological frameworks, and SLA-based approaches. For those interested in off-the-shelf solutions, references have been provided in the preceding text and the Resources section below. However, it is strongly recommended that language teachers develop their own systems using the methodological framework provided or adapting one of the other approaches. It should also be mentioned that while courseware and website evaluation is often a solitary activity, there are advantages to doing such evaluations with one or more colleagues or at least comparing notes on the product of evaluative activities. This is especially the case where the evaluation is being done for a curriculum that extends beyond a single instructor's class. Actively involving a group of instructors and other stakeholders such as support staff or the students themselves in the process will likely lead to more reliable results that participants are more enthusiastic about implementing.

Courseware/tutorial app and website evaluation remain an important area of CALL and there are indications its role may be increasing, particularly in the domain of empirical evaluation as tracking systems improve. However, for most language teachers, courseware and website evaluation at its core will remain primarily a judgmental process, though ideally with some empirical follow-up of the types described in the previous section. Yet even at the judgmental level, thorough courseware evaluation of the type often mandated by published checklists and procedures is a time-demanding process that will be impractical for many classroom teachers. The question remains then, which evaluation procedure to select. Robb & Susser suggest an answer:

> The vendor who explains everything, the colleague who remembers everything, the checklist that covers everything, and the framework that suggests everything do not exist and if they did, would probably be impossible to use. Consequently, software selection is still very much an art honed by experience. (2000: 49)

Reflecting on the material and procedures provided in this chapter is an important step in mastering that art. However, the challenge remains for the individual – or group in the case of collective evaluation – to gain the experience needed to determine a compatible CALL evaluation procedure that is practical and consistently yields useful results.

Questions for Reflection

1. Recall the three major types of evaluations: checklists, methodological frameworks, and SLA-based approaches. If you had to evaluate a piece of courseware today for possible use in your class,

which approach, or combination of approaches, would you use and why?

2. Visit the *CALICO Journal* site at
   https://journals.equinoxpub.com/index.php/CALICO
   and type "review" into the search box to bring up courseware and app reviews. Select one that seems relevant to your current or future teaching and read it critically. Think about (1) what useful information is provided, (2) what support the reviewer offered for the judgments made, and (3) what information was not provided that you would have found helpful. If possible, compare your own experiences working with this program with the reviewer's opinion.

3. Locate a piece of language learning courseware (like Duolingo) and find one activity in it. Using the model in Figure 3, see whether you can describe the interactional sequence of an item. What could you tell students about using the courseware that would help their deliberation and consolidation?

4. This chapter has focused on evaluating courseware and websites aimed for learner use, but there are also websites that include resources for teachers, such as lesson plans. How could you use the methodological framework in section 4 to help evaluate the resources on such websites? For an example, see http://iteslj.org/Lessons/

5. If you are currently teaching or have recently taught a language class, think about the kinds of CALL courseware support materials that could either be integrated into it or made available to students for supplementary work. How would you go about locating such materials once you identify the need?

6. If you have never learned a language using tutorial courseware, try to find some at your institution or on the web and experience CALL from the learner's perspective. Reflect on how your experience as a learner can inform evaluation decisions you make as a teacher of a language you know well.

7. Using the methodological framework in section 4 as a guide, design a 10–15 item evaluation checklist for web resources with a teacher fit that incorporates your own language teaching approach-based evaluation criteria. You can connect this to a specific class you are currently teaching or plan to teach.

Case Studies

Case Study 1: Evaluating supplementary material for a class

You are teaching a class of advanced beginning (ACTFL novice mid to high or Common European Framework A2) language learners. The textbook that was chosen for you by the previous instructor is structurally based and does not seem to be working well with this group of students or with your more communicatively-oriented approach. Unfortunately, you cannot abandon the textbook altogether. You have developed some in-class and out-of-class activities that allow students to engage more with the language and one another, but additionally, you would like to find one or two online sources that would give the students some additional guided listening and vocabulary activities at about the right level.

One colleague has mentioned using a Google search for suitable material. Another has suggested visiting the websites of several major textbook publishers to see if supplementary materials they provide for their textbooks would be helpful in supplementing yours. You don't have a lot of time to explore these options in depth, but you hope that one or the other will lead you to something that will be consistent with your needs. As a start, take a look at http://www.esl-lab.com (for English) or http://multidict.net/clilstore/ (for many other languages).

Discussion Questions:
1. What would be a good idea to do first before visiting any of these sites?
2. Assume you were going to use Chapelle's framework as the basis for your evaluation. Which of the six criteria do you think would be most important in this situation? Least important? Why?
3. Assume you were going to use the methodological framework approach to develop a checklist for your specific purposes (supplemental listening and vocabulary), keeping in mind you are trying to balance a structure-focused textbook with developing some communicative proficiency. What are some of the checklist items you would put under teacher fit and learner fit and why? How does your list compare with the listening and vocabulary sections of the NFLRC checklist for multimedia software at http://nflrc.hawaii.edu/networks/nw31/evaluation_checklists.htm?

Case Study 2: Evaluating courseware alternatives for a language center

A committee of three foreign language teachers at a university language center has been tasked by the administration to evaluate three popular commercial multi-skill language apps – for the purposes of (1) supplementing the current first-year curriculum to move to a more "blended" format and (2) providing the option of independent study for first-year students unable to take the regular classes. Despite any misgivings members may have, the committee's charge is to rank the three in terms of their overall quality and consistency with the objectives of the current curriculum and provide a rationale for that ranking.

Assume that you have been brought in to advise the committee on developing and implementing an evaluation procedure for the three programs. What would you tell them?

Discussion Questions:
1. Beyond those stated in the preceding description, what are some of the most important considerations in this situation?
2. What are two or three options for an evaluation procedure? What are the pros and cons of each in this situation? Which would you choose and why?
3. If the committee had only two weeks to put together this report, on top of their regular full-time teaching load, what sort of *expedited* evaluation procedure would you recommend to them?

Ideas for Action Research Projects

1. After selecting a piece of tutorial software or web-based task or activity on the basis of one of the evaluation frameworks described in this chapter, try it out with your students. Collect observational data and data on outcomes to determine in what ways it did, and did not, work as expected. Try in particular to determine the source of any obvious breakdowns or areas of confusion or frustration, as well as ways in which the students may have been able to complete the exercise, activity, or task without engaging in the expected learning processes. On the basis of those results, reflect on how they either reinforced or challenged your approach to evaluation, your own language teaching approach, or your understanding of your students as language learners using technology. Use the results to inform subsequent choices.

2. Teacher evaluation is important, but if students are to be the end users of a piece of courseware or a website, then getting their impressions can be beneficial as well. This is especially true in the era of mobile apps. Besides providing an additional source of insight, student evaluation can be a motivating factor for them and potentially lead them to using the material in an informed way. Develop a simple evaluation procedure for your students based on selected concepts from this chapter appropriate to their age and language proficiency level (for example, novice to low intermediate students might evaluate using their L1, while intermediate and beyond might use the target language). Have them use this procedure and collect the data from it. Then, reflect on how the students' evaluations compare with your initial one. Use the results to inform subsequent use of the evaluated material as well as to aid in selecting new material.

References

Boling, E., and Soo, K.-S. (1999). CALL issues: Designing CALL software. In J. Egbert and E. Hanson-Smith (eds.), *CALL environments: Research, practice, and critical issues*, pp. 442–457. Alexandria, VA: Teachers of English to Speakers of Other Languages.

Bradin, C. (1999). CALL issues: Instructional aspects of software evaluation. In J. Egbert and E. Hanson-Smith (eds.), *CALL environments: Research, practice, and critical issues*, pp. 159–175. Alexandria, VA: Teachers of English to Speakers of Other Languages.

Burston, J. (2003). Software selection: A primer on sources and evaluation. *CALICO Journal*, 21(1), 29–40. https://doi.org/10.1558/cj.v21i1.29-40

Byrd, P. (2001). Textbooks: Evaluation for selection and analysis for implementation. In M. Celce-Murcia (ed.), *Teaching English as a second or foreign language*, pp. 415–427. Third edition. Boston: Heinle.

CALICO Journal (2018). Learning technology review guidelines. Available at https://www.equinoxpub.com/home/wp-content/uploads/2018/04/CALICO_LearningTechnologyReviewGuidelines.pdf

California Language Teachers' Association (n.d.). Evaluation form for Web lessons. Available through the Internet Archive: https://web.archive.org/web/20120516045155/http://www.clta.net/lessons/evalform.html

Chapelle, C. (2001). *Computer applications in second language acquisition: Foundations for teaching, testing, and research*. Cambridge: Cambridge University Press. https://doi.org/10.1017/CBO9781139524681

Colpaert, J. (2006). Pedagogy-driven design for online language teaching and learning. *CALICO Journal*, 23(3), 477–497. https://doi.org/10.1558/cj.v23i3.477-497

Council of Europe (2001). *Common European framework of reference for language: Learning, teaching, assessment.* Cambridge: Cambridge University Press. Available at https://rm.coe.int/1680459f97

Davies, G. (2009). ICT4LT CALL software and website evaluation forms. In Davies G. (ed.) *Information and communications technology for language teachers (ICT4LT),* Slough, Thames Valley University [online]. See the Web Archive: https://web.archive.org/web/20160323084210/ http://www.ict4lt.org/en/evalform.doc

Egbert, J., & Hanson-Smith, E. (eds.). (1999). *CALL environments: Research, practice, and critical issues.* Alexandria, VA: Teachers of English to Speakers of Other Languages.

Fischer, R. (2004). How do students use CALL reading materials, and how do we know that they do? Paper presented at the 11th CALL conference: *CALL and research methodologies,* Antwerp, September 2004.

González-Lloret, M. (2015). *A practical guide to integrating technology into task-based language teaching.* Washington, DC: Georgetown University Press.

Healey, D., & Johnson, N. (1997/1998). A place to start in selecting software. *Computer Assisted English Language Learning Journal,* 8(1). Also available at http://www.deborahhealey.com/cj_software_selection.html

Hubbard, P. (1988). An integrated framework for CALL courseware evaluation. *CALICO Journal,* 6(2), 51–72.

Hubbard, P. (1996). Elements of CALL methodology: Development, evaluation, and implementation. In M. Pennington (ed.), *The power of CALL,* pp. 15–33. Bolsover, TX: Athelstan.

Hubbard, P. (2001). Extending & enhancing interactional sequences in tutorial CALL. Paper presented at CALICO symposium, Davis, CA, March 2001.

Hubbard, P. (2013) Making a case for learner training in technology-enhanced language learning environments. *CALICO Journal,* 30(2), 163–178. https://doi.org/10.11139/cj.30.2.163-178

Hubbard, P,. & Bradin Siskin, C. (2004). Another look at tutorial CALL. *ReCALL,* 16(2), 448–461. https://doi.org/10.1017/S0958344004001326

Jamieson, J., Chapelle, C., & Preiss, S. (2004). Putting principles into practice. *ReCALL* 16(2), 396–415. https://doi.org/10.1017/S0958344004001028

Jamieson, J., Chapelle, C., & Preiss, S. (2005). CALL Evaluation by developers, a teacher, and students. *CALICO Journal,* 23(1), 93–138. https://doi.org/10.1558/cj.v23i1.93-138

Kolaitis, M., Mahoney, M., Pomann, H., & Hubbard, P. (2006). Training ourselves to train our students for CALL. In P. Hubbard & M. Levy (eds.), *Teacher education in CALL.* Amsterdam: John Benjamins. https://doi.org/10.1075/lllt.14.26kol

Leakey, J. (2011). *Evaluating computer-assisted language learning: An integrated approach to effectiveness research in CALL.* Bern: Peter Lang. https://doi.org/10.3726/978-3-0353-0131-1

Levy, M. (1997). *Computer-assisted language learning: Context and conceptualization.* Oxford: Clarendon/Oxford University Press.

Levy, M., & Stockwell, G. (2006). *CALL dimensions: Options and issues in computer assisted language learning.* Mahwah NJ: Lawrence Erlbaum.

Lightbown, P., & Spada, N. (2013). *How languages are learned* (4th edition). Oxford: Oxford University Press.

Longman English Interactive [computer software] (2003). New York: Pearson.

National Foreign Language Resource Center (Hawaii). Multimedia software evaluation checklist. www.nflrc.hawaii.edu/NetWorks/NW31/evaluation_checklists.htm

National Foreign Language Resource Center (Hawaii). Software database. www.nflrc.hawaii.edu/NetWorks/NW31/software_eval/

Phillips, M. (1985). Logical possibilities and classroom scenarios for the development of CALL. In C. Brumfit, M. Phillips, & P. Skehan (eds.), *Computers in English language teaching*, pp. 25–46. New York: Pergamon.

Reinders, H., & Pegrum, M. (2016). Supporting language learning on the move: An evaluative framework for mobile language learning resources. In B. Tomlinson (ed.), *SLA research and materials development for language learning*, pp. 219–231. New York: Routledge.

Richards, J., & Rodgers, T. (1982). Method: approach, design, procedure. *TESOL Quarterly*, 16(2), 153–68. https://doi.org/10.2307/3586789

Robb, T., & Susser, B. (2000). The life and death of software. *CALICO Journal*, 18(1), 41–52. https://doi.org/10.1558/cj.v18i1.41-52

Romeo, K., & Hubbard, P. (2010). Pervasive CALL learner training for improving listening proficiency. In M. Levy, F. Blin, C. Siskin, and O. Takeuchi (eds), *WorldCALL 2008: Global perspectives on computer-assisted language learning*. New York: Routledge.

Rosell-Aguilar, F. (2017). State of the app: A taxonomy and framework for evaluating language learning mobile applications. *CALICO Journal*, 34(2): 343–358.

Son, J. B. (2005). Exploring and evaluating language learning web sites. In J. B. Son, and S. O'Neill (eds.) *Enhancing learning and teaching: Pedagogy, technology and language*, pp. 215–228. Flaxton, Australia: Post Pressed. Available at http://eprints.usq.edu.au/820/

Son, J. B. (2010). A model for the evaluation of language learning websites. Website: http://www.usq.edu.au/users/sonjb/projects/web_reviews/

Susser, B. (2001). A defense of checklists for software evaluation. *ReCALL*, 13(2), 261–276. https://doi.org/10.1017/S0958344001001021a

Thorne, S. (2003). Artifacts and cultures-of-use in intercultural communication. *Language Learning & Technology*, 7(2), 38–67.

Torres, D. (2015). Hello-hello – Language on the go [courseware review]. *CALICO Journal*, 32(3), 600–608.

Underwood, J. (1984). *Linguistics, computers, and the language teacher: A communicative approach.* Rowley, MA: Newbury House.

Resources

ICT4LT Software and website review forms. Downloads as a doc: http://www.ict4lt.org/en/evalform.doc

California Language Teachers' Association. (n.d.) Internet activities for foreign language classes. Website evaluation form that addresses the 5C's – see the Web Archive:
https://web.archive.org/web/20120516045155/
http://www.clta.net/lessons/evalform.html

CALICO Journal Review Form.
https://www.equinoxpub.com/home/wp-content/uploads/2018/04/CALICO_LearningTechnologyReviewGuidelines.pdf

National Foreign Language Resource Center (Hawaii). Multimedia software evaluation checklist.
www.nflrc.hawaii.edu/NetWorks/NW31/evaluation_checklists.htm.

National Foreign Language Resource Center (Hawaii). Software database.
www.nflrc.hawaii.edu/NetWorks/NW31/software_eval/.

Son, J. B. (2010) http://www.usq.edu.au/users/sonjb/projects/web_reviews/ (reviews of websites using a specific evaluation model).

About the Author

Philip Hubbard is Senior Lecturer in Linguistics and Director of the English for Foreign Students Program at the Stanford University Language Center. A professional in computer-assisted language learning (CALL) for over 30 years, he has published in the areas of CALL theory, research, methodology, listening, teacher education, learner training, and evaluation. Over the past three decades, he has served CALICO as a member of two executive boards and as its president (2015–16). He was previously the courseware review editor for the *CALICO Journal* and is a current member of the journal's editorial board. His recent projects focus on CALL as a transdisciplinary field, teacher support for informal language learning, and teaching reflectively with technology.

Index

CPSIA information can be obtained
at www.ICGtesting.com
Printed in the USA
BVHW042034070821
613305BV00001B/1